Unwrapping Goethe's Weimar

Studies in German Literature, Linguistics, and Culture
Edited by James Hardin
(*South Carolina*)

Unwrapping Goethe's Weimar

Essays in Cultural Studies and Local Knowledge

Edited by
Burkhard Henke,
Susanne Kord,
and
Simon Richter

CAMDEN HOUSE

Copyright © 2000 the Contributors

All Rights Reserved. Except as permitted under current legislation,
no part of this work may be photocopied, stored in a retrieval system,
published, performed in public, adapted, broadcast, transmitted,
recorded, or reproduced in any form or by any means,
without the prior permission of the copyright owner.

First published 2000
by Camden House

Camden House is an imprint of Boydell & Brewer Inc.
PO Box 41026, Rochester, NY 14604–4126 USA
and of Boydell & Brewer Limited
PO Box 9, Woodbridge, Suffolk IP12 3DF, UK

ISBN: 1–57113–194–9

Library of Congress Cataloging-in-Publication Data

Unwrapping Goethe's Weimar: essays in cultural studies and local
   knowledge / edited by Burkhard Henke, Susanne Kord, and Simon
   Richter
       p.   cm. – (Studies in German literature, linguistics, and
   culture)
   Rev. papers from the 2nd Davidson German Studies Symposium held in
   Feb. 1997 at Davidson College, N.C.
   Includes bibliographical references and index.
   ISBN 1–57113–194–9 (alk. paper)
   1. Goethe, Johann Wolfgang von, 1749–1832—Homes and haunts-
-Germany—Weimar (Thuringia) Congresses. 2. Weimar (Thuringia,
Germany)—Description and travel Congresses. 3. Weimar (Thuringia,
Germany)—Social life and customs Congresses. 4. Tourism—Germany-
-Weimar (Thuringia) Congresses. I. Henke, Burkhard, 1962–
II. Kord, Susanne. III. Richter, Simon. IV. Davidson German
Studies Symposium (2nd: 1997: Davidson College) V. Series:
Studies in German literature, linguistics, and culture (Unnumbered)
DD901.W4U6   1999
943'.224—dc21   99–42723
                                                                                                              CIP

A catalogue record for this title is available from the British Library.

This publication is printed on acid-free paper.
Printed in the United States of America

Contents

Preface   vii

Abbreviations of Works, Journals, and Archives Frequently Cited   ix

Introduction

Like a Box of Chocolates...
Simon Richter   1

Selling Weimar by the Kilo

1: Goethe®. Advertising, Marketing, and Merchandising the Classical
Burkhard Henke   15

2: Weimar Classicism and the Origins of Consumer Culture
Daniel Purdy   36

Weimar and the Senses

3: Floating Heads: Weimar Portrait Busts
Catriona MacLeod   65

4: Music in Weimar circa 1780: Decentering Text, Decentering Goethe
Annie Janeiro Randall   97

Performativity and Transgression in Weimar

5: War and Dramaturgy: Goethe's Command of the Weimar Theater
Karin Schutjer   147

6: From Werther to Amazons: Cross-Dressing and
   Male-Male Desire
   Susan E. Gustafson   166

Women in Weimar

7: Sartorial Transgressions: Re-Dressing Class and Gender
   Hierarchies in Masquerades and Travesties
   Elisabeth Krimmer   191

8: Women Writers and the Authorization of
   Literary Practice
   Linda Dietrick   213

9: The Hunchback of Weimar: Louise von Göchhausen
   and the Weimar Grotesque
   Susanne Kord   233

Wrapping Up the Weimar Myth

10: Creation and Constipation: *Don Carlos* and Schiller's
    Blocked Passage to Weimar
    Stephanie B. Hammer   273

11: Skeletons in Goethe's Closet: Human Rights, Protest,
    and the Myth of Political Liberality
    W. Daniel Wilson   295

12: The Weimar Myth:
    From City of the Arts to Global Village
    Gert Theile   310

Preface

THIS BOOK is the refined and distilled result of the *Second Davidson German Studies Symposium: Approaches to the City of Weimar*, which was held at Davidson College, North Carolina, in February 1997. All of the participants, some of whom are contributors to this volume, had one thing in common: they were wrapped up in Weimar. Seizing the opportune moment that history provided — Weimar's designation as "Kulturstadt Europas 1999" [Culture City of Europe 1999], the celebration of Goethe's two hundred and fiftieth birthday, and the ascendancy of Cultural Studies as a scholarly paradigm — the editors have assembled a book that unwraps Weimar in the sense of opening up new perspectives on the culture of a city we thought we knew too well.

This volume would not have been possible without a great deal of generous and collegial support. The editors would like to thank all those who contributed to this volume and those in Weimar who looked kindly upon it. Special thanks are due to Hansford Epes and Thomas P. Saine for their editorial help, James Hardin, Jim Walker, and Cheryl Branz for their professional support, Scott Denham for his translation of Gert Theile's essay, and Larisa Zgonjanin for her help in the raw stage of the essays. To Barbara Bloom and the Weimar 1999 — Kulturstadt Europas GmbH [Culture City of Europe, Inc.] we would like to extend our gratitude for giving us permission to use their artwork. We are also grateful to Liliane Weissberg for her perceptive comments at an early stage of the project — it was she who called our attention to the pertinence of the metaphor of unwrapping. Finally we would like to thank Davidson College, Georgetown University, the University of Pennsylvania, and Barbara Motyka from the DAAD New York for their financial support.

While we and our contributors have made every effort to contact all copyright owners of pictures, we wish to apologize to any we may have missed. Our thanks to all those whose generous permission to reproduce pictures has made it possible for us to include these materials here.

For this volume, the editors have by and large followed the fifth edition of the *MLA Handbook for Writers of Research Papers*, ed. Joseph Gibaldi (New York: MLA, 1999), with occasional recourse to the fourteenth edition of *The Chicago Manual of Style* (Chicago: Chicago UP, 1993). We have generally tried to make this volume as friendly to the readers of English as possible. All German titles and terms, save those that have found their way into the English vocabulary, are translated on their first occurrence in an essay; all quotations are provided in the original followed by English translations. Translations are those of the author unless otherwise stated.

We have capitalized Cultural Studies and put up with its monolithic appearance as a matter of fairness since we did the same for terms that are generally read as monolithic, especially epoch references. That is true in particular of Weimar Classicism, though we decided to retain lower case for any variants of the classical.

Burkhard Henke
Susanne Kord
Simon Richter
July 1999

Abbreviations of Works, Journals, and Archives Frequently Cited

GOETHE'S works are cited throughout from the Münchner Ausgabe (MA), with occasional letters taken from the Frankfurter Ausgabe (FA), the Gedenkausgabe (GA), or the Sophienausgabe (WA). Unless they are the author's, all translations of Goethe's works are cited from the Suhrkamp/Princeton edition (SE). Schiller's plays, poems, and aesthetic writings are cited from the Nationalausgabe (NA), some of his letters are taken from other specified sources. Weimar archives are frequently abbreviated, as are Bertuch's and Wieland's journals. The abbreviations and editions below appear here rather than in individual lists of works cited.

Goethe and Schiller Editions

FA Goethe, Johann Wolfgang von. *Sämtliche Werke. Briefe. Tagebücher und Gespräche.* Frankfurter Ausgabe. Eds. Dieter Borchmeyer et al. 40 vols in 2 secs. Frankfurt a. M.: Deutscher Klassiker Verlag, 1985–.

GA Goethe, Johann Wolfgang von. *Artemis-Gedenkausgabe der Werke, Briefe und Gespräche.* Ed. Ernst Beutler. 24 vols. Zurich: Artemis, 1948–54. (3 add. vols. 1960–71).

MA Goethe, Johann Wolfgang. *Sämtliche Werke nach Epochen seines Schaffens.* Münchner Ausgabe. Eds. Karl Richter et al. 20 vols. Munich: C. Hanser, 1985–98.

NA Schiller, Friedrich von. *Schillers Werke.* Nationalausgabe. Eds. Julius Petersen et al. 42 vols. Weimar: Hermann Böhlaus Nachfolger, 1943–.

WA Goethe, Johann Wolfgang von. *Goethes Werke.* Weimarer Ausgabe (Sophienausgabe). Ed. im Auftrage der Großherzogin Sophie von Sachsen. 143 vols. in 4 secs. Weimar: Hermann Böhlaus Nachfolger, 1887–1919.

Goethe Translation

SE　　Goethe, Johann Wolfgang von. *Goethe. The Collected Works*. Eds. Victor Lange, Eric Blackall, and Cyrus Hamlin. 12 vols. New York: Suhrkamp, 1983–89.

Goethe, Johann Wolfgang von. *Goethe. The Collected Works*. Princeton Paperback Edition (identical pagination). Eds. Victor Lange, Eric Blackall, and Cyrus Hamlin. 12 vols. Princeton: Princeton UP, 1995.

Journals

Modejournal　　*Journal der Moden*. Eds. Friedrich Justin Bertuch and Georg Melchior Kraus. Vol. 1. Gotha: Ettingersche Buchhandlung 1786.

Journal des Luxus und der Moden. Eds. Friedrich Justin Bertuch and Georg Melchior Kraus. (Ed. Carl Bertuch from 1807–12). Vols. 2–27. Weimar: Industrie-Comptoir, 1787–1812.

Journal für Luxus, Mode und Gegenstände der Kunst. Ed. Carl Bertuch. (Ed. Heinrich Döring from 1815) Vol. 28–30. Weimar: Industrie-Comptoir, 1813–15.

Journal für Literatur, Kunst, Luxus und Mode. Ed. Heinrich Döring. (Ed. Stephan Schütz from 1825). Vols. 31–41. Weimar: Industrie-Comptoir, 1816–26.

Journal für Literatur, Kunst und geselliges Leben. Ed. Stephan Schütz. Vol. 42. Weimar: Industrie-Comptoir, 1827.

Modejournal rpt.　　Bertuch, Friedrich Justin, and Georg Melchior Kraus, eds. *Journal des Luxus und der Moden*. Abridged Edition. Ed. Werner Schmidt. 4 vols. Rpt. Hanau: Müller and Kiepenheuer, 1967–70.

Merkur	*Der Teutsche Merkur.* Eds. Christoph Martin Wieland, Friedrich Justin Bertuch, K. L. Rheinhold, and K. A. Boettiger. Weimar: Im Verlag der Gesellschaft, 1773–89.
	Der Neue Teutsche Merkur. Ed. Christoph Martin Wieland. Weimar: Landes-Industrie-Comptoir, 1790–1810.

Archives

AAB	Herzogin-Anna-Amalia-Bibliothek, Weimar
GSA	Goethe- und Schillerarchiv, Weimar
ThHStAW	Thüringisches Hauptstaatsarchiv, Weimar

Introduction

Simon Richter

Like a Box of Chocolates...

1999 IS THE YEAR of the city of Weimar. A bundle of anniversaries and celebrations — Goethe's two hundred and fiftieth birthday, seven hundred and fifty years of Weimar's existence, the hundredth anniversary of the Bauhaus — not to mention the general good will in the wake of unification, all came together to win for the city the designation of "Kulturstadt Europas 1999" [Culture City of Europe 1999]. Weimar and the Federal Republic have responded to this honor with ingenuity and resources. It would have been so easy to revel piously in the myth of Goethe's Weimar, that story begun already by Goethe and his admirers in his lifetime and perpetuated by generations of German teachers in Germany and abroad. We all know how the story goes: the young Goethe called from patrician Frankfurt to join the impetuous Duke Carl August who had only just assumed power from his mother, the revered Anna Amalia; how first under her reign and even more under the influence of her son and Goethe, Weimar became an Athens on the Ilm, attracting scores of illustrious writers, artists, philosophers, musicians, actors, and singers, many of whose names live on, others of whom are largely forgotten. This was Goethe's Weimar, visited by many, it is true, but more often imagined, a virtual village of urbane cultivation, packaged, as it were, for the consumer of culture.

Fortunately, the city of Weimar resisted the snares of nostalgic and uncritical commemoration, thanks in large part to Bernd Kauffmann, Director of Weimar 1999 — Kulturstadt Europas GmbH, and his imaginative staff. A visit to the Weimar website gives plentiful evidence of a determined and comprehensive effort to celebrate Weimar in all its historical and contemporary complexity and with all the technological, scholarly, and artistic means available at the turn of the twenty-first century. The Weimar production of Hans Magnus Enzensberger's controversial *Nieder mit Goethe: Eine Liebeserklärung* (Down with Goethe: A Declaration of Love, 1995 and 1996) is indicative of the tone — an irreverent reverence for the Goethe phenomenon. What the city is doing with Goethe's legendary Gartenhaus casts a light on tourism in the age of cyberspace reproduction. The real or virtual visitor to Weimar will encounter Goethe's Gartenhaus, for example, in three modes: as historical building for external viewing, necessarily spared the hordes of daily tours; as total material duplicate for the experience of its interior; and as virtual space accessible over the World Wide Web. Countless avant-garde theater, dance, and film projects (among them an *Urfaust Rap* directed by Michael Simon) combine with mainstream cultural offerings such as Schiller's *Wallenstein* (1798–99) or Branford Marsalis on the saxophone. A whole array of exhibitions call attention to aspects of Weimar forgotten or unknown. Artists from all over the world have been commissioned to produce works of their own imagining that respond to Weimar in spatial and temporal ways.

Barbara Bloom, an American conceptual artist from New York, is one of eight artists so commissioned. So provocative and so telling is her response to Weimar that we have chosen the title for this volume — *Unwrapping Goethe's Weimar* — in allusion to her project. There is, in our view, an important analogy between her efforts and ours in assembling the Cultural Studies essays that make up this volume. By unwrapping Bloom's project, we can at the same time demonstrate what is at stake in approaching Goethe's Weimar from the perspective of Cultural Studies.

For several months Bloom's artwork was on sale to tourists in city souvenir shops for the improbable price of DM 20. Perhaps you were one of them or can easily imagine yourself there. You peruse the Weimar curios and mementos, the ginkgo leaves and Goethe mugs, the Goethe brandy and other products analyzed below in Burkhard Henke's essay on "Goethe®," and notice a white box that resembles a book with the title: *Weimar. Vergangenheit ... Zukunft. Und jetzt?* (Fig. 1). Imprinted with an ancient map of Weimar on the cover and bearing the name Barbara Bloom and the year 1995 on its spine, nothing prepares you for the box's contents. Unwrapping the plastic that seals it, you lift its faux cover and find yourself looking at a box of chocolates complete with an iconographic guide to assist you in your selection of the chocolate blocks wrapped in gold foil through which the contours of a stamped silhouette or insignia appear. On the inside cover you encounter a quotation from Nietzsche, another of Weimar's famous inhabitants, even if he was, in his madness, unaware of his presence in the city and in the exploitative care of his sister. Casting an eye on the chocolate legend (Fig. 2), you realize you may choose from

Anna Amalia, the Hotel Elephant, Charlotte von Stein, Johann Wolfgang von Goethe, the Princes' Vault, Friedrich von Schiller, Franz Liszt, Friedrich Nietzsche, Harry Graf Kessler, the Museumsplatz-Gauforum, the Bauhaus, and Ernst Thälmann. To paraphrase Forrest Gump, Weimar is like a box of chocolates.

Inside the wrapping of each of the chocolates, there is a folded slip of paper bearing pictures and texts, an assemblage of historical and visual material over which to ruminate as you let the bittersweet chocolate melt in your mouth. Goethe's chocolate is accompanied by a picture of wallpaper samples from his extensive collection; on the other side you find a picture of his mineral collection and an excerpt from a British novel by Bruce Chatwin that indirectly comments on Goethe's collecting mania. The slip accompanying Schiller shows nine different portraits of the poet and quotes from Michail Gerassimov's account of the morbid confusion surrounding Schiller's authentic skull, as well as from Gombrich's reflections on the aesthetics and meaning of portraiture. Anna Amalia includes a picture of the library named in her honor, as well as a portrait detail of her lap with an open book in her hands. The reverse chronicles the fortunes of the library and joins to it a list of significant street name changes dating from 1841 to 1991 that illustrate the political vicissitudes of the city: "Brauhausstraße, Kaiserin-Augusta-Straße, Straße der SA, Steubenstraße" [Brewhouse Street, Empress Augusta Street, Street of the Storm Troopers, Steuben Street]. The accompanying leaflet for the Hotel Elephant shows a picture of a now missing commemorative plaque over the hotel fireplace that celebrated the fact that Hitler had slept there twenty-six times. Flipping the page, you see a picture of Hitler at the hotel entrance, as well as an anecdote from 1789 and an excerpt from the hotel's own promotional material from 1994 that completes the picture. In the latter the reader is invited to join the company of the many luminaries who frequented or slept at the Elephant. Goethe and Schiller, we are proudly told, ate at the hotel. Friedrich Hebbel, Franz Grillparzer, Johann Sebastian Bach, Felix Mendelssohn-Bartholdy, Clara Schumann, Franz Liszt, Richard Wagner, Anton Rubinstein, and Leo Tolstoy, among others, slept there. For obvious reasons Hitler is not mentioned. Bloom herself steered clear of producing a Buchenwald chocolate, though necessary allusions to the Nazi past make several chocolates extremely bitter.

It is remarkable to what an extent the complexity and subtle brashness of Bloom's Weimar project coincides with the efforts of Cultural Studies generally and with our intentions in this book specifically. The unlikely, but so apt combination of Weimar's mythological grandeur with the triteness of a box of chocolates perfectly captures the spirit in which Cultural Studies seeks to question and reverse past canons of taste and hierarchy. The box of chocolates does not jettison the canon, but it makes a point of including figures regularly excluded (women for so long, or Ernst Thälmann or others for political reasons). Long revered figures, a Goethe, a Schiller, are not toppled from their places, but questions are posed concerning the myths that surround them. Who is the authentic Schiller? What manias were at work in Goethe? Bloom calls attention to the sense in which Weimar is a politicon, a troubled locus of ideological projection and contestation. By imprinting the cultural icons of Weimar on chocolate, she further underscores the transitory and consumable quality of art. We may reflect on the ephemeral cultural production of Goethe's Weimar, not merely the occasional poems enshrined in editions, but the skits and songs, the handwritten journals and improvised plays, the musical accompaniments and the scribbles and drawings, the lives aesthetically lived and only haphazardly recorded that together made up part of the everyday of Weimar culture. Cultural Studies brings us back to Weimar, sends us to archives and other sources on a quest for what was forgotten, concealed, revised, or transformed.

When Christo was finally permitted to wrap the Berlin Reichstag in 1995, he fixed the world's attention on this building and all it had meant in previous generations and what it could mean in the future. By wrapping the Reichstag, he unwrapped it. Bloom's box of chocolates performs a similar function. Like Christo, she explicitly calls attention to the crass market logic that grips our society to the point of litigious copyright battles over the brand names "Goethe" and "Salve." At the same time, in a dialectical move, she reverses that logic, tugs at the bows and ribbon and wrapping paper, and thereby unwraps Weimar, not that it may appear as it authentically was, but that it may appear anew. This is precisely what Cultural Studies asks us to do. We who have so long been wrapped up in Goethe must go back to the city and its archives, back to the musical compositions and suppressed and forgotten texts of its female participants, and begin to consider the processes involved in producing the myth of Goethe's Weimar. The Weimar that emerges as a result of such efforts (and some of them are represented in the essays that follow) will be more complex, more diverse than the one we are accustomed to. It will leave a bittersweet taste, like Bloom's chocolates do, not because of an iconoclastic and destructive desire that might be thought to motivate some of these efforts — in most instances this is not the case — but rather because cultural production in any time necessarily unfolds in a material and political context, involves relations of power, and succeeds by and large in reliance on mechanisms of exclusion. By retooling our perspective on Weimar to take into account the pressing concerns of race, class, gender, and sexuality, we perceive a bifurcated picture of Weimar that on the one hand seems splendidly dynamic, still revolving around Goethe, but certainly not in his control, nor doing so only with reverence, while, on the other hand, we become increasingly aware of the class and gender inequities that were a condition for Weimar's flourishing high and hybrid culture.

It has been a long time since scholars took a sustained look at the culture of Goethe's Weimar. Bruford's *Culture and Society in Classical Weimar*, published in 1961, duly furnishes an account of social demography and the many other mundane circumstances that make up everyday life. He provides a detailed rendering of the many cultural institutions: the literary, scholarly, and social clubs, the amateur theater company, and Friedrich Justin Bertuch's commercial projects (treated in Daniel Purdy's essay in this volume). Indeed, in the first pages of his foreword, Bruford tellingly quotes from Raymond Williams's pathbreaking book, *Culture and Society* (1958), in clear recognition that the field of literary and cultural history has been altered. Williams, of course, would go on to be closely associated with the founding of British Cultural Studies, also known as the Birmingham School. For all his awareness of a significant shift, and for all his attention to the material details of culture broadly understood, Bruford yet remains captive to the German definition of culture as "Bildung," as the education of humanity, as a master narrative forcefully and brilliantly modeled in the lives and work of Weimar's luminaries: Goethe, Wieland, and Herder. The critical edge, the associative logic, and the nose for mischief that characterize contemporary Cultural Studies have no place in Bruford's representation of Goethe's Weimar.

In 1994 a voluminous lexicon appeared with the title *Goethe's Weimar*, written by Effi Biedrzynski. Still in the thrall of a consuming reverence for Goethe, it nonetheless widens the field considerably and places countless evocative details into the hands of prospective Cultural Studies scholars. Individual entries for musicians, singers, and composers, as well as for Anna Amalia and Goethe, for example, allow the reader to infer the crucial role that music played in the life of Weimar. In our volume, musicologist Annie Janeiro Randall uses her own extensive archival work in Weimar as an occasion for "Decentering Text, Decentering Goethe," and reveals a pattern of collaboration between Goethe and women musicians, poets, and singers that faintly anticipates the discrediting of Brecht's authorship in the sense that literary history also typically erases Goethe's female collaborators. Other details collected by Biedrzynski document the international diversity of Weimar, particularly the French and British who lived there and were part of the cultural scene. Charles Gore, originally of Yorkshire, and his two daughters, are among them. He first met Goethe in Rome as a friend of the artist Philipp Hackert, and decided in 1791 to move permanently to Weimar. Someone she fails to mention, however, is Jean Joseph Mounier, who fled France and opened an educational institute in the abandoned and dilapidated Belvedere palace. Funded by Carl August, with a French faculty and largely British students interested in philosophy, politics, law, and the arts, Mounier's institute seems an anomalous riff in the cultural geography of Weimar. Hans Tümmler delicately hints at profound cultural misunderstandings between the students and the city's inhabitants, "die wohl doch über die Grenzen üblichen Jugendunfugs hinausgingen und sogar die Gerichte beschäftigten" [that exceeded the limits of the usual youthful pranks and even involved the courts; Tümmler 44].

The lives of many of Weimar's citizens and residents call out for the sort of attention only Cultural Studies can provide. Bertuch, as Daniel Purdy's essay shows at length, is an exemplar of the cultural politics that Cultural Studies typically focuses on, and was a master in the marketing of classical Weimar, a key participant in the development of the myth of Goethe's Weimar. Strained relations with Goethe aside, Bertuch had an uncanny sense for the commercial possibilities of high culture. Barbara Bloom's box of chocolates is in the best tradition of Bertuchian enterprise. Catriona MacLeod picks up the thread in her analysis of the commodification and marketing of classical sculpture, focusing in particular on the Weimar court sculptor Gottlieb Martin Klauer. In a third essay, Stephanie Hammer examines Friedrich Schiller's tortured relation to commodification.

Another Weimaranian whose presence ruffles the appearance of classical Weimar is August von Kotzebue, an enormously popular playwright whose plays were performed all over Germany and in such major cities as Madrid, Boston, Paris, Moscow, and St. Petersburg (and frequently, in the late eighteenth and early nineteenth centuries, even in Charleston, South Carolina). Born and raised in Weimar, Kotzebue was exiled from the city in a move engineered by Goethe because of a play, *Die Weiber nach Mode* (Women After the Latest Fashion) that transparently made fun of all the luminaries of Weimar, including Anna Amalia. Nonetheless, Goethe continued to produce Kotzebue's plays in the court theater, shrewdly aware of their enormous popularity. Further altercations with Goethe and his aura ensued. In the aftermath of the Napoleonic Wars, Kotzebue was murdered in Mannheim in 1819 by a fanatical fraternity brother. Although the present volume contains no discussion of Kotzebue, it seems appropriate to name him here, and to recognize in him Goethe's pop-culture Doppelgänger. As teachers of the Age of Goethe and German Classicism, we have to wonder why Kotzebue is not on our syllabi. Goethe certainly knew that his plays, if not his person, had a place in Weimar.

Similarly the noble Einsiedel family may provide for fresh perspectives on Goethe's Weimar. All the world seems to know about Carl August and his arrangement with Caroline Jagemann, virtuoso theater talent and Carl August's longtime mistress. But what of Emilie von Einsiedel, née von Münchhausen, with whom the young duke played "wer besser küssen könne" [who can kiss better; qtd. in Biedrzynski 76]? In 1785, married to Christian Ferdinand von Werthern, she staged her own death, allowing a straw doll to be buried in her stead, in order to join August von Einsiedel on an expedition to Africa. The travelers made it as far as Tunisia but were forced to turn back due to plague. Cultural Studies undeniably has an eye for scandal and sensation, not only for the pleasure of indulging in them, but for the social and cultural fractures that inevitably come to light. What, indeed, do we know of the imperial and colonial fantasies of Weimar that might have occasioned the Einsiedels's enterprise? What sexual and moral codes were in play that caused Emilie to resort to such extravagant means to release herself from her marriage? German Studies is still awaiting a thorough study of gender and sexuality in Weimar. The present volume makes several contributions: Elisabeth Krimmer looks at the ritual and courtly forms of masquerade and cross-dressing, while Susan Gustafson focuses on the homosocial camaraderie and cross-class-dressing of the "Weimar boys." Linda Dietrick and Susanne Kord assess the ramifications of gender for literary production, Dietrick in an analysis of the female literary market along the lines of Bourdieu, while Kord coins the new term Weimar Grotesque to challenge Weimar Classicism in the person of Louise von Göchhausen.

Of all the contributors to *Unwrapping Goethe's Weimar*, none has so significantly and permanently forced a revision of our image of the city as a locus for the harmonious coexistence of humane culture and political power as has Daniel Wilson. His essay on the "Skeletons in Goethe's Closet" is only the latest in an on-going investigation of the politics of Goethe's Weimar. Beginning with his book on the infiltration of secret societies by Goethe and Carl August and continuing through his critical analysis of the Nazi-era scholarship that idealized the latter's reign for political ends, Wilson has now published the results of years of research in the city archives of Weimar with particular attention to the issue of human rights. *Das Goethe Tabu* was published in Germany in 1999, a book that will certainly elicit strong responses in the German press. For this book, Wilson looks, among other things, into the matter of Goethe's complicity in selling Weimar's prisoners as soldiers to fight in the Revolutionary War in North America. Soldiering is also at stake in Karin Schutjer's account of Goethe's command of the Weimar theater. In an analysis of Goethe's writings on the French campaign as well as his directorial efforts in the Weimar Theater, Schutjer points out a sustained and disconcerting analogy between them. Casting doubt on Goethe's exemplary humaneness is, of course, nothing new: we need only think of Ortega y Gasset's essay in *The Dehumanization of Art*. Doing so by intensely motivated archival research and by the analysis of discourses usually not linked, however, is indicative of the kind of contribution Cultural Studies makes.

The final essay in *Unwrapping Goethe's Weimar* is by Gert Theile, one of the key inventive and enterprising minds in Bernd Kauffmann's Weimar 1999 — Kulturstadt Europas GmbH. Trained as a Germanist in Leipzig in the days of the German Democratic Republic, employed by the Stiftung Weimarer Klassik [Weimar Classics Foundation] before unification, Theile embodies the Bertuchian spirit of Weimar: effervescent and irreverent wit combined with irrepressible enterprise. His critical reflections on the myth of Weimar and his challenges for its future and its future scholarship, the very challenges he poses to himself, round off our collection of essays, not in the sense of providing a conclusion, but in bringing home the point that the unwrapping of Goethe's Weimar is an ongoing project, a gargantuan task. Even as this introduction is being written, the packaging of Goethe and Weimar continues. In an article with multiple punning titles — "Paper Towel Offers Absorbing Wisdom" and "Spill Blotters Run Deep" — the *Washington Post* of 15 April 1998 reports about a paper towel produced by the Georgia-Pacific Corporation that features life-cheering quotations from none other than Goethe. In a telling gesture, Christa Sammons of the Beinecke Rare Book Library at Yale University made sure to secure a case of the paper towels for the library's collection of Goetheana. As Christo and Bloom have taught us, the wrapping and unwrapping proceed in tandem. Like Bloom's box of chocolates, and like the present volume, the cataloging of paper towels in one of the nation's most prestigious libraries is a perfect emblem of the pressures and opportunities of our times. 1999 will come and go. If the efforts of Bernd Kauffmann and Gert Theile, of Barbara Bloom, and the contributors to *Unwrapping Goethe's Weimar* have any purchase at all, we, who continue to be wrapped up in Weimar, will have them to thank for a Weimar image that is new and improved.

— University of Pennsylvania

Works Cited

Biedrzynski, Effi. *Goethes Weimar: Das Lexikon der Personen und Schauplätze.* 3rd ed. Zurich: Artemis and Winkler, 1994.

Bruford, W. H. *Culture and Society in Classical Weimar 1775–1806.* Cambridge: Cambridge UP, 1962.

Enzensberger, Hans Magnus. *Nieder mit Goethe: Eine Liebeserklärung. Requiem für eine romantische Frau. Ein Liebeskampf in sieben Sätzen.* Frankfurt a. M.: Verlag der Autoren, 1995.

Ortega y Gasset, José. *The Dehumanization of Art.* Princeton: Princeton UP, 1993.

Tümmler, Hans. *Das klassische Weimar und das große Zeitgeschehen. Historische Studien.* Cologne and Vienna: Böhlau, 1975.

Washington Post. 15 April 1998.

Weimar online — Stadtinformationssystem. 13 May 1999. <http://www.weimar.de/>

Williams, Raymond. *Culture and Society. 1780–1950.* London: Chatto and Windus, 1958.

Wilson, Daniel W. *Geheimräte gegen Geheimbünde: Ein unbekanntes Kapitel der klassisch-romantischen Geschichte Weimars.* Stuttgart: Metzler, 1991.

———. *Das Goethe-Tabu: Protest und Menschenrechte im klassischen Weimar.* Munich: dtv, 1999.

———. "Tabuzonen um Goethe und seinen Herzog. Heutige Folgen nationalsozialistischer Absolutismuskonzeptionen." *Deutsche Vierteljahrsschrift für Literaturwissenschaft und Geistesgeschichte* 70 (1996): 394–442.

Fig. 1: Barbara Bloom, Weimar. Vergangenheit ... Zukunft. Und jetzt? *(Past ... Future. And now?). Book cover with spine for a box of twelve chocolates, 1995 (courtesy of Barbara Bloom).*

Anna Amalia

Hotel Elephant

Charlotte von Stein

Johann Wolfgang von Goethe

Fürstengruft

Friedrich von Schiller

Franz Liszt

Friedrich Nietzsche

Harry Graf Kessler

Museumsplatz - Gauforum

Bauhaus

Ernst Thälmann

Fig. 2: Barbara Bloom, Weimar. Vergangenheit ... Zukunft. Und jetzt? *(Past ... Future. And now?). Chocolate legend on the enclosed leaflet, 1995 (courtesy of Barbara Bloom).*

SELLING WEIMAR BY THE KILO

BURKHARD HENKE

Goethe®. Advertising, Marketing, and Merchandising the Classical

As if Goethe readers needed a reminder, the registration sign attached to the poet's name will let them know that they are not so much readers of literary works as they are consumers of culture.¹ Once emptied out and chained to the ultimate sign of commodification, the name "Goethe" appears to have wandered beyond the realm of mere linguistic signifier to a place where we can hardly make it out beneath the piles of merchandise. What was the reason for that kind of Wanderlust? Shall we call Goethe's commodification a deformation, a distortion, a desecration even? Or is this commercial purpose behind the construction of Goethe as a myth no more or less abusive than any other? To what extent was Goethe involved in his own commodification? A cursory look at the early packaging stages of the Goethe myth will lead us to the art of advertising and merchandising the classical in today's Weimar, specifically to the registered trademark of a brandy named *Johann Wolfgang von Goethe*. I will conclude with my thoughts on the curious for-profit nationalism with which such merchandise is sold as the classical.

Marketing Culture Around 1800

There is plenty of evidence — factual, anecdotal, or otherwise — that Goethe had already become a legend in his own lifetime. One of Goethe's secretaries, Friedrich Theodor Kräuter, for example, is said to have asked Goethe's barber for a curl off the poet's distinguished head. He was told no. "Those are all counted," was the answer, "they are being shipped for sale in Frankfurt" (Ebersbach 100). We know from many accounts that Goethe's home at the Frauenplan square had turned into a virtual museum late in his lifetime. Its aging inhabitant attracted visitors by the hundreds from Europe and America, all of whom were hoping to catch a glimpse of the living legend. Though pre-dating that phenomenon, the following anecdote gives us an idea of the sorts of audiences which Goethe was willing to grant (Ebersbach 59).

"A certain Herr Tieck wishes to see you," the servant announced. On the strength of his publications Ludwig Tieck was so assured of his own celebrity in Weimar that he did not deem it necessary to have himself recommended in advance as a visitor to Goethe's home. Initially, Goethe instructed his servant to send Tieck off but changed his mind in an instant and came down. "You wished to see me?" "Certainly, Herr Geheimrat," replied Tieck. Then Goethe slowly turned full circle and said, "Well, you are seeing me." Since the visitor appeared rather dazed and had apparent difficulty in determining what to make of the show, Goethe asked "Did you see me?" "Undoubtedly," Tieck replied. "Well, then, you may go." And with these words Goethe turned again toward the door. "Just one moment, Herr Geheimrat, if I may," added Tieck. "What is it?" Tieck then started digging in his pocket and asked: "How much for the sightseeing?"

As the anecdote would have it, Goethe did eventually let Tieck in but that may not be the point. What is interesting is the fact that the story introduces us to the notion of an already commodified Goethe. We see a multi-talented man who knows he has already become a living cultural landmark, yet does not seem to mind much. On the contrary, he appears actively to participate in his own commodification. The son of a well-to-do merchant, Goethe always knew how to market his books to publishers and himself to others. Once in Weimar, there were few who possessed Goethe's talent, leverage, and his occasional callousness to jockey for position the way he did; even fewer decided to fictionalize and mythologize themselves as openly as Goethe did in *Dichtung und Wahrheit* (From My Life: Poetry and Truth, 1811–33); none was able to gather around him the kind of public relations staff that Goethe had in Eckermann, Zelter, and company.

Acknowledging Goethe's own complicity in his commodification is not to say that Goethe is actually responsible for creating the structure necessary for such exploits. That credit rightly belongs to Friedrich Justin Bertuch, a man of letters whose translation of *Don Quichote* cost him much of his eyesight but brought him the starting capital necessary to become a businessman. Bertuch first organized Goethe's commodification and, as Daniel Purdy shows in the following essay, can generally be credited (or discredited) for molding Weimar's consumer culture and the bourgeois taste that became its driving force. Innovative entrepreneur that he was, Bertuch was clever enough to make a fortune selling culture high and low. What is more, his influence on Weimar culture around 1800 can hardly be underestimated. Could it be that Bertuch shaped the same cultural space in firmer and more lasting ways than the town icon Goethe? Certainly, it is ironic that his name should have been more widely known in the Europe of 1800 than the name of the man whose likeness Bertuch was so eager to sell (Hohenstein 83).

For all we know, Goethe never cared much for Bertuch's distribution of mass culture, nor for Bertuch himself for that matter. When Goethe encouraged court sculptor Martin Gottlieb Klauer to make busts of famous contemporaries, Bertuch encouraged mass production — much to Goethe's chagrin (Hohenstein 55, 78; also Catriona MacLeod in this volume), although perhaps not to his surprise and certainly not to his monetary disadvantage. Bertuch advertised art and culture for sale in the *Intelligenzblatt*, a supplement of Bertuch's *Journal des Luxus und der Moden* (Journal of Luxury and Fashion, 1786–1827, abbr. as *Modejournal*; see "Works Frequently Cited") that functioned, like much of the content of the journal proper, as one massive, thinly veiled advertisement for Bertuch's enterprise. In today's terms, it was a mail order catalogue (Hohenstein 56). In its first issue of January 1786, the advertising supplement offered Klauer's modern busts of, among others, Goethe, Wieland, Herder, Gellert, Jacobi, Voltaire, and yes, Bertuch himself (*Modejournal* vi; MacLeod in this volume). Later issues of that same year then contained advertisements by the fan factory of Vienna which offered fans featuring profiles of Lavater's physiognomy as well as fans number twenty and twenty-one, "Lotte at Werther's grave," and "Lotte, unconscious, with Albert" (see, for example, June 1786: xlvii, xlviii). Issues of later years saw more of the same, from advertisements of Goethe's works to medallions portraying Goethe, Wieland, and Herder (see, for example, February 1787: xiii; April 1787: xxxii; March 1789: lvi). By 1788 — Goethe was still in Italy — the semiotic boundary between the work and the man appears to be dissolving, clearing the way for the myth and the commodity that Goethe is today. The enterprise of marketing and merchandising the great national poet, advocate of humanity, had been rung in.

Advertising in Today's Weimar

These days, Goethe sells more than ever before, not just in Weimar but especially in Weimar. In the absence of any major commercial chains in the downtown area, the ubiquitous use of Goethe's name, image, and words for commercial purposes faces little competition. No billboards, let alone flashy neon signs are permitted to disturb the classical peace. There is ostensibly no Marlboro Man in the marketplace of Weimar other than Goethe. Weimar, it would appear, has cast its lot with the poet, and in a regional economy dependent on the service industry, the city is no doubt cashing in on the service of His name. No longer drained by an exhausting pilgrimage, the modern-day grail seeker partakes of the consecration of Goethe's name. That consecration has been performed in a variety of ways and venues ever since Goethe established a career here, though it was most pronounced during the nineteenth century. Today it still takes place at the same historic venues, such as Goethe's home at the Frauenplan, his Gartenhaus, or his tomb, but also in the seemingly less sacred places, such as the Goethe pharmacy or the Goethe Café. Goethe's name is for sale — now and then, here and there — and it may be no coincidence that the bookstores in the Schillerstraße are nestled between the Bayerische Vereinsbank on Goetheplatz 5, and the Commerzbank in Schillerstraße 16. The modern-day grail seeker cannot help but be confused. Where does the official keeper of the grail, the not-for-profit organization called Stiftung Weimarer Klassik [Weimar Classics Foundation] keep that grail? In the offices near the City Palais or in its profitable souvenir shop near the marketplace?

In semiological terms, Goethe's name is a signifier that carries meaning. When the Weimar Tourist Information advertises its package deals, entitled "Reisen zu Goethe" (Travels to Goethe) and "Essen wie zu Goethes Zeiten" (Dining as in Goethe's Time), it ostensibly invites us to travel back in time to a point of historical and cultural immediacy where Goethe the man will be brought back to life in our company. Spending a so-called Goethe Weekend in the Treff Hotel Weimar promises a similar experience whose pseudo-historicity can already be savored in the confines of the hotel's major ballrooms: Goethe 1, Goethe 2, Goethe 3. Incidentally, all major hotels in Weimar have named at least one conference room or ballroom after Goethe — and those hotels that were in business before unification had done so even before western capitalists received license to show them how to do it better. The hotels thus establish a connection between hotel and poet around the signifier "Goethe." The word and its concept are preserved in the associative total of both, the sign "Goethesaal" [Goethe Room] in the Weimar Hilton. We may interpret this sign to mean something like, "The name of this room is 'Goethe' because we, as a hotel in the very city in which Goethe lived and wrote, would like to express our appreciation of Goethe's attainments and celebrate him by naming one of our rooms after him."

It is of course not all that difficult to recognize another level of signification, one which Roland Barthes has termed *metalanguage* or *myth*. On that level, a second-order semiological system is constructed by reducing the sign "Goethesaal" to the role of a new signifier which is now wed to a new signified in order to produce the mythical sign. That second, global signification may be explained in the following terms. By reducing "Goethesaal" to a mere signifier, the myth strips it of all its fullness, its rich pool of associations and ambiguities. We see the image of an empty room stripped of meaning. We are no longer encouraged to consider the man in his historical context, nor are we any longer aware of the shape and size of the room, its lighting perhaps, its uses, its own history. The name "Goethesaal" is still there, but it "thickens," as Barthes would have it; Goethe's name "becomes vitrified, freezes into an eternal reference" (Barthes 125). Only after the Weimar Hilton has condemned Goethe to an instrumental signifier, a gesture, can the myth unfold its motivation and acknowledge the presence of the signified through the signifier. Its signification may be summed up in the form of a triangular identification.

> We have named this room the 'Goethesaal' because the Hilton is as great as the man himself was, because the authority by which we name this room is equivalent to the authority that Goethe's name has come to command, and because its excellence is commensurate with the cultural and social standing you, our distinguished guest, bring to our establishment and which you, by the very act of choosing Hilton, have already further cemented.

To put it more bluntly, "Goethe sells."

Naming its noblest ballroom after Goethe is but one of many ways in which the Weimar Hilton, to stick with the example, constructs the Goethe myth for financial profit. Banished to the outskirts of the downtown area, the Hilton compensates for its lack of immediacy by taking the liberty of renaming that which may not fit the bill: the not so desirable location on the Belvederer Allee at the very end of the "Park on the Ilm" is quietly transformed into a much more attractive location "directly at the Goethepark," suggesting a natural path to the heart of German Classicism. Can we expect Goethe's *Geist*, his ghost, mind, and spirit, to meet us halfway on our stroll from the Hilton to the Gartenhaus (see Weissberg)?

The move from sign to myth, from the first to the second semiological system, hinges on the successful stripping away of the full meaning of the signifier. Only once "Goethe" the sign is drained of meaning and reduced to a gesture can "Goethe" become the signifier of the metalinguistic myth. This is not a process of obliteration, as Barthes points out, but rather one of deformation. The signifier is no longer permitted to convey anything but self-contained form. It is "uni-form" in its most literal sense. Nothing illustrates that better than another one of the Hilton's distortions, the invitation to go see "the world famous Goethe- and Schillerhaus," put in the singular as if the buildings were one and the same, much like the Goethe and Schiller monument. It is myths like these that make money, both directly and indirectly. Directly, by attracting guests to the Hilton, to the Weimar Classics Foundation, to the city of Weimar, the state of Thuringia; indirectly, by perpetuating a myth of a different kind, that of a symbiotically creative relationship between Goethe and Schiller. Packaged together they stand as one statue in front of the National Theater, corporeal evidence of a myth from which not only publishers and bookstores have been profiting for almost two full centuries.

What works for high culture works for low culture. In Weimar's advertising world we are likely to encounter Goethe in many more guises. We may see his image next to a portrait of Schiller's on the Telekom phone card, entitled "Kulturstadt Europas 1999," or we may be enticed to purchase Weimar porcelain because it features a silhouette of Goethe's head to explicate the slogan, "Weimar Porzellan. Inspired by Great Masters." We may see reproductions of Goethe in the form of busts not only in the Weimar Hilton but also in the Weimar Classics Foundation's shop and countless offices, both public and private. And, frequently, we will see Goethe's works being put to profitable use, his color circle of 1810 on the Weimar Card, for instance. The engraver in Schlossgasse 11 attempts to sell his goblets, pill boxes, and embossed cigarette cases with the same Goethe words with which he offers a gold replica of Goethe's and Christiane Vulpius's wedding bands: "Everything good that happens, works not alone." There is a good deal of irony in these attempts of commodifying Goethe by selling his own commodities or material possessions. Moving backwards on the signifying chain, we never get to Goethe, only to his possessions.

It is the big businesses, rather than the small, that appropriate Goethe's words most systematically. "Vom Eise befreit sind Strom und

Bäche" [Freed of ice are stream and creeks], we read not in *Faust* (MA 6.1: 560; 903) but in an advertisement of the InterCity Hotel Weimar enticing us to join its version of the Easter walk through the Park on the Ilm. "Come with me to Ettersburg ...." We do not know what Goethe planned to do up there with Charlotte von Stein, but it is quite clear why the Wimare Immobilien GmbH wants us to heed the call from the distant past. It is selling homes for its new development, cashing in on the beautiful scenery and an idyllic version of history.

The whole package, finally — that of Goethe's name, image, and works — is marketed for consumption in the form of a ginkgo biloba leaf, traditionally one of the most popular souvenirs the city has to offer. In Weimar, the ginkgo leaf continues to be mass-reproduced in all imaginable kinds of jewelry and sweets, from brooches, earrings, and necklaces to chocolates, pralines, and pastry. The sign is thus stripped of its material origins since all those products carry the decided advantage that they do not smell like that hellish blend of rotten eggs and sweat-soaked socks with which the fruit of the ginkgo tree charms its admirers every spring. What keeps the high number of jewelers in business is, first and foremost, Goethe's relationship to that extraordinary tree, culminating in a poem whose facsimile copy will invariably accompany any display of the ginkgo leaf. Some portrait of Goethe is bound to complete the picture.

What makes the phenomenon of Weimar's ginkgo biloba so interesting is the fact that this robust tree with its extract and various representations forms a mythical network within the larger network of the Goethe myth. Weimar tourists may well begin a ginkgo journey with a visit to the tree which Goethe himself is said to have planted across from the Anna Amalia library. Along the way, then, the tourist will pass numerous jewelry and sweets stores, will be staring this or that Goethe image in the face, will be tempted to read again Goethe's poem, may come across some ginkgo pills in the drugstore, and finally take a break from the tiring ginkgo tour by having a bite to eat at an Asian restaurant named *Ginkgo*. In a supreme marketing coup, the uniqueness of the tree — half conifer, half deciduous — has been intrinsically tied to the uniqueness of the poet, so much so that with every softgel of 50:1 concentrated ginkgo extract, the consumer of the cerebral stimulant can hope to edge ever closer to the intellectual heights of that most famous of planters who made it all possible. Goethe's original deed, then, is magically preserved and reproduced in every pill, in every cookie, in every earring. Consecrated in "the magic system of advertising" (Williams), the cult figure of an educated German bourgeoisie is no longer being celebrated as opium, as Carl von Ossietzky once saw it, but exalted and consumed as ginkgo extract. If we cannot touch the true Goethe, we are at least allowed to eat him as our Last Supper.

Weimar has many attractions to offer; its rich history comprises far more than just Goethe's life and letters or the consumable representations thereof. The consumer tourist, however, may not notice that in Weimar's Goethean landscape. One may be purchasing a set of Goethe slides only to find oneself in Schiller's, not Goethe's old home. One may enter a liquor store and find that a liter of wholesome Schiller wine is in fact cheaper than Goethe tea. Goethe cups may be on display in the company of others, portraying, say, Johann Sebastian Bach and Franz Liszt. In the morning, it may be a note on the front entrance of the Bauhaus that alerts us to the temporary closure of Goethe's Gartenhaus. For lunch we may treat ourselves to Goethe's favorite dish, "Tafelspitz mit Meerrettich" [boiled fillet of beef with horseradish], a dish that will cost us DM 15.50 and that now makes us wonder whether we should not have applied the money toward the purchase of a Goethe barometer. As we feast, our eyes may well wander over to the German National Theater and we may recall the various productions it has seen, productions of plays, of an ill-conceived but democratic constitution, of deadly weaponry. In the afternoon, then, we may spot an advertisement in the Bahnhofstraße, en route to Buchenwald perhaps, inviting us to ride horses in Goethe's tracks. Are we perhaps better off simply following in Goethe's footsteps, joining, as the Weimar Hilton suggests in one of its many classical brochures, the organized tour that promises to re-enact Goethe's Easter walk of 1777? That would no doubt acquaint us with the children of the Wieland, Herder, and von Stein families and, moreover, remind us that Goethe was not the only one shooting birds, hunting Easter eggs, and enjoying fireworks.

While the city is surely greater than the man, Goethe is the one figure indispensable to the modern myth the city has invented for itself. Not a single tourist attraction in Weimar is free of its association with Goethe because Goethe himself has been turned into a mythical system, a complex semiological system of representations that is capable of reproducing ad infinitum Goethe's life and letters in ever new form. To say that his mythical presence dominates the current Weimar market is not an exaggeration. This town is Goethe's town. Even where the Goethe myth is parodied, as in an advertisement of the Autonomous Culture Center where "Goethe meets Nina [Hagen]," even where the commercial construction of the myth is humorously exposed, as in the well-known poster of Donald Duck in the Campagna, and even where that myth is ostensibly desecrated, as in the poster of a beat-up Goethe under the heading "What else needs to happen?," such desecration only serves to point to the seemingly eternal consecration of the myth. Just in case the public needed contemporary literary proof of the firm grip which the Goethe myth holds over Weimar, Hans Magnus Enzensberger's provocative play, cast as a talk show and subversively entitled *Nieder mit Goethe* (Down with Goethe, 1995), provided it — and did so live in Weimar, in print, on television, on the internet (Fig. 1). Four of Goethe's contemporaries were put on stage to attack Goethe the man, the poet, the lover, and the politician. As if to exhibit to the entire country Weimar's helplessness in rebelling against Goethean authority, the characters never deliver. In the end the production revealed itself to be nothing more than what was already conceded in the play's sappy subtitle, *Eine Liebeserklärung* (A Declaration of Love). The event sold beyond expectations.

Marketing Culture Today: The Case of Goethe International

Recognizing that a powerful advertising system constantly works to reconstruct, market, and sell Weimar as Goethe's Weimar, it is reasonable to conclude that Goethe outsells the city. With its many streets named after poets and thinkers Weimar is literally carved up by signifiers of Germanistik, yet the city possesses no capital greater than her favorite son. While Goethe draws the consumer tourist to provincial Weimar today, the preservation and perpetuation of Goethe's myth will guarantee the economic future of an entire region dependent on tourism. The myth produces instant revenue also because it attracts businesses and their investments. One such business is Groth & Consorten, a Hamburg-based firm which made a name for itself when it joined forces with Thuringia's ministry of economics to call into being the program "Reisen und Genießen entlang der Klassikerstraße" (Traveling and Indulging along the Road of Classicism). More recently, Groth & Consorten opened an office right on the Weimar marketplace for its subsidiary, the Goethe® International. MarkenvertriebsGmbH. For the time being, the corporation Goethe® International distributes only two trade-marked products of Groth & Consorten, brandy and pralines, but intends in the future, according to a local Thuringian newspaper, to market and distribute internationally exclusive writing accessories, china, and glassware as well (*Thüringische Landeszeitung* of 5 September 1995). The brand name under which these products are currently being sold, and presumably will be sold in the future, is *Johann Wolf-*

gang von Goethe. As a trademark, that brand name is registered to the ownership of Groth & Consorten with the German Patent Office in Munich (*Warenzeichenblätter 2.21: G 33572/ 33 WZ*).

It is here, in the official library of signs, where one discovers the legal truths in trademarked myths. In Munich one learns, for instance, that there is more than one trademark by the name of Goethe, Johann Wolfgang von Goethe, or Geheimrat Goethe; but one also learns that such proliferation is still a far cry from the ninety-four entries registered in Mozart's name between 1954 and 1994 — which include the famous Mozart liqueur (not to be confused with the Amadeus liqueur), and the even more famous "Mozart-Kugeln," or "Mozart Balls." As for Goethe, the man could hardly complain about the multifariousness of the products to which he lends his name. While others have registered the name for wine, travels, candy, and the presentation of avant-garde music, Groth & Consorten has ensured its rightful use of the name *Johann Wolfgang von Goethe* and the image of Goethe's head in the Campagna in a series of patents dating back to February of 1983 (a 1994 registration runs under the name of "Goethe" alone). Included in the long list of goods to be distributed under Groth's auspices are: wines, liqueurs, chocolates (including those containing alcohol), chewing gum (except for medicinal purposes), ice cream, cigars, cigarettes, chewing tobacco, snuff, lighters, matches, posters, stationery, fountain pens, napkins, calendars, china, silverware, pottery, coffee, tea, sugar, rice, tapioca pudding, bread, honey, molasses, baking powder, sauces (excluding dressings), spices, ice, mustard, vinegar, and many more. Even though this list has been compiled from five separate registered entries, it is nonetheless impressive. But baffled as we are, we may still ask ourselves what vinegar and molasses have to do with Goethe? Why would the name Goethe sell products as apparently unsuited for mythification as these? In a flood of virtually indistinguishable products the brand name will set Groth's product apart from scores of others. Furthermore, the brand name Goethe is advantageous because Goethe's name recognition value is extremely high — probably second in Germany only to that of Adolf Hitler, and certainly comparable to the name recognition carried in the United States by select sports and entertainment figures. We can assume that *Air Goethe* would not be selling a sandal anywhere on this globe, or that the likeness of Michael Jordan would not be selling much cognac (though one never knows, of course).

The difference in this example is two-fold. On the one hand, the use of a personal name as brand name will be successful only when the consumer recognizes, or rather mis-recognizes, a "natural" relationship between name and product: Michael Jordan drinking Gatorade, Goethe reading a book. On the other hand, we can generally maintain that money-making proceeds "from a specific work upon values, social needs, and cultural wishes: in short, from dreams" (Rey 34). What distinguishes the appeal of the living body from that of the dead mind is the distinction between two consuming dreams: that of identification ("I want to be like Mike" because I value what Mike is and therefore dream) and that of possession ("I want to have Goethe" because I value such *Bildungsbesitz*, a synthesis of education, cultivation, and material possession). The first is more apt to advertise, the second more fit to market. Given the two criteria of a "natural" name-product relationship and the fulfillment of dreams, it is unlikely that Goethe vinegar will ever be much of a marketing success. (It is very likely that the product will never appear on the market in the first place since it is used by Groth & Consorten solely as a defensive sign, that is, an a priori trademark designed to preempt and block potential competition.) By the same token, the two criteria serve to explain why Goethe as a brand name is much better suited to sell fine brandy than molasses.

For all intents and purposes, *Goethe Weinbrand* has been a hit. This brandy exists in two substantially priced varieties, the regular version and the even more expensive *Extra*. We may liken them to, say, *Iphigenie* and *Faust*, for *Goethe Weinbrand* is passed on to the consumer as if it were a cultural artifact in and of itself, a distillate of literature and culture. To clarify in theoretical terms this move toward the satisfaction of cultural desire, we may apply Pierre Bourdieu's concept of capital to our analysis.[2] Bourdieu's theory goes beyond a purely economic definition in that he, generally speaking, views capital as any accumulable resource that wields power. As a result, he mainly distinguishes between economic capital (most frequently money) and immaterial, symbolic forms of capital, such as social capital (consisting largely of resources based on connections and group membership) and cultural capital (educational credentials, cultural competence to appreciate art). What makes Bourdieu's model so useful in describing cultural practices is that it allows for an interplay between the various types of capital. To Bourdieu, any type of capital can not only be accumulated and dispensed but is also convertible from one form to another.

If we apply this model to our discussion, we may formulate the marketing strategy of Groth & Consorten along the following lines. With the purchase of a bottle of *Goethe Weinbrand*, consumers are invited to "distill" symbolic capital from economic capital. What they stand to gain in this transaction is an increase mostly in cultural capital which in turn can be converted into prestige: being recognized by others as possessing cultural knowledge, an education, a sophisticated taste, and so forth. The price for being able to define the self in such a way is not all that high, especially when the presumed target group for the product is the upper middle class. A bottle of *Goethe Weinbrand* buys one an education, and if this is the essence of Goethe in a bottle, then the brandy surely makes the lack of action in *Iphigenie* more palatable. It smoothes and distills the ambiguities of *Faust* into an aromatic whole and brings the loftiness of Goethe's summum opus right into the consumer's stomach. The brandy, we may presume, is to be enjoyed with effects far more pleasurable than those of the German lessons in the Gymnasium.

Notwithstanding the culturally motivated relationship between Goethe and brandy, there is of course nothing in the distilled liquid that would make the connection to Goethe a semantically intrinsic one. Unlike the Köstritz brewery, for example, which can claim Goethe as one of its early customers and which can thus infer the right to depict him in the Campagna with a glass of dark beer in his hand, *Goethe Weinbrand* has to rely on other means of creating a "natural" link between name and product. It does so by producing a mythical signification, a second-order meaning of *Goethe Weinbrand*, which is anything but arbitrary. In vino veritas. The distilled truth of *Goethe Weinbrand* reveals itself in a bouquet of four major second-order connotations, all of which are passed on as attributes shared by poet and product, and all of which are subsumed under the concept of consumption. First, there is the attribute "old," connoting history, lasting, aged, mature, tradition, the latter being important as a principle of legitimacy, particularly for a new brand. Second, "German": the discreet sign is always defined by that which it is not. The product is *Weinbrand*; it is neither French cognac nor British brandy. Third, Goethe connotes "quality." By association the brandy is fine, excellent, perhaps even noble and aristocratic, certainly exceptional, a choice selection, if not the epitome of greatness. Quality has its price and is available only to select few. The incantation reads, "*Johann Wolfgang von Goethe Weinbrand Extra. So erlesen wie sein Name*" [as distinguished as its/his name]. Lastly, Goethe connotes "culture," unequivocally positive high culture, discriminating taste, sophisticated enjoyment, pleasure of beauty. All put together, *Goethe Weinbrand* promises the buyer nothing short of acquiring, possessing, and consuming "old German quality culture."

Much more so than literature, or literary criticism, for that matter, marketing is "at once the most powerful agent of cultural change and of cultural stability at work in the contemporary world" (Sherry 442). The flagship advertisement disseminated by Goethe® International shows not only how the four connotations are visually conveyed but how they relate to the network of the Goethe myth (Fig. 2). Here the link between Goethe and the brandy is established by placing pictures of both side by side. We see Tischbein's portrait of Goethe's head in the Campagna (1786–88) reproduced both as a framed circular detail of the painting and as the trade-marked imprint on the bottle itself. (We are spared the familiar but ever curious sight of the left leg extending into eternity and a left shoe gracing Goethe's right foot.) On the bottle the connotation "old" is literally impressed as authenticity: the trademark looks much like an eighteenth-century seal, a sign of authority further affirmed by the reproduction of Goethe's signature near the top of the bottleneck. The qualitative link between Goethe and the brandy is established not only by positioning a snifter right underneath Goethe's nose but also by a manipulation of color. Compared to Tischbein's original painting, the entire portrait of Goethe has been darkened. But while the hat appears much darker, the red of his collar has been altered so that it conforms to and becomes one with the brownish-red color of both liquor and bottle.

By far the most revealing manipulation, however, is the organization of the advertisement around nationalistic sentiment. The colors black, red, and gold are demonstratively presented as the German flag near the very top of the bottle, placed right above the words "Deutscher Weinbrand." But the colors are also contained in the presentation of the bottle itself, including the label. We can further identify the colors in the portrait of Goethe's head with its golden hair, the brandy-red collar, and the darkened black of his hat. Last but not least the colors are again visible in the top part of the ring framing the detail (see also Fig. 3).

What are we to make of this strong emphasis on the "German"? The advertisement reproduces and affirms the Goethe myth. To the consumer tourist, that myth has always been a German myth in the streets of Weimar. Bottled up, however, the myth takes the form of a nationalistic image of German supremacy. It is constituted much like the advertisements discussed earlier. The complexities of Goethe, his works and their reception, are reduced the moment he is transformed into the signifier of a myth. He becomes a lifeless icon, a monument as monolithic as the bottle on which his eye is fixated, only to be called back to life by an injection of conservative bourgeois values. That transformation is all the more forceful in this case because name and image are here used not merely as advertising vehicles but as a brand, an authorized and registered trademark. The prerequisite for the construction of the mythical signifier is explicitly demanded by the legal definition of the brand. For purposes of distinction, any brand must possess as its chief property "unified, instantly recordable (flat or two-dimensional), easily remembered form" (*Markengesetz* § 3, "Warenzeichen" 1363). While trademarking is a legally binding guarantee of consistently high or improved quality, the banal claim of any brand will always be the — explicit or implicit — promise that it is *better* than the rest. When the cultural supremacy attributed to the German national author is augmented by the investment of superiority in the brand as brand, when both are subsequently placed into an advertising context that is structured around signs of the "German," then Groth & Consorten has indeed constructed a nationalistic myth. Even where that myth does not flaunt its nationalistic character, it remains imbued with a sense of aristocratic arrogance. "Bitten Sie doch einfach/ Johann Wolfgang von Goethe zu Tisch" [Why not simply ask/ Johann Wolfgang von Goethe to your table? Fig. 4].

Far from re-enacting Anna Amalia's Monday *Tafelrunde* [roundtable; see Susanne Kord's essay in this volume] and rekindling any socially progressive function of negotiating class, gender, and age boundaries, the message in the bottle is a profoundly conservative one, more akin to the nationalistic tradition of Wilhelmine Germany than to Weimar circa 1800 or the early movement towards a culture nation (see Gert Theile's contribution to this volume). The voluminous literary histories of the nineteenth century relied on the early conflation of Goethe and his works and re-drew the local boundaries of city and duchy in order to produce a Goethe myth that could be sold by a militaristic state: Goethe's Weimar as the German, Weimar Classicism as German Classicism. It is only because Groth & Consorten is so far from matching the marketing success of its predecessor that the mythification for corporate profit does not appear to be particularly alarming. In its ineffectiveness it may well prove amusing.

Vested Interests

To the best of my knowledge, Groth & Consorten is struggling, perhaps because its advertising strategy is not very innovative and only mildly playful, perhaps because the competition is too stiff. But the myth of Goethe and Weimar as essentially German remains a powerful one that is exploited by many whose motives are far more honorable than those of Groth & Consorten. Today, the list of those groups and institutions that have a vested interest in Goethe's commodification and the circulation of the Goethe myth is lengthy. It ranges from the

German government and its branches (from the German Academic Exchange Service to the Goethe Institutes) to the governments of cities and states, to cultural foundations such as the Weimar Classics Foundation. Abroad the state and its agents find themselves in an environment that is just as competitive and therefore requires as firm an appropriation of the national Goethe myth as that of businesses, companies, and corporations; academic departments, theaters, and museums; publishers and bookstores. All are to some extent invested in propagating the Goethe myth for purposes as diverse as commerce and tourism, sales and student enrollments, political and moral authority.

There was no trademark law in the territories of the Holy Roman Empire of the German Nation. Had there been one, Goethe would have likely done exactly what Bernd Kauffmann, the President of the Weimar 1999 — Kulturstadt Europas GmbH and a lawyer by trade, did shortly after his appointment, that is register the poet's name (incidentally along with that of virtually all other prominent figures in Weimar history) with the German Patent Office. The move, we may assume, was designed to salvage "Goethe" and everything he embodies to the Weimar guardians: a traditional notion of high German culture, *our* culture, *our* Weimar, on the one hand; the profit to be derived from the control, mass-marketing, and merchandising of the sign on the other. Taken together, the two purposes demonstrate quite clearly that the dichotomy between high culture and low advertising does not hold up, not in 1999 and not in Goethe's lifetime.

The Goethe experience to which Tieck was treated, the privilege of bringing to life and setting in motion a revolving monument, was already the consumption of a commodity, put up for sale by owner. As consumer tourists today we eat and drink and consume and devour the Goethe we cannot touch, knowing that when we seek his essence, the "real" Goethe in the "here and now," we can never hope to get much closer than to his material possessions. But we can and should visit Weimar today and we should go for a stroll; the kind of engaging walk that will help us get to know again the city and its history, the people that lived there circa 1800, but also those who lived everyday lives there in 1900 as well as in 1999. We should walk the streets of Weimar with our minds and our senses — imaginatively, virtually, and critically — and joyfully use an ever-fluctuating local knowledge (Geertz) as our best defense against the temptation, presented by so many of the city's historical layers of consumer culture, to appropriate nationalism while walking. That is not only in our interest but also in that of the European culture city Weimar.

—Davidson College

Notes

[1] For an introduction and an overview of the range of cultural criticism, see During's *Cultural Studies Reader*; for German Cultural Studies, see *A User's Guide*, eds. Denham, Kacandes, and Petropoulos. My own thoughts on the matter (Henke 399–415) have led to this essay, and I would like to thank Liliane Weissberg, Stephanie Hammer, Hansford Epes, and Margaret McCarthy for their suggestions and criticism.

[2] See Bourdieu, *Distinction*, *Logic of Practice*, and *Language and Symbolic Power*; see also Linda Dietrick's essay in this volume.

Works Cited

Barthes, Roland. *Mythologies*. Trans. Annette Lavers. New York: Hill and Wang, 1972.

Bourdieu, Pierre. *Distinction. A Social Critique of the Judgement of Taste*. Trans. Richard Nice. Cambridge, MA: Harvard UP, 1984.

———. *Language and Symbolic Power*. Trans. Gino Raymond and Matthew Adamson. Ed. John B. Thompson. Cambridge: Polity P. Cambridge, MA: Harvard UP, 1991.

———. *The Logic of Practice*. Trans. Richard Nice. Cambridge: Polity. Stanford: Stanford UP, 1990.

Calhoun, Craig. "Habitus, Field, and Capital." *Bourdieu: Critical Perspectives*. Eds. Craig Calhoun, Edward LiPuma, and Moishe Postone. Chicago: U of Chicago P, 1993. 61–88.

Denham, Scott, Irene Kacandes, and Jonathan Petropoulos, eds. *A User's Guide to German Cultural Studies*. Ann Arbor, MI: U of Michigan P, 1997.

During, Simon. "Introduction." *The Cultural Studies Reader*. Ed. Simon During. London and New York: Routledge, 1993.

Ebersbach, Volker. *Ein geborener Genießer. Goethe-Anekdoten*. Winsen and Weimar: Hans Boldt, 1995.

Enzensberger, Hans Magnus. *Nieder mit Goethe: Eine Liebeserklärung. Requiem für eine romantische Frau. Ein Liebeskampf in sieben Sätzen*. Frankfurt a. M.: Verlag der Autoren, 1995.

Geertz, Clifford. *Local Knowledge: Further Essays in Interpretive Anthropology*. New York: Basic Books, 1983.

Gesetz über den Schutz von Marken und sonstigen Kennzeichen (Markengesetz — MarkenG). 25 October 1994.

Henke, Burkhard. "Cultural Studies, the Eighteenth Century, and the Uses of the German Classics." *A User's Guide to German Cultural Studies*. Eds. Scott Denham, Irene Kacandes, and Jonathan Petropoulos. Ann Arbor, MI: U of Michigan P, 1997. 399–415.

Hohenstein, Siglinde. *Friedrich Justin Bertuch (1747–1822) — bewundert, beneidet, umstritten. Übersetzer mit Verdiensten. Dichter ohne Talent. In Weimar kluger Verwalter der fürstlichen Privatschatulle, erfolgreicher Herausgeber und Verleger, Freund Goethes. Ein Kapitalist und Philanthrop der Aufklärung*. Berlin and New York: Walter de Gruyter, 1989.

Rechtswörterbuch. Ed. Hans Kauffmann. 11th ed. Munich: C. H. Beck, 1992.

Rey, Alain. "From Money to Dream: A Return Ticket." *Marketing and Semiotics. New Directions in the Study of Signs for Sale*. Ed. Jean Umiker-Sebeok. Berlin, New York, Amsterdam: Mouton de Gruyter, 1987. 31–37.

Sherry, John F. "Advertising as a Cultural System." *Marketing and Semiotics. New Directions in the Study of Signs for Sale*. Ed. Jean Umiker-Sebeok. Berlin, New York, Amsterdam: Mouton de Gruyter, 1987. 441–61.

Thüringische Landeszeitung. 5 September 1995.

Warenzeichenblätter. Teil 2: Eingetragene Zeichen. Ed. Deutsches Patentamt. Munich: Wila, 1954–1994.

Weissberg, Liliane. *Geistersprache: Philosophischer und literarischer Diskurs im späten 18. Jahrhundert*. Würzburg: Königshausen and Neumann, 1990.

Williams, Raymond. "Advertising: the magic system." *The Cultural Studies Reader*. Ed. Simon During. London and New York: Routledge, 1993. 320–36.

Fig. 1: Advertisement sticker for the Weimar performance of Hans Magnus Enzensberger's Nieder mit Goethe: Eine Liebeserklärung *(Down with Goethe: A Declaration of Love, 1995; courtesy of Weimar 1999 — Kulturstadt Europas GmbH).*

Fig. 2: Advertisement sticker for Goethe Weinbrand: "Johann Wolfgang von Goethe Brandy Extra. As distinguished as its name" (courtesy of Groth & Consorten).

Fig. 3: Advertisement sticker for Goethe Weinbrand (back): "Behind this door, Johann Wolfgang von Goethe is waiting for you" (courtesy of Groth & Consorten).

BITTEN SIE DOCH EINFACH
JOHANN WOLFGANG VON GOETHE ZU TISCH.

JOHANN WOLFGANG VON GOETHE WEINBRAND.
SO ERLESEN WIE SEIN NAME.

Fig. 4: Advertisement in form of a place card. "Why not simply ask Johann Wolfgang von Goethe to your table? Johann Wolfgang von Goethe Weinbrand. As distinguished as its name" (courtesy of Groth & Consorten).

2

DANIEL PURDY

Weimar Classicism and
The Origins of Consumer Culture

FRIEDRICH JUSTIN BERTUCH (1747–1822) was a Weimar publisher and manufacturer whose immensely popular publica-tions introduced provincial Germans to the fashions of distant cities. His *Journal des Luxus und der Moden* (Journal of Luxury and Fashion, 1786–1827, abbr. as *Modejournal*; see "Works Frequently Cited") sought to educate non-aristocratic Germans on the subtleties of French and English luxuries. In its pages, Bertuch formulated a consumer aesthetic that integrated clothing, cosmetics, household objects, and other instruments of daily life with the activities and labor of the ordinary "Bildungsbürger" [educated and cultivated bourgeois]. An adherent of the Enlightenment and an advocate of English liberal economic policy, Bertuch sought to replace the aristocratically representative order of Francophile luxuries with a consumer culture that brought decorative objects and fashion goods under a labor-intensive regime of domesticity. Rather than symbolize rank, consumer goods were supposed to facilitate mental and physical productivity as well as comfort. These new consumer wares were, according to Bertuch, more practical as well as affordable; and thereby allowed the dispersed and provincial German middle classes to participate in the newly emerging cosmopolitanism of the Western European urban bourgeoisie.

In addition to encouraging consumption, Bertuch's *Modejournal* was intended to foster domestic industries dedicated to supplying German consumers with inexpensive and useful products. Bertuch considered the support of industry to be a fundamental tenet of his plan to reformulate the practices of German consumers. To that end he established the *Modejournal* as a kind of "mail-order catalogue." Readers were encouraged to write to Bertuch to purchase the products described in the *Modejournal*. To respond to readers' demands for consumer goods, Bertuch established in Weimar his Landes-Industrie Comptoir, a facility we would now designate as a proto-industrial factory. Through these publishing and manufacturing ventures, Bertuch quickly became the wealthiest private citizen in Weimar. When it came to administrative matters, he was Goethe's Doppelgänger, a non-aristocrat, who by dint of his special skills had the ear and trust of the duke. In 1775 Bertuch was placed in charge of the duke's treasury and personal finances, a position he maintained until his business obligations led him to resign in 1796. His publications included the *Allgemeine Literaturzeitung* (General Literary Newspaper, 1785–1849) and *London und Paris* (1798–1805), although some of his most profitable ventures were series dedicated to natural history, geography, and children's literature. As his career took off, he expanded his country home so that a year after the *Modejournal* appeared Körner reported that he lived in the most beautiful and tastefully decorated house in Weimar.[1]

From the moment the *Modejournal* appeared in 1786, it stood in an intimate and thus awkward relation to the literary culture that made Weimar famous. Bertuch made no claim that fashion wares were works of art, despite the fact that they shared a clear neoclassical aesthetic (Figs. 1–3). In legitimating the *Modejournal*, Bertuch was far more concerned with the moral and economic arguments against its publication than with aesthetic critiques. The regulation of dress and consumer practices had been a long-standing prerogative first of medieval cities, and then of absolutist princes. The first obstacles to Bertuch's efforts to disseminate elite styles to a broad middle-class reading class came from pastors and cameralists concerned about the deleterious effects of introducing a taste for luxury to the German provinces. To preempt charges that the *Modejournal* encouraged personal bankruptcy and national indebtedness, Bertuch argued that a rational, indeed often critical, discussion of luxury goods in the *Modejournal* was a far more persuasive means of regulating consumer habits than sumptuary laws which by the end of the eighteenth century had become too rigid for an increasingly mobile society with its growing class differentiations.

In place of sumptuary laws, Bertuch advocated a functional and personalized consumer ethic that claimed to liberate the individual as a productive and expressive member of a new cosmopolitan society. By adopting the standards of taste which Bertuch claimed were already established in foreign capitals, Germans would escape the accumulated obligations of the "Stände" [feudal, or corporate, estates]. Bertuch juxtaposed the codified layers of feudal dress with a restrained, utilitarian style that focused on the body as a natural organism and the person as an intellectual and economic producer. This affirmative standard of taste invoked a concept of the body not very different from the neoclassical conception of the artwork as a harmonious entity. In the case of the *Modejournal*, the organic unity included the material objects of everyday life. The *Modejournal's* interest in the tasteful arrangement of household things was not confined to decorations or clothes. The terms *fashion* and *luxury* covered a spectrum of goods, ranging from those intimately connected to the consumer's body and extending to architectural structures that stood in a less fluid and more detached relation. The title page of the first issue of January 1786 announced:

> Die Gegenstände des Journals sind [...] 1) weibliche und männliche Kleidung; 2) Putz; 3) Schmuck; 4) Nippes; 5) Ammeublement; 6) alle Arten von Tische- und Trink-Geschirre, als Silber, Porcellain, Gläser usw.; 7) Equipage, sowohl Wagen als Pferdezeug, und Livréen; 8) Häuser- und Zimmer-Einrichtung und Verzierung; 9) Gärten und Landhäuser. (*Modejournal* rpt. 1: 30)
>
> [The objects of this journal are (...) 1) feminine and masculine dress; 2) adornment; 3) jewelry; 4) ornamentation; 5) furniture; 6) all forms of tableware, including silver, porcelain, and glassware; 7) riding equipment, including coaches, gear, and liveries; 8) interior and exterior design; 9) gardens and country homes.]

All these products had once been subject to sumptuary laws. Within absolutist society, they had been the envied status symbols of the upper aristocracy. Bertuch's journal brought them under the emerging utilitarian, or rather disciplinary, regime of bourgeois tastes, thereby introducing new mechanisms of social control into sectors of society that had long stopped complying with sumptuary laws. Instead of restricting consumption on the basis of cost, as sumptuary laws did, Bertuch's *Modejournal* fostered conformity to a pragmatic, understated, yet expensive standard of "good taste."

At the end of the eighteenth century the task of organizing the diverse practices and objects of upper-class consumption had become more difficult as these conventions and commodities separated from the formalized rituals of courtly celebrations. The loss of legitimacy suffered by courtly etiquette in the latter half of the eighteenth century was brought on, in part, by the functionalization of the symbolic authority invested in the king's body. In a limited sense, the *Modejournal* adapted the courtly principle that all decorations, ceremonies, installations, celebrations and earthly activities reflect the magnificence of the king. Bertuch set the parameters of his own journalistic enterprise by defining "Mode" and "Luxus" as those objects that enhance the bodily comfort, pleasure, and appearance of the individual consumer. By making universal claims about the importance of comfort and social graces in all human interactions, the *Modejournal* applied the principle to bourgeois households that all things must integrate themselves with operations of "the body."[2] What distinguished the *Modejournal's* effort to arrange domestic objects around a human body was its total reconceptualization of what the body did and the recognition that its own consumer aesthetic was concerned with the bodies of many different individual property owners, rather than that of a single monarch.

The importance of the body as a conceptual anchor for the many diffuse objects, beliefs, and social rituals that comprised fashionable consumer culture was apparent on the journal's title page. Bertuch's list, as quoted earlier, moves outward from the body. As the types of objects are counted off, beginning with clothing and ending with country homes, they are set in concentric circles removed at different distances from their owner. These circles mark different degrees of intimacy between the owner and the object. The title page's list reveals the perspective of bourgeois fashion judgment which, rather than approaching the individual from afar (as in the ceremonial spaces of princes), sizes up the overall figure from a close distance (as if from across a private room) and then moves in to examine details before backing away to consider the individuals' relation to their domestic environment. Not only does the list suggest the manner in which individuals examine each other, it also suggests an imaginary sequence with which the individual constructs his or her persona, not unlike a person dressing a doll.[3] First the body is covered, then the face decorated with cosmetics and jewelry, then material things are placed in proximity to the body — decorations which refer to the figure. As the focus moves away from adorning the body, objects are introduced which bring it into circulation with others. Furniture, tableware, and carriages share the common goal of enabling public intercourse through the satisfaction of bodily requirements. The first items listed approached the respective parts of the body, the second half grasps the entire body as a thing to be situated within an arena. These items are less intimate, less likely to bear the personal mark of their owner, not as closely tailored to her physical form. The last two categories listed are architectural — wall coverings and building facades. They stand at the greatest remove from the body's specialty. As fixtures, they do not respond to its organic fluidity, to its emotions, health, age, or education. They are also least likely to be replaced and most readily treated as backdrops, inflexible signifiers of the class or aesthetic tradition to which the owner belongs, imprecise references to personal particulars. Yet within the *Modejournal's* framework, the fact that an object was not in direct contact with the body of its owner (as in the case of the front facade of a building) did not mean that his or her personal and intimate needs were ignored. Each layer in the concentric circle of objects arrayed around the body was joined to every other layer by the formal principle that their design should be based upon their role in the individual's mental and physical life.

The integration of clothes with bodily functions became the model for designing other types of goods. Just as clothes were supposed to satisfy the specific needs of the person who wore them (as opposed to clothes representing a social class), so must every object within a household be designed to comply to the personal requirements of the inhabitants. Bertuch spells out this sequential logic during the *Modejournal's* first year of publication. "Die Kleidung bestimmt das Ammeublement der Zimmer, die Tafel, den Umgang, die Equipage, die Bedienten und dergleichen. Es muß alles akkordiren, sonst nimmt sichs nicht aus" [Clothing determines the type of furniture in a room, the table setting, the social intercourse, riding equipment, servants, and the like. Everything must be in accord, otherwise nothing will look right; October 1786: 352]. Later he extended the design principle to include architecture. Even at its furthest remove from the physical presence of the owner, objects must respond to his needs and provide him comfort.

> Ein Hauß sollte von Rechtswegen immer den Bedürfnissen der Lebensart und Verhältnissen des Hausherrn so angemessen seyn und anpassen, als der Rock seinem Leibe. Wenigstens fordre ich dies von ihm, wenn er sich's neu erbaut. (October 1788: 381)
>
> [A house by rights should suit the needs, lifestyle, and social standing of the master as closely as his jacket fits around his chest. At least that is what I demand of him when he builds it from the ground up.]

Disciplinary interests were never foremost in the language of the *Modejournal*, yet the question of setting limits on consumption was impossible to dispel. Bertuch concluded his cautious introduction to the *Modejournal's* first issue by stating:

> So viel, dünckt uns, sey hier hinreichend, sowohl über die sehr unbestimmte und unschicklich so gestellte Frage: ist Luxus schädlich oder nützlich? unsere Meinung zu sagen als auch un-

> sern Lesern einen richtigen Maasstab dazu in die Hände zu geben. (*Modejournal* rpt. 1: 27–28)
>
> [This much, it seems to us, is sufficient to both express our opinion concerning the very ill-defined and awkwardly phrased question "Is luxury harmful or beneficial?" and to press an accurate yardstick into the hands of our readers, so that they will be able to make such determinations.]

Articles might insist on the practicality of a given garment or product, but these assertions always went hand in hand with an evaluation of its appearance. At times the regulatory interests of the *Modejournal* were unmistakable. For example, between 1789 and 1791 numerous articles advocated the abandonment of expensive mourning clothes. Letters from readers were often printed thanking the *Modejournal* for pointing out the hazards of some particular product or practice. This overt language of Enlightenment social reform was generally subsumed by the more enthusiastic celebration of new styles and their superiority over older fashions. Bertuch sought not to be held responsible for the harmful consequences of consumption. He insisted that the *Modejournal* was primarily an archive of style. Its function was to describe, critique, and disseminate fashion.

> Wir sind Geschicht-Schreiber des Luxus, nicht seine Priester, kennen genau die Rechte und Gränze, welche der Historiker hat, und werden sie gewiß in keinem unseren Werke, auf irgend eine Art überschreiten [...]. Wir maaßen uns die Gabe und den Amt, Moralisch-Kranke zu heilen, nicht an; und überlassen sie dem, welchem sie gegeben ist. (March 1786: 138)
>
> [We are the history writers of luxury, not its high priests. We know exactly what privileges and limitations an historian has, and will not exceed them in any way in any of our works. We wish to assume neither the ability nor the office of curing moral illness. We leave that to those who have that ability.]

Ultimately the *Modejournal* did take clear positions on the personal and social value of commodities, however within the optimistic free-market model of the late Enlightenment, these utilitarian interests were completely consistent with the expectations of tasteful opinion. Bertuch's attitude was in line with Christian Garve's assertion:

> So hat der Kreislauf der Moden und Meubeln, durch alle Abentheuerlichkeiten, durch welche er in der Reihe vergangner Jahrhunderte bis auf unsre Zeit hindurchgegangen ist, doch im

Ganzen unsre Kleidung bequemer und einfacher gemacht, als beydes bey unsern Vorfahren gewesen ist. (Garve 291)

[The cycle of fashion, despite all the outrageousness it has provided over the last few centuries, has made our clothes more comfortable and simpler than those worn by our ancestors.]

Providing the Bildungsbürgertum with news of the latest styles from abroad fit neatly with the overall project of the Enlightenment, for the spread of cosmopolitan tastes amounted to a re-organization of German domestic life. The *Modejournal* praised its own efforts when it published the following account of German fashion advancement:

Wenn auch die kleinern Städte Teutschlands im Fortschritte der Aufklärung weit hinter ihren größern Schwestern zurückbleiben, so kann man ihnen doch den Ruhm nicht versagen, daß sie in Ansehung der Moden alles thun, um jenen gleich zu kommen. (*Modejournal* rpt. 1: 200)

[Even if Germany's smaller towns have lagged behind their bigger sisters in accepting Enlightenment progress, one cannot deny them praise for doing everything to be their equals in matters of fashion.]

It was precisely that the Bildungsbürgertum was dispersed across the German countryside that made it possible for Weimar to serve as the generator for the newly emerging fashion culture. The German intelligentsia, as well as the nascent business classes, were dependent upon written information in a way that London merchants were not. Aside from printed sources, aspiring Germans had no means of participating in an urban, cosmopolitan society. Excluded from princely courts, which in Germany were even more contemptuous of commoners than their English and French counterparts, the middle class and its literary offshoots were obliged to rely on textual mediation in escaping the particular traditions of the immediate locality. Fashion in Germany thus relied on a literate populace, just as every other movement of the Enlightenment did.

The more fundamental, theoretical challenges to fashion culture were raised by Goethe and Schiller in the 1790s. The "problem" of fashionable commodities appears in their writings as a background phenomenon, as an example of failed artistic expression. Goethe's introduction to the short-lived journal *Propyläen* (Propylaea, 1798–1800), and a few related essays which never made it into publication, directly address the popularity of antique reproductions in Germany (see also Catriona MacLeod's essay in this volume). While not the most prominent of Goethe's aesthetic writings, his distaste for the commercial marketing of imitation Greek vases has reverberated far beyond the initial context of the eighteenth century's enthusiasm for antiquity. The most important descendant of Goethe's critique is Walter Benjamin's famous discussion of the reproducibility of art (471–508), itself a repetition of Goethe's own complaints about the mechanical recreation of Greek antiquity. When Goethe warns in "Kunst und Handwerk" (Art and Craftsmanship, presumably written 1797) that "kluge Fabrikanten und Entrepeneurs haben die Künstler in ihren Sold genommen und durch geschickte mechanische Nachbildungen die eher befriedigten als unterrichteten Liebhaber in Kontribution gesetzt" [Clever manufacturers and entrepreneurs have taken artists into their pay and through skillful mechanical reproductions have found buyers more interested in gaining satisfaction than education; MA 4.2: 120–21], he is beginning to articulate the most important aesthetic critique of commodity culture Germany has produced. The continuity between Goethe's concerns and the Frankfurt School's more elaborate confrontation with the culture industry is so remarkably smooth that one feels almost deceived by Benjamin for not citing his obvious neoclassical source.

The aesthetic principles of Weimar Classicism have always been strongly associated with Goethe's Italian journey (1786–88). However, many of its theoretical features are a result of developments which occurred in the city of Weimar itself, namely Friedrich Bertuch's highly successful marketing of antiquity in the form of consumer goods. Put simply and coyly, Weimar Classicism was as much a product of Weimar as it was an experience of Italy. The negative reactions of Goethe, Schiller, and Herder to the *Modejournal* were instrumental in creating the theory that "true art" is autonomous from pressures of societal demands, be they political or fashion-oriented. Their aesthetic theory of the 1790s can be understood in local terms as a factional struggle within Weimar over the boundaries between commerce and art. To that end Goethe's short pieces for the *Propyläen* attempt to establish a clear boundary between antique art and the Greco-Roman fashions depicted in Bertuch's *Modejournal*.

Most histories of aesthetic theory in eighteenth-century Germany automatically assign Goethe and Schiller legitimacy for their rejection of popular tastes without considering the pedagogical function of fashion culture in constituting "Bürgerlichkeit" [bourgeois mentality]. These commentaries frequently dismiss the similarities between Bertuch's advocacy of Greek style in fashion and Goethe's and Schiller's arguments concerning the "proper" imitation of Greek art, by implying that the eighteenth-century fashion for antiquity was itself an imitation and simplification of Weimar Classicism. Both movements — the fashionable and the theoretical — are intertwined when examined on the local level of Weimar. Instead of asking how much of Weimar Classicism can be found in eighteenth-century fashion, we might ask: why were Weimar classicists so afraid of their own fashionableness?

A vast amount of research has been devoted to the minute goings-on in Weimar, and yet a great deal of this research has been presented so as to re-affirm the originality and decisiveness of the town's literary geniuses. This bias, I believe, accounts for the fact that Bertuch's private papers have never been published or documented, even though they have been available in the Goethe and Schiller Archive for decades. Bertuch the entrepreneur represents a side of Weimar history that has been characterized as conflicting with the aesthetic principles of neo-classicism; I will argue, however, that his *Modejournal* belongs very much to Weimar culture once it is understood as having had economic and material dimensions. The formal principles of classicism were clearly intended as a means of distancing art from mass consumption, yet Bertuch's representation of "antikisierte Mode" [neo-antique fashion] was too closely allied with the goals and methods Goethe and Schiller espoused for us not to consider the many ways in which Weimar's fashion publications overlapped with their literary competitors. Both classicism and Bertuch's *Modejournal* appreciated the harmonious beauty of organic structures. Both enjoyed the integration of practical necessity and form. Both grounded their own discourse in an idealized conception of the human being in which everyday material life was organized according to the requirements of the spirit (or intellect). The one point in which they diverged was in their estimation of the historical significance of these organic structures. Did they participate in an eternal unity or were they throw-aways readily replaced by new integrations of form and matter? Was harmony a condition that could last beyond a very limited context? Did it exist only for a brief here and now, or could it be rediscovered endlessly by those who had the right means of understanding?

The questions discussed in this essay, I believe, go to the heart of Cultural Studies. The classical concept of "Kunstautonomie" [autonomy of art] stands behind German literary criticism's traditional dismissal of both "non-literary" texts and the material culture of ordinary life. By showing through historical and theoretical arguments that Weimar Classicism was already embedded in a fashion culture even as it sought to define itself in opposition to mass consumption, I wish to lower the barriers between traditional literary criticism and Cultural Studies. My project does not seek to describe the "cultural background" of Weimar's literary movements, in the manner of cultural historians such as W. H. Bruford. Rather I want to challenge the legitimacy of such categories as "foreground/background" and "original/imitation." Cultural Studies raises a theoretical challenge to literary criticism's disciplinary boundaries, by questioning how and why the distinction between "high art" and every other form of symbolic expression first came into existence and continues to be maintained within academic disciplines. Although it might at times want to bury itself in the obscure and the esoteric, Cultural Studies ought not just skip over the monadic work of art, and search for new, more exciting material to champion; it is far better served by an examination of all social objects that seeks to understand the discursive operations which separate art from material culture.

For all the historical significance of Goethe's comments on commodity culture, they are also a response to the context of Weimar. The "clever manufacturers" who draw artists onto their payroll were not just famous foreign entrepreneurs such as England's Josiah Wedgwood. Friedrich Bertuch clearly represented the practices Goethe and others found threatening. He is not mentioned by name in Goethe's essays on consumer culture precisely because he was such an important local figure. Goethe refrained from citing the immediate object of his complaint, and instead cast his argument in the abstract terms of aesthetic theory and generalizing social commentary.

When it came to discussions of policy, Bertuch and Goethe nurtured a collegial aversion to each other. For all the prominence of Bertuch's publications, not once did Goethe publish an important piece in the *Modejournal* (for Bertuch's role in the publication of "Das Römische Carneval" [The Roman Carnival, 1789] see MA 3.2: 547–53). When the journal ran an unfriendly overview of local stage productions, Goethe insisted, as director of Weimar theater, that he be allowed to supervise and, on occasion, suppress the *Modejournal's* reviews. Their antipathy was tempered by collegial forbearance, yet they managed to avoid each other for years at a stretch. Neighbors unable to expel each other, they extended their studious disavowal of one another in their writing. The *Modejournal* eschewed most purely artistic topics. Bertuch was far too tactful a businessman to risk a direct confrontation with the duchy's leading light. In fact, he took the opposite tack. His essays on fashion implicitly challenge Goethe's pointed distinctions between art and entertainment by blithely ignoring the fact that they were aimed at him.

Bertuch elaborated a standard of taste that came very close to Goethe's and Schiller's celebration of Greek and Roman antiquity. Not the modest reporter of foreign trends he claimed to be, Bertuch insisted that clothes and interior decorations stand in a formal relation to the physical and social needs of the individual consumer. The *Modejournal* claimed that the highest standard of taste consisted of an organic arrangement of individual commodities, wherein each garment and appliance complemented as well as integrated itself into the larger structure of the household. Individual trends might vary over time, Bertuch acknowledged, but the particular requirements of domestic life were more consistent, and thus should determine the arrangement of consumer goods. Pragmatic utility provided a loosely defined necessity upon which Bertuch sought to construct a stable notion of "good taste."

According to Bertuch's *Modejournal*, consumer goods were required to address the individual in his 'natural' condition, as well as in his social interactions. The natural body was presumed to exist outside the obligations of polite companionship. A double imperative insisted that certain bodily features could not and should not be altered. The color of skin, eyes, hair were treated as primary conditions in the creation of beauty. Their alteration through cosmetics and dyes would never be convincing enough to compete with the idealized unadorned body. To demonstrate the failure, as well as the harmful effects of cosmetics, the *Modejournal* of February 1787 cited the example of veteran stage actors, whose faces would be covered with rashes and lesions brought on by powders and creams made from lead, mercury, and quick silver (53). The old actor's agony served as a warning to the fashionably young: by trying to enhance the allure of the body the individual ultimately brings about its disfigurement. By personalizing clothes, cosmetics, and hair styles so that they "brought out the natural beauty" of the individual, the *Modejournal* claimed that its readers would rise above transitory trendiness. Their beauty would last longer and appeal universally, as one letter to the editor claimed:

> Wenn man uns mit glänzenden buntschäckigen [...] Gewändern behangen, angestaunt, höchstens Minuten lang bewundert, so werden wir in sauberer, einfacher Kleidung, wovon Farbe und Form unserm Teint und Wuchs anpaßt, immer gefallen. (November 1789: 461)
>
> [If we were adored for a few moments while we were draped in glittering and brightly colored garments, then we will forever find favor if we wear clean, simple clothes whose color and cut match our skin tone and figure.]

Modern aesthetics has seen many versions of Bertuch's distinction between rapidly changing fashion trends and a temporally detached standard of taste. At the turn of the twentieth century, movements in the decorative arts and architecture defined themselves in part through a division between *style* as a formal expression that defines the spirit of an epoch and *fashion* as the constantly fluctuating, empty ornamentation of commodities (see Schwartz; Wigley). Goethe formulates a similar distinction when he outlines his understanding of the difference between artistic creation and mechanical production of fashion goods.

> Eine Materie erhält durch die Arbeit eines echten Künstlers einen innerlichen, ewig bleibenden Wert, anstatt daß die Form welche durch einen mechanischen Arbeiter selbst dem kostbarsten Metall gegeben wird immer in sich bei der besten Arbeit etwas unbedeutendes und gleichgültiges hat, das nur so lang erfreuen kann als es neu ist [...]. (MA 4.2: 119)
>
> [Through the work of a true artist, a material obtains an inner, eternally lasting value, whereas the form given even to the most costly metal by mechanical craftsmen always has, even in the best work, something insignificant and indifferent in it which can please only as long as it is new (...).]

The term mechanical referred not only to the production of goods but also to the "automatic" and uncritical manner in which consumers adopted new trends. The form of a fashion article, Goethe suggested, amounted to nothing more than its position in time, its place in a series of products that is destined to extend beyond its own moment, thereby negating its own identity. Form in fashion was not a substance that defined the character of a commodity, rather it occurred only within an artificially constructed schema. The isolated product itself was a disposable part in an open-ended chain.

Goethe argues that luxury, as opposed to "der wahre Reichtum" [real riches] consists in a cyclical substitution of household objects. The sheer value of his possessions does not suffice, according to Goethe, in establishing an individual's status as a consumer.

> Der Luxus besteht nach meinem Begriff nicht darinnen daß ein Reicher viele kostbare Dinge besitze, sondern daß er Dinge von der Art besitze, deren Gestalt er erst verändern muß um sich ein augenblickliches Vergnügen und vor andern einiges Ansehen zu verschaffen. (MA 4.2: 119)
>
> [Luxury, to my mind, does not consist in the rich man's possession of many costly things, but rather that he possesses things whose form he first has to change in order to procure a momentary pleasure for himself as well as the respect of others.]

Herein lies one of the fundamental shifts in the history of consumer culture. Aristocratic culture had its changing trends in style, yet they were associated with dynastic changes or shifts in monarchical alliances, not the inextricable movement of a social system beyond even the symbolic control of an individual. The bourgeois consumer culture that emerged at the end of the eighteenth century was driven by a cycle of change that required alterations that were not justified by monarchical authority; baffling even their most loyal adherents, these new fashions rolled across society with greater frequency than ever before and with no better explanation than that it was expected for all members of good society to keep up. The rationale for change had shifted from the expediencies of displaying one's standing in the absolutist hierarchy to the obligation to position oneself within the sway of public opinion. The *Modejournal*'s great value to its readers was its ability to keep them better informed about these shifts in taste than any other periodical (or other media, for that matter).

The phrase "real riches" suggests both material and spiritual wealth. The ideal consumer combined these two by possessing expensive objects that were also aesthetically and morally edifying, therefore not subject to the arbitrary whims of fashion. The proof of an object's true value was that its owner could enjoy it throughout his life, growing ever more pleased with it the more he grew to understand it.

Goethe provides two illustrations of the hermeneutic process through which an aesthetic form contributes to its owner's ongoing education. The first is a paraphrase from Homer in which an artisan has produced a belt so exquisite that he could justly be praised for the rest of his life, just as the belt's owner could always find pleasure in wearing it. Goethe intends to contrast the longevity of the ancient belt with modern fashion which never preserves a garment for so long. Goethe might be seen as arguing in favor of a modern design concept that eschews all appeals to passing tastes. However, in the absence of a community that bestows praise as Homer does, the individual who insists on wearing the same garment his life long becomes something of an eccentric, a sentimental fetishist of Werther's variety (see Purdy 160–65; also Susan Gustafson's essay in this volume). What amounts to high praise in the heroic world of the *Iliad* comes across to the cosmopolitan eighteenth century as a churlish refusal to alter one's appearance as tastes change. As the example shows, the "real riches" are predicated upon a community that recognizes them. By holding fast to his Homeric sensibility, Goethe implicitly suggests the formation of an heroic anti-fashion, a masculine refusal to play along with the stylish whimsy.

While not making an explicit appeal to sexual difference, Goethe's attitude, with its invocation of antiquity, provides a rationale for the gendered division of modern fashion culture — a split that has in large part been predicated upon the claim that masculinity in dress and consumption depends on a stubborn insistence on preserving objects because they have some intrinsic worth unrecognized by communal opinion. More than just the refusal to play along with the fashion game, the masculine gesture has always sought to protect the timeless value of the things to which it clings. This insistence on extra-social value has hardly undermined fashion culture; indeed, since the eighteenth century, it has served as a primary rationale for consumption. Long before blue jeans and white tee-shirts, Bertuch lauded the solidity and durability of the newest products from England.

> Die geschmackvolle Simplicität und Solidität, welche England allen seinen Fabrikwaaren zu geben hat, ist für uns Teutsche so ausserordentlich empfehlend und anlokend, daß das Wort Englisch, englische Waare, schon dermalen einen unwiderstehlichen Zauberreitz für uns hat, und beynah ein Synonym der Vollkommenheit und Schönheit bey Werken des Kunstfleißes worden ist. (*Modejournal* rpt. 1: 75)

> [The tasteful simplicity and solidity which England gives to all its factory products, is, for us Germans, so extraordinarily attractive and commendable that the words "English" and "English commodity" have an irresistible and magical allure, so much so that they have become virtual synonyms for perfection and beauty in craftsmanship.]

The *Zeitung für die elegante Welt* (Newspaper for the Elegant World, 1801–59), Bertuch's later competition, acknowledged the defensive character in masculine dress when it wrote in 1802:

> Bei unserer männlichen Kleidung ist nur nie an das Idealische zu denken; sie ist recht herzlich positiv. Es ist alles Mögliche gewonnen, wenn sie von dem Charakter des Unmännlichen, des Karikaturmäßigen frei ist. Die Engländer bleiben für uns darin Muster; sie verbinden das Kleidende mit dem Bequemen.[4]

> [The important thing in men's clothing is that it should always be assertive and never dreamy. Anything is possible, so long as the clothes avoid the unmasculine and anything akin to caricature. The English are the model for this, they provide comfort while assuring that one is well-dressed.]

Masculinity consists of a double move: the rejection of the "unmasculine" (a purely negative and reactive gesture), and the preservation of some non-symbolic value (what the above passages refers to as "positiv," in contrast to "das Idealische"). Goethe's praise of Homer's admiration for the ancient belt seeks to fend off cyclical tastes while protecting the artistic production as epitomized within the epic. In arguing for an aesthetic tradition that in part defines itself apart from the twists and turns of opinion, Goethe's essay unintentionally traces out a distinction that within dress culture amounted to the difference between high fashion in women's wear and professional respectability in male attire. Rather than give preference to one argument or the other by granting precedence to the demands of gender analysis or aesthetics, we might pause to consider that both the autonomy of art and the "Great Masculine Renunciation," as J. C. Flügel called the eighteenth century's costume change (110), are simultaneous developments in the history of Weimar's cultural production.

The Villa Borghese in Rome, Goethe's second example of "wahrer Reichtum," combines financial wealth and political rank with aesthetic value. Built in Rome at the beginning of the seventeenth century by the powerful Cardinal Scipione Borghese, the villa had long drawn the admiration of foreign tourists (Heilmann 98). In 1644, the exiled nobleman John Evelyn described its gardens as "an elysium of delight [...] [that] abounded with all sorts of delicious fruit and exotic simples, fountains of sundry inventions, groves and small rivulets." Inside, Evelyn found a vast collection of artworks. "The walls of the house are covered with antique incrustations of history [...]. In a word, nothing but what is magnificent is to be seen in this Paradise" (Bray 115–16). In 1782, the Casino was built on the grounds specifically to house the collection. Clearly impressed, Goethe wrote: "Der Prinz Borghese besitzt was niemand neben ihm besitzen, was niemand für irgend einen Preis sich verschaffen kann" [The Prince Borghese owns what no one besides him can have, things which cannot be bought at any price; MA 4.2: 120]. On a material level, the Villa hardly serves as a reason why eighteenth-century Germans should not buy fashionable porcelain from England. Few would deny that living in a Roman palace with Renaissance masterpieces was far more pleasurable and satisfying than collecting Wedgwoods in Saxony. If we ignore for a moment the auratic allure of Borghese's masterpieces, a very difficult move especially for Goethe, then we are left with the point that the Prince was a collector of unique and edifying objects. Herein lies the relevance for Goethe's critique of the *Modejournal*. Better to collect unique things, which in their particularity illuminate the formal relations of nature and man, than to purchase a reproduction of an antiquity simply because it is in style. More than the objects, it is the mentality of the collector Goethe singles out — his insistence on finding unique and instructive materials.

But Goethe does not, indeed cannot, forget the substance of the villa's collection. That it consists of antique and Renaissance paintings and sculptures adds literal riches to the collection's aesthetic or spiritual wealth. It places the collection at the beginning of a communication sequence that moves from Italy to northern Europe via English factories. The obvious, superior alternative, from Goethe's perspective, is to travel to Italy, to see its ruins as unique pieces within an archaeological whole, rather than have them come up to Germany decontextualized by manufacturers and ignorant opinion. Implicitly aligning himself with the Borghese family, Goethe allows being a connoisseur to substitute for consumption. Superior knowledge of the origins of Greek and Italian copies provides riches that compensate for not possessing the art. There is no denying that the Italian art collector combines the pleasures of material ownership and aesthetic understanding, while the distant German is left with a choice between knowing, perhaps more than the actual owner, or buying a copy produced without the aesthetic intention and quality of the original. Given the constraints of this situation, Goethe prefers the immaterial choice.

Bertuch has a far more literal-minded and at the same time illusive conception of the fashion commodity's value. He did, for one, share Goethe's amazement at the enthusiasm with which the German public took to English products.[5] The fetish-character that English goods had acquired in Germany did require correction, Bertuch reasoned, however not through a critique of their false representation of art. Instead, the demand for English goods ought to be mobilized to produce equivalent German manufacturing. "Es ist bekanntlich Plan und Zweck dieses Journals [...] Teutschland auf seinen eignen Kunstfleiß aufmerksamer zu machen" [It is the plan and purpose of this journal to make Germany more aware of its own industry; *Modejournal* rpt. 1: 81–82]. Heightened consumer demand coupled with state support could foster domestic enterprise, thereby allowing German states to compete directly with English industries.

Fashionable objects also had an intellectual or spiritual value, for Bertuch was not just an adherent of eighteenth-century theories that claimed luxury consumption increased economic production. For him the value of consumer goods could also be found in their elusiveness. Commodities were always a means to end. They were always in transition, facilitating activities that were not solely of their own construction. Discursively, fashion borrowed enormously from other fields, always combining a lot of everything else. In this sense fashion operated as a formal principle of synthesis. Nothing was sacred before the need to always invent a new image. "Nur das unbegreifliche Talent, Rom und Athen, China und Augsburg in sich zu vereinigen und zu verschmelzen, das ist nicht von sonst" [(Fashion has) the unbelievable talent of combining Rome and Athens, China and Augsburg by synthesizing them into one, an accomplishment which is no mean feat; *Modejournal*, May 1797: 262; qtd. in Kröll and Göres 65; see Fig. 4].

For Goethe, this mechanical process was synonymous with aesthetic emptiness, whereas Bertuch's journal equated it with the advancement of manufacturing techniques, the improvement of commodities and the overall elevation of civilized life. Bertuch fervently maintained that the net effect of the cyclical obsolescence and invention of consumer goods was to make ordinary existence more comfortable and more beautiful. Seen with historical hindsight, the wheel of fashion testified to the heights of cultivation a given epoch had attained. In so doing, he adapted an argument already current within absolutist justifications of luxury. As he writes in the *Teutscher Merkur* (German Mercury, 1773–89) of November 1785:

> In der That charakterisiert sich eine Nation durch nichts auffallender und deutlicher, als durch die Art des Luxus, den sie treibt, und den Geist ihrer Moden; und eine treue Geschichte der Moden nur einiger der wichtigsten Völker von einem Paar hundert Jahren her, würde gewiß ein höchst interessanter Beytrag zu einer künftigen philosophischen Geschichte des menschlichen Geistes seyn. (187)
>
> [In actuality, a nation cannot characterize itself more clearly and distinctly than through the forms of luxury it practices and the spirit of its fashions. An accurate history of fashion (...) would be a highly interesting contribution to any philosophical history of the human spirit.]

Instead of serving as signs of a monarch's past greatness, luxury goods were, according to Bertuch, indications of the advancement of the human spirit. Whereas the baroque prince would have shown future kings the extent of his own power by saturating his domestic space with designs marking his rule, the Enlightenment, Bertuch felt, would demonstrate the productivity and complexity of its own thought by protecting, comforting, and adoring the universal individual's natural body. As Norbert Elias has shown, luxury goods within the absolutist court functioned primarily as indications of rank; their ability to satisfy the physical needs of existence, such as providing warmth and sustenance, were outweighed by their symbolic meaning (Elias, esp. chapter five). The bourgeois fashion sensibility that Bertuch so successfully represented reversed this relation by creating a table of needs which were deemed more important than any display of wealth or rank. Any judgment of rank was deferred to a later date, to some undefined future that would compare entire social systems, as opposed to individual monarchs. This historical argument eliminated any interest in judging the aesthetic accomplishments of individuals, be they monarchs serving as patrons or poetic geniuses creating autonomous works of art.

Bertuch's journal took for granted that fashion was a product of a social consensus; it came into being through the formation of a consensus. No great fashion divas appear in his journal, only mythical persons, such as the anonymous Parisian courtesan who inadvertently invents a new European trend by wearing her hair differently one night. Even this imaginary moment of serendipitous creation requires collective action to transform a single chance act into a recognizable trend. Because society is the agent of fashion, all judgments in Bertuch's journal are made between different epochs, rather than separate individuals. A very clear example of Bertuch's historical and ethnographic conception of fashion is most obvious in an article published at the turn of the nineteenth century (Fig. 5). The accompanying commentary does not satirize the neoclassical style unduly, nor does it mock the ungainly manners of the baroque. Rather the author claims to view each in isolation "um den Geist ihrer Zeit besser zu entwickeln" [in order to elaborate better the spirit of its time; *Modejournal* rpt. 2: 65]. Both pairs are catalogued for some future archivist, that is to say for some later historical perspective that would compare its own material culture with the Empire and the baroque. The passing of fashions, their inherent transitoriness, makes them an all the more successful encapsulation of the historical moment in which they were considered new.

The long-term goal of the *Modejournal* was to record the many short-lived fads as a cumulative process. Even ridiculous, immoral, and down-right disturbing trends — like the Revolution's guillotine — were valid material for the *Modejournal's* readers. While presenting its first detailed account of the beheading machine in Paris, Bertuch reiterated his claim that the journal was not bound by the rules of morality or even necessarily good taste. Rather he conceived his project as an archive of social practices, one which ought not shy from delineating the unbearable or the unappealing.

> Hoffentlich bedarf es bey unsern Lesern keiner Entschuldigung, daß wir einen so schauerlichen Gegenstand hier aufnehmen, und hart neben weit süßere Gefühle erweckende Bilder in unserer Galerie aufstellen. Wir schreiben ja kein Damen-Journal oder ein Toiletten-Werk, worinn man nichts als Nectar und Ambrosia sucht, und nur Wohlgerüche aus Elysium athmen will. Dies sey Andern überlassen. Nein, wir schreiben die Chronik des Geistes unser Zeit, in so fern er von der Mode beherrscht, geleitet, und geformt wird; und aus diesem Standpuncte sieht man leicht, daß unser Feld der Beobachtungen sehr groß, und die Erscheinungen darauf höchst verschieden und abstechend sind. (*Modejournal* rpt. 1: 314–15)
>
> [Hopefully our readers will not require an apology because we have taken up such a horrifying topic and placed it directly adjacent to images in our gallery that evoke far sweeter emotions. We are not writing for a ladies journal nor a cosmetics magazine, where one finds nothing but nectar and ambrosia and the perfumes of Elysium. We leave that to others. No, we are writing the chronicle of the spirit of our times to the extent that it is formed, directed, and dominated by fashion. From this point of view it will be easy to discern that our field of observation is very wide and that the objects that appear therein are varied and provocative.]

Bertuch's claim of autonomy from moral censure might remind one of arguments defending Goethe's *Die Leiden des jungen Werthers* (The Sorrows of Young Werther, 1774) against the claim that it was an immoral work worthy of censorship because it depicted an illicit love affair and advocated suicide. The one key difference would be that Bertuch's claim for autonomy was predicated upon the historical veracity for his text, whereas Goethe sought expressly to downplay any connection his novel had with real historical events. Both authors did, however, insist on the truthfulness of their work, whether it be historical or literary. Embedded in Bertuch's concern for historical accuracy was an ideological interest in constituting a German national identity within the framework of a European cosmopolitan society. Both the German and the European components were crucial to Bertuch's understanding of his *Modejournal's* mission: to foster German consumer culture by elaborating upon the finer accomplishments of European taste and industry. Neither the European nor the German element could be taken for granted.

Each successive style, as it came and went, left its trace in the *Modejournal*, so that over time an imaginary reader might look back over the previous decades of fashion and thereby recognize the progressive advance of civilization as it manifested itself in the decorations and appliances of domestic life. Far from distracting the intellectual, the successive waves of furniture designs, architectural movements, medicinal practices, and sartorial preferences would lead a thoughtful reader to characteristics of individual societies and epochs. From its very inception, German writing on fashion had an historical consciousness. Unable to indulge in elegant surfaces for their own sake, the *Modejournal*, and its many smaller competitors, insisted that fashion be an object of analysis almost from the moment it came into being. The transitoriness of a given fad was recognized immediately, subjecting it to the question of whether it deserved to exist. German fashion discourse, at least in its early bourgeois phase, was highly critical of its own standing, always seeking to legitimate itself. Eager to please, German writing on fashion integrated the arguments made against itself. Indeed, as the *Modejournal's* many critical articles prove, fashion writing was often its own worst critic. Bertuch did not conceive of fashion as existing outside critical theory. It should come as no surprise that his own standard of good taste was predicated upon an organic model not very different from the ideal of beauty postulated by classicism, nor should we be surprised that short lived styles were characterized as incremental steps in the progressive advancement of humanity. Classicism's critique of commodity culture all too often presumed that the fashion-conscious were not self-conscious on a theoretical level. Friedrich Justin Bertuch's *Journal des Luxus und der Moden* goes a long way toward dispelling that impression.

—Columbia University

Notes

[1] For a complete biography see Feldmann.
[2] "Es ist eine auffallende Bemerkung, die man macht, wenn man die Geschichte der Menschheit etwas aufmerksamer studirt, daß Gefallen an Putz und Hang zu Moden allen Völkern der Erde so allgemein eigen sind. Selbst die Wilden von Amerika, die in den finstersten Wäldern wohnen, wo sie sich kaum Hütten bauen, und oft nicht für die ersten Bedürfnisse des Lebens sorgen, sind so für ihre Schönheit besorgt, als kaum die erste Coquette von Europa" [If one studies the history of mankind somewhat more carefully, one will make the rather interesting observation that a pleasure in bodily decoration and a tendency towards fashion is general to all peoples of the earth.

Even the savages of America, who live in the darkest forests where they build themselves huts and often are unable to provide the most basic necessities of life for themselves, even they are concerned about their own beauty in much the same manner as the foremost Coquette of Europe; *Modejournal* rpt. 1: 28].

[3] Bertuch announced that the *Modejournal* intended to counter-act the foreign influence of fashion dolls (see rpt. 1: 28). For a discussion of how fashion dolls were employed to spread new styles throughout Europe, see McKendrick 42–47. The *Modejournal* of September 1786 reported on a society in London which offered twenty-four life-size dolls striking different "attitudes" (335). In November 1791 and January 1792, the *Journal* offered fashion dolls complete with the newest wardrobes for sale.

[4] *Zeitung für die elegante Welt*, 30 January 1802, 104.

[5] One letter to the editor noted: "Sie haben mehrmals in Ihrem Journale Teutschland für der Anglomanie gewarnet, und ziemlich sich vorausgesagt, daß unsre reiche, luxuriose und genießende Welt von der Französischen auf die Englische Modesucht übergehen, und sich mit heißem Durste in dieß Meer stürzen werde. Ihre Prophezeihung scheint zum Theil schon richtig erfüllt zu seyn, zum Theil es noch zu werden; denn es ist unverkennbar, daß Anglomanie in allem, was sich auf Luxus, Wohlleben und Genuß bezieht, mehr als jemals bey uns allgemein wird" [In your journal, you have warned Germany often against "Anglomania" and have predicted well how our wealthy and luxuriating classes would switch from the French to the English fashion addiction, drowning their hot thirst in this vast sea. Your prophecy seems in part to have already been fulfilled and in part to be coming true in the near future, for it is unmistakably true that in all matters of luxury, high-living, and connoisseurship Anglomania has become universal; *Modejournal*, December 1794: 602; qtd. in Kröll and Göres 51].

Works Cited

Benjamin, Walter. "Das Kunstwerk im Zeitalter seiner technischen Reproducierbarkeit (Zweite Fassung)." *Gesammelte Schriften.* Eds. Rolf Tiedemann and Hermann Schweppenhäuser. Vol. 1. Frankfurt a. M.: Suhrkamp, 1980. 471–508.

Bray, William, ed. *The Diary of John Evelyn.* Akron, OH: St. Dunstan Society, n.d.

Elias, Norbert. *The Court Society.* Trans. Edmund Jephcott. Oxford: Basil Blackwell, 1983.

Feldmann, Wilhelm. *Friedrich Justin Bertuch.* Saarbrücken: Carl Schmidtke, 1902.

Flügel, J. C. *The Psychology of Clothes.* New York: International UP, 1971.

Garve, Christian. "Über die Moden." *Versuche über verschiedene Gegenstände aus der Moral, der Literatur und dem gesellschaftlichen Leben.* Ed. Kurt Wölfel. Rpt. Hildesheim: Georg Olms, 1985. 119–294.

Heilmann, Christoph. "Die Entstehungsgeschichte der Villa Borghese in Rom." *Münchner Jahrbuch der bildenden Kunst* 24 (1973): 97–158.

Kröll, Christina and Jörn Göres, eds. *Heimliche Verführung: Ein Modejournal 1786–1827.* Düsseldorf: Goethe Museum, 1978.

McKendrick, Neil. *The Birth of a Consumer Society: The Commercialization of Eighteenth-Century England.* Bloomington: Indiana UP, 1982.

Purdy, Daniel. *The Tyranny of Elegance: Consumer Cosmopolitanism in the Era of Goethe.* Baltimore: Johns Hopkins UP, 1998.

Schwartz, Frederic. *The Werkbund: Design Theory and Mass Culture before the First World War.* New Haven: Yale UP, 1996.

Wigley, Mark. *White Walls, Designer Dresses: The Fashioning of Modern Architecture.* Cambridge, MA: MIT P, 1995.

Zeitung für die elegante Welt. Ed. Heinrich Laube. Leipzig: Voß, 1801–1859.

Fig. 1: A young woman in a tunic made of white silk with arabesque embroidering, 1796 (courtesy of Staatliche Museen zu Berlin, Kunstbibliothek/Lipperheidesche Kostümbibliothek).

Fig. 2: Fashionable ball gown, 1802 (courtesy of Staatliche Museen zu Berlin, Kunstbibliothek/Lipperheidesche Kostümbibliothek).

Fig. 3: Two female busts, one wearing a satin bonnet, the other a half veil, both coifed in the antique manner, 1802 (courtesy of Staatliche Museen zu Berlin, Kunstbibliothek/Lipperheidesche Kostümbibliothek).

Fig. 4: A woman wearing a robe with silver trim in the Chinese style and an antique Greek hairstyle, 1802 (courtesy of Staatliche Museen zu Berlin, Kunstbibliothek/Lipperheidesche Kostümbibliothek).

Fig. 5: Comparison of fashions at the beginning (1701) and the end (1801) of the eighteenth century (courtesy of Staatliche Museen zu Berlin, Kunstbibliothek/Lipperheidesche Kostümbibliothek).

Weimar and the Senses

3

CATRIONA MACLEOD

Floating Heads:
Weimar Portrait Busts

> Here is a portrait. Place it on the
> mantelpiece, for it must be in an elevated
> place, and practice physiognomy.
> — Goethe to Charlotte von Stein

SCULPTURE OCCUPIES A CENTRAL SPACE in eighteenth-century aesthetics, as well as in the culture of classical Weimar. With the new understanding and appreciation of Greek Antiquity, theorists such as Winckelmann, Diderot, and Herder had privileged sculpture over painting in their hierarchy of the arts, favoring sculpture as a paradigm of the aesthetic object and emphasizing its corporeal qualities and sensual appeal. Emblematic of these concerns, the viewing experience of the Juno Ludovisi stands at the center of Schiller's *Über die ästhetische Erziehung des Menschen* (On the Aesthetic Education of Man, 1795). Schiller, positing the modern sensibility as fragmented and dissociated, nevertheless describes the harmonizing of antagonistic drives, the integration of the viewer, through the aesthetic experience of the Juno (NA 20: 359–60). The fetishistic aspects of the interest in sculpture are readily apparent. Herder's treatise on sculpture, for example, presents the idealized, determinedly non-realistic sculptural form as protection against the fragmentation and disintegration of the spectator's body: an antidote to human mortality, a restoration of lack. According to Lacan's psychoanalytic model, a critical moment in the psychological development of an infant occurs when the child recognizes his image in a mirror — an image that appears stable, unified, fixed, but that is associated with the child's experience of "le corps morcelé" [the body in pieces]. Tellingly, Lacan stresses the narcissistic dimension of the fantasy of wholeness by describing this version of the self as "the statue in which man projects himself" (2). Sculpture display practices of the late eighteenth century seem to reinforce such a Lacanian reading of the viewer-statue relationship: occasionally portrait busts were set in mirror-backed niches, following an arrangement in the collection at the Villa Albani in Rome, thus producing doubled reflections of observer and sculpture. The fetishistic function of the statue is confirmed anecdotally by Goethe's account of meeting a melancholic young poet and prescribing the youth his colossal Juno bust as an antidote to "Zersplitterung" [fragmentation] — Goethe's sculpture collection serving here as a means of re-collecting the aesthetically and emotionally dissipated self (Eckermann 77).

Yet such a projection of wholeness depends on the viewing of a Juno bust: itself a partial body and, moreover, a plaster copy of the Roman original. The huge head, some five feet high and mounted on a plinth, dominates the interior of Goethe's house and occupies a mirrored room of its own, the so-called "Junozimmer" (Fig. 1). This apparently contradictory association of the whole body, the original (the antique statue) and the body part, the copy (the portrait bust that becomes an art and fashion staple of classical Weimar) is one that this essay seeks to explore. The techniques of reproducing antique sculptures in plaster stress the association of copying and partiality: the plaster copy of a full figure statue is necessarily composed of an assemblage of body parts from a succession of molds (Haskell and Penny 83), and is crafted from a non-durable material inferior to marble. Goethe's "Vorschläge den Künstlern Arbeit zu verschaffen" (Suggestions on How to Create Work for Artists, 1832) ascribes, significantly, a compensatory function to the portrait bust, the production of which Goethe favors as a practical means of preserving the implicitly endangered art of sculpture (MA 6.2: 185).[1]

I observe a link between the aesthetic project of Weimar Classicism, so frequently expressed in writings on antique sculpture by such theorists as Herder, Schiller, Goethe, and Moritz, and the social practices and implications of sculpture collecting and fabrication during this period. How, I ask, was aesthetic cultivation, as it came to be made emblematic in the identificatory viewer-statue relationship, diffused within society more generally? This is to highlight the points of contact and exchange between what have been termed by the cultural theorist Aleida Assmann the "monumental" and the "documentary" aspects of culture: on the one hand, those "monumental" cultural productions that stage themselves as self-conscious signs, bearers and transmitters of collective meaning, and, on the other hand, the allegedly unreflected "documents" or traces of the quotidian sphere, which I argue, to pursue Assmann's observations to their logical conclusion, are related here to a process of miniaturization. More specifically, I want to link the experience of fragmentation and its anticipated suspension in the aesthetic experience with the popularity in late eighteenth-century Weimar of the classicizing portrait bust. I also emphasize the economic and cultural value assigned to this partial representation of the celebrity body, circulating as it does within and beyond the borders of Weimar and serving as it does as the embodiment of Weimar culture.

Goethe had begun buying plaster copies of antique sculptures while in Frankfurt, from traveling Italian merchants, was an avid collector of plaster casts of antiquities he had viewed in Rome, and had also acquired some genuine marble fragments on his Italian travels. His house was filled with such pieces, by the time of his death numbering as many as ninety-three sculptures. All of those who considered themselves cultivated in Weimar, it seemed, shared this enthusiasm for sculpture, as a letter by the dramatist Maximilian Klinger indicates in which the visitor expresses astonishment at the range of antique copies to be found in the town:

> Hier ist die ganze Statue von Ganymed, das Höchste, was des Künstlers Herz geboren. Die Gruppe von Laokoon. Die Statue von Antinous. Der Vatikanische Apoll. Und Vieles! Auch herrliche Büste [...]. Wieland hat Vieles, der Herzog Alles, und auch Goethe. Unter diesen Göttern zu wandeln! (Qtd. in Geese 29)

> [The statue of Ganymede is here intact, the highest creation ever born of an artist's heart. The Laocöon group. The Antinous statue. The Vatican Apollo. And so much more! Also a magnificent bust (...). Wieland has a great deal, the Duke has everything, and Goethe too. Oh, to wander among these gods!]

In July 1781, Wieland's literary-political monthly *Der Teutsche Merkur* (The German Mercury, 1773–89), with its goal of bourgeois cultivation or *Bildung*, included an announcement of Weimar court sculptor Gottlieb Martin Klauer's line of busts and medallions depicting Weimar notables: "Bey dem Fürstl. Hofbildhauer, Hrn. Klauer, in Weimar, sind Gipsabgüsse der Abbildungen zu haben, welche derselbe von Herder, Goethe, und Wieland, sowol en buste als en Medaillon vor kurzem nach dem Leben verfertigt hat" [Plaster casts are now available — busts as well as medallions — of the statues of Herder, Goethe, and Wieland recently modeled from life by the Weimar court sculptor Herr Klauer; qtd. in Geese 45]. By September 1782, Klauer advertised in the *Merkur* three additions to his inventory: Raynal, Villoisson, and Oeser. Bertuch's *Journal des Luxus und der Moden* (Journal of Luxury and Fashion, 1786–1827), instrumental in the creation of Weimar's consumer culture and the propagation of bourgeois good taste (see Purdy in this volume), also contained in the July 1787 *Intelligenzblatt* [advertising supplement] an advertisement for relatively affordable plaster casts of classical subjects by Klauer. Klauer had by then set in motion a veritable assembly-line for his works, producing plaster casts of Weimar and foreign celebrities, in addition to his classical line, for export in other parts of Germany as well as abroad (the advertisement in the *Modejournal* assures prospective buyers that sculptures will be carefully packed for shipping near and far). Copies of Klauer's Weimar busts were commissioned from as far afield as St. Petersburg, and other markets included the Baltic, Scandinavia, Switzerland, and Holland. Bode even mentions a commercial inquiry from New York (Geese 44 and Bode 263–64). Klauer's stock by 1787 ranged from a large, full-figure Medici Venus at sixteen talers to small busts of Homer and Cicero at a few talers apiece, or for the same sum, plaster busts of such contemporary cultural icons as: Voltaire, Raynal, Villoisson, Goethe, Wieland, Herder, Jacobi, Bode, Bertuch, Musäus, Oeser, Gellert, Lavater, Fürstenberg, Hemsterhuis, or Sterne. An original bust, such as that of Oeser, would be priced at around thirty-two talers (Bode 259). Over the decade Klauer's range of Weimar busts would expand from his first portraits of the ducal family and other court figures to include the town's poets and scholars, but also government officials, as well as portraits of famous visitors (Raynal, Villoisson, Hemsterhuis, Fürstenberg, and Lavater, for example, belong to this latter category). These transients could in this way be made permanent residents of Weimar, fixed in statue form as part of the local pantheon. One may read this as suggestive of a desire in classical Weimar to fashion itself as a plenitudinous cultural body. Although the fetishistic spirit is usually applied to the dead, here it was predominantly the living who became its object. Clearly, cost and relative ease of transportation facilitated the expansion of Klauer's line of portrait busts. That Klauer advertised his merchandise both in the *Merkur* and the *Modejournal*, one of the earliest fashion magazines in the world, tells us something about the broad popular appeal of his sculptures. Klauer's line was marketable not only to the intellectual readership of Wieland's journal (who, significantly, were the target audience for the portraits of Weimar intellectuals, to which they were invited to subscribe): it was also aimed at a public interested in the niceties of etiquette, in the latest French and English fashions for men, women, and children, in furniture, bric-à-brac, silverware, china, carriages, garden design, or wallpapers. The advertising in the *Modejournal* was far more extensive, featuring classical as well as contemporary sculptures, in addition to architectural and garden ornaments. Carrying advertisements in French, Italian, and English, the *Modejournal* sought, in addition to cultivating good taste, to further Weimar trade and commerce throughout Germany, as well as on a wider European market. Thus Klauer, as the *Modejournal* documents, found himself competing with the line being produced by the English "Artificial-Stone-Manufactory" of Coade: Coade advertised in the August 1788 issue of the *Modejournal* with an extensive price-list of about a thousand pieces, ranging from a nine-foot statue of a river-god at one hundred guineas, to two or three dozen classical pieces, to busts of Homer, to members of the British royal family, on the cheaper side, at two guineas. Klauer responded by October 1789 with his own workshop producing a line of "Toreutikawaren"[2] in a fired ceramic material more durable than plaster, at about a quarter the price of the English firm. In the 1790s there were fewer commissions for new busts, but the demand for copies rose. Both Klauer's workshop and factory throve commercially until his death in 1801, so much so, that in 1792 he published his own illustrated catalogue with sixty items, and in 1800 a second edition in two volumes (priced at one taler each), with one hundred and thirty pieces. In 1800, Bertuch, who had become his commercial representative, published a list of one hundred and eighty-five sculptures by Klauer, with twenty-eight portrait busts retailing at two talers each.[3]

Born in Rudolstadt, Thuringia, in 1742, Klauer was appointed court sculptor in Weimar by Duchess Anna Amalia in 1773. In 1779, Klauer's courtly patron sponsored his study trip to the celebrated Mannheim antiquities collection that constituted a kind of surrogate Roman experience for Germans who could not travel south. Klauer's prolific production of plaster-casts began in 1781, and included copies of almost all of the sculptures in the Mannheim Antikensaal, themselves copies of antique originals. Following the Mannheim visit Klauer departed radically from the baroque and rococo tradition in which he must have been schooled and immersed himself in Lavater's *Physiognomische Fragmente* (Science of Physiognomy, 1775–78). Klauer's works were available to a wide German consumer public through Bertuch, through the Rost art dealership in Leipzig and the Daveson dealership in Braunschweig, as well as through the Fürstenberg porcelain factory, which manufactured miniaturized figurines after several of Klauer's so-called "moderne Büsten" [modern busts]. Numerous aristocratic estates and their grounds, as well as bourgeois homes in and around Weimar, were decorated with Klauer's sculptures and ornamental stonework. Despite this commercial success, or rather because of the mass-production that brought about the success, Klauer occupied an ambiguous zone within classical Weimar — a position that may be compared with that of his patron, Bertuch, whose wide-ranging entrepreneurial efforts, culminating in the founding of the "Industrie-Comptoir," met with outright hostility within Weimar. (Herder went so far as to accuse Bertuch of cheapening and ruining "genuine" Greek taste; see Feldmann 96.) Klauer's workshop, in addition to its output of classical and contemporary sculpture, produced among other items gravestones, garden furniture and ornaments, vases, pedestals, plaster picture-frames, and architectural details — Bertuch's catalogue lists the full array of products. The sculptor's announcement in the *Modejournal* might be preceded by advertising for an Erfurt jeweler and followed by a notice extolling the merits of a certain brand of Leipzig wallpaper. All of this supplied the evidence for Goethe of Klauer's aesthetic descent into "den neuen, leeren Dekorations-Gusto" [the new and empty mania for decoration] and rendered Klauer an unsuitable candidate in his eyes to execute a public monument to Carl August (FA 29: 226–27; see also the discussion of monuments in the *Propyläen* [Propylaea, 1798–1800], MA 6.2: 182–83). Paradoxically, then, Goethe and other Weimar intellectuals challenged the mass production of objects catering to Grecophile tastes at home and abroad, while this very system of production was instrumental in exporting the image of Weimar as classical center. As Daniel Purdy demonstrates more fully in this volume, both "high" and "popular" culture participate in the neoclassical project.

It is important to take into account Goethe's instrumental role in the formation of Klauer's sculptural gaze, and not simply in his commissioning and circulating of his own portraits or in his classical self-fashioning. I return to both of these below, as examples of Weimar Classicism's inclination to mold itself as its own monument. Goethe was a regular and critical presence in Klauer's studio.[4] In commissioning a full-figure portrait of the six-year-old Fritz von Stein in 1779 after having first ordered a bust, for example, Goethe demonstrates both his own preference for the wholeness of the naked Greek body and his desire to impose his own aesthetic vision or education on the Weimar court sculptor (Fig. 2). Goethe expressed his satisfaction that Klauer was finding the commission at last the occasion for "ein übergroß Studium" [a colossal study; FA 29: 156], once again suggesting the monumental totality of the classical body, for Goethe the ideal sculptural model. Indeed, Klauer's visit to Mannheim followed closely on the heels of the Stein commission. The sculpture of Fritz von Stein remains unique among Klauer's works, the only full-figure and nude statue of a living contemporary. The full-figure sculpture, importantly, is of a child; hinting at a certain nostalgic vision of the lost totality of childhood. The sculpture is also displayed in the intimate setting of Tiefurt, Anna Amalia's summer residence, and did not make its way on to Klauer's export lists. With this one important exception, contemporaries are portrayed only in the inherently fragmented bust form, clothed, while Klauer's figural works are representations of mythological beings or copies of classical works. The lengthy merchandise catalogues also strictly differentiate between the two sculpture types, with the more expensive, larger classical works privileged in the lists. Klauer's illustrated catalogues, in fact, contain images only of these classical statues.

"Setzen Sie es [das Bild] aufs Camin, denn es muß hoch stehen, und üben Sie die Physiognomik" [Place it on the mantelpiece, for it must be in an elevated place, and practice physiognomy], Goethe wrote to Charlotte von Stein in December 1780, presenting her with a portrait bust of himself by Klauer (qtd. in Bode 260.). Display practices have seldom been analyzed in their own right, and have often been understood as neutral techniques. But as Peter Wollen suggests in his introduction to the volume *Visual Display* (1995), they may conceal or reveal tensions between image and onlooker: "Above all, it is necessary to place the myriad contemporary forms of display in a historical context [...]. Each historic period has its own rhetorical mode of display, because each has different truths to conceal" (Cooke and Wollen 10). Any visitor to Weimar is confronted with an apparently unending series of sculptures — in gardens, in libraries, in museums, on the marketplace — that tends to blur analysis. What does Goethe's statement about the "correct" display form for his own portrait reveal about its historical context, as well as about the imaginary power of display?

In domestic settings, the private venue of bourgeois self-cultivation, Klauer's sculptures would commonly have been placed high up on ledges or on plinths of his own manufacture, above eye-level and beyond the range of touch, their elevated position in a room drawing the eye of the viewer upward: this hierarchy of the gaze is further reinforced by the downward glance typical of the neoclassical portrait bust (Fig. 3), a gesture that problematizes the specularity that appears central to the classical viewer-sculpture relationship. As Lavater puts it, upon receiving a bust of Goethe as a gift from Carl August, "wie wird er [Goethe] niedersehen, anbeten und anbeten lehren" [How he will look down, adore and teach adoration; qtd. in Geese 59].[5] Goethe's own sculpture collection (Fig. 4) reveals much about the display arrangements common during this period and their varied stagings of the viewer-sculpture relationship: the free-standing classical figure, the bust (classical or contemporary) placed on a pedestal at eye-level, and the contemporary bust set high up on a recessed wall plinth. As if to underscore the centrality of the gaze in this room, each of the two doors to the Büstenzimmer is crowned, as it were, with a classical fragment representing a gigantic pair of eyes — a Minerva mask and a Jupiter mask. The experience of the classical full-figure statue appears markedly different from that of the bust in its tactile immediacy, at least as suggested by Goethe's recollections of his visit to the Mannheim Antikensaal: "ein Wald von Statuen, durch den man sich durchwinden, eine große ideale Volksgesellschaft, zwischen der man sich durchdrängen mußte" [A forest of statues through which one made one's way, a huge, ideal society, through which one had to force one's way forward; MA 16: 535]. Despite the almost unbearable physical intimacy of the statues, Goethe emphasizes the power of the viewer in Mannheim to shape his aesthetic experience, thanks to the movable pedestals on which many of the statues were placed as well as to the viewer's ability to alter and control conditions of light and shade: this is an interactive display technique not employed in Weimar, to the best of my knowledge. Goethe's introduction to the *Propyläen* (1793) also underlines the mobility of the viewer's position: the utility of "ein Überblick, ein Seitenblick über und auf" [an overview, a side view across and over; MA 6.2: 15] is posited as essential to the visual experience of corporeal totality. Herder too writes extensively of the observer's multi-positional viewing of an Apollo figure — "sein vielverändertes Umherschauen, oder sein sichtliches Umhertasten" [his ever-changing look or his visual touch; 415] — which is explicitly intended to counter two-dimensionality. The viewer of the portrait bust is cast into a different position, reminiscent of Goethe's description of the art connoisseur in the introduction to the *Propyläen*:

> Zur Kenntnis, zur Einsicht sind aber weit mehrere Menschen fähig, ja man kann wohl sagen, ein jeder, der sich selbst verleugnen, sich den Gegenständen unterordnen kann, der nicht, mit einem starren, beschränkten Eigensinn, sich und seine kleinliche Einseitigkeit in die höchsten Werke der Natur und Kunst überzutragen strebt. (MA 6.2: 22)
>
> [Many more individuals are capable of knowledge and insight, indeed one can say that all are, who have the capacity to deny themselves, who can subordinate themselves to the objects, and who are not fixated, in their stubborn and limited willful-

ness, on projecting themselves and their trivial one-sidedness on to the highest works of nature and art.]

In Lacanian terms, as Žižek has argued in his recent work on the gaze (125), the eye viewing the object is on the side of the subject, while the gaze is on the side of the object, thus ensuring that when one looks the object, here the statue, is always gazing back. The placement of the statues in niches can also be said to work against the tactile three-dimensionality that is at the heart of the statue-viewing experience for theorists such as Herder. According to Herder, the eye, the deficient organ of perception that has gained primacy in the modern age, has access only to the two-dimensional, to "Fläche" — a word that is negatively freighted throughout his major essay *Plastik* (Sculpture, 1778). In the case of this display mode, however, the sculpture is already somewhat flattened out and is available to the viewer's gaze only from a reduced number of angles, a display mode that anticipates the prevalent visual citation of portrait busts in paintings, drawings, and silhouettes of the same period, as well as in mass-circulation print media.[6] Corresponding to the loss of mobility of the viewer is also the physical stasis suggested by the limbless bust — compared with, for example, the dynamism of a full-figure Apollo Belvedere.

Klauer's sculptures were also, however, publicly displayed in garden and park settings, thus attesting to their dual function as decorative objets d'art and as cultural monuments offered to the eye of a wider public. Together with sculptures of Wieland and Herder completed in the same year, Klauer's 1781 bust of Goethe was, for example, exhibited in the so called Lobhölzchen [Grove of Honor] in the Tiefurt Park (Schmidt 34). And in 1791, in a lecture to the Freitagsgesellschaft [Friday Club], Goethe called for a public retrospective of Klauer's works, emphasizing the monumental role of the sculptures in communicating Weimar culture to foreign visitors, as well as to posterity. Goethe also stressed in these comments the need to re-collect Klauer's works, to re-assemble the classical body of art from "manches, was zerstreut liegt" [much that is scattered; GA 12: 674]. If Weimar Classicism understood, created, and viewed itself through classical sculpture — Hannelore Schlaffer speaks of its desire literally to embody the past (195) — then it also marketed itself in the form of sculpture, of a collectible Goethe bust. I also want to suggest the cultural, and perhaps more important, the currency exchange value possessed by the Weimar celebrity busts. It is no accident that the origins of the portrait genre in sculpture have been associated with developments in coinage

(Boardman 239), and that Klauer's line of busts was marketed alongside a line of medallions of the same subjects.

Klauer traded his Weimar merchandise, including the best known busts, with the important Rost art dealership in Leipzig, in exchange for access to antique sculptures which Klauer could then copy and add to his own, ever-expanding list. Geese notes (186) that the Rost catalogue of 1796, for example, listed thirteen Klauer busts modeled from life in Weimar, portraits which Rost in turn could copy and distribute. Also according to Geese (186), the Rost dealership held a unique inventory of sculptures. The owner of the business, through a special dispensation by the pope, had access to the finest plaster casts, modeled on the original Roman sculptures; he also had the right to copy twenty-five sculptures from the Dresden collection of antiquities; and the Dresden collection had acquired in 1782 a unique, extensive collection of plaster-casts that had once belonged to the artist Anton Raphael Mengs (1728–79) and that comprised eight hundred and thirty-three works. Weimar as classical center was able to assemble its classical collections through the adroit marketing of its own cultural luminaries as classical icons. But beyond this, the body part (portrait bust) became tradable for the desired whole body — the antique, more precisely classical Greek sculptural tradition, whose idealizing tendency, as Boardman observes "militates against individualizing characteristics of body or features" (239) and thus against portraiture.

Throughout Europe, the portrait bust, a staple of many sculptors' trades, assumed increasing importance in secular and domestic settings from the mid-eighteenth century on. The commercial success of the form may be explained as a result of growing popular interest in individual psychology, as well as of the cult of genius, coupled with Lavater's enormously influential work on physiognomy. Italian travel literature also begins to show signs of new physiognomic interest, directed more at Roman portrait busts than at figural Greek statues (Schneider 106). Klauer's oeuvre might have received even less critical attention than it has had it not been for the persistence of such visual obsessions well into the twentieth century — as evinced by books with such titles as *Die Bildnisse Goethes* (The Portraits of Goethe), *Goethe im Bildnis* (Goethe in Portrait), *Goethe: Seine äußere Erscheinung* (Goethe: His Outward Appearance), or even *Wie sah Goethe aus?* (What Did Goethe Look Like?), as well as by the author of the only monograph on Klauer, Walter Geese, who in his 1935 study finds the significance of the sculptor's legacy in its utility as a source of physiognomic information, of "das Wissen um das Aussehen der Großen Weimars" [knowledge about the appearance of the Weimar greats; Geese 39].

Lavater, who had received a plaster bust of Goethe as a gift from Carl August of Weimar in 1781, explicitly used the sculpture as a model for two drawings in his scientific collection. It is the second of Klauer's Goethe busts, decidedly idealized and classical in style (Fig. 5). Lavater further abstracts and monumentalizes the representation by in the first plate designating the bust simply as the image of "Genius," and in the second plate having his artist set the sculpture within a niche and crop the lower portion of the bust, in order to focus all attention on the iconic genial head, for Lavater *the* significant part of the human body. Finally, Klauer's Goethe bust enters mass circulation in the 1820 French edition of Lavater's *Physiognomische Fragmente* in the flattened and reusable form of a silhouette, a genre that reductively abstracts from the three-dimensional corporeal qualities of classical sculpture (Fig. 6).[7] Barbara Stafford aptly terms the silhouette, which became increasingly popular after the publication of Lavater's work, a "body print" (98). Interestingly, a process of reduction and omission also occurred with Klauer's busts: as they were mass produced from the original sculptures in plaster or ceramic, the tendency was to eliminate or abridge the shoulder and chest area, thus further repressing the less desirable "lower" body of Weimar Classicism.[8] The cropping of the body was in practical terms a reflection of economic considerations — Bode notes (268) that if a customer requested a portrait bust including the subject's chest in addition to his or her head and neck the cost would increase by two talers, thus in most cases at least doubling the price of the work. Lavater's physiognomy, which takes the dissections of anatomical science as its model and also makes extravagant use of sculptural tools such as plaster casts as well as of the new and modish silhouette genre, is dependent on the fragmentation of the body — Lavater is fascinated with severed body parts such as lips, eyes, noses, and foreheads — and in the case of the silhouette on its directional projection into a two-dimensional image; yet, like the portrait bust, these fragments, as Rotraut Fischer and Gabriele Stumpp show in their work on physiognomy, are supposed in synecdochic fashion to suggest a whole, the sum of the parts.

I want to mention here a fascinating series of physiognomic drawings from Lavater's collection by an unknown artist; the images depict the developmental stages from frog to poet and from lion to Apollo, both of which culminate in the image of Goethe. Interestingly, the Dutch surgeon Petrus Camper (1722–89) had in the 1760s and 1770s devised a system of measurements to gauge the development from ape to Apollo, presenting the Apollo Belvedere as the supreme form, and even mathematically reconstructing the sculpture's "skull." Thus,

Lavater, whose "Animalitätslinie" [animality line; that is, a series of drawings that show the developmental stages leading from animal to human being] had been conceived of in response to Camper's, conflates Goethe with a classical statue, the Apollo Belvedere, a move I see as symptomatic.[9]

In the final part of my essay, I want to discuss Klauer's series of Goethe busts, as well as works by two other sculptors.[10] My interest in Klauer's evolving representations or constructions of Goethe is motivated more by what they have to tell us about cultural self-representation and self-stylization than by the psychologizing of genius — "what did Goethe look like?" — that, as I indicated earlier, has tended to be the focus of criticism (Beutler 266). What is most striking about Walter Geese's evaluation of Klauer's Goethe sculptures is its recourse to eighteenth-century aesthetic associations of sculpture and wholeness, "der ganze Mensch" [the whole human being]: only the plastic representation of the poet, Geese insists, can convey the plenitude of the genial individual, the unity of human thought, emotion, and action (64–65; see also Beutler 268). Yet this organic "wholeness," supposedly proper to sculpture, expresses itself in the reduced and fragmentary genre of the portrait bust. The discourse of synthetic naturalness and the prevalent view of Klauer as the consummate realist (Beutler 267; Geese 7, 37) are also questionable, of course, when one considers the highly codified and stylized aesthetic vision of Goethe as Greek that prevailed in Weimar and that was marketed so successfully beyond the city limits. As we will see, these are the opposite of naturalistic or objective portraits. It is important to contrast Klauer's vision of Goethe with the decidedly more realistic priorities of his other Weimar portraits. Goethe, it should be stressed, is never portrayed by Klauer in contemporary clothing, indeed successive sculptures become increasingly antique in style, while others who are the subject of several portrait busts, such as Carl August, may be shown both in classical and in modern garments. If one compares Klauer's vision of other Weimar personalities with that of Goethe, one is also struck by the more naturalistic version of the human body that can emerge. A 1782 bust of Bode, for example, presents its subject literally warts and all (Fig. 7). Significantly, however, it is Goethe's portraits of Goethe that have consistently been praised as the sculptor's most enduring achievement.

Klauer's first bust of Goethe — the only portrait bust he executed before the visit to the Mannheim antiquities collection — was commissioned by Goethe in 1778 and sculpted from gray limestone quarried near Weimar (Fig. 8). The stone, deemed comparable in quality to marble, had been discovered by Goethe himself in the ruins of the

Weimar castle, which had burned down in 1775. It inaugurates a non-realistic, classical plastic style which will typify subsequent sculptural representations of Goethe in Weimar. The artist who heightened such stylization was the Swiss sculptor Alexander Trippel: his marble bust of 1787 was modeled in Italy after a recently discovered antique Apollo original (MA 15: 474–75) and depicts Goethe with a flowing mane of curls, as a demi-God (Fig. 9). Goethe recorded in his memoirs of his Italian journey his satisfaction at the idealized representation, observing that he had nothing against bequeathing this view of his appearance to posterity (MA 15: 480). In addition to Apollonian features, Trippel's statue also possesses elements of martial Alexander iconography — the stylized eyes and the general's cloak. A companion piece to a bust of Frederick II of Prussia, who had died in 1786, the bust in one version shows a tragic mask in brooch form fastening the poet's cloak, while Friedrich wears a pin depicting a Medusa head.

To return to Klauer's Goethe busts, his second sculpture, probably completed around 1780 and inspired by Klauer's stay in Mannheim, is markedly more classicizing in style than the first (Figs. 5 and 10). In the first bust, Goethe's hair is coifed in a contemporary style; two years later, the poet wears a Greek taenia or headband in his hair, which is now styled in classical fashion, and he is draped in antique robes. It seems likely that Klauer here represents Goethe in his role as Orestes, which Goethe had performed to great acclaim in the April 1779 stage première of his *Iphigenie auf Tauris*. As Gisela Sichardt notes in her study of Goethe's early theatrical activities in Weimar, it was the first time Weimar had witnessed a theatrical production in Greek costume, and the effect was sensational (79). Luise von Göchhausen testified: "Ich habe ihn [Goethe] in meinem Leben noch nicht so schön gesehen" [I have never in my life seen him look so beautiful] while the Weimar physician Christian Hufeland declared that "man glaubte einen Apollo zu sehen. Noch nie erblickte man eine solche Vereinigung physischer und geistiger Vollkommenheit in einem Mann" [you thought you were looking at an Apollo. Never had such a unity of physical and spiritual perfection and beauty been seen in a man; qtd. in Geese 58]. In a sense, this is a doubly monumental image of Goethe: the representation through Klauer's classical lens of Goethe's own classical self-representation. Goethe himself gave copies of this bust to Charlotte von Stein, Prince August of Gotha, and Jenny Voigt, among others (Bode 260). Advertised in the *Merkur* in 1781 in plaster copies, and produced in multiple variants, most of which represented only Goethe's head and neck, this image must have been in wide circulation, and it also, significantly, inaugurated Klauer's trade in copies.

Finally, I want to turn to the statue which Klauer executed after Goethe's Italian journey and which, as is evident from the brooch fastening Goethe's cloak and the modeling of the hair, must have been influenced by Trippel's Apollo-like sculpture, a plaster copy of which had arrived in Weimar in 1790 (Fig. 11). Most striking about this sculpture is its overt sensuality — its flowing hair, full lips and bare chest. It is the only one of Klauer's wide range of portrait busts to suggest the classical nude body — one is reminded of Goethe's sense of aesthetic mission in guiding Klauer's sculptural vision of Fritz von Stein. Yet while the full-figure statue of Fritz von Stein was intended to convey corporeal wholeness and ideality, no other work by Klauer so strongly embodies the contradiction identified by art historian Gundolf Winter as inherent in the latter sculptural genre: that of wholeness versus fragmentation (87–88). In Klauer's final representation of Goethe, the strong diagonal line of the classical drapery underscores the cutting of the body intrinsic to the portrait bust.

As a postscript and contrast to Klauer's oeuvre, I turn now to the sculpture of Goethe by Berlin sculptor Johann Gottfried Schadow, which marks a distinct break with the earlier Weimar representations (Fig. 12). Schadow's 1823 marble bust was not commissioned by Goethe, and, tellingly, was not publicly exhibited in Goethe's lifetime, remaining in the possession of the artist's family until 1887. Here, Goethe, sporting a medal and contemporary clothing, appears to my eye as a world-weary Weimar courtier and statesman. The question of costume had come to the forefront of theoretical deliberations in the so called "Kostümstreit": the antique "natural" body favored in the eighteenth century versus the more realistic priorities of the nineteenth century. One is reminded of Hegel's deliberations on whether or not to give modern clothing to portrait statues of contemporaries: he sidesteps the thorny issue with the suggestion that it is precisely for this reason that it is better to produce busts only (749). Schadow departs radically from the pathos of earlier classicizing works, in a way that was not appreciated by his subject, whose objections to the sculpture emphasized that it was in his view "kleinlich" [small-minded, petty], that is, simply not monumental enough (Schmidt 34). Indeed, the plaster bust was so inexpensive that almost any middle-class pater familias could afford a commemorative sculpture by the middle of the nineteenth century, thereby ensuring the demise of the genre and the rise of a new trend towards full-figure monuments. Years later Franz Biberkopf in Alfred Döblin's *Berlin Alexanderplatz* (1929) will deliberate ponderously on which merchandise he can most profitably deal in as a traveling salesman, mousetraps or "Gipsköppe" [plaster heads; 63].

In conclusion, I want to address the place of Klauer's work in the commodification and packaging of Weimar Classicism in the twentieth century. Having remained in obscurity throughout the nineteenth century, Klauer came to public attention again with Wilhelm Bode's reassessment of his oeuvre in the early years of this century and with Bode's efforts in having the portrait busts — many of which appear to have been languishing in storage for decades — exhibited publicly in Weimar (Bode 242). Klauer's Goethe busts have strategically been placed on a cultural pedestal by subsequent German regimes, needless to say with starkly varying agendas. Only two years after the end of World War I and the founding of the Weimar Republic, Hans Wahl celebrated the loan of Klauer's 1790 Goethe bust to the Goethehaus in Weimar, in an essay that remarkably associates the permanent return of the sculpture from Berlin with the birth of a new nation. The drafters of the new constitution had paid a visit, of course, to the Goethehaus and had been fascinated by the sculpture:

> Der Gedanke, in Goethes Haus für alle Zeiten eine Erinnerung an die Tagung der Deutschen Verfassunggebenden National-versammlung in der Goethestadt zu hinterlassen, führte zur Erwerbung der Leihgabe durch die Nationalversammlung und deren Stiftung an das Goethe-Nationalmuseum. So erinnert dieses wichtige Dokument für die Erkenntnis von Goethes äußerer Erscheinung in seiner Unterschrift an ein Stück der Geschichte tiefster Not des deutschen Vaterlandes, und spätere und — wir hoffen es — glücklichere Geschlechter werden doppelt ergriffen vor dem edlen Kunstwerk haltmachen. (8)

> [The idea that a souvenir of the drafting of the constitution by the German National Assembly could be left behind in the city of Goethe led to the acquisition of the loan by the National Assembly and its donation to the Goethe Nationalmuseum. Thus the commemorative plaque beneath this important document of Goethe's outward appearance reminds us of a historical moment in which our German Fatherland experienced the deepest despair, and future and — we hope — more fortunate generations will feel doubly moved when they stand before the noble work of art.]

The description of the sculpture privileges the sense of touch, recommending that observers close their eyes and use their fingers to appreciate the sensuality of the work, in a move strikingly antithetical to the primacy of the eye in sculptural display of late eighteenth-century Weimar. Here Goethe's bust serves as a fetishistic mechanism for mastering historical and human loss: its compensatory function corresponds to Freud's understanding of collection as a part of the work of mourning or compensation for loss, which in his 1916 essay "On Transience" is associated with the catastrophic experiences of the war (307). In 1949, following the greatest catastrophe of all, the bicentennial of Goethe's birth was celebrated with an exhibition in Marburg of the more than forty Klauer busts from the Kippenberg collection, with central place given to Klauer's Goethe series. The illustrated brochure to an extensive 1972 Weimar exhibition in the Wittumspalais — an exhibition prompted by the principles of "Kulturpolitik" promulgated by the SED at their sixth party conference — does not hesitate to place Klauer as the exponent of classical realism in a tradition extending from the bourgeois revolutions to classicism to socialist realism. Handrick's brochure is illustrated, to my mind revealingly, with Klauer's earliest and most "realistic" Goethe bust of 1778. On a recent trip to Weimar, I was struck by a prominently displayed plaster replica of Klauer's Goethe bust of 1790, available for sale at the Weimar Classics Foundation's gift shop, and at DM 170 a decidedly up-market tourist souvenir (at the other end of the price scale, postcards of Klauer's Fritz von Stein sculpture and of his Göchhausen bust can be had for only DM 1). Klauer's commercial vision, then, proves enduringly appealing and marketable in the contemporary cultural packaging of Weimar.

—University of Pennsylvania

Notes

I would like to thank the organizers of the Davidson Symposium on Weimar culture, as well as the other participants at the conference, in particular Daniel Purdy and Liliane Weissberg, for their encouragement with this project, their stimulating conversation, and helpful suggestions. I am further grateful for the comments of Eric Downing and Jane Brown. My audience at the University of Pennsylvania conference *Body Parts/ Partial Bodies* also offered valuable insights. Finally, I wish to acknowledge the generous assistance I received from the Griswold Fund at Yale University, which made possible a research trip to Weimar and face-to-face encounters with many of the sculptures I discuss in this essay.

[1] One of the more peculiar popular cultural manifestations of the relationship between corporeal wholeness (classical statue) and fragmentation (modern body) is surely the late eighteenth-century fashion for prostheses serving to make modern partial bodies conform to the ideal body of the statue — pad-

ded inserts for men's white stockings that would enable their wearers to mimic the muscular calves of classical marble figures (Thiel 291). The tropes of Greek wholeness and modern fragmentation are central to the aesthetic writings of Weimar Classicism, as for example in the opening passages of the *Propyläen*, with their stress on antique "Vollkommenheit" [perfection] as opposed to the "Stückwerk" [fragmentary work] produced by the moderns (MA 6.2: 9). By metaphorical association, the classical past is embodied in Italy, a country described as a monumental body of art (MA 6.2: 26). Goethe stresses that the modern artist "dismemberer" — whose highest subject is the human body — must have as his ultimate the representation of "ein schönes ungetrenntes Ganzes" [a beautiful undivided whole] (MA 6.2: 14). Note also the hierarchy in aesthetic pleasure outlined by Goethe as it relates to the tropes of original and copy: least satisfactory is the experience of looking at a clumsy fragmentary copy of a classical statue, then follows the pleasing vision of a more expertly executed plaster cast and finally the delight at seeing a complete original (MA 6.2: 21–22). On the modern human being as a copyist, see Schlaffer. For a stimulating discussion of artistic representations of the fragmented body, see Nochlin.

[2] A technical term deriving from the Greek *toreutikos* for "relief work," toreutic refers to the art of working in metal or ivory, for example embossing or chasing. More generally, the term comes into use for sculpture in metal. Geese suggests a further connection between Greek bronzes and eighteenth-century fired ceramic sculptures, noting that ceramic works such as those by Coade or Klauer were often blackened so as to suggest their antique models (47). I would stress, in this connection, the use of an inferior material in the copying of antique sculpture, whether it was ceramic imitating bronze or plaster standing in for marble.

[3] For a sense of typical incomes in Weimar, see Bruford's index "The Structure of Weimar Society in 1820 on the Basis of Income" (428–31). Bruford categorizes as "upper class" an income level of six hundred to over three thousand talers per annum. Klauer's salary from Carl August, at two hundred talers, put him at the low end of the craftsman class.

[4] Beutler points out that Goethe also presided over many of the portrait sessions at Klauer's workshop, for instance at those of Duchess Luise, Herder, Elisa von der Recke, and Jacobi (266–67).

[5] Brentano offers an ironic perspective on the divine condescension of the Goethe bust in a letter to Savigny of 1803, in which he reports of a visit to the sculptor Tieck's Weimar studio. His comments show an awareness of the tendency to trivialization and pastiche inherent in the transformation of a classical head into a reproducible display-cabinet ornament: "die Form behält er [Tieck] und jeder Abguß kostet wieder zwei Louisd. so können sie ja auch zu einem Hausgözzen kommen. Wollen Sie nicht den Göthe von ihm, ich will ihn ihnen besorgen, er wäre schön auf dem Eckschrank" [He (Tieck) re-

tains the mold and each cast costs two louis d'or — so that you can become the proud owner of a domestic idol. If you want his Goethe I'll arrange the matter, he would look good on top of the corner cupboard; 115].

[6] See for example Lavater's use of Klauer's Goethe bust as a silhouette in his *Physiognomic Fragments* (vol. 6, facing page 155), discussed below, the repeated appearance of busts in Weimar silhouette art (Kroeber 33, 73, 87, 89, 101, 111), and Angelika Kauffmann's 1788 drawing *Die Musen des Dramas huldigen Goethe* (The Dramatic Muses Pay Homage to Goethe), in which Goethe is depicted as a bust on a pedestal, after Trippel's marble sculpture (Goethehaus, Weimar). The Kauffmann drawing itself entered mass circulation as an etching for the title page of vol. 8 of the Göschen edition of Goethe's works, in 1789. See Maul and Oppel 95.

[7] Not surprisingly, Herder is scathing on the subject of the silhouette (499–500).

[8] Alice Kuzniar linked the erasure of the body in classical Weimar with attitudes towards popular culture in her remarks at the Davidson Symposium.

[9] See the excellent exhibition catalogue *Goethe und die Kunst* (Schulze 212–13). The catalogue also reproduces the two evolutionary series in Lavater's collection (216–17).

[10] Other noted busts of Goethe were sculpted by Alexander Trippel (1787), Christian Friedrich Tieck (1801 and 1820), Carl Weisser (1807), Christian Daniel Rauch (1820), Johann Gottfried Schadow (1823), and Pierre Jean David d'Angers (1829–31). For images of these works, see Schulze 181–87.

Works Cited

Assmann, Aleida. "Kultur als Lebenswelt und Monument." *Kultur als Lebenswelt und Monument*. Eds. Aleida Assmann and Dietrich Harth. Frankfurt a. M.: Fischer, 1991. 11–25.

Beutler, Ernst. "Taten und Ruhm von Gottlieb Martin Klauer." *Essays um Goethe*. 4th ed. Vol. 1. Wiesbaden: Dietrich, 1948. 265–73.

Boardman, John. *Greek Sculpture: The Classical Period*. London: Thames and Hudson, 1985.

Bode, Wilhelm. "Martin Klauer, der Bildhauer im klassischen Weimar." *Stunden mit Goethe*. Vol. 5. Berlin: E. Mittler, 1909. 241–88.

Brentano, Clemens. *Historisch-Kritische Ausgabe*. Eds. Jürgen Behrens, Konrad Feilchenfeldt, Wolfgang Frühwald, Christoph Perels, and Hartwig Schulz. Vol. 31. Stuttgart: Kohlhammer, 1975–.

Bruford, Walter Horace. *Culture and Society in Classical Weimar 1775–1806*. Cambridge: Cambridge UP, 1962.

Cooke, Lynne and Peter Wollen, eds. *Visual Display: Culture Beyond Appearances*. Seattle: Bay P, 1995.

Döblin, Alfred. *Berlin Alexanderplatz*. Munich: Artemis and Winkler, 1993.

Eckermann, Johann Peter Eckermann. *Gespräche mit Goethe in den letzten Jahren seines Lebens*. Ed. Fritz Bergemann. Frankfurt a. M.: Insel, 1981.

Feldmann, Wilhelm. *Friedrich Justin Bertuch*. Saarbrücken: Pecheur, 1902.

Fischer, Rotraut and Gabriele Stumpp. "Das konstruierte Individuum: Zur Physiognomie Johann Kaspar Lavaters und Carl Gustav Carus'." *Transfigurationen des Körpers*. Ed. Dietmar Kamper. Berlin: Reimer, 1989. 123–43.

Freud, Sigmund. "On Transience." *Standard Edition of the Complete Psychological Works*. Trans. and ed. James Strachey. Vol. 14. London: Hogarth P, 1953–74. 303–7.

Geese, Walter. *Gottlieb Martin Klauer: Der Bildhauer Goethes*. Leipzig: Insel, [1935].

"Goethe, seine Freunde und Zeitgenossen im Werk Gottlieb Martin Klauers." *Goethe: Ausstellungen aus der Sammlung Kippenberg*. Marburg/Lahn: Marburger Presse, 1949. 7–15.

Handrick, Willy. *Gottlieb Martin Klauer: Der Bildhauer der Goethezeit*. Weimar: n.p., 1972.

Haskell, Francis and Nicholas Penny. *Taste and the Antique: The Lure of Classical Sculpture 1500–1900*. New Haven: Yale UP, 1981.

Hegel, Georg Wilhelm Friedrich. *Aesthetics: Lectures on Fine Art*. Trans. T. M. Knox. Vol. 2. Oxford: Clarendon, 1975.

Herder, Johann Gottfried. *Plastik. Werke*. Ed. Wolfgang Pross. Vol. 2. Munich: C. Hanser, 1987. 401–542.

Kroeber, Hans Timotheus. *Die Goethezeit in Silhouetten*. 1911. Introd. Lutz Unbehaun. Rudolfstadt: Hain, 1996.

"Kunst-Artikel der Klauerschen Toreutica-Fabrik zu Weimar." *Verzeichnis von Kupferstichen, Kunst- und andern Waaren welche im Fürstlich. Sächs. privil. Industrie-Comptoir zu Weimar in Menge zu haben sind*. GSA 06 5257.

Lacan, Jacques. "The Mirror Stage." *Ecrits: A Selection*. Trans. Alan Sheridan. New York: Norton, 1977. 1–7.

Lavater, Johann Kaspar. *L'Art de connaître les hommes par la physiognomie*. 10 vols. Paris: de Pélasol, 1820.

Maul, Gisela and Margarete Oppel, eds. *Goethes Wohnhaus*. Munich: C. Hanser, 1996.

Nochlin, Linda. *The Body in Pieces: The Fragment as a Metaphor of Modernity*. London: Thames and Hudson, 1994.

Schlaffer, Hannelore. "Antike als Gesellschaftsspiel." *Analogon Rationis: Festschrift für Gerwin Marahrens zum 65. Geburtstag.* Eds. Marianne Henn and Christoph Lorey. Edmonton: M. Henn and C. Lorey, 1994. 193–207.

Schmidt, Martin H. *"Ich mache mir eine Büste von Goethe": Schadows Widerstreit mit Goethe.* Frankfurt a. M.: Peter Lang, 1995.

Schmölders, Claudia. "Das Profil im Schatten: Zu einem physiognomischen 'Ganzen' im 18. Jahrhundert." *Der ganze Mensch: Anthropologie im 18. Jahrhundert.* Ed. Hans-Jürgen Schings. Stuttgart: Metzler, 1994. 242–59.

Schneider, Klaus. *Natur — Körper — Kleider — Spiel. Johann Joachim Winckelmann: Studien zu Körper und Subjekt im späten 18. Jahrhundert.* Würzburg: Königshausen and Neumann, 1994.

Schulze, Sabine, ed. *Goethe und die Kunst.* Stuttgart: Hatje, 1994.

Sichardt, Gisela. *Das Weimarer Liebhabertheater unter Goethes Leitung: Beiträge zu Bühne, Dekoration und Kostüm unter Berücksichtigung der Entwicklung Goethes zum späteren Theaterdirektor.* Weimar: Arion, 1957.

Stafford, Barbara Maria. *Body Criticism: Imaging the Unseen in Enlightenment Art and Medicine.* Cambridge, MA: MIT P, 1992.

Thiel, Erika. *Geschichte des Kostüms: Die europäische Mode von den Anfängen bis zur Gegenwart.* Wilhelmshaven: Heinrichshofen, 1980.

Verzeichnis der Toreutica-Waare der Klauerschen Kunst-Fabrick zu Weimar. Vol. 1. Weimar: n.p., 1792.

Wahl, Hans. *Martin Gottlieb Klauers Goethebüste 1789/ 1790.* N.p.: n.p., 1920.

Winter, Gundolf. *Zwischen Individualität und Idealität: Die Bildnisbüste.* Stuttgart: Urachhaus, 1985.

Žižek, Slavoj. *Looking Awry: An Introduction to Jacques Lacan through Popular Culture.* Cambridge, MA: MIT P, 1991.

Fig. 1: Juno Ludovisi. Plaster bust in the Juno room of Goethe's house on the Frauenplan square. Photograph: Angelika Kittel (courtesy of Stiftung Weimarer Klassik).

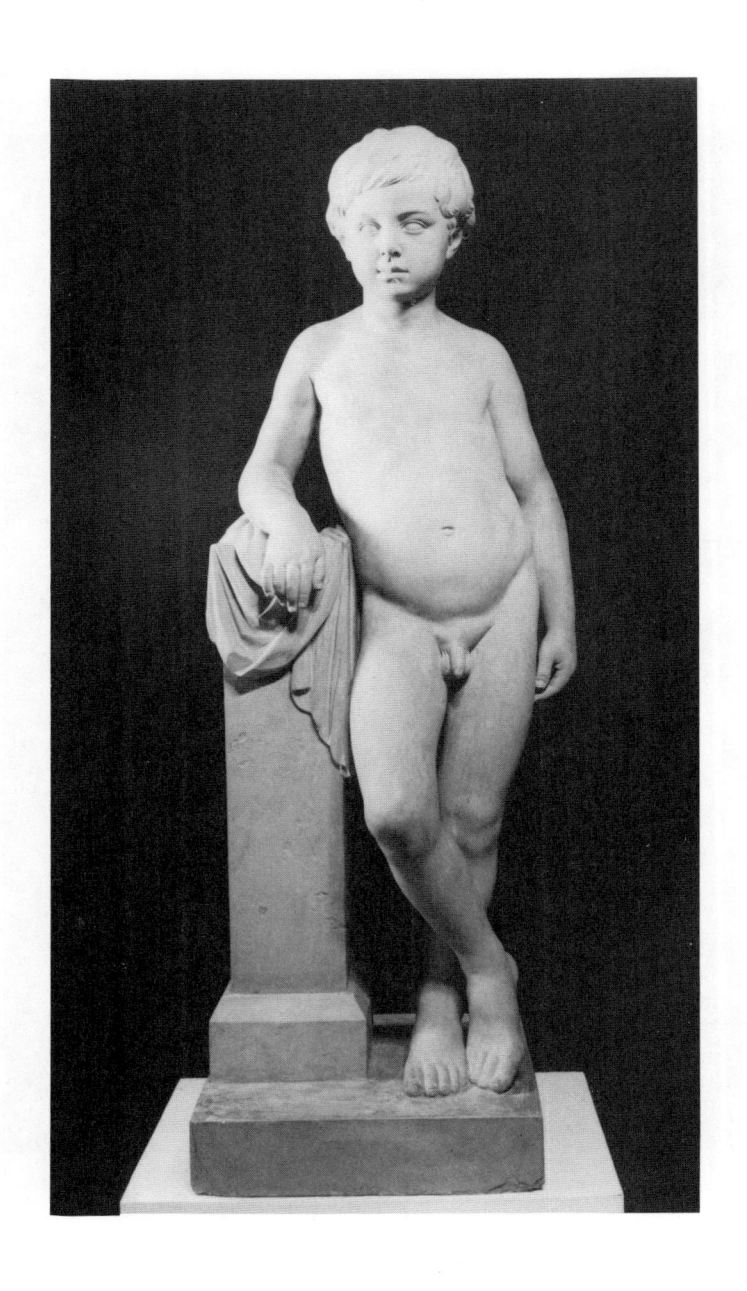

Fig. 2: Fritz von Stein. Limestone sculpture by Klauer, 1779. Schloss Tiefurt (courtesy of Stiftung Weimarer Klassik).

Fig. 3: Verzeichnis der Toreutica-Waare der Klauerschen Kunst-Fabrick zu Weimar *(Index of Teurotic Wares from the Klauer Art Factory at Weimar)* 1: Plate VIII. Weimar 1792. AAB 31.4: 58 e1 *(courtesy of Stiftung Weimarer Klassik)*.

*Fig. 4: Bust room in Goethe's house on the Frauenplan.
Photograph: Angelika Kittel (courtesy of Stiftung
Weimarer Klassik).*

Fig. 5: Johann Wolfgang von Goethe. Plaster bust by Klauer, 1780. Wittumspalais. Photograph: Angelika Kittel (courtesy of Stiftung Weimarer Klassik).

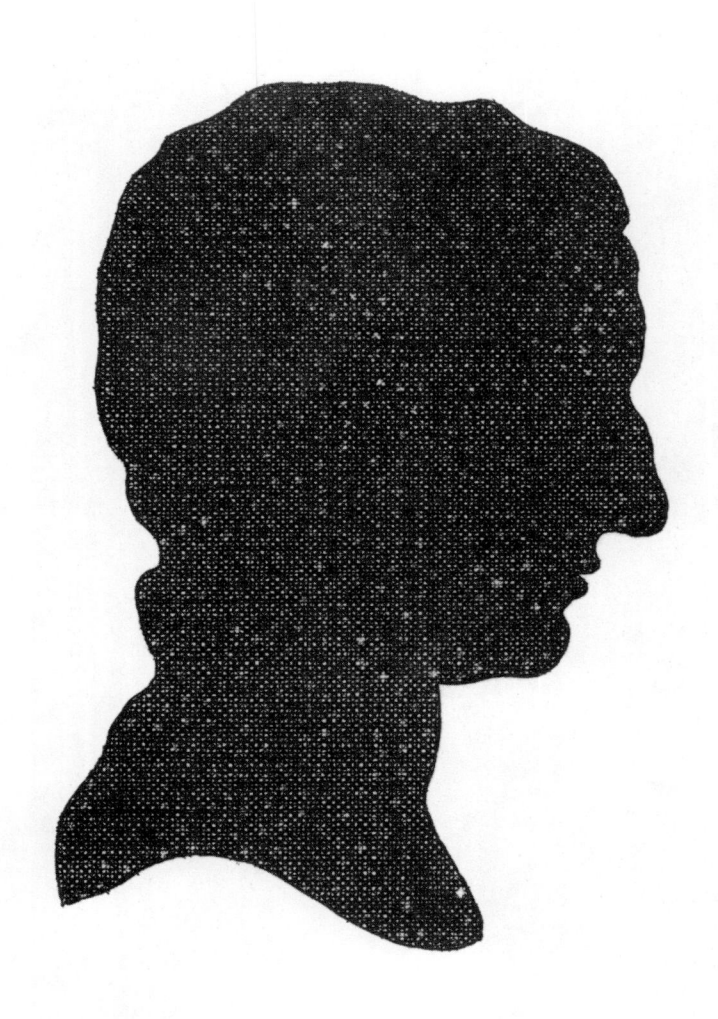

Fig. 6: Johann Kaspar Lavater, L'Art de connaître les hommes par la physiognomie *(The Science of Physiognomy, 1820; courtesy of Beinecke Library, Yale University).*

Fig. 7: Johann Joachim Christoph Bode.
White clay bust by Klauer, 1782. Photograph: Angelika Kittel
(courtesy of Stiftung Weimarer Klassik/Museen).

Fig. 8: Johann Wolfgang von Goethe.
Plaster bust by Klauer, 1778–79. Photograph: Angelika Kittel
(courtesy of Stiftung Weimarer Klassik/Museen).

Fig. 9: Johann Wolfgang von Goethe. Marble bust by Alexander Trippel, 1790. AAB. Photograph: Sigrid Geske (courtesy of Stiftung Weimarer Klassik).

Fig. 10: Johann Wolfgang von Goethe. Bronzed plaster bust by Klauer, 1780. Photograph: Angelika Kittel (courtesy of Stiftung Weimarer Klassik/Museen).

Fig. 11: Johann Wolfgang von Goethe. Bronzed plaster bust by Klauer, 1790. Photograph: Angelika Kittel (courtesy of Stiftung Weimarer Klassik/Museen).

Fig. 12: Johann Wolfgang von Goethe. Plaster bust by Johann Gottfried Schadow, circa 1823. Photograph: Angelika Kittel (courtesy of Stiftung Weimarer Klassik/Museen).

4

ANNIE JANEIRO RANDALL

Music in Weimar circa 1780: Decentering Text, Decentering Goethe

EXPLORING WEIMAR'S MUSICAL PAST from the perspective of Cultural Studies exposes a rich vein of material that has remained relatively untouched by literary, historical, and musicological scholars and throws into question several aspects of the constructed tradition of Goethe's Weimar. Considering music in Weimar as more than a faint aural backdrop to the production of literature is problematic due largely to the constraints of traditional disciplinary boundaries, paradigms, and practices within which researchers customarily operate.

Other limitations, including blind spots concerning the cultural contributions of women and the material aspects of art production have made the topic of music in Weimar particularly inaccessible. However, an expanded view of each discipline's procedures and acceptable objects and subjects of study allows for examination of works outside the narrow boundaries of late eighteenth-century canons, and exploration of the social, economic, and political aspects of art production. With these changes in disciplinary perspectives it becomes possible to create a listening post from which to begin hearing the integral musical dimension of many of the poems and plays produced in Weimar circa 1780.

Each section of the following discussion takes as its point of departure one of the issues just raised: the first section examines the social and material underpinnings of musico-literary activity at the court of Weimar circa 1780; the second details the centrality of women — Anna Amalia and Corona Schröter — in the creation of Weimar's musical identity; and the third presents *Proserpina* (1778 and 1787) as a case study of the interpenetration of musical and literary spheres in Weimar circa 1780. A concluding section reviews the problems of analyzing collaborative works and the implications inherent in the premise that literature and music were interdependent cultural practices in Goethe's Weimar.

Music and Image circa 1780

The carefully cultivated image of Weimar as an intellectually elite court of creative, enlightened polymaths owes much to its reputation for music making; nearly all members of Anna Amalia's court circle took part in the cultural practice of making music. For those familiar with Weimar and its environs, it is not difficult to imagine music in virtually every locale: in large formal ballrooms of the palace; in Anna Amalia's rooms at the Wittumspalais; in Goethe's house on Frauenplan and in his Gartenhaus; along the banks of the river at Schloss Tiefurt; in the gardens at Ettersburg; at Herder's church; and on the stage of the court theater. While Anna Amalia and Corona Schröter were the most musically active and high-profile of Weimar's residents, the musical activities of Wieland, Bertuch, Herder, Goethe, Seckendorff, Ernst and Caroline Wolf, among others, contributed to the construction of Weimar's identity as the "court of the muses." These activities included not only the performance and composition of music, but also writings on musical aesthetics and the creation of texts for musical treatment. Of these, most time, energy, and financial resources were spent on the production of musico-literary stage works for performance in the private court theater. Productions became increasingly elaborate and expensive, to the point that the bills associated with the group's activities became so numerous that they required the court treasurer to create a separate accounting book (Figs. 1 and 2).[1]

In the eight-year heyday of the private court theater, from 1775 to 1783, Anna Amalia's circle mounted sixty-six stage productions and gave a hundred and eleven performances (Sichardt 130–69 and 175–88). Two thirds of the productions were spoken plays by contemporary French and Italian authors such as Molière, Beaumarchais, Voltaire, Gozzi, and Goldoni, while twenty were musico-dramatic pieces. The majority of them were created collaboratively by the composers and writers of the court circle; Anna Amalia, Karl von Seckendorff, Ernst Wolf, Corona Schröter, and Johann Kranz composed music to texts, mostly comedies, by Goethe, Friedrich Hildebrand von Einsiedel, and Seckendorff (see the final section of this essay for a full listing of the twenty works). Herder, Wieland, and Bertuch also collaborated on musico-dramatic works, working with composers both in and outside Weimar. Wieland's collaborations with the composer Anton Schweitzer resulted in three operas and Herder also produced opera libretti and at least one cantata text, *Osterkantate* (Easter Cantata, 1782) which was set to music by Kapellmeister Ernst Wilhelm Wolf.[2] Bertuch provided the text for his single known musico-dramatic venture, *Polyxena*, for treatment by Anton Schweitzer.

In the same time period, from about the mid-1770s to the mid-1780s, while Herder was undertaking his folk song research, members of the Weimar court created over two hundred musico-poetic pieces, from Lieder and arias to ballads, airs, and ariettes, all mainly in German but some also in French and Italian. Most of these pieces were published in Lieder collections by composers Karl von Seckendorff and Corona Schröter and sold throughout the central and northern parts of the German-speaking lands.[3] Schröter and Seckendorff were joined by other Weimar composers such as Mimi von Oertel, Caroline Wolf, Johann Kranz, and Ernst Wolf in setting to music poems by poets both in and outside Weimar, among them Goethe, Herder, Caroline Rudolphi, Sophia Albrecht, Johann Jung, Johann Michaëlis, Hölty, Matthisson, Gotter, and Klopstock. In addition to printed song collections, many of the pieces were published in Wieland's *Teutscher Merkur* (German Mercury, 1773–89) which registered some two thousand subscribers (Stoll 58).[4] Other songs composed in Weimar circulated only among a select court inner circle; these include the five songs that appeared between 1781 and 1784 in the hand-copied *Tiefurt Journal* (see Burkhardt 13–19).

Given the number of writers in Weimar circa 1780, it is not surprising that the court produced such a large number of text-centered musical works. However, instrumental musical works were also popular, and dozens of large and small-scale compositions were composed by members of the court, principally Anna Amalia, Wolf, and Seckendorff. Along with their own compositions, ranging from solo keyboard works and keyboard concertos to oratorios and cantatas, Anna Amalia's circle also sought out solo, chamber, and orchestral works by well-known contemporary composers such as Haydn, Paisiello, Mozart, Lombardini-Sirmen, and Stamitz. The court favored the rococo, galant, and Sturm und Drang musical styles, signaling its knowledge of the latest fashions in music, as determined by the music then current in Vienna, Paris, and Italian opera centers.

In addition to numerous musical works, several essays on the subject of musical aesthetics and music education were produced by members of the Weimar court circle. These included Anna Amalia's unpublished and undated manuscript "Gedanken über die Musik" (Thoughts on Music); Herder's critical writings, most notably "Über die Oper" (On Opera) and "Tanz und Melodrama" (Dance and Melodrama); and various essays on musical aesthetics by Wieland, Wolf, and Seckendorff.[5] The latter were published in the *Merkur*, and, like the *Merkur*'s songs, enjoyed wide circulation.

From this overview it is clear that the scope of musical endeavor in Weimar was both broad and deep, and that the creation of the court's reputation as a center of musico-literary activity was aided considerably through exposure in Wieland's *Merkur*. Although the court lacked the wealth to make its cultural mark by displaying that ultimate signifier of political power, a large resident musical establishment — which, in the late eighteenth century, would have been made up of separate church and theater orchestras and choruses, virtuosic vocal and instrumental soloists, and an opera house — Weimar invented and occupied a middle ground situated between the few wealthy, politically powerful courts of the cultural mainstream and the smaller courts of the provincial, cultural backwaters. Despite a comparatively short roster of resident musicians and the financial inability to maintain a renowned composer or large orchestra, the court was still able to use music as a means of claiming status as a participant in European high culture. By capitalizing both on the fame of its authors and the predilections of its small but prolific band of aristocratic, professional, and non-professional musicians, Weimar's leaders cultivated a unique, hybrid musico-literary culture. Wieland's *Merkur*, arguably "Germany's nearest approach to a national cultural institution" (Boyle 241), became the indispensable medium in which they publicized that culture beyond the boundaries of the duchy of Saxe-Weimar.

This pragmatic but also serendipitous cross-fertilization of music and literature in Weimar was facilitated and embodied by Anna Amalia and Corona Schröter, both adept at literature and languages, and highly trained in music. Corona Schröter's celebrity was as important as Anna Amalia's personal involvement and patronage in elevating Weimar's provincial cultural profile. As the only bona fide professional musician among Anna Amalia's inner circle, with a reputation established across Europe before arriving in Weimar in 1776, Schröter's participation conferred musical legitimacy on the court's hybrid projects, guaranteeing them a much-coveted degree of respect in circles outside of Weimar. The duchess's and Schröter's activities and public personae made it possible for Weimar to portray itself convincingly not only as a literary court, but as a musical court as well.

At the Center of Musical Life:
Anna Amalia and Corona Schröter

Anna Amalia's influence, visibility, and financial means as Weimar's head-of-state for sixteen years (and, in matters cultural, as the power behind the throne for many years after), allowed her to promote her own musico-literary activities along with those of her circle. The centrality of music in Anna Amalia's life manifested itself in her seemingly ceaseless activity as a performer, composer, and patron of music. While her music making was, of necessity, private, her identity as a musician was long-lived and widespread. She missed few opportunities to establish and reinforce her musical identity in the minds of Weimar's residents, court visitors, guest artists, and visiting statesmen. Anna Amalia was known in musical circles in cities and courts outside of Weimar through regular mention of her name and activities in music journals and by way of dedications or appearances on subscriber's lists in music publications.[6]

In addition to prefatory dedications in printed music scores and news reports in music journals that kept her musical identity before the public,[7] Anna Amalia saw to it that most of her official portraits portrayed her with a musical instrument or a piece of music in her hand. The consistent presence of musical imagery coupled with the absence of traditional icons of religious virtue or civic power (such as bibles, crucifixes, swords, horses, or military uniforms) suggests not only Anna Amalia's devotion to music, but her desire to personify Weimar's musical image.[8]

Although she wished to be known as a composer, most of Anna Amalia's music was composed for performance at private court gatherings or for private theater productions and thus remained unpublished in her lifetime. Among her unpublished works are: *Erwin und Elmire* (1776; text by Goethe), *Das Jahrmarktsfest zu Plundersweilern* (The Yearly Fair at Trashville, 1778; text by Goethe), and *Die Zigeuner* (The Gypsies, 1780; text by Einsiedel).[9] In addition to these three musical stage works, Anna Amalia composed several instrumental pieces: an oratorio that appears to be no longer extant (see Hiller n. 17), three orchestral works (Sonatina in G; Sinfonia for oboes, flutes, bassoon, violins, viola, and bass; Sinfonia for flutes, horns, bassoon, violins, viola, and bass), and a keyboard quartet. The quartet, Divertimento per il Pianoforte, Clarinetto, Viola e Violoncello (Divertimento for Pianoforte, Clarinet, Viola, and Violoncello; circa 1780), is the only work of hers to be published in her lifetime (Fig. 3).[10]

A further dimension of Anna Amalia's role in shaping Weimar's musical life was her activity as a patron of music. She patronized, for instance, the Italian violin virtuosa, composer, and protégé of Tartini, Maddalena Lombardini Sirmen, who was invited to Weimar during her tour of European courts and cities and was paid highly for her several concerts in Weimar.[11] The artist for whom Anna Amalia's patronage had the farthest ranging consequences and with whom she worked most closely was the singer and actress Corona Schröter (1751–1802). Anna Amalia's association with Schröter was the most beneficial for Weimar in terms of advancing the agenda of establishing a high-profile musical presence for the court.

Given the ambition of the Weimar court to position itself among mainstream European cultural circles, and the fact that music was a principal medium through which participation in high culture was displayed, the hiring of Corona Schröter was both strategically wise and economically shrewd. Upon joining the court in 1776 with the title "Hofsängerin" [Court Singer] and a life stipend of four hundred talers per year, the court acquired not only the fame that came with Schröter's celebrity status, a highly valued commodity under the circumstances, but also several talents — singer, composer, actress, and painter — for the price of one stipend. Schröter was most immediately important to the court as a singer and actress; the cachet attached to her participation in the court theater created the impression that its productions were on a par with those produced on the stages of Leipzig, Paris, and London on which Schröter had performed. In the cases of some of the collaborative musico-dramatic works that emerged in the years following Schröter's arrival, the impression is accurate: *Erwin and Elmira, Lila, Die Fischerin* (The Fisher Woman, 1782),[12] and *The Yearly Fair at Trashville* are on a par with both the Weisse/Hiller collaborations in Leipzig and the Favart/Duni collaborations in Paris, while the melodrama *Proserpina* compares favorably with Benda's and Gotter's melodramas.

Although the court theater took most of Schröter's time in the years 1776 to 1782 (she took the lead in virtually all private theater productions, both musical and nonmusical), her musical activities were not confined to the private performances of the court theater. In contrast to Anna Amalia, whose passion for instrumental music engaged her as much as her musico-dramatic collaborations, Schröter focused on song composition when she was not involved in acting or singing in the court's theatrical productions. Although more than three hundred of her vocal compositions are thought to be lost, at least fifty songs survive.[13] Because they sold well both in and outside of Weimar, Schröter's two publications helped propagate Weimar's image as a musico-literary court and even establish a distinct musico-poetic genre known as the "Weimar Lied" (see Herrmann 109–12). An example of the Weimar Lied is Schröter's "Die ersten Blümchen" (The First Small Flowers, 1780), printed in the *Merkur* (Ex. 1). Several of the songs Schröter offered to the public in her first Lieder collection of 1786 were from her musical setting of the private theater's 1782 production of *Die Fischerin*, among them the first known musical setting of Goethe's "Erlkönig" (King of the Elves), the opening number of *Die Fischerin*.

Schröter's and Goethe's *Fischerin* and Weimar's other musico-dramatic works from this period are so clearly musical in conception and collaborative in their realization that each might be used as a rich example of the interdependence of musical and literary spheres in Weimar circa 1780.[14] *Proserpina* is singled out for closer scrutiny here for a number of reasons: first, of the many musico-dramatic collaborations from this period, *Proserpina* integrates music and text most closely and in sophisticated ways; second, its genre, the melodrama, links Weimar to a musical fashion in the courts and cities with which Weimar wished to establish cultural parity; third, the particular musical, literary, and dramatic demands and devices of the genre serve to highlight areas of likely collaboration; and fourth is the fact that this work was set to music not once, but twice in Weimar at Goethe's behest, hence underlining the integral nature of its musical component (Eberwein). A final reason for focusing on *Proserpina* is its veneration as an important Goethe text. While the other works mentioned above are read rarely and are marginalized as "occasional pieces," the familiarity of *Proserpina*'s text stands in stark contrast to the obscurity of its music. The problems of separating music from text, and the opposite effects of viewing both elements simultaneously, may in the case of *Proserpina* be more readily apparent than in a discussion of a less familiar work. In this discussion of *Proserpina* I will first locate the work within the context of the private theater's collaborative productions and the then-current taste for melodrama. Following this is an examination of the close integration of musical gestures and poetic/dramatic devices in *Proserpina*. I suggest that the complex weaving together of music and text in this piece reflects, in microcosm, the interdependence of musical and literary spheres in Weimar circa 1780.

The Private Theater's Musico-Dramatic Tastes and the Craze for Melodrama

Before 1776 the private theater favored works that had been successes on the stages of London, Paris, and Hamburg. These included translations or reworkings of plays such as Voltaire's *Nanine* (1749), Cumberland's *West Indian* (1771), and Lessing's *Minna von Barnhelm* (1767). But after 1776, due to the creative symbiosis of Anna Amalia's musical coterie, Goethe, and Schröter, the group focused increasingly on works of its own creation. This situation prevailed from 1775 until the last performance of the private theater in March 1783. Of the private theater's sixty-six productions and one hundred eleven performances, at least twenty were musico-dramatic works, of which fifteen were by Weimar composers. These works include:

Das Milchmädchen und die beiden Jäger (The Milkmaid and the Two Hunters, 1775–76); Anseaume/Duni?
Die beiden Geizhälse (The Two Misers, 1775–76); Grétry/Falbaire
Le Maître en droit (The Master of Law, 1775–76); Legrand?/Legrand?
Erwin und Elmire (Erwin and Elmira, 1775–76); Goethe/Anna Amalia
Der Fassbinder (The Cooper, 1775–76); Audinot/Faber?
Lila (Lila, 1777); Goethe/Seckendorff
Proserpina (Proserpina, 1778); Goethe/Seckendorff
Der Barbier von Sevilla (The Barber of Seville, 1778); after Beaumarchais/ ?
Das Jahrmarktsfest zu Plundersweilern (The Yearly Fair at Trashville, 1778); Goethe/Anna Amalia
Iphigenie auf Tauris (Iphigenia in Tauris, 1779); Goethe/Ernst Wilhelm Wolf
Die Laune des Verliebten (The Lover's Caprice, 1779); Goethe/Seckendorff
Claudine von Villa Bella (Claudine of Villa Bella, 1779); Goethe/Seckendorff
Orpheus und Eurydike (Orpheus and Eurydice, 1779); Einsiedel/Seckendorff
Robert und Kalliste (Robert and Calliste, 1780); Seckendorff/Seckendorff
Jery und Bätely (Jery and Betty, 1780); Goethe/Seckendorff

Die Vögel (The Birds, 1780); Goethe/Wolf
Die Zigeuner (The Gypsies, 1780); Einsiedel/Anna Amalia
Minervens Geburt, Leben und Taten (Minerva's Birth, Life, and Deeds, 1781); Goethe/Seckendorff
Die Fischerin (The Fisher Woman, 1782); Goethe/Schröter
Zobeis (Zobeis, 1782); Einsiedel after Gozzi/Seckendorff?[15]

The repertoire of 1775–76 contains just two works which had been in the Seyler company's repertoire: *Das Milchmädchen und die beiden Jäger* (The Milkmaid and the Two Hunters) and *Der Fassbinder* (The Cooper), and none from the previously favored librettist-composer teams of Weisse/Hiller, Heermann/Wolf, Wieland/Schweitzer, and Gotter/Benda. This absence is telling in view of the fact that works by these writers and composers accounted for nearly half of the thirty-one musical pieces presented by Seyler's troupe just a few years earlier, and is particularly pointed as both Wolf and Wieland were Weimar residents. Wieland was deeply interested in the development of a distinctly German operatic style, and the private theater provided him with a unique venue in which he could pursue his theories on the relationship of music and dramatic text (see his "Versuch über das Teutsche Singspiel, und einige dahin einschlagende Gegenstände," or "Essay On the Singspiel and Other Such Matters"). Yet Wieland and Schweitzer's works found no place in the private theater's repertoire, nor was any work by Wieland performed in the years 1775–83.[16]

Ernst Wilhelm Wolf, Weimar's Kapellmeister and a favorite of Duchess Anna Amalia, was also shunned by the private theater. He composed music for only two productions in the years 1775–83, Goethe's *Iphigenie auf Tauris* in 1779 and *Die Vögel* in 1780.[17] The music for these works is no longer extant, and it is impossible to know whether Wolf's compositions were incidental or integral to the plays. Although six of Wolf's operas were in the Seyler troupe's repertoire, none was performed by the private theater. They were *Die Dorfdeputierten* (The Village Representatives), *Die treuen Köhler* (The Loyal Charcoal Burners), *Das Rosenfest* (The Festival of Roses), *Der Abend im Walde* (The Evening in the Woods), *Ceres*, and *Das grosse Loos* (The Grand Prize). Heermann was the librettist for the first four, while Einsiedel and Bertuch, respectively, provided texts for the last two.[18]

Weisse and Hiller's works may also have seemed to be out of touch with the aesthetic objectives of the private theater. Although French works were popular, as evidenced by the preponderance of French pieces in 1775–76, it seems that German adaptations of French opérascomiques, such as *Lottchen am Hofe* (Little Lotte at Court) and *Die*

Jagd (The Hunt), both of which were in the Seyler troupe's repertoire during its Weimar residency, had fallen from favor (see Pendle, "French Styles in Europe" and "Opéra Comique in Paris"). It is possible that in their adaptations of opéras-comiques Weisse and Hiller, like Wieland, went too far — for the private theater's taste — in their reshaping of characters along ethical and moral lines.[19]

Herder is yet another of Weimar's residents whose interest in musical drama found no outlet in the private theater. He too favored ethical themes in his libretti, and seems to have regarded the light, comic style that prevailed in the productions of the private theater as frivolous. In contrast to his collection of folk songs (1778–79), which had a great impact on Weimar musical life and whose texts found their way into Seckendorff's and Schröter's published song collections, Herder's opera libretti aroused no interest among members of the Weimar private theater.

Melodrama, on the other hand — a musico-dramatic genre featuring intensely declaimed monologues in which text is typically delivered via underscored speech rather than singing — was of great interest to the musically fashion-conscious members of the "court of the muses" and Seckendorff composed his setting of Goethe's *Proserpina* (1777) soon after the first melodramas in German appeared. Melodramas of the era included those by Franz Aspelmayer (*Pygmalion*, 1772), Peter Winter (*Lenardo und Blandine*, 1783), Georg Benda (*Ariadne auf Naxos*, 1775), Anton Schweitzer (*Pygmalion*, 1772), and Franz Beck (*Pandore*, 1789).[20] Rousseau's *scène lyrique*, *Pygmalion* (Lyrical Scene, Pygmalion, music by Coignet, with two numbers by Rousseau) was the catalyst for the 1770s flowering of the melodrama genre in Germany, and both Franz Aspelmayer and Anton Schweitzer set as melodramas German translations of Rousseau's text. Aspelmayer's version was first performed at Vienna's court theater in 1772, while Schweitzer's version had its first performance by the Seyler company in Weimar in the same year. Georg Benda also set a translation of Rousseau's *Pygmalion* in 1779 in Gotha.

Benda's melodramas enjoyed the widest circulation among these, and were likely models for Seckendorff in his setting of *Proserpina*. Mozart too admired the Gotha composer's melodramas, and his letters of winter 1778 suggest their character and reasons for their popularity.

> I cannot remember whether I told you anything about this type of drama the first time I was here [in Mannheim]. On that occasion I saw a piece of this kind performed twice and was absolutely delighted. Indeed, nothing has ever surprised me so much, for I had always imagined that such a piece would be quite ineffective! You know, of course, that there is no singing

in it, only recitation to which the music is like a sort of obbligato accompaniment to a recitative. Now and then words are spoken while the music goes on, and this produces the finest effect. The piece I saw was Benda's *Medea*. He has composed another one *Ariadne auf Naxos* and both are really excellent. You know that of all the Lutheran Kapellmeisters Benda has always been my favorite and I like these two works so much that I carry them about with me. (Anderson 631)[21]

While the subject of Rousseau's text resonated with composers and audiences, the devices of the literary Sturm und Drang had at least as much to do with shaping the literary style of the melodrama as *Pygmalion*.[22] In fact, *Pygmalion's* original music was probably unknown in German speaking lands. The melodrama's distinctive musical identity (sudden changes in texture, dynamics, mood, key, and registration; dramatic use of silence) was shaped by the German court composers Aspelmayer, Schweitzer, and Georg Benda, who in turn were influenced by Graun's and Hasse's recitative style, C. P. E. Bach's sentimental pieces, and probably Haydn's many so-called Sturm und Drang works of the years 1765–73 (for example, Haydn's Symphonies 39, 49, and 59).

The genre's emphasis on an intensely emotional situation within a single, continuous time frame required small casts and modest staging — highly appealing features given the musical and dramatic conditions at the neighboring courts of Gotha and Weimar. Following *Pygmalion's* example, the Gotha and Weimar melodramas emphasized single characters, making them ideal "star vehicles" for talents such as Corona Schröter in Weimar, and Johann Böck, Charlotte Brandes, and Sophie Seyler, who were all members of the Seyler company that had performed Schweitzer's *Pygmalion* in Weimar in 1772 and 1773, and Benda's *Ariadne* and *Medea* in Gotha in 1775.[23]

Emulating Benda, yet wanting to add their own twists to the genre, Seckendorff and composers such as Neefe (*Sophonisbe*, 1776) and J. F. Reichardt (*Ino*, 1779) included singing in their melodramas. Though Benda's melodramas contained only spoken text and musically underscored speech (text spoken over a musical accompaniment), they maintained their popularity until the first decade of the nineteenth century. The addition of vocal music posed problems for the genre in that few actors and actresses had sufficient training in music to sing any but the simplest of musical roles. Though Neefe and Reichardt's additions were limited to the chorus, the addition of singing opened the door to the possibility — explored by Seckendorff in *Proserpina* — that the lead characters could sing as well. Lack of musical training meant that the principal characters could not bring to their roles a musical virtuosity that was on par with their dramatic virtuosity. In other words, the relative quality of their singing and speaking would be wildly divergent, and perhaps unintentionally comic. Schröter, with whom Goethe and Seckendorff collaborated on *Proserpina,* was an exception who combined rare gifts for both dramatic declamation and vocal performance.

Word and Tone:
Proserpina's Interdependent Texts

Influenced by Schweitzer's and Benda's melodramas, and working in a court with expectations of high literary quality in its musico-dramatic products, Goethe and Seckendorff created a melodrama in which they freely alternated singing, speaking, underscored speech, and accompanied measured speech in the demanding role of Proserpina. *Proserpina* was not, however, an independent work in its first performance of 30 January 1778, but the fourth act of Goethe's six-act play *Der Triumph der Empfindsamkeit* (Triumph of Sensibility, 1787). It was later performed as an independent melodrama on 10 June 1779. The text publication of *Proserpina* in the *Merkur* of February 1778 (Fig. 4), shortly after the play's first performance but without any mention of it, suggests that Goethe conceived the work simultaneously as an independent piece and as part of a larger work, both with music. Supporting the conclusion that *Proserpina's* original conception was as a musico-dramatic work is the fact that the text of the 1778 *Merkur* publication and that copied by Seckendorff into his 1777 score are virtually identical (Figs. 4 and 5). That Goethe and Seckendorff intended *Proserpina* expressly for Corona Schröter seems obvious, as there was no other artist at the Weimar court who could have performed the work convincingly, given its musical and dramatic demands.

In *Der Triumph der Empfindsamkeit,* Schröter played the role of Queen Mandandane, a woman who, to the dismay of her husband King Andrason (played by Goethe), was susceptible to the charms of Prince Oronaro (played by Philip Seidel, Goethe's valet). Acts one through three establish Oronaro's false sensibility through the parodic language of his disingenuous interactions with Mandandane and her ladies-in-waiting, and his taste for "artificial nature" (Blackall 54).

In what must have been a marvel of set design as well as a visual parody of the excesses of sensibility, Oronaro's valet Merkulo — whom the prince refers to as his "Naturmeister, Directeur de la nature" [master of nature; MA 2.1: 176] — follows the prince wherever he goes, transporting several large cases that contain "nature"; the most beautiful birdsong but also moonlight (MA 2.1: 177). In such a setting of artificial nature, which the prince prefers because it spares his sensitive nerves from the unpleasant smells and uncomfortable temperatures of "real" nature (MA 2.1: 177), this "empfindsamste Mann von allen Männern" [most sensitive of all men, MA 2.1: 175] declaims a speech in the style of a melodrama. Preceding his speech, the stage directions read: "Die feierliche Musik geht fort, die Wasserfälle fangen an zu rauschen, die Vögel zu singen, der Mond zu scheinen" [Solemn music begins, the waterfalls begin to flow, the birds sing, the moon shines; MA 2.1: 183]. Despite his self-proclaimed passions, the prince falls asleep during his own speech. Perhaps suggesting that the melodrama genre is so boring that it requires music to awaken the audience, Goethe writes in his stage directions:

> Während der letzten Kadenz, da die Instrumente die Stimme zu lange nachahmen, setzt sich der Prinz auf eine Rasenbank, und schläft endlich ein. Man gibt ihm verschiednemal den Ton an, damit er einfallen und schließen möge; allein er rührt sich nicht, und es entsteht eine Verlegenheit im Orchester; endlich sieht sich die erste Violine genötigt die Kadenz zu schließen, die Instrumente fallen ein, die Laube geht zu, der mittlere Vorhang fällt nieder. (MA 2.1: 184)

> [During the last cadence, the instruments imitate the voice for a long while. The prince sits down on a grassy bank and falls asleep. Several times he is given his note as a cue, but he does not respond; there is embarrassment in the orchestra, and finally, the first violin is compelled to finish the phrase. The other instruments join in, the scene closes, and the curtain falls.]

Unfortunately, the incidental music described here has not survived.

In act four, the narrative of acts one through three is suspended while Queen Mandandane performs the monodrama *Proserpina,* her performance contrasting sharply with Oronaro's comical, soporific effort in act three. In the persona of Proserpina, Queen Mandandane expresses her personal despair through Proserpina's story of abduction, abandonment, seduction, and captivity. Just as Mandandane (as Proserpina) resigns herself to a life in Hades, her husband Andrason interrupts and Proserpina, mistaking Andrason for Pluto, Proserpina's captor, flees offstage. Although the above-quoted stage directions indicate that the only music in the fourth act of *Der Triumph der Empfindsamkeit* was a short, mood-setting prelude, they confirm the presence of the orchestra. Given the 1777 date of Seckendorff's manuscript, it is likely that the full musical version of the monodrama was performed in January (Fig. 6).

In acts five and six, Andrason and the ladies-in-waiting use a life-size doll resembling Queen Mandandane to expose Oronaro to Mandandane as a fraud. The doll, hollowed out and stuffed full of such books as Rousseau's *La Nouvelle Héloïse* (1760) or Goethe's *Die Leiden des jungen Werthers* (1774), is the prince's undoing, as he is unable to distinguish it from Mandandane. The queen, displeased that Oronaro has mistaken a doll for her, finally recognizes the prince's shallowness, and returns to her husband with a wish to rejuvenate their marriage. By placing Oronaro's ludicrous monologue and Mandandane's highly affecting monodrama back-to-back, Goethe contrasts sensibility's charlatans with its true believers. As the play's title indicates, the poseur is exposed and sensibility triumphs.

Similarities between Seckendorff's musical treatment of *Proserpina*, Schweitzer's 1772 setting of *Pygmalion*, and Georg Benda's 1775 *Ariadne auf Naxos* and *Medea* are numerous. They include short spoken phrases introduced, accompanied, or followed by music that mirrors the sentiment of the text; affective use of major and minor modes; and occasional soloistic writing for bassoons and violoncelli within the context of the basic late eighteenth-century orchestral complement. Supplementing Benda's musical and text-setting practices, Seckendorff created his own devices; most notably he used singing and measured speech as additional means of text delivery, deployed the varied types of text delivery in rapid succession, and included clarinets in the orchestra. While both Benda and Seckendorff used underscored speech, Seckendorff employed the device fourteen times, whereas Benda used it only twice, preferring his speeches interpolated between musical phrases and reserving underscored speech for moments of heightened emotion only (Bauman, *German Opera* 85, 114–15). Moreover, Seckendorff also made use of instrumental affect to add layers of nuance to the text.

While each of these devices is worthy of close attention, the use of four types of text delivery in *Proserpina* and the apparent assignment of different values to them in a hierarchy of meaning are of particular interest. These four types of text delivery are singing, underscored speech, accompanied measured speech, and unaccompanied speech. Singing and unaccompanied speech represent the extreme ends of the expressive range, while underscored speech and accompanied measured speech occupy the middle ground between them (see appendix).[24]

Set in high relief are those parts of the text which carry crucial emotional and narrative information through the medium of song. Seckendorff uses singing judiciously to make his points most forcefully and economically. Only ten numbers of the work's total of thirty-one employ singing (nos. 3, 4, 20, 26, 28, 31a, 31c, 31e, 31f, 31g), and only fifty-two lines out of a total of two hundred and sixty-nine are sung. The sung portions of *Proserpina* convey the following information: Proserpina's sense of despair; Ceres's fury at Proserpina's abduction and her futile attempt to rescue her daughter; Proserpina's entreaty to her father, Jupiter, to save her from Hades; Proserpina's plea for a reprieve from punishment for eating and enjoying the pomegranate; denial of her wishes and eternal damnation. Thus, all crucial elements of the story are sung, while their emotional content is conveyed simultaneously through the music. The discontinuity of the melodic line in "Halt einmal" [stop right now; no. 3; Ex. 2], caused by constant insertion of rests, is magnified by the single line of spoken text that breaks up the singing. Proserpina's despair, underlined by chromaticism, the minor mode, and prominently placed augmented fourths, becomes more palpable as fifteen numbers pass before she sings again, as though despair had robbed her of that ability. The figure accompanying her as she sings "Endlos liegen sie vor dir die Trauergefilde/ und was du suchst, liegt immer hinter dir" [Endlessly stretch before you fields of sorrow,/ And what you seek forever lies behind you; SE 7: 274; 3–4] foreshadows the song of the damned in no. 31, its identical rhythm suggesting that, though she rails against her fate, she knows that her destiny is fixed. By contrast, her song in no. 28, "Laß dich geniessen" [Let me enjoy you; SE 7: 278; 183], confirms her innocent enjoyment of the pomegranate in its use of the major mode, virtually no chromaticism, continuous rhythms, and a single meter. As it is the longest continuous piece of music in the work (except for the overture and postlude), and the most aria-like of the sung portions, Seckendorff signals that this is the climactic point of the piece.

Underscored speech (Ex. 3) and accompanied measured speech (Ex. 4) are used in fourteen instances (nos. 10, 11, 16, 17, 18, 20, 23, 25, 26, 27, 30, 31b, 31g, 31h), a total of fifty-three lines. Whereas song is used to convey elements of the story line and Proserpina's emotional state, Seckendorff appears to reserve the two types of musically accompanied speech for Proserpina's immediate reactions to specific aspects of her fate: indignation and irony (nos. 10, 11, 16, 18, 20,30, 31b, 31g, 31h); and nostalgia and regret (nos. 23, 25, 26, 27). Seckendorff sets what may be considered the work's most dramatically intense lines of text as accompanied measured speech:

> Was hab ich verbrochen,
> Daß ich genoß?
> Ach, warum schafft
> Die erste Freude hier mir Qual?
> [...]
> Warum sind Früchte schön,
> Wenn sie verdammen? (204–7, 229–30)
>
> [What crime have I committed,
> In my enjoyment?
> Ah, why does this first joy
> Bring me pain?
> (...)
> Why should fruit be beautiful,
> If it brings damnation? (SE 7: 279)]

This passage is framed by the Chorus of the Damned singing "Du bist unser!" [You are ours! SE 7: 279].

Spoken text (Ex. 5) accounts for the remaining one hundred and sixty-four lines of text. Throughout, Seckendorff uses unaccompanied speech to elaborate on the information that has been given to us in concentrated form through song. Proserpina establishes emotional and narrative motifs in the songs, which she then spins out in unaccompanied speech. She follows each of her songs with elaborative speech, heightened by musically underscored reactions. With the exception of "Let me enjoy," which is followed by music of a radically different nature (signifying her punishment for tasting the pomegranate), the material that follows the songs usually takes up the song's musical motifs. Seckendorff does not develop or vary these significantly, but uses fragments of them to punctuate the elaborative speeches. The rapid succession of different types of text delivery was facilitated by Schröter's expertise in both singing and acting; the degree of difficulty in executing such rapid changes required nothing less.

Problems and Conclusions

The exact degree to which Goethe, Seckendorff, and Schröter collaborated on *Proserpina* is difficult to determine. We know from other contexts (*Jery und Bätely*, principally; see Pendle, "Transformation") that Goethe did not share Seckendorff's compositional tastes, and may have enjoyed, in the creation of this piece, a certain license to offer suggestions to Seckendorff given the logocentric nature of the melodrama genre.[25] Schröter and Goethe are known to have worked together on drawings, song settings, and even on the revisions of *Iphigenie*.[26] Taking this into consideration, and given the difficulty of notating and performing measured and accompanied speech, it is probably safe to assume that Schröter, herself a composer, would have offered notational strategies (such as placement of fermatas, cues, dynamic and tempo markings) and interpretive suggestions to Seckendorff and Goethe. The close atmosphere of the private theater and the daily contact its denizens had with one another were factors highly conducive to the sharing of ideas; it stretches credulity that Seckendorff, Goethe, and Schröter would not have collaborated on a project which by its very nature demands it.

Collaboration is particularly difficult to trace in the absence of documentation, and within a tradition of historiography that views the Weimar theater exclusively through the lens of Goethe. However, collaboration can, and should, be inferred in certain types of works and under certain conditions. The contributions of performers are especially elusive, though, as seen in the case of *Proserpina*, they are well worth investigating: would Goethe and Seckendorff have attempted such an ambitious musico-dramatic project had Schröter not been present? The concept of sole authorship seems strained at best upon restoring the musical dimension to stage works such as *Proserpina*.

Considering the musico-dramatic works circa 1780 in the form in which they were originally conceived and performed results in an adjusted historical perspective in which Goethe is decentered and shares the stage with Seckendorff, Anna Amalia, Schröter, and Wolf, who emerge as co-authors of works that are generally thought of as having been authored by Goethe alone. Text itself is also decentered in this reoriented view, as the restored musical component requires the reader to focus on the interplay of text and music rather than on text and music as discrete entities. Material conditions must also be considered when attempting to understand Weimar's musico-literary cultural practices and products circa 1780, for the court's financial limitations created a situation in which the musical and literary spheres overlapped of necessity. Within this environment of financial limitation and cultural ambition, the musical and literary spheres of Weimar's "muses" operated interdependently from at least 1775 to 1783, producing many stage works and Lieder which seem due for critical re-appraisal.

—Bucknell University

Notes

I am grateful to Susanne Kord, Burkhard Henke, and Simon Richter for their insightful editorial suggestions, and to many of the participants in the *Second Davidson German Studies Symposium: Approaches to the City of Weimar* (February 1997) whose research has greatly enriched my understanding of Weimar's cultural life.

[1] The sum of 1,239 talers can be put in perspective by considering the fact that Corona Schröter and Wieland each received yearly stipends of 400 talers. Therefore, the cost of the private court theater's 1777 productions was the equivalent of three years' income for a well-paid member of the court.

[2] Wieland's and Schweitzer's operas were all first performed in Weimar: *Aurora* (24 October 1772), *Alkeste* (28 May 1773), and *Die Wahl des Herkules* (Hercules's Choice, 4 September 1773). Herder's texts included *Melusine* (1769), *Brutus* (1772–74), *Sokrates* (1774), *Tod der Naemi* (Naemi's Death, 1793–96), and *Ariadne-Libera* (1802). See Kirby 316–29.

[3] Seckendorff was especially influenced by Herder, as shown in his *Volks- und andere Lieder* (Folk- and Other Songs, 1779–82), and *Zwölf Lieder mit Begleitung des Pianoforte* (Twelve Songs Accompanied by Pianoforte, n.d.). See also Schröter, *Fünf und zwanzig Lieder in Musik gesetzt* (Twenty-five Songs Set to Music, 1786), and *Gesaenge mit Begleitung des Fortepiano* (Songs Accompanied by Pianoforte, 1794).

[4] Twenty-nine songs in piano-vocal score were published in the *Merkur* from 1774 to 1785. Most were by Weimar composers and varied in length from five measures to fifty-six measures long.

[5] See Wieland, "Versuch über das Teutsche Singspiel, und einige dahin einschlagende Gegenstände" (Essay on the German Singspiel and Other Such Matters) in *Merkur* (July 1775): 63–87; also Seckendorff, "Versuch einer Berichtung des jetztigen Zustands der Tonkunst in Italien" (Essay on the Current Condition of Music in Italy) in *Merkur* (May 1776): 169–86 and "Etwas von der musikalischen Edukation" (Of Musical Education) in *Merkur* (December 1776): 212–28; finally, Wolf, "Was ist wahre Musik? und wie erhält man sie?" (What Is True Music? And How Is One to Obtain It?) in *Merkur* (February 1783): 231–39.

[6] For instance, Ernst Wolf's *Sei Sonate per il Clavicembalo Solo* (Six Sonatas for Clavicembalo Solo, 1774), a collection of keyboard pieces sold throughout the Empire and also in Paris and London, contains a dedication in Italian to Anna Amalia. Amid the generic hyperbole of such dedications, Wolf's description of his patron as "la più perfetta conoscitrice" [the most perfect connoisseur] stands out: it places Anna Amalia among "Kenner" [connoisseurs, or serious musicians], a term of respect distinct from "Liebhaber" [lover] which was used to describe amateur musicians of lesser skills.

[7] A news item, published in Hiller's *Wöchentliche Nachrichten und Anmerkungen die Musik betreffend* (Weekly News and Comments on Music) reports the performance of an oratorio composed by Anna Amalia, which shared the stage with a work by the esteemed Berlin court composer C. H. Graun (d. 1759): "Ein nicht minder bewundernswürdiges Beyspiel findet die Musik an Ihre Durchl. der verwittweten Herzoginn von Sachsen-Weimar. Diese erhabene Verehrerin der Musik macht derselben nicht allein durch ihre Stärke auf dem Flügel Ehre; sondern die Composition erhält auch nicht selten aus Ihrer Feder ansehnliche und sehr wohl gerathene Vermehrungen; wie denn in vergangener Fasten außer dem Tod Jesu vom seel. Capellmeister Graun, noch ein Oratorium, von der Composition der Durchlauchten Herzoginn, am Hofe zu Weimar aufgeführt worden ist" [An equally admirable example of a musician is found in her Highness, the widowed Duchess of Saxe-Weimar. This sublime worshipper of music graces music not only with her skillful keyboard playing, but also with the praiseworthy and well-crafted compositions which pour from her pen, one of which, an oratorio by her Highness the Duchess of Weimar, was performed during Lent, alongside *Christ's Death* of the late Kapellmeister Graun, at the Court of Weimar; 317].

[8] A 1771 formal portrait by J. F. Loeber pictures her seated near a harpsichord flanked by her bewigged, teenaged sons Carl August and Constantine, while a slightly later, informal portrait by Georg Melchior Kraus (1774) shows her dressed casually, her left arm resting on a sidetable piled with pieces of music, books, and a flute. The most famous portrait from Anna Amalia's regency (by J. E. Heinsius, 1770) bears her coat of arms and shows her seated next to a double manual harpsichord with an open music manuscript positioned on it, in full view. This seems to have been Anna Amalia's favorite official portrait as several, large scale copies of it were made for display in various royal residences. A later painting from 1780, also by Heinsius, shows the duchess with no musical instrument, but with a piece of music scrolled in her hand in the traditional pose of a composer. All paintings mentioned are in the possession of the Stiftung Weimar Klassik.

[9] The latter is also known as *Adolar und Hilaria* and was, like the other two, first performed in Weimar. When read or studied today, these texts are rarely considered in their original musical settings, and are typically dismissed as occasional pieces, unconnected to the literary or musical mainstream. Reading the words alone misses the flavor of the German Singspiel, French opéra-comique, Italian opera buffa, and English ballad opera traditions that are evident in the music. As comic stage works of the late eighteenth century, these works are fully in keeping with German adaptations of contemporary French and Italian musical style, thus placing the works firmly in the European mainstream circa 1780. On both textual and musical levels they contain ribald humor, many moments of slapstick hilarity, and dry commentary on bourgeois manners. They also play on sexual, racial, ethnic, and class stereotypes.

[10] It is likely that Anna Amalia's objective in publishing this work was to establish a *public* reputation as a composer. To her private court circle, who knew her compositions and heard her perform almost on a daily basis, there was nothing to prove; yet, those outside of her immediate circle would have had no opportunity to have heard her perform or to know the level of her compositional skill. The dedications, news reports, appearances on subscription lists, and even her portraits could suggest, but not demonstrate that she was an accomplished composer. Treading carefully within the narrow confines of class and gender propriety, the Divertimento allowed her to publicly display her skills as a composer of professional ability without actually crossing the line into the professional, masculine, symphonic domain. A mid-sized chamber work in two, binary movements, the Divertimento was "serious" enough to distance Anna Amalia from the dilettantism associated with small-scale song composition, yet not so serious as to invite association with the artisan-composer class. The fact that she put the piece up for sale (at the price of eight groschen) guaranteed that the music would circulate in places that Anna Amalia could never go personally, and was thus a means of extending her reputation as a serious musician.

[11] See court account books for the year 1778–79 in ThHStAW A 935: 1004. Keyboard reductions of two of Sirmen's concertos have been found in Anna Amalia's private library suggesting that Anna Amalia played these works herself, possibly with Sirmen when the violinist visited the court.

[12] *Die Fischerin*, one of many of Schröter's musical collaborations with Goethe (her published *Lieder* contain many settings of Goethe texts), represents the only extant court theater production for which she was the composer. She also acted and sang in this broad peasant comedy. Performed outdoors on the grounds of Schloss Tiefurt, *Die Fischerin's* climactic scene takes place among torch-lit barges floating down the river toward the audience. Schröter's deft musical handling of this comedy, centering on the plight of Dortchen and her disaffected husband and father, reflect her dry musical wit and the rigorous musical training she received from J. A. Hiller in Leipzig. Schröter's connection to Hiller, who was renowned as a pedagogue, scholar, and also as the era's most successful composer of Singspiele, was no doubt another reason Anna Amalia, Carl August, and Goethe were so anxious for Schröter to join the court: her experience of Hiller and Weisse's many successes in Leipzig was an invaluable first-hand resource for composers at court who, like Seckendorff and Anna Amalia, prided themselves on keeping abreast of new musical fashions.

[13] In addition to the publications cited above, Gerber refers to three hundred and sixty arias by Schröter (4: 122). Along with two other songs mentioned in a 6 March 1801 letter of Charlotte Schiller, namely "Der Taucher" (The Diver, 1797) and "Würde der Frauen" (Women's Dignity, 1795), both based

on Schiller's eponymous poems, these arias are no longer extant (Urlichs and von Schiller 2: 132).

[14] The musical conception is most obvious in the use of both prose and verse, indicating speaking alternating with singing. Collaboration is evident upon examination of different versions of these works' texts: each contains textual additions and deletions that most likely resulted from the suggestions of the composers and/or the performers.

[15] Author's names are followed by composer's names; questionable attributions are indicated by a question mark. For sources, see Bauman, *North German Opera*; Sichardt.

[16] Though Wieland's *Merkur* was much sought after as a tool of publicity, his ideas on music and drama were often contrary to those of the members of the private theater, and appear to have been unwelcome. Goethe's satirical play *Götter, Helden und Wieland* (Gods, Heroes, and Wieland; 1773) ridiculed Wieland's self-importance in matters of dramatic theory, and while both writers seemed to agree on the primacy of text in musico-dramatic works, they differed on the issue of ethical and moral qualities of the characters. According to Wieland, characters should express morally and ethically enlightened views which educate and inspire the audience. The characters in the private theater plays from this period are driven less by morals and ethics than by lust, naïveté, and social convention. This difference in outlook may have been enough to prevent Wieland from joining, or wanting to join, the activities of the private theater.

[17] J. F. Reichardt's later setting of a monologue of *Iphigenie* is still extant in his *Goethe's Lieder, Oden, Balladen und Romanzen*.

[18] These works were among the most popular in Seyler's repertoire and, along with two other works by Wolf — *Das Gärtnermädchen* (The Gardener Girl, 1769; 1774) and *Ehrlichkeit und Liebe* (Honesty and Love, 1776; 1794) — were published in the form of keyboard-vocal scores. It may be that Wolf's fondness for da capo arias and relatively complex accompaniment figures conflicted with the folksong-inspired preference for strophic songs with simple accompaniments. Wolf's stance may have been regarded as stodgy, and his participation not encouraged. See Brockt 51.

[19] The private theater shifted its focus away from such issues, and concentrated attention on plots arising from characters' problematic encounters with social convention and traditional gender roles. This is not to say that the private theater quarreled with the notion that theater serves a didactic purpose: they appear simply to have established a didactic agenda that diverged from that of Wieland and Weisse. It should be added that while the Weisse/Hiller works were expunged from the repertoire, Hiller's musical style was well-represented in the compositions of the Weimar composers Anna Amalia, Seckendorff, and Hiller's pupil Corona Schröter. This is particularly evident in Schröter's *Die Fischerin* of 1782.

[20] Melodramatic passages appear in Mozart's operas *Zaide* (composed 1779–80) and *Thamos König in Ägypten* (Thamos, King of Egypt; composed between 1773 and 1779), Cherubini's *Les deux journées* (The Two Days, 1800) and *Medée* (Medea, 1797), as well as Grétry's *Richard Coeur-de-Lion* (Richard Lionheart, 1784; 1786). Mozart's music to *Semiramis* (text by Otto Heinrich von Gemmingen), which may have been a melodrama, is no longer extant.

[21] Mozart's letters of 1778 describe the Mannheim performances of Benda's works which had their premieres in Gotha in 1775.

[22] Texts such as Goethe's *Götz von Berlichingen* (1772), and Bürger's *Lenore* (1773) may have had some influence on the musical style of melodrama.

[23] Facsimile scores of Benda's works can be found in Bauman, *German Opera* 4: iii. In addition to continued performances in Vienna until about 1810, Benda's *Ariadne* stayed in the public eye through publication of its keyboard-vocal score in 1778 and full score in 1781. Bauman notes that the publication of any large-scale work in full score format was highly unusual in late eighteenth-century Germany, and its occurrence serves to underline the work's importance. Benda's influence was especially great in Mannheim where Christian Cannabich and Franz Beck, after hearing *Medea* and *Ariadne,* composed their own melodramas *Elektra* (1780–81) and *Pandore*. The parts for Beck's *Pandore* were published in Paris in 1789, and represent one of the last successful independent melodramas.

[24] Underscored speech resembles film scoring in which speaking occurs against a musical backdrop. Though musical and verbal information are constantly interacting in underscored speech, words, beats, and pitches do not require close coordination. In contrast, accompanied measured speech begins, proceeds, and ends at precise musical points and must be carefully synchronized and cued. — In the appendix, line numbers corresponding to most modern editions of *Proserpina* appear at the extreme left of the first column. Seckendorff's sections are numbered 1 through 31 in the second column; the length of each is indicated by the measure numbers. The third column shows the instrumentation of each section, with arrows (→) showing changes within the course of the section. The last four columns follow the progress of tempo, meter, key, and dynamics throughout the piece, again, using arrows to show changes.

[25] Goethe may have destroyed some of Seckendorff's settings of his works, for example, *Die Laune des Verliebten* and *Jery und Bätely*. As the scores of *Proserpina* and *Lila* were out of Goethe's reach, having been given as birthday gifts to Princess Luise, it is impossible to know whether these too would have disappeared had Goethe had access to the manuscripts. An indication that Goethe was not satisfied with Seckendorff's work is the fact that he commissioned Karl Eberwein circa 1814 to compose a new musical score to his *Proserpina* text. See earlier note.

[26] In a letter to Charlotte von Stein of 17 April 1781 Goethe writes, "Crone [*sic*] ist heut mit mir. Ich hab an Iphigenien übersetzt und werds noch mit ihr" [Corona is with me today. I am working on Iphigenia and will continue to do so with her; Petersen 1.2: 344].

Works Cited

Anderson, Emily ed. *The Letters of Mozart and his Family*. London: Macmillan, 1966.

Anna Amalia. "Gedanken über die Musik." GSA 36/ VII: 18.

Bauman, Thomas. *North German Opera in the Age of Goethe*. Cambridge and New York: Cambridge UP, 1985.

Blackall, Eric A. "Goethe's *Proserpina* in Context: The Two Faces of *Empfindsamkeit*." *Patterns of Change: German Drama and the European Tradition*. Eds. Dorothy James and Silvia Ranawake. New York, Berne, Frankfurt a. M., Paris: Peter Lang, 1990. 45–58.

Boyle, Nicholas. *Goethe, the Poet and the Age*. Oxford: Clarendon P, 1991.

Brockt, Johannes. *Ernst Wilhelm Wolf (Leben und Werk): Ein Beitrag zur Musikgeschichte des 18. Jahrhunderts*. Breslau: Striegauer Anzeiger, 1927.

Burkhardt, C. A. H. *Das Tiefurter Journal. Literarische Studie*. Leipzig: F. L. Herbig, 1871.

Gerber, Ernst Ludwig. *Neues historisch-biographisches Lexicon der Tonkünstler 1812–1814*. Vol. 4. Rpt. Graz: Akademische Druck- and Verlagsanstalt, 1966.

Herder, Johann Gottfried von. "Über die Oper." *Sämtliche Werke*. Ed Bernard Suphan. Vol. 4. Berlin: Weidmann, 1877–1913. 483–86.

———. "Tanz und Melodrama." *Sämtliche Werke*. Ed. Bernard Suphan. Vol. 13. Berlin: Weidmann, 1877–1913. 329–46.

Herrmann, Ernst. "Das Weimarer Lied in der 2. Hälfte des 18. Jahrhunderts." Universität Leipzig: Ph.D. dissertation, 1929.

Hiller, J. A., ed. *Wöchentliche Nachrichten und Anmerkungen die Musik betreffend*. Rpt. Hildesheim and New York: Georg Olms, 1970.

Kirby, Frank. "Herder and Opera." *Journal of the American Musicological Society* 15 (1962): 316–29.

Pendle, Karin. "The Transformation of a Libretto: Goethe's *Jery und Bätely*." *Music and Letters* 55.1 (1974): 77–88.

———. "Opéra Comique as Literature: The Spread of French Styles in Europe, ca. 1760 to the Revolution." Unpubl. typescript, 1991.

———. "Opéra Comique in Paris in the Eighteenth Century." Unpubl. typescript, 1991.

Petersen, Julius, ed. *Goethes Briefe an Charlotte von Stein.* Leipzig: Insel-Verlag, 1923.

Seckendorff, Karl von. "Etwas von der musikalischen Edukation." *Der Teutsche Merkur* (December 1776): 212–28.

———. "Versuch einer Berichtung des jetztigen Zustands der Tonkunst in Italien." *Der Teutsche Merkur* (May 1776): 169–86.

Sichardt, Gisela. *Das Weimarer Liebhabertheater unter Goethes Leitung.* Weimar: Arion Verlag, 1957.

Stoll, Karin. *Christoph Martin Wieland: Journalistik und Kritik.* Bonn: Bouvier, 1978.

Urlichs, Carl, and Emilie von Schiller, eds. *Charlotte von Schiller und ihre Freunde.* 3 vols. Stuttgart: J. G. Cotta, 1860–65.

Wieland, Christoph Martin. "Versuch über das Teutsche Singspiel, und einige dahin einschlagende Gegenstände." *Der Teutsche Merkur* (July 1775): 63–87.

Wolf, Ernst Wilhelm. "Was ist wahre Musik? und wie erhält man sie?" *Der Teutsche Merkur* (February 1783): 231–39.

Musical Works Cited

Anna Amalia. Divertimento per il Pianoforte, Clarinetto, Viola e Violoncello. Weimar: Ambrosius e Zahn, n.d. AAB MUS IVf: 4.

———. Sinfonia [ms.: flutes, horns, bassoon, violins, viola, bass]. N.d. AAB Hofmarschallamt 3810.

———. Sinfonia [ms.: oboes, flutes, bassoon, violins, viola, bass]. N.d. AAB MUS IIIc: 110.

———. Sonatina in G di Amalia cembalo obligato [ms.: orchestra and keyboard]. N.d. AAB MUS IVf: 1.

———, and Friedrich Hildebrand von Einsiedel. *Die Zigeuner* [ms.: keyboard-vocal score]. 1780. N.d. AAB MUS IIc: 2 and MUS IIa: 11.

———, and Johann Wolfgang von Goethe. *Erwin und Elmire* [ms.: keyboard-vocal score]. 1776. AAB MUS IIc: 1.

———, and Johann Wolfgang von Goethe. *Das Jahrmarktsfest zu Plundersweilern* [ms.: keyboard-vocal score]. 1778. AAB. MUS IIa: 2 and MUS IIb: 53.

Bauman, Thomas, ed. *German Opera 1770–1800.* IVON. New York: Garland, 1985.

Eberwein, Karl. *Proserpina* [ms.: orchestral score]. 1815. GSA

Reichardt, J. F. "Monolog der Iphigenia" [*sic*]. *Goethe's Lieder, Oden, Balladen und Romanzen.* Leipzig: Breitkopf und Härtel, 1809–11.

Schröter, Corona. *Fünf und zwanzig Lieder in Musik gesetzt.* Weimar: Annoch bey mir selbst und in Commission der Hoffmannischen Buchhandlung, 1786.

———. *Gesaenge mit Begleitung des Fortepiano.* Weimar: Industrie-Comptoir, 1794.

———, and Johann Wolfgang von Goethe. *Die Fischerin* [ms.: keyboard-vocal score]. 1782. AAB.

Seckendorff, Karl von, and Johann Wolfgang von Goethe. *Proserpina, ein Monodrama in einem Aufzuge* [ms.: orchestral score]. 1777. Hessische Landes- und Hochschulbibliothek, Darmstadt. MUS ms 1013.

———. *Volks- und andere Lieder.* 3 vols. Weimar: Karl Ludolf Hoffmann, 1779–82.

———. *Zwölf Lieder mit Begleitung des Pianoforte.* Leipzig: Breitkopf und Härtel, n. d.

Wolf, Ernst Wilhelm. *Sei Sonate per il Clavicembalo Solo.* Leipzig: Breitkopf, 1774.

———, and Johann Gottfried von Herder. *Osterkantate.* Leipzig: Breitkopf, 1782.

Appendix: Seckendorff's Setting of Goethe's *Proserpina*

KEY: singing = *italicized*; underscored speech = underlined; accompanied measured speech = **boldface, underlined**; unaccompanied speech = plain text.

Text	Number	Instrumentation	Performance Indications	Meter	Key	Dynamics
	1 (overture) mm. 1-23	hn 1, 2; cl 1, 2; ob 1, 2; fl 1, 2; vln 1, 2; vla; bsn; bass	Allegro furioso	2/2	b	[f]
Proserpina	2 mm. 24-54	ob; vln; vla; bsn; bass → + fl	Sostenuto → Largo molto	4/4	d → D	[mf] → p
Halte! halt einmal, Unselige! Vergebens Irrst du in diesen rauhen Wüsten hin und her! [line 2 spoken between mm. 67 & 68]	3 mm. 55-67	hn; ob; fl; vln; vla; bsn; bass	Allegro	2/4	d	p
Endlos liegen vor dir die Trauergefilde, Und was du suchst, liegt immer hinter dir.	4 mm. 68-78	hn; cl; vln; bsn; bass	Andante	2/2	F	p
5 Nicht vorwärts, **Aufwärts auch soll dieser Blick nicht steigen!** [spoken between mm. 87 & 88]	5 mm. 79-87	hn; ob; vln; vla; bsn; bass	Allegro	2/2	C	p → f
Die schwarze Höhle des Tartarus Verwölbt die lieben Gegenden des Himmels, In die ich sonst 10 Nach meines Ahnherrn froher Wohnung Mit Liebesblick hinaufsah!	6 mm. 88-99	vln; vla; bsn; bass	Allegro	2/2	Bb → g	[f]

4 • Music in Weimar circa 1780 • 123

No.	Text	Instrumentation	Tempo	Meter	Key	Dyn.
7 mm. 100-29	Ach! Tochter du des Jupiters, Wie tief bist du verloren! [spoken between mm. 99 & 100] Gespielinnen! Als jene blumenreichen Täler Für uns gesamt noch blühten, 15 Als an dem himmelklaren Strom des Alpheus Wir plätschernd noch im Abendstrahle scherzten, Einander Kränze wanden, 20 Und heimlich an den Jüngling dachten, Dessen Haupte unser Herz sie widmete: Da war uns keine Macht zu tief zum Schwätzen, Keine Zeit zu lang, Um freundliche Geschichten zu wiederholen, 25 Und die Sonne Riß leichter nicht aus ihrem Silberbette Sich auf, als wir voll Lust zu leben, Früh im Tau die Rosenfüße badeten. [spoken between mm. 129 & 130]	hn; cl; ob; vln; vla; bsn; bass	[none given]	4/4	C	pp
8 mm. 130-44	O Mädchen! Mädchen! 30 Die ihr, einsam nun, Zerstreut an jenen Quellen schleicht, Die Blumen auflest, Die ich, ach Entführte! Aus meinem Schoße fallen ließ, 35 Ihr steht und seht mir nach, wohin ich verschwand! [spoken between mm. 144 & 145]	fl; vln; vla; bsn; bass	Adagio con affetto	3/4	Bb	pp
9 mm. 145-51	Weggerissen haben sie mich, die raschen Pferde des Orkus; Mit festen Armen [spoken between mm. 151 & 152]	fl; vln; vla; bsn	Tempo precedente	3/4	Bb → f	p

124 • UNWRAPPING GOETHE'S WEIMAR

Text	§ / mm.	Instrumentation	Tempo	Meter	Key	Dynamics
Hielt mich der unerbittliche Gott! 40 Amor!, Ach, Amor floh lachend auf zum Olymp -- Hast du nicht, Mutwilliger, Genug an Himmel und Erde? Mußt du die Flammen der Hölle Durch deine Flammen vermehren? [spoken between mm. 156 & 157] 45 <u>Herunter gerissen</u> <u>In diese endlosen Tiefen!</u> <u>Königin hier!</u> <u>Königin?</u> [166-172] Vor der nur Schatten sich neigen! [spoken between mm. 172 & 173] 50 Hoffnungslos ist ihr Schmerz! Hoffnungslos der Abgeschiedenen Glück, Und ich wend es nicht [spoken between mm. 178 & 179]	10 mm. 152-78	hn; ob; vln; vla; bsn; bass	Allegro assai → un puoco piu adagio → Andante	4/4	C	p → pp
Den ernsten Gerichten Hat das Schicksal sie übergeben; [spoken between mm. 179 & 180] 55 Und unter ihnen wandl ich umher, <u>Göttin! Königin!</u> <u>Selbst Sklavin des Schicksals!</u> [underscored in mm. 189-91]	11 mm. 179-91	hn; cl; ob; fl; vln; vla; bsn; bass	Allegro	4/4	Bb	f → p
Ach! das fliehende Wasser Möcht ich mit dem Tantalus schöpfen, 60 Mit lieblichen Früchten ihn sättigen! Armer Alter! Für gereiztes Verlangen gestraft! -- [spoken between mm. 203 & 204]	12 mm. 192-203	ob; vln; vla; bass*	Andante lamentabile	12/8	G	p → mf → p

No.	Text	Instrumentation	Tempo	Meter	Key	Dyn.
13 mm. 204-9	In Ixions Rad möcht ich greifen, Einhalten seinen Schmerz! 65 Aber was vermögen wir Götter Über die ewigen Qualen! Trostlos für mich und für sie, Wohn ich unter ihnen und schaue Der armen Danaiden Geschäftigkeit! [spoken between mm. 209 & 210]	ob; vln, vla, vc;* bsn 1, 2;* bass	Allegro	12/8	e	[p]
14 mm. 210-29	70 Leer und immer leer, Wie sie schöpfen und füllen! [spoken between mm. 213 & 214] Leer und immer leer! Nicht einen Tropfen Wassers zum Munde, Nicht einen Tropfen Wassers in ihre Wannen! [spoken between mm. 217 & 218] 75 Leer und immer leer! [spoken between mm. 221 & 222] Ach, so ists mit dir auch, mein Herz! Woher willst du schöpfen? -- Und wohin? [spoken between mm. 229 & 230]	hn; ob; vln; vla; bass	Allegro	4/4	D	p
15 mm. 230-35	Euer ruhiges Wandeln, Selige, Streicht nur vor mir vorüber; 80 Mein Weg ist nicht mit euch! In euern leichten Tänzen, In euern tiefen Hainen, In euerer lispelnden Wohnung, Rauschts nicht von Leben wie droben, 85 Schwankt nicht von Schmerz zu Lust Der Seligkeit Fülle. -- [spoken between mm. 235 & 236]	vln; vlc;* bsn; bass	Adagio grazioso	6/8	G	p
16 mm. 236-61	Ists auf seinen düstern Augenbraunen, Im verschlossenen Blicke?	hn; fl; vln; vlc;* bsn; bass → ob. replace	Adagio grazioso → Allegro (m.	6/8	G → e → G	pp

[spoken between mm. 249 & 250] Magst du ihn Gemahl nennen? [spoken between mm. 252 & 253] 90 Und darfst du ihn anders nennen? [underscored in m. 254] Liebe! Liebe! Warum öffnetest du sein Herz Auf einen Augenblick? Und warum nach mir, 95 Da du wußtest, Es werde sich wieder auf ewig verschließen? [spoken between mm. 261 & 262]		fl. at Allegro → fl. replace ob. at Adagio	242) → Adagio grazioso (m 256)			
Warum ergriff er nicht eine meiner Nymphen, Und setzte sie neben sich Auf seinen kläglichen Thron? 100 Warum mich, die Tochter der Ceres? [underscored in mm. 278-89 (senza tempo)] O Mutter! Mutter! Wie dich deine Gottheit verläßt Im Verlust deiner Tochter, Die du glücklich glaubtest, [spoken between mm. 283 & 284]	17 mm. 262-83	hn; ob; vln; vla; bsn; bass → fl. replace hn. & ob. at Adagio	Allegro di molto → senza tempo (m. 278-79) → Adagio (m. 280)	3/4	C	p → pp
105 **Hinspielend, hintändelnd ihre Jugend!** [mm. 285-87] Ach, du kannst gewiß Und fragtest nach mir, Was ich bedürfte? Etwa ein neues Kleid 110 Oder goldene Schuhe? Und du fandest die Mädchen An ihre Weiden gefesselt, Wo sie mich verloren, Nicht wieder fanden,	18 mm. 284-87	vln; vla; bass	Andante	4/4	Bb	a mezzo vocè

		Text	Scoring	Tempo	Meter	Key	Dynamics
		115 Ihre Locken zerrauften, Erbärmlich klagten, Meine lieben Mädchen! -- [spoken between mm. 287 & 288]					
19	mm. 288-312	Wohin ist sie? [spoken during fermata in m. 299] Wohin? rufst du. [spoken during fermata in m. 301] Welchen Weg nahm der Verruchte? [spoken during fermata in m. 303] 120 Soll er ungestraft Jupiters Stamm entweihen? [spoken during fermata in m. 305] Wohin geht der Pfad seiner Rosse? [spoken during fermata in m. 310]	cl; vln; vlc;* bass → ob. replace cl. at Allegro, bsn. added	Tempo di prima adagio assai → Allegro (m. 298)	2/4	Eb	p → f
20	mm. 313-67	Fackeln her! Durch die Nacht will ich ihm verfolgen! Will keine Stunde ruhen, bis ich sie finde 125 Will keinen Gang scheuen, Hierhin und dorthin. Dir blinken deine Drachen mit klugen Augen zu, Aller Pfade gewohnt, folgen sie deinem Lenken: In der unbetretnen Wüste treibt dichs irre -- 130 Ach, nur hierher, hierher nicht! Nicht in die Tiefe der Nacht, [spoken during fermata in m. 364] Unbetreten den Ewiglebenden, [spoken during fermata in m. 365] Wo, bedeckt von beschwerendem Graus, Deine Tochter ermattet! [underscored in m. 366]	hn; ob; vln; vla; bass	Furioso	2/4	Ab → E (m. 334) → Ab (m. 352)	f → p alternation
21	mm. 367-68	[no text]	vln; vla; bass	Adagio	2/4	Ab	morendo

#	Measures	Text	Instrumentation	Tempo	Meter	Key	Dynamics
22	mm. 369-77	135 Wende aufwärts, [spoken during rest in m. 370] Aufwärts den geflügelten Schlangenpfad, [spoken between mm. 373 & 374] Aufwärts nach Jupiters Wohnung! [spoken between mm. 374 & 375] Der weiß es, Der weiß es allein, der Erhabene, 140 Wo deine Tochter ist! [spoken between mm. 377 & 378]	vln; vla; bass → + fl. at m. 375	Andante → Allegretto (m. 371)	4/4	Db → Bb (m. 375)	f
23	mm. 378-400	**Vater der Götter und Menschen!** **Ruhst du noch oben auf deinem goldnen** **Stuhle,** Zu dem du mich Kleine So oft mit Freundlichkeit aufhubst, 145 In deinen Händen mich scherzend Gegen den endlosen Himmel schwenktest, Daß ich kindisch droben zu verschweben bebte? [mm. 393-400] Bist dus noch, Vater? -- [spoken between mm. 400 & 401]	hn; ob; fl; vln; vla; bass	Maestoso	4/4	Eb	f → pp
24	mm. 401-8	Nicht zu deinem Haupte, 150 In dem ewigen Blau Des feuerdurchwebten Himmels, [spoken between mm. 408 & 409]	hn; ob; fl; vln; vla; bass	Maestoso	4/4	Eb	f → p → f
25	mm. 409-15	**Hier! Hier! --** **Leite sie her!** [m. 410] Daß ich auf mit ihr 155 Aus diesem Kerker fahre! [spoken between mm. 411 & 412] Daß mir Phöbus wieder	vln; vla; bass	Adagio → Allegro molto (m. 411) → Adagio (m. 413)	4/4	Eb	p → f → p

	Seine lieben Strahlen bringe, Luna wieder Aus den Silberlocken lächle! [spoken between mm. 415 & 416]					
26 mm. 416-71	160 *O du hörst mich,* *Freundlichlieber Vater,* *Wirst mich wieder,* *Wieder aufwärts heben;* *Daß, befreit von langer schwerer Plage,* 165 *Ich an deinem Himmel wieder mich ergötze!* **Letze dich, verzagtes Herz!** [mm. 466-468] Ach, Hoffnung! Hoffnung gießt In Sturmnacht Morgenröte! [spoken between mm. 471 & 472]	hn; fl; vln; vla; bsn; bass	Andante	3/4	F	sotto voce
27 mm. 472-98	170 **Dieser Boden** **Ist nicht Fels, nicht Moos mehr;** Diese Berge Nicht voll schwarzen Grauses! [mm. 472-77] **Ach, hier find ich wieder eine Blume!** [mm. 481-82] 175 **Dieses welke Blatt,** **Es lebt noch,** **Harrt noch,** **Daß ich seiner mich erfreue!** [mm. 486-88] **Seltsam!** [m. 494] seltsam! 180 Find ich diese Frucht hier? Die mir in den Gärten droben Ach! so lieb war -- [spoken between mm. 498 & 499]	hn; ob; fl; vln; vla; bass	Allegro assai	2/2	D	f → p alternation

(Sie bricht den Granatapfel ab.)

#	Text	Instrumentation	Tempo	Meter	Key	Dynamics
28 mm. 499-517	*Laß dich genießen,* *Freundliche Frucht!* 185 *Laß mich vergessen* *Alle den Harm!* *Wieder mich wähnen* *Droben in Jugend,* *In der vertaumelten* 190 *Lieblichen Zeit,* *In den umduftenden* *Himmlischen Blüten,* *In den Gerüchen* *Seliger Wonne* 195 *Die der Entzückten,* *Der Schmachtenden ward!* (*Sie ißt einige Körner.*) *Labend! Labend!*	fl; vln; vla; bsn; bass	Grazioso	6/8	G	p
29 mm. 518-34	Wie greifts auf einmal Durch diese Freuden, 200 Durch diese offne Wonne Mit entsetzlichen Schmerzen, Mit eisernen Händen Der Hölle durch! -- [spoken between mm. 534 & 535]	hn; ob; vln; vla; bsn; bass	Andante	3/4	C → c	f
30 mm. 535-69	**Was hab ich verbrochen,** 205 **Daß ich genoß?** **Ach, warum schafft** **Die erste Freude hier mir Qual?** [mm. 537-40] Was ists? Was ists? -- [spoken between mm. 543 & 544] Ihr Felsen scheint hier schrecklicher herabzuwinken,	hn; ob; vln; vla; bsn; bass	Andante → Allegro (m. 541)	4/4	c	p → f

Text	No.	Instrumentation	Tempo	Meter	Key	Dynamics
210 Mich fester zu umfassen! Ihr Wolken tiefer mich zu drücken! [spoken between mm. 546 & 547] Im fernen Schoße des Abgrunds Dumpfe Gewitter tosend sich zu erzeugen! Und ihr weiten Reiche der Parzen 215 Mir zuzurufen: [spoken between mm. 567 & 568] Du bist unser! [spoken between mm. 569 & 570] Die Parzen (unsichtbar) *Du bist unser!* *Ist der Ratschluß deines Ahnherrn:* *Nüchtern solltest du wiederkehren;* 220 *Und der Biß des Apfels macht dich unser!* *Königin, wir ehren dich!*	31 (a) mm. 570-96	vln; vla; "fond."* SATB chorus	Allegro maestoso	4/4	c	[none given]
Proserpina **Hast du gesprochen, Vater?** **Warum? Warum?** Was tat ich, daß du mich verstößest? 225 Warum rufst du mich nicht **Zu deinem lichten Thron auf!** Warum den Apfel? [spoken during fermata in m. 606] O verflucht die Früchte! [spoken during fermata in m. 607] **Warum sind Früchte schön,** [spoken during first two beats of m. 608] 230 **Wenn sie verdammen?** [underscored in last two beats of m. 608]	31 (b) mm. 597-608	vln; vla; bass	Grave → Allegro (m. 606)	4/4	c	f → p alternation
Die Parzen *Bist nun unser!*	31 (c)	vln; vla; fond.;	Tempo precedente	4/4	c	[none

Text	Measures	Instrumentation	Tempo	Time	Key	Dynamics
Warum trauerst du? / *Sieh, wir ehren dich,* / *Dich o Königin!*	mm. 609-26	SATB chorus	piu Allegro			given]
Proserpina / 235 O hätte der Tartarus eine Tiefe / Daß ich euch drein verwünschte! / [spoken between mm. 626 & 627]						
O wäre der Cozyt nicht euer ewig Bad, / Daß ich für euch / Noch Flammen übrig hätte! / [spoken between mm. 631 & 632]	31 (d) mm. 627-31	ob; vln; vla; bsn; bass	Piu Allegro	4/4	c	f
240 Ich Königin / Und kann euch nicht vernichten! / [spoken between mm. 633 & 634] / In ewigem Haß sei ich mit euch verbunden! / [spoken between mm. 635 & 636] / *So schöpfet, Danaiden!* / *Spinnt, Parzen! Wütet, Furien!* / 245 *In ewig gleiche Qual!* / Ich beherrsche euch, / [spoken between mm. 639 & 640] / Und bin drum elender als ihr alle. / [spoken between mm. 641 & 642]	31 (e) mm. 632-41	hn; ob; vln; vla; bass	Allegro assai	4/4	c	p → f con fuoco (m. 640)
Die Parzen / *Du bist unser!* / *Wir neigen uns dir!* / 250 *Bist unser! unser!* / *Hohe Königin!*	31 (f) mm. 642-81	hn; ob; vln; vla; bsn (divisi); fond; SATB chorus	Allegro di molto	4/4	c	p → f alternation
Proserpina / *Fern! Weg von mir*						

Text	Section / mm.	Instrumentation	Tempo	Meter	Key	Dynamics
Sei eure Treu und eure Herrlichkeit! / Wie baß ich euch! / 255 Und dich, wie zehnfach hass ich dich -- / [spoken between mm. 681 & 682]						
Abscheu und Gemahl, / **O Pluto! Pluto!** [mm. 683-685] / **Weh mir! Ich fühle schon** / **Die verhaßten Umarmungen!** [mm. 687-88]	31 (g) mm. 682-707	vln; vla; bass → hn; ob; bsn; fond; SATB added (m. 691)	Allegro → piu Andante (m. 686) → Allegro molto (m. 691)	4/4	c	f → p alternation
Die Parzen / 260 *Unser! Unsre Königin!*						
Proserpina / Warum reckst du sie nach mir? [m. 709] / Recke sie nach dem Avernus! [m. 712]	31 (h) mm. 708-22	vln; vla; bass	Allegro assai	4/4	Db → mod (m. 720)	f → p alternation
Rufe die Qualen aus stygischen Nächten empor! [mm. 715-16] / Sie steigen deinem Wink entgegen, / [spoken between mm. 719 & 720] / 265 Nicht meine Liebe. / [spoken between mm. 720 & 721] / **Gib mir das Schicksal deiner Verdammten!** / Nenn es nicht Liebe! -- / Wirf mich mit diesen Armen / In die zerstörende Qual! / [spoken between mm. 722 & 723]						
[no text]	31 (i) mm. 723-46	hn; cl; ob; fl; vln; vla; bsn; bass	Allegro furioso	2/2	b → D	f

Ex. 1: Corona Schröter, "Die ersten Blümchen"
(The First Small Flowers). Merkur, June 1780
(courtesy of Stiftung Weimarer Klassik).

Ex. 2: Line 1, no. 3, sung text. Karl von Seckendorff's setting of Goethe's Proserpina, 1777 (courtesy of Hessische Landes- und Hochschulbibliothek, Darmstadt).

Ex. 3: Line 55, no. 11, underscored speech.
Karl von Seckendorff's setting of Goethe's Proserpina, 1777
(courtesy of Hessische Landes- und Hochschulbibliothek,
Darmstadt).

Ex. 4: Line 45, no. 10, accompanied measured speech. Karl von Seckendorff's setting of Goethe's Proserpina, 1777 (courtesy of Hessische Landes- und Hochschulbibliothek, Darmstadt).

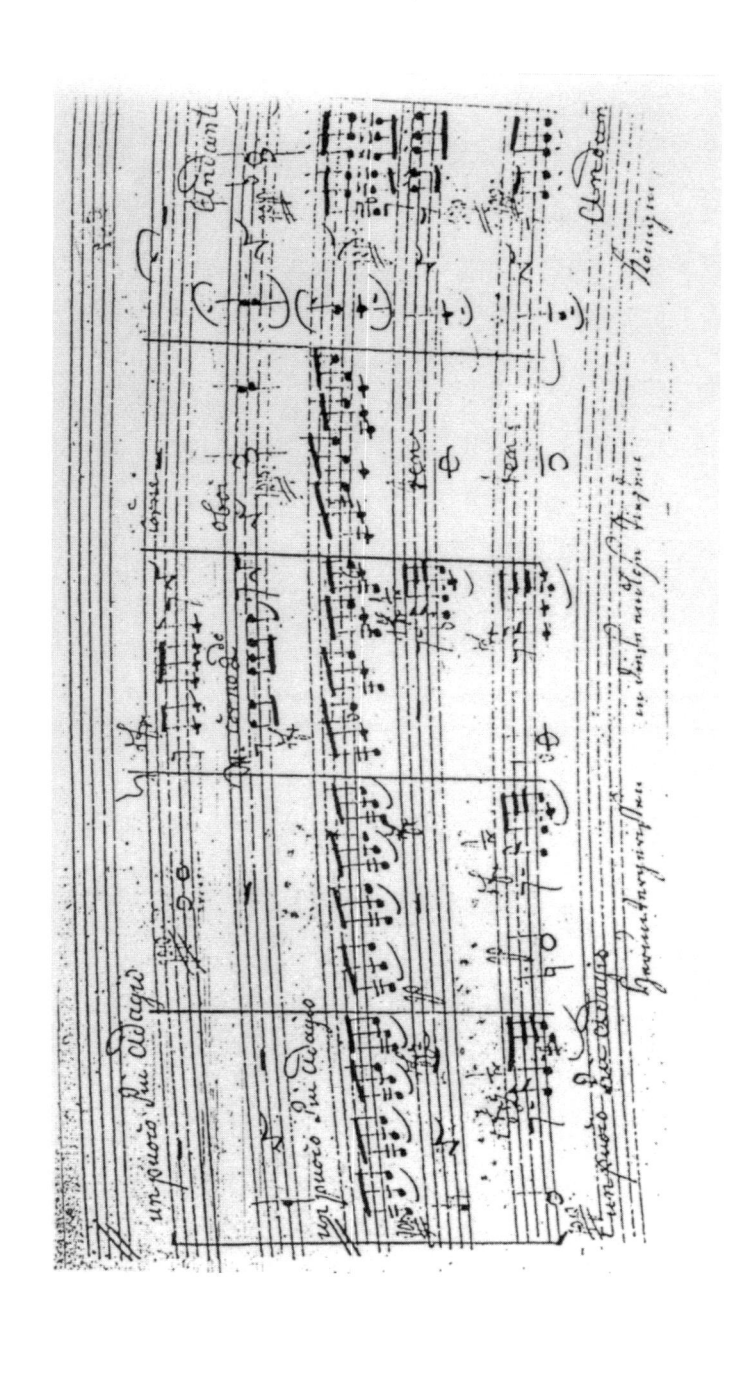

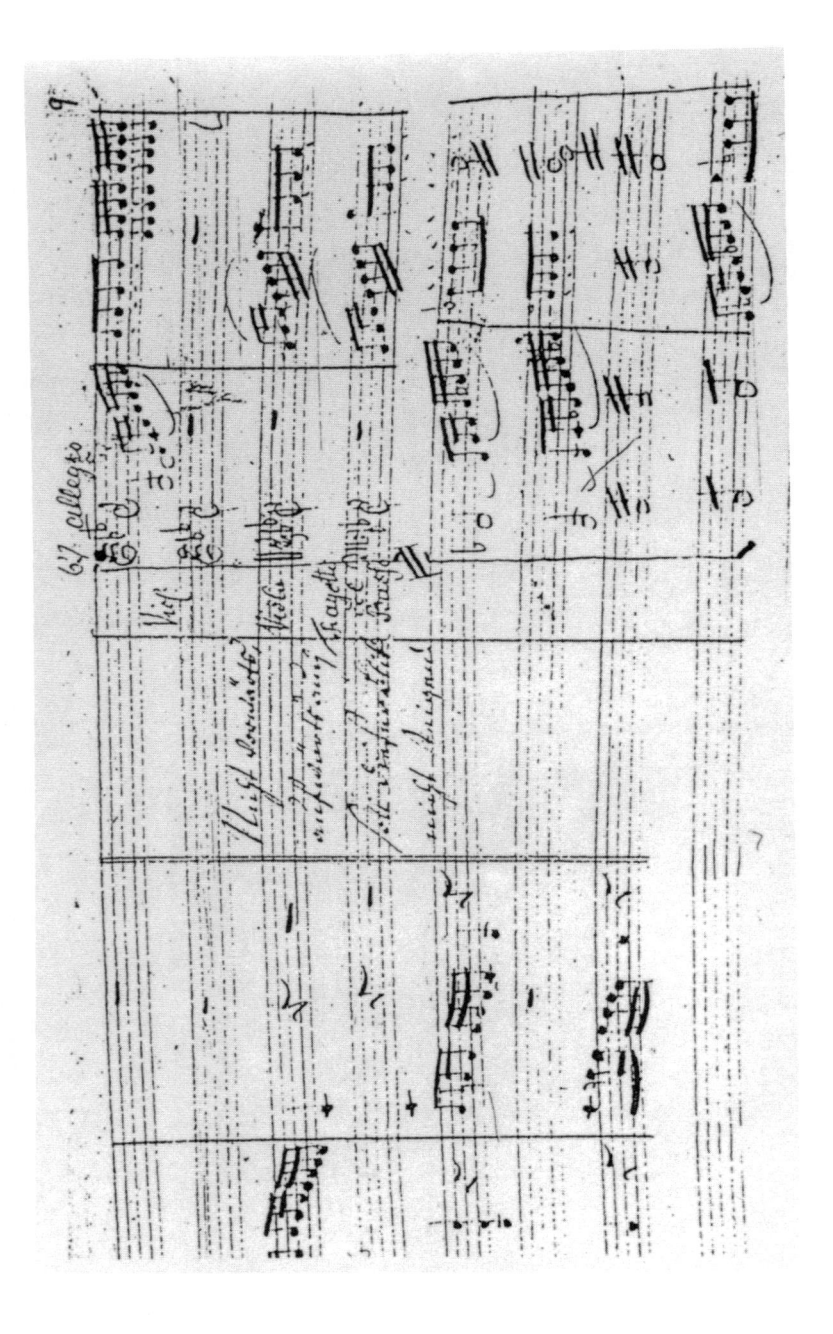

Ex. 5: Line 5, no. 5, unaccompanied speech. Karl von Seckendorff's setting of Goethe's Proserpina, 1777 (courtesy of Hessische Landes- und Hochschulbibliothek, Darmstadt).

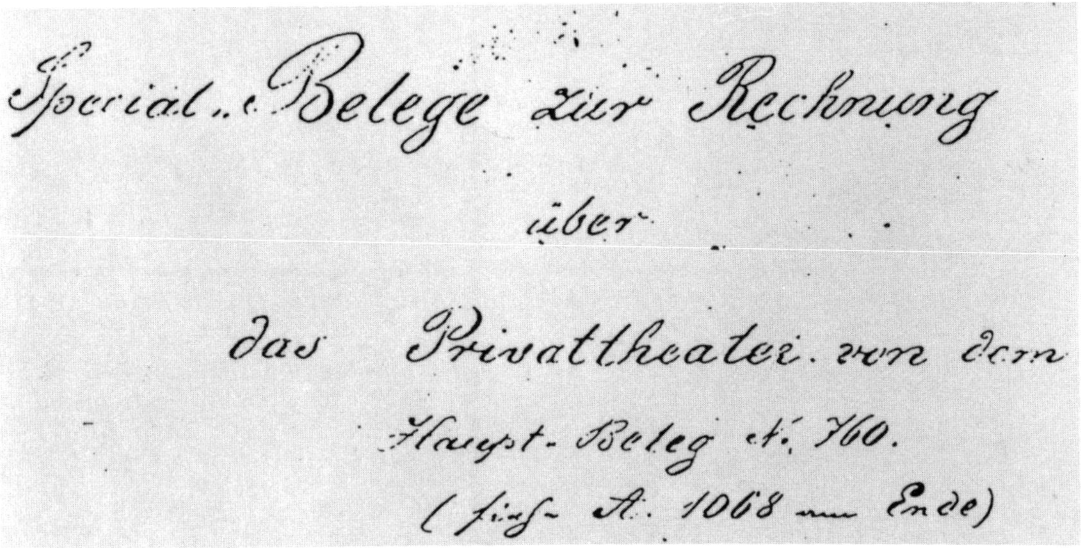

Special-Belege zur Rechnung

über

das Privattheater von dem

Haupt-Beleg d: 760.

(fisch- N: 1068 — Ende)

Fig. 1: Title page of one of the private theater's special account books, circa 1780 (courtesy of ThHStAW).

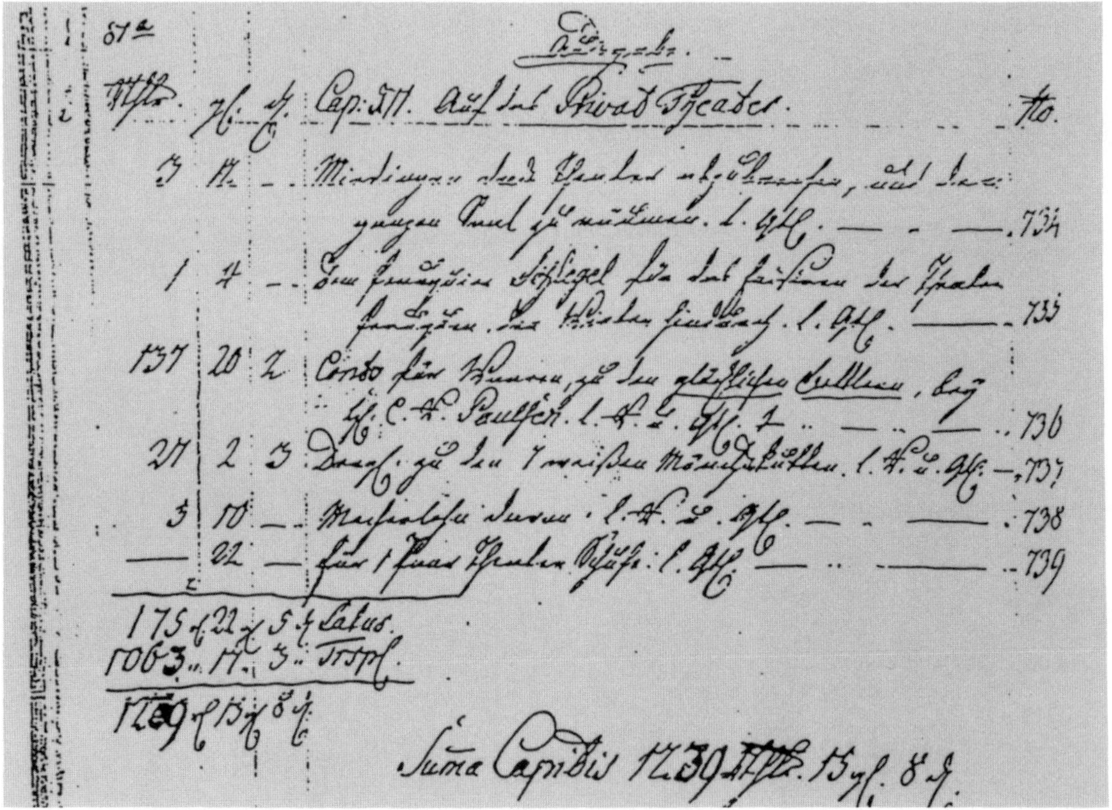

Fig. 2: Itemized expenses for the private theater, circa 1780 (courtesy of ThHStAW).

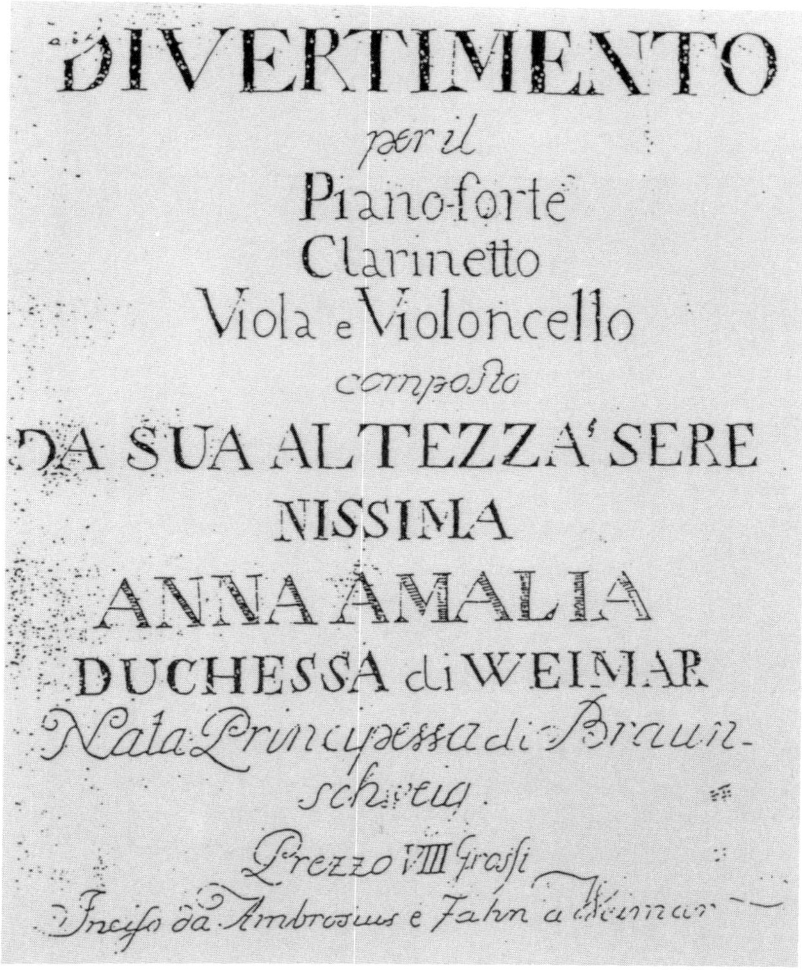
DIVERTIMENTO
per il
Piano-forte
Clarinetto
Viola e Violoncello
composto
DA SUA ALTEZZA' SERE
NISSIMA
ANNA AMALIA
DUCHESSA di WEIMAR
Nata Principessa di Braun-
schweig.
Prezzo VIII Grossi
Inciso da Ambrosius e Zahn a Weimar

Fig. 3: Title page of Anna Amalia's Divertimento, circa 1780 (courtesy of Stiftung Weimarer Klassik).

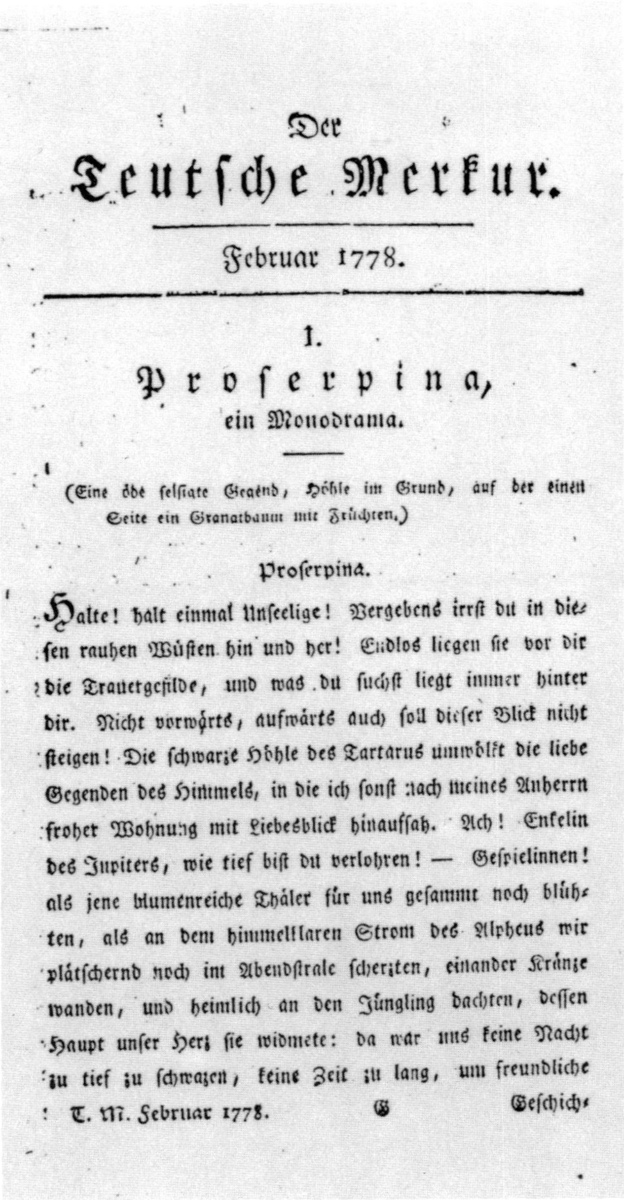

Der Teutsche Merkur.

Februar 1778.

1.
Proserpina,
ein Monodrama.

(Eine öde felsigte Gegend, Höhle im Grund, auf der einen Seite ein Granatbaum mit Früchten.)

Proserpina.

Halte! halt einmal Unseelige! Vergebens irrst du in diesen rauhen Wüsten hin und her! Endlos liegen sie vor dir die Trauergefilde, und was du suchst liegt immer hinter dir. Nicht vorwärts, aufwärts auch soll dieser Blick nicht steigen! Die schwarze Höhle des Tartarus umwölkt die liebe Gegenden des Himmels, in die ich sonst nach meines Anherrn froher Wohnung mit Liebesblick hinaufsah. Ach! Enkelin des Jupiters, wie tief bist du verlohren! — Gespielinnen! als jene blumenreiche Thäler für uns gesammt noch blühten, als an dem himmelklaren Strom des Alpheus wir plätschernd noch im Abendstrale scherzten, einander Kränze wanden, und heimlich an den Jüngling dachten, dessen Haupt unser Herz sie widmete: da war uns keine Nacht zu tief zu schwazen, keine Zeit zu lang, um freundliche

T. M. Februar 1778.　　G　　Geschich-

Fig. 4: Goethe's Proserpina *as it appeared in the* Merkur *of February 1778 (courtesy of Stiftung Weimarer Klassik).*

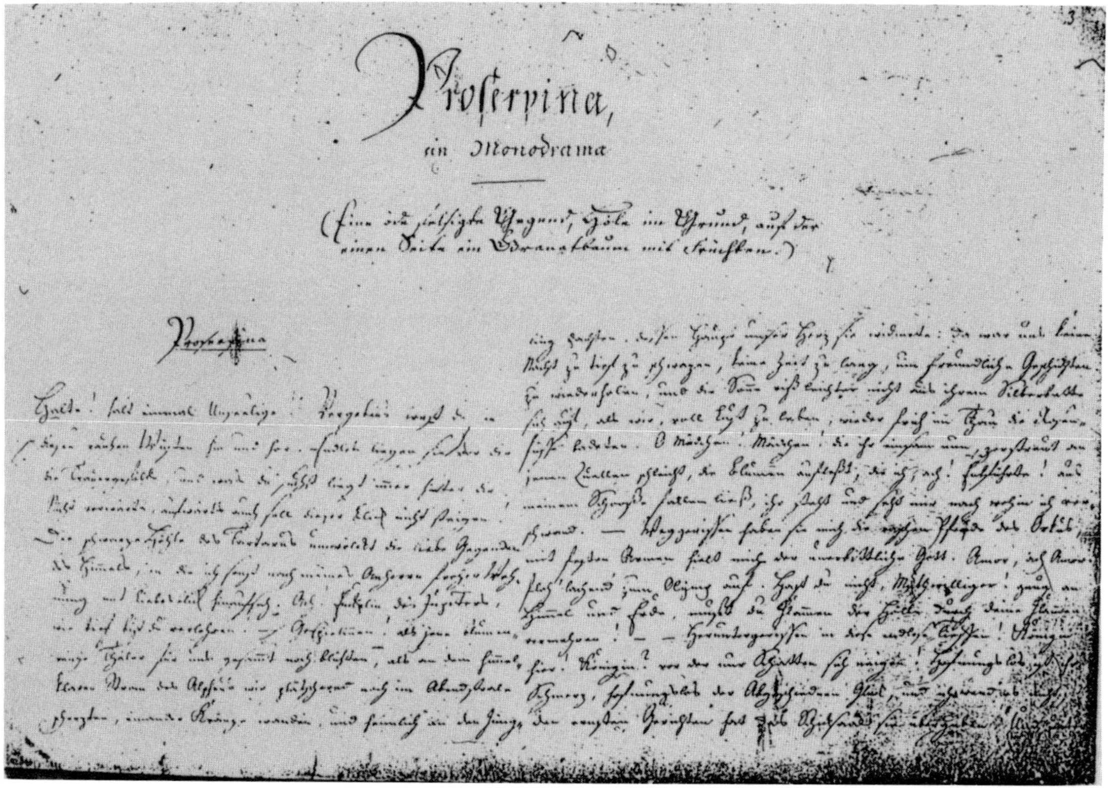

Fig. 5: Goethe's Proserpina as it appeared in Karl von Seckendorff's score, 1777 (courtesy of Hessische Landes- und Hochschulbibliothek, Darmstadt).

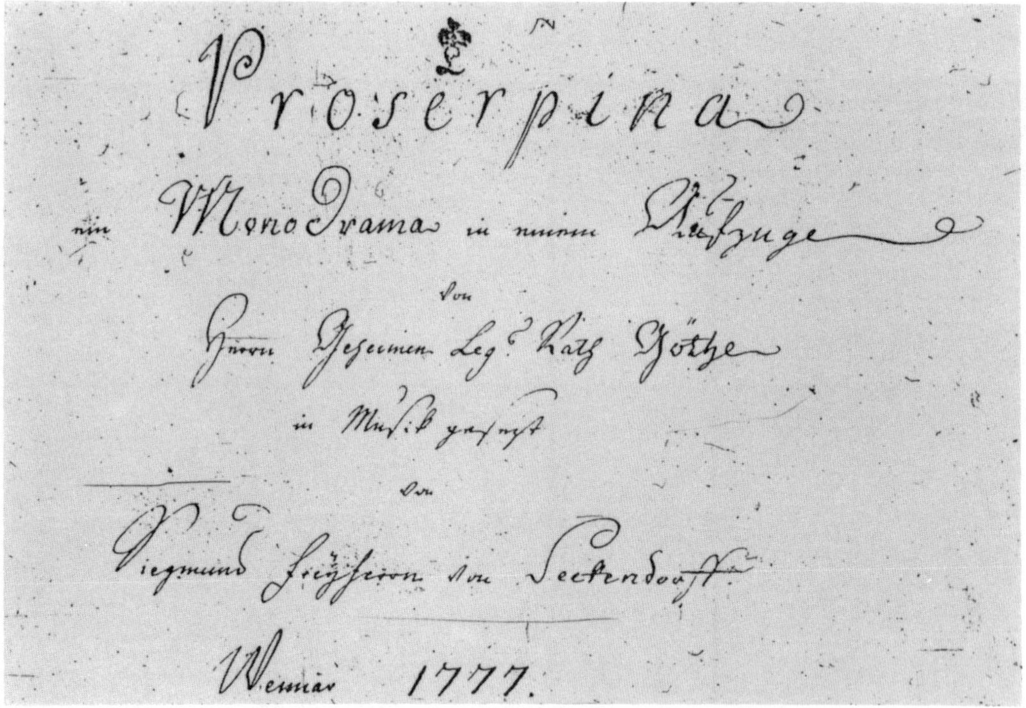

Proserpina

ein MonoDrama in einem Aufzuge

von

Herrn Geheimen Leg. Rath Göthe

in Musik gesetzt

von

Siegmund Freyherrn von Seckendorff

Weimar 1777.

Fig. 6: Title page of Karl von Seckendorff's setting of Goethe's Proserpina
(courtesy of Hessische Landes- und Hochschulbibliothek, Darmstadt)

PERFORMATIVITY AND TRANSGRESSION IN WEIMAR

KARIN SCHUTJER

War and Dramaturgy:
Goethe's Command of the Weimar Theater

THE HISTORIES OF WAR AND THEATER have long been entwined. From Aeschylus and Aristophanes to Brecht and beyond, European theater has often treated war as its province. And war in turn has often been viewed in the West as a kind of drama, as military expressions like "the theater of operations" seem to imply. In Shakespeare's prologue to *Henry V*, for example, the chorus invokes as the object of imitation for its own humble stage the grander theater of politics and war — which has a kingdom as its stage, princes as actors and monarchs as audience. Analogies between theater and military are intimations of an underlying semiotic continuity between the two institutions. The military strives not just to exercise brute force but also to produce a compelling spectacle, "to elaborate a poetics of power, not [merely] a mechanics" (Geertz 123).[1] The theater is not only a compelling spectacle but a public occasion that bears a complicated relationship to the social powers that underwrite or permit it. As theater and the military thus define their own social roles with respect to both power and persuasion, they often engage in crucial cultural negotiations with each other.[2]

A struggle over the roles of these two institutions was played out in the Weimar court theater under Goethe's direction during the uncertain years after the French Revolution. In the small duchy of Weimar the structural and causal links between the theater and the military were clear enough. Goethe was both theater intendant and court minister; his duke, Carl August, was both an involved theater patron and commander of his own troops as well as, with interruptions, an officer in the Prussian army.[3] From the beginning of Goethe's tenure in 1791, the Weimar theater evolved in the shadow of military concerns. As political events heated up, the theater had to compete against the military for limited finances[4] as well as for administrative attention.[5] In his first three years as director of the court theater, Goethe was twice drawn away by military events: at his duke's request, he participated as an observer first in the Coalition's campaign in France and then in the siege of Mainz. While Prussia left the First Coalition in 1795 through the Peace of Basel, there was no ultimate sense of security in Weimar from the conflict that was consuming much of Europe. Eventually the war would indeed make its way to Weimar: after Napoleon's troops took the town on 14 October 1806, Goethe's theater remained closed for over two months.

But the deeper crisis for the theater had to do with its cultural and social significance in relationship to the military. In the wake of the French Revolution a shift in the social meaning of the military gave rise to an uncertainty concerning the role of the theater. Goethe, often in close collaboration with Schiller,[6] struggled to re-invent a theater that could compete for popular feeling and loyalties with a new revolutionary army.

In order to delineate this transformation, I will turn first to the traditions and expectations surrounding these two institutions in Germany prior to 1789. Theater had a quite remarkable status for some German writers and thinkers in the latter half of the eighteenth century: it was to serve as the very cradle of a national consciousness. In the late 1760s, Lessing outlined the project of a national theater in his *Hamburgische Dramaturgie*. A generation later, Schiller echoed Lessing in his lecture "Was kann eine gute stehende Bühne eigentlich wirken?" (What Can a Good Permanent Stage Actually Achieve? 1785) when he claimed that a national stage would forge a nation (NA 20: 99). Of course in order to understand the conception of "nation" informing this vision, one must think beyond nineteenth-century forms of nationalism. For Schiller as for Lessing, a "nation" implied a common culture rather than a united government or a biological race. Above all, "nation" in Schiller's essay means a solidarity beyond the distinctions of class, region, and individual life situation. Theater could be the vehicle for overcoming such differences because, in Schiller's view, it brings a diverse audience together around a compelling spectacle that addresses both the heart and the understanding.

In Goethe's unfinished novel *Wilhelm Meisters Theatralische Sendung* (Wilhelm Meister's Theatrical Calling, written between 1777–86), the protagonist Wilhelm dreams of being the founder of such a national theater.[7] Much more than in the later, completed version of the novel, *Wilhelm Meisters Lehrjahre* (Wilhelm Meister's Apprenticeship, 1795–96), this early version explores theater's relationship to the military. Theater and military emerge here as two entirely distinct institutions that complement each other but do not compete: the military neither does offer a compelling model of social relations nor is the theater capable of creating a sustainable order.

In the novel Wilhelm meets an officer, Herr von C., whose love of theater and German literature in general helps compensate for his harsh profession.

> In einem strengen Dienste, wo alles seit Jahren in der bestimmtesten Ordnung ging, wo alles abgemessen, die eherne Notwendigkeit allein die Göttin war, der man opferte, wo die Gerechtigkeit zur Härte und Grausamkeit ward und der Begriff von Mensch und Menschheit gänzlich verschwand, war seine gute Seele [...] gänzlich verdruckt, seine Gefühle abgestumpft und fast zu Grunde gerichtet worden. (MA 2.2: 155; bk. 3, ch. 11)

> [His good soul (...) was completely suppressed, his feelings deadened and almost destroyed in a service where for years everything had followed the most predetermined of paths, where everything was measured, where iron necessity was the sole goddess to whom one made sacrifices. There justice had turned harsh and cruel, and any concept of humankind and humanity disappeared.]

Before he heads off to participate in a war, Herr von C. ventures a comparison between war and theater. War, he suggests, is a theater, "wo man ernsthaftere Stücke aufführt, wo jeder seine Rolle nur einmal spielt" [where more serious plays are being performed, where each acts his part only once; MA 2.2: 198; bk. 4, ch. 11]. Wilhelm objects to the comparison with theater, assuming that war offers immeasurably greater opportunities for fame and self-realization. The officer concedes then that the comparison is indeed inappropriate but for a deeper reason: war is for him not a public performance or a matter of self-representation at all. He is motivated by neither passion nor a desire for glory. War is simply a matter of obligation and luck.

It is the military, however, which within the novel secures the order that makes theater possible, for theater often has an unpredictable outcome. When an audience becomes outraged and violent toward a bad actor, a detachment of guards moves in to save him. When the public order dissolves as war approaches, Wilhelm's troupe of actors cannot safely continue its performances and must seek safe haven, first in a court, then in the distant city of "H." During this journey, in response to rumors of hostile *Freikorps* in the area, the group arms itself for defense as if it were a small militia.[8] When the group is attacked, Wilhelm's "Heerführerschaft" [military leadership] reveals itself to be a charade. Thus in the novel's vision, theater needs the military for peace and security, just as the military needs the theater to foster the humanity and social solidarity it is incapable of forging.

The war in which Herr von C. fights is usually assumed to be the Seven Years' War (Köpke 372), and the military in which he serves is presumably the Prussian army of Frederick II. Frederick's army was the great success story and dominant military model of the era — for observers not only in Weimar but throughout Europe. Foreign armies studied Prussian successes and religiously reproduced Prussian formations and drills. Indeed, "in all things military the Prussian example was eagerly emulated" (Rothenberg 19). But as a model for social relations, the Prussian army could hardly seem compelling, above all to anyone of bourgeois extraction like Goethe. The army was organized according to rigid class distinctions. Only sons of the nobility were generally eligible to become officers — but even for these it was often a harsh life that began in boyhood. The common soldiers were a motley mix of conscripted peasants and mercenaries kept in line by endless drilling and brutal corporal punishment. The high number of foreign recruits limited the development of any collective identity based on a common homeland.[9] The rest of the soldiers, in Frederick's own estimation, were "Taugenichtse," "Wüstlinge," "ungeratene Söhne," or "wilde Gesellen," who all "zu ihrem Kriegsherrn ebensowenig ein innerliches Verhältnis haben wie Ausländer" [good-for-nothings, libertines, wayward sons, or wild fellows whose relationship to their commanders is no closer than that of foreigners; qtd. in Kuczynski 69]. If nonetheless feelings of loyalty developed among the troops (Rothenberg 17; Kuczynski 80; Marwitz 43), this feeling was not viewed as the foundation or aim of the military.

With the French Revolution the dominant military paradigm shifted from Frederick's ideal of a "kunstvolle und vollkommene Maschine" [artificial and total machine; qtd. in Latzel 81] to the people's army of the French. In 1789 the French National Assembly declared that a public force protecting the rights of man and of the citizen is "instituted for the advantage of all, and not for the private benefit of those to whom it is entrusted" (qtd. in Paret 44). In the first years of the Revolution royal control of the army gave way: old officers resigned or fled; new ones, loyal to the cause, were appointed by the Assembly or elected by their own men. The ranks were filled first with volunteers, then with draftees. In 1793 the Convention instituted a *levée en masse* on the principle that the army belonged to the people and the entire

French people constituted the army (Rothenberg 95–100). While naturally in practice the new French army also relied on training, discipline, and hierarchies of command,[10] it came to represent to a stunned Europe something much more spontaneous: the drive for equality, the force of national feeling, and the authority of the citizen.

The Prussian and Austrian armies first met this new citizen army when they invaded France in 1792. Their impregnable confidence was suddenly shattered when at Valmy their advance was halted by French troops, whose rallying cry was "Vive la nation!" (Haswell 89). Goethe, who had accompanied Carl August on this campaign, claims to have proclaimed at the end of the day of fruitless cannon fire that this time and place marked the beginning of a new epoch in world history (MA 14: 385). Indeed, this encounter with a powerful and passionate army that stood for a "nation" ultimately constituted a mirror stage for a Germany that was culturally and politically fragmented.[11] In 1797, in an analysis of the continuing success of the French military, the Prussian officer Gerhard von Scharnhorst identified national pride and popular belief in the country's cause as a key to French military power (Scharnhorst 105). After Prussia had been devastated by France in 1807, Scharnhorst and other military officers would try to reform the Prussian military into more of a people's militia with the hope "that the new army would be the school of a new nation" (Craig xv).

Thus Goethe's first years at the Weimar theater coincided with a gradual paradigm shift in the meaning of the military and with the emergence of the army as a potential vehicle for a national consciousness. Goethe's theatrical prologue of 7 May 1791, which inaugurated his tenure with the theater, still invokes Wilhelm's vision of the national theater:

> Von allen Enden Deutschlands kommen wir
> Erst jetzt zusammen; sind einander fremd
> Und fangen erst nach jenem schönen Ziel
> Vereint zu wandeln an [...]. (WA 1.13.1: 22–25)

> [We come together only now from all corners of Germany;
> We are foreign to each other,
> And are just beginning to wander
> United toward that beautiful goal.]

And yet the complementary relation laid out in the earlier novel between a spontaneous, humanizing theater and a disciplined army that could secure order would come increasingly into question. The well-drilled Prussian army was not a certain bulwark against this new kind of national military collective. At the same time, this new brand of army converged in unmistakable ways with the theater. Its promise of a nation founded on liberty, brotherhood, and equality echoed in more radical ways the moderate reformist goals of the German theater. How then could the theater present itself as an alternative to the citizen army?

Despite its fictionalized, even novelistic character (see Saine 193), Goethe's *Campagne in Frankreich 1792* remains the best source on Goethe's understanding of this new threat. Here Goethe conceives the new citizen army as something close to a mob, associating the stream of volunteers with the participants in the September massacres:

> aber diese [Freiwilligen] in den gräßlichen ersten Septembertagen, durch die reißend fließenden Blutströme, aus der Hauptstadt ausgewandert, brachten Lust zum Morden und Rauben mehr als zu einem rechtlichen Kriege mit. [...] Man durfte sie nur undisciplinirt loslassen, so machten sie uns den Garaus. (MA 14: 393)
>
> [these volunteers, who had poured out of the capital through the torrents of blood that were flowing in those horrible early September days, brought with them more of a lust to rob and murder than to wage legitimate war (...). They had only to be turned loose without any discipline and they would be the death of us. (SE 5: 659)]

Goethe here laments the passing of a model of legitimate war that assigned clear and distinct roles to civilians and soldiers and allowed for a kind of protocol in warfare. In his account, both soldiers and civilians behave in unpredictable ways. Captive French soldiers commit suicide for the cause (MA 14: 358, 360); French civilians serve as spies or engage in guerrilla warfare (MA 14: 394, 412). Meanwhile Goethe observes the coalition troops contributing to the crisis through their own transgressions of discipline and injustices against French civilians. As new collective hatreds and loyalties challenge conventional categories, a crisis emerges for Goethe concerning the recognition and interpretation of other individuals.[12]

Since Goethe associated the Revolution with a militant mob, his theater's unique defense against revolutionary impulses would be its emphasis on individuality. In his essay with Schiller "Über epische und dramatische Dichtung" (On Epic and Dramatic Poetry, 1797), Goethe outlines some of the basic features of drama as genre. Drama, according to the essay, renders events fully in the present (MA 4.2: 126). The spectator is called upon to follow the action passionately, that is, "sich nicht zum Nachdenken erheben" [not rise to reflect; MA 4.2: 128]. The focus of the audience's attention and passion — what the drama renders fully present — is the specific individuality of the actor.

> [Der Mime] stellt sich als ein bestimmtes Individuum dar, er will daß man an ihm und seiner nächsten Umgebung ausschließlich Teil nehme, daß man die Leiden seiner Seele und seines Körpers mitfühle, seine Verlegenheiten teile und sich selbst über ihn vergesse. (MA 4.2: 128)
>
> [(The actor) represents a specific individual and wants us to concentrate exclusively on him and his immediate surroundings. His goal is to make us empathize with his mental anguish and his physical suffering, share his difficulties and forget ourselves. (SE 3: 194)]

Theater spectatorship thus inspires identification with another individual to the point of self-forgetting. Essential, though, is Goethe's and Schiller's claim that this self-forgetting immersion could serve a higher good; the subject of tragedy, like that of epic, should be "rein menschlich, bedeutend und pathetisch" [humane, significant, and elevated; MA 4.2: 126/SE 3: 193). Theater spectators, unlike a revolutionary collective, focus on individual fates while remaining bound to general human ideals.

One can thus find in Goethe's theater during these years repeated attempts to disarm or demystify the forces of war through an emphasis on individuality. For example, in his prologue (1793) to Goldoni's comedy *La Guerra* (The War), Goethe promises that here the horrors of war will not emerge. Instead, the spirit of frivolity will find its way into war. Familiar emotions like love will conquer even in the field: "Ihr werdet sehen daß die Liebe sich/ So gut in's Zelt als in die Häuser schleicht" [You will see that love slinks into the tent as well as into houses; WA 1.13.1: 18–19]. The second half of the prologue then turns to lament Weimar's one great hardship in the current war: the duke, who is "verehrt, bewundert, und geliebt von allen" [honored, admired, and loved by all; 39] is absent due to the conflict. The speech concludes, "Er lebe! Lebe für uns, wie wir für ihn!" [May he live, live for us, as we do for him; 49]. Thus the prologue summons the gentle, domestic emotions of the comic theater as an antidote to the horrors of war. If love succeeds even in the field, the final profession of love for a representative individual is its own form of resistance to "this evil war." Significantly, this collective love is professed for an aristocratic lord in battle against revolution.

The focus on individuality, which in the above case aimed to reinforce a traditional collective identity, could also be deployed to undermine a radical, hostile one if the frightening and mysterious forces of revolution or war could be unmasked as the comprehensible follies of an individual. In Goethe's satirical play *Der Bürger-General* (The Citizen-General, 1793), the French Revolution seems to have infiltrated a small German village. Yet Schnapps, the apparent emissary of the Revolution and self-proclaimed "citizen-general," turns out to be no more than a two-bit con-man attempting to cheat his fellow villagers out of their breakfast. Harmony is restored not only with the revelation of Schnapps's trickery, but also as the lord recognizes that Schnapps presents no true danger to the land and treats him with mercy. Thus the humanity of all is restored as the threat of revolution is defused. According to Goethe's assistant, Anton Genast, this popular and oft performed play was viewed by the people as a "kleine Schlacht" [little battle] which Weimar fought against France (57).

Schiller's three-part tragedy *Wallenstein*, which premiered on the Weimar stage in 1798 and 1799, also follows this strategy of taking apart war by taking apart an individual, in this case Albrecht Wallenstein, the renowned commander in the Thirty Years' War. In his prologue of 12 October 1798 introducing the play and dedicating the remodeled Weimar theater, Schiller establishes a parallel between Wallenstein's chaotic age and the uncertainty of the present, since the "alte feste Form" [old and solid form] which finally emerged out of the Thirty Years' War is now in ruins. The trilogy begins with *Wallensteins Lager* (Wallenstein's Camp), a tableau of a destructive "kingdom of soldiers." The soldiers enjoy freedom (but only as a license to destroy), the equality granted by an uncertain fortune, and a solidarity through the figure of their commander. Wallenstein has created this army but is also seduced and led astray by it. Though in the prologue Schiller advises us that the general's crime is the result of the charismatic military power he holds over his soldiers, the next two parts of the trilogy increasingly dispel the aura created around Wallenstein by his army — following Schiller's dictum in the prologue: "Doch euren Augen soll ihn jetzt die Kunst,/ Auch eurem Herzen menschlich näher bringen" [Art will contrive to bring him nearer/ To both your eyes and hearts as only human; Hinderer 10].[13] Thus dramatic character study offers a protection from a violent crowd: if the individual threatens to create a mob and this moblike collective in turn inflates the authority of the individual, theater's solution is to demystify and bring back into perspective the individual. Such a strategy might have seemed especially crucial as Napoleon emerged on the scene.

Yet despite this apparently programmatic attempt to set theater up as the school of a humane, but non-revolutionary, German public, Goethe was quietly, even from the beginning, skeptical about the entire enterprise.[14] Certainly in practice the Weimar theater never could rely on a stable, orderly public. For example, unruly incidents involving students from Jena led Goethe in June 1797 to bid the marshal's office to station one or two hussars on the right side of the audience in addition to those already standing at the door (Linder 146–47). But the stability of the spectator's position was put to its most extreme tests when Goethe took part as an observer in the campaign in France and the siege of Mainz.

Richard Fisher has noted the abundance of theater metaphors in the *Campagne in Frankreich*. For example, the phrase "Kriegstheater" [theater of war] shows up several times in the text including in the very first and last paragraphs. Fisher also notes that Goethe's position in relation to certain battle scenes he describes is like that of a spectator in the theater. But Fisher views the theater spectatorship as a normative ideal, a sovereign, immune stance above the battle fray. Fisher writes: "the role of the 'Zuschauer' (spectator) in metaphors derived from the theater is that of a sage who sees through the action unfolding before him" (245). He overlooks the ways in which this very ideal is undermined by Goethe's experience of the war.

In Goethe's description of the siege of Verdun early in the campaign one can perhaps still attribute a positive valence to the theater analogy. Goethe describes the bombardment of the city as if it were a firework display, noting the particularly powerful effect produced by the battery on one side, which was *playing* with incendiary rockets that sent quarters of the city up in flame (MA 14: 354). But then he focuses his gaze, indeed his field glasses, on the individual figures on the city walls.

> Unsere Ferngläser, dorthin gerichtet, gestatteten uns auch dieses Unheil im Einzelnen zu betrachten; wir konnten die Menschen erkennen, die sich oben auf den Mauern dem Brande Einhalt zu tun eifrig bemühten, wir konnten die freistehenden, zusammenstürzenden Gesparre bemerken und unterscheiden. (MA 14: 354)
>
> [Our telescopes, trained in that direction, permitted us to see this damage in detail; we could make out the people on top of the walls trying hard to stop the fires, and we could see and distinguish the collapsing beams. (SE 5: 631)]

Then Goethe describes the varied response to this spectacle among a random crew of spectators: "Dieses alles geschah in Gesellschaft von

Bekannten und Unbekannten, wobei es unsägliche, oft widersprechende Bemerkungen gab und gar verschiedene Gesinnungen geäußert wurden" [All this was observed in the company of both friends and strangers, who made indescribable, often contradictory comments and expressed widely divergent sentiments; MA 14: 354/SE 5: 631]. This scene can remind us of the model of spectatorship advanced in the essay "Über epische und dramatische Dichtung" (On Epic and Dramatic Poetry, 1797). The viewer is focused on the fate of specific individuals — here, on the figures racing to put out the fires in the beleaguered city. Judging by the indescribable and often contradictory remarks of the audience, the sight is deeply affecting, perhaps in the generally humane and significant way that Goethe and Schiller promise for the theater in their essay.

But if here we can attribute an independent, even critical thrust to spectatorship, that independence erodes as the campaign continues. At Valmy, the epoch-making standoff that halted the allied advance, the cannon volleys back and forth absorb all into the conflict. Spectators come under fire and those under fire can do nothing but watch: "Und so blieb alles eigentlich nur Zuschauer und Zuhörer, was im Feuer stand und nicht" [And thus in fact we remained only spectators and listeners, whether under fire or not; MA 14: 382/SE 5: 650]. Later in the cannonade Goethe experiences the total erosion of these distinctions between self and spectacle. Driven by boredom as well as an incorrigible drive for adventure, Goethe rides out to a dangerous ridge facing the French, who were before him in an amphitheater formation, in order to experience a phenomenon called cannon fever. With the cannon balls whizzing around him, Goethe experiences a total feverish absorption in his surroundings: "Es schien als wäre man an einem sehr heißen Orte, und zugleich von derselben Hitze völlig durchdrungen, so daß man sich mit demselben Element, in welchem man sich befindet, vollkommen gleich fühlt" [It seemed as though I were in a very hot place, and thoroughly permeated by that same heat, so that I felt completely at one with the element in which I found myself; MA 14: 384/SE 5: 651–52]. In the very middle of this battle theater, Goethe experiences complete identity with the spectacle. This war has eliminated the position of spectator, destroyed all objectivity or perception of difference. The theater itself is implicated in this crisis, for Goethe's description of cannon fever recalls the language of "complete presence" and "self-forgetting" in Goethe's and Schiller's essay "Über epische und dramatische Dichtung."

The analogy between theater spectatorship and violence takes its most sinister form in an event after the siege of Mainz. Goethe describes the explosive tension surrounding the flight of French sympathizers after the city has been reoccupied. A mob of townspeople pulls one well known "clubbist" by his feet from a carriage and beats him mercilessly. While his distinctive build and looks — short and heavy with a broad, pockmarked face — had made him immediately identifiable to the crowd, now all his limbs are broken and his face has been rendered unrecognizable. A guard at last intervenes to take the beaten man into a farmhouse where, now lying on straw, he remains the object of the crowd's taunts and insults. The officer at last tries to hinder the onslaught and begs Goethe too to stay away from this "traurigsten und ekelhaftesten aller Schauspiele" [saddest and most disgusting of all spectacles; MA 14: 545/SE 5: 768]. This extreme spectacle amounts to voyeurism and violence, where all boundaries and difference are lost. The incident begins with the identification of a distinctive individual, but ends with the bloody effacement of all of his recognizable individual features.

Thus the humane, productive identification in the service of general ideals that Schiller and Goethe hope for in the theater depends upon an apparently fragile, unstable sensibility that seems to be related on a continuum to voyeurism and violence. The specific individuality which Goethe and Schiller place at the core of dramatic reception seems easily transgressed. This sense of danger and uncertainty in the theater comes out further in a passage in the *Campagne in Frankreich* where Goethe explicitly compares diplomats to theater directors and, by extension, military troops to a troupe of actors. Actors, like soldiers, are exposed to an uncertain fate: "die Truppe [muß,] so gut sie kann, aufs beste herausgestutzt das Resultat ihrer Bemühungen dem Glück und der Laune des Publikums überlassen" [Decked out in the fanciest costumes, (they) must do as well as they can and leave the final judgment on their efforts to fortune and the whims of the public; MA 14: 419/ SE 5: 678]. Thus the fate of actors at the hands of the public is like the fate of soldiers in battle.

Perhaps one can locate in this instability some of the logic behind the peculiar style of dramaturgy Goethe developed in the Weimar theater. At the end of the *Campagne in Frankreich*, as Goethe relates his return to Weimar, he discusses the shortcomings of the theater at the time. Goethe felt his actors lacked a basic "Grammatik" of acting (MA 14: 503). He criticizes the "Natur- und Konversationston" [natural and conversational tone] that was then in vogue in the theater. According to Goethe, this tone is praiseworthy and gratifying only "wenn er als vollendete Kunst, als eine zweite Natur hervortritt, nicht aber wenn ein jeder glaubt nur sein eigenes nacktes Wesen bringen zu dürfen" [if it gets to the point of being a perfected art, a second nature, but not if everyone believes he has only to reproduce his own naked person in order to merit applause; MA 14: 503/SE 5: 738]. Goethe uses the same metaphor of nakedness and exposure in reference to Aurelie in the *Lehrjahre,* who is unable to separate her self from the character she plays and who, according to her brother, "wird noch eh'stens ganz nackt auf das Theater treten, und dann wird erst der Beifall recht willkommen sein [one of these days she will appear stark naked on the stage, and then they will really applaud; MA 5: 354; bk. 5, ch. 16/SE 9: 214]. Indeed, Aurelie feels prostituted by her admirers and deteriorates physically due to her exertions on stage.[15] I contend that in order to avoid exposing his own actors in such a personal way on stage, Goethe worked to outfit them with an inviolable artistic armor. Their individuality and naturalness on stage had to become second nature, the product of self-alienation and artifice. According to the same passage in the *Campagne in Frankreich,* he thus began to study acting techniques that were based on tradition and to employ "gewisse Regeln und Anordnungen" [certain rules and precepts; MA 14: 503/SE 5: 738].

In collaboration with Schiller, Goethe came to develop an idealized, anti-naturalistic Weimar style, for which Greek and Roman antiquity, French Classicism served as inspirations. This approach involved a rhythmic mode of declamation, a stylized vocabulary of gestures, and careful arrangement of actors on stage to form a harmonious composition. Experimentation with theatrical masks (beginning in 1801 with a production of Terence's comedy *The Brothers*) was also, according to Goethe, an important step forward for the theater (see "Weimarisches Hoftheater," MA 6.2: 692–703). Borchmeyer has seen in the Weimar style, particularly in its evocation of an ancien régime French Classicism, an opposition to the unrestrained fantasy and "naturalism" associated with the French Revolution (Borchmeyer 358–59). A military metaphor comes out clearly in Schiller's prologue to the *Braut von Messina* (Bride of Messina, 1803), where he describes his use of the classical chorus as an attempt, "dem Naturalism in der Kunst offen und ehrlich den Krieg zu erklaeren" [openly and honestly to declare war on naturalism in the arts; qtd. in Borchmeyer 352].

Weimar's chief theatrical weapon against the French Revolution becomes an ever more controlled and disciplined individuality. Since, as we have seen, the individuality of the actor moves and transports the audience but is also vulnerable to transgression and violence, the art of theater demands the effective but careful deployment of the actors' primary instruments — their bodies and voices. Goethe's "Regeln für Schauspieler" (Rules for Actors, 1803) establishes speech and bodily movement as the key components of the actor's art. Goethe pays close attention to the details of gesture, delivery, and movement in his actors and emphasizes precise self-control: "Jeder Teil des Körpers stehe daher ganz in seiner Gewalt, so daß er jedes Glied, gemäß dem zu zielenden Ausdruck, frei, harmonisch und mit Grazie gebrauchen könne" [Therefore every part of the actor's body should be under his control so that he may be able to use each limb freely, harmoniously, and gracefully in accord with the expression called for; MA 6.2: 735]. Klaus Schwind sees here Goethe's attempt to inscribe expression on his actors' bodies, to force them, in the name of art, to internalize his own control over them (83). Even a more sympathetic modern critic has compared the "Regeln" to a book of military drill (Hinck 12). Many of Goethe's contemporaries clearly also viewed his approach to his actors as excessively regimented, even dehumanizing. For example, the rhythmic style of declamation Goethe advocates in his "Regeln" causes the playwright and director August Klingemann to describe some of Goethe's actors as "Automate" and "Sprechmaschinen" [automatons and speech-machines; qtd. in Schwind 101]. By contrast, Goethe's assistant Anton Genast defended Goethe against the apparently widespread charge, "daß er die Bühne wie ein Schachbrett betrachtet habe, dessen lebendige Figuren nur nach seinem Willen sich stellen und ihre Plätze wechseln dürfen" [that he viewed the stage as a chessboard, the living figures of which had to position themselves and change places only according to his will]. Such critics, Genast claims, do not understand Goethe's "hohes geistiges Streben," that is, the high spiritual aspiration behind Goethe's strategies (54).

Goethe's control over his actors, however, extended beyond his detailed stage directions. Beginning in 1793, the Weimar theater adopted a set of laws, modeled on those of other German theaters, which regulated behavior in rehearsal and performance and prescribed fines for many infractions. Goethe, who as privy councilor commanded more state authority than most German theater directors, went well beyond these regulations to punish his actors for their misbehavior on and off stage, occasionally with such severe penalties as house arrest and short periods in jail (Linder 34ff.). In a parody of Goethe's "Regeln" published anonymously in 1808, the actor Carl Wilhelm Reinhold — who spent sixty hours in jail after a fight with other actors (Linder 118) — alludes to Goethe's severity: "Jedes Spiel, jede Gesticulation, jeder Ausdruck der Stimme, wodurch ein Charakter nueanciert und scharf bezeichnet werden könnte, ist bey Gefängnisstrafe verboten" [Every performance, every gesticulation, every expression in the voice that could mark a character in a distinct and nuanced way is punishable with a jail sentence; qtd. in Schwind 105].

Goethe's intention was to mold his actors into artists and dignified representatives of public life (Linder 101–17). That his theatrical ideal was not the military is clear enough from his instruction to his actors not to stand like soldiers (MA 6.2: 737). In the "Vorspiel auf dem Theater" of *Faust I* (Prologue in the Theater, 1808), Goethe treats with some irony the poet's unrealistic fantasy of an almost drill-like control. The poet brags:

> Wenn aller Wesen unharmon'sche Menge
> Verdrießlich durch einander klingt;
> Wer teilt die fließend immer gleiche Reihe
> Belebend ab, daß sie sich rhythmisch regt? (MA 6.1: 539; *Pr.* 144–47)

> [When all existence's discordant roar
> Grates on the soul — who then divides
> The rushing ever-recurrent file,
> Reviving it, making it beat in order?" (Jarrell 9)]

In an essay on the Weimar theater published in 1802, Goethe complains rather of a lack of control, of all the factors that served to "tyrannize" the director ("Weimarisches Hoftheater," MA 6.2: 693). Nevertheless, in his attempt to counter this "tyranny," to create a controlled individuality in his actors, Goethe sometimes reduced his actors to a machine-like function that recalls uncannily the conventional role of subordinate soldiers. That irony is particularly trenchant in an incident of 1809, reconstructed by Schwind. The young actor Eduard Deny was required, as an employee of the court, to seek permission to marry from the theater commission, which consisted of Goethe and two other members. In a document signed by Goethe, the commission turned down Deny's request citing the various burdens the young woman, an actress, would present both to the actor and to the theater. Deny appealed to the duke. In a further memorandum the commission used a new argument: that a marriage would reduce the actor's appeal.

> Der Zuschauer will nicht nur ästhetisch und sittlich sondern auch sinnlich gerührt seyn. Ein unberührtes Mädchen, ein unbescholtener Jüngling bringen in passenden Rollen ganz andere Empfindungen hervor, ihr Spiel schließt Herz und Gemüth

auf eine ganz andere Weise auf, als Personen von denen das Gegentheil bekannt ist. (Qtd. in Schwind 71)[16]

[The spectator wants to be moved not only aesthetically and morally but also sensually. An untouched girl, an unblemished boy elicit in appropriate roles entirely different feelings. Their performance opens heart and soul in entirely different ways than do persons of whom the opposite is known.]

In an unofficial note, Carl August complained of "Goethescher Unsinn," of Goethe's "tirrannei" and "Herrschsucht" [Goethean nonsense, tyranny and thirst for power; qtd. in Schwind 71]. In his official decision reversing that of the commission, Carl August noted that up until then no case had come up where permission to marry had been denied — except in the case of common soldiers (qtd. in Schwind 72). In the interest of art Goethe had attempted to control his actor's expressive resources, to exploit in particular the young man's presumed bodily integrity. But in his disposition over the body of his actor for a public purpose, he had treated his actor very much like a common soldier. Did Goethe in his reaction to the French Revolution unwittingly create an acting troupe in the image of the well-drilled troops he once defined theater against? To recall, in *Wilhelm Meisters Theatralische Sendung* the order and discipline of the Prussian army complemented but did not compete with the freedom, spontaneity, and solidarity across class lines deemed possible in the theater. As the French army came to represent these same ideals in militant form, Goethe had to redefine the role of the theater as a conservative institution. The Weimar theater strove to distinguish itself from and yet compete with a revolutionary citizen-army for the loyalty of the local public. In close collaboration with Schiller, Goethe worked to develop the theater's focus on individuality as a defense against what he viewed as the moblike army of the Revolution. But the category of individuality and the position of the spectator emerged as unstable in Goethe's experience of war. Goethe's classical style of dramaturgy, his strictness, even severity with his actors all aimed to reinforce this category of the individual. If this discipline went so far that Goethe's actors began to recall the well-drilled automatons of Frederick's army, there was nonetheless this important difference: discipline in the theatre was imposed in the name of an expressive individuality.

The next chapter in this story would have to address a parallel transformation of the soldier in the Prussian military. Just as Goethe's theater turned to discipline and control as a defense against the Revolution, so would Prussian military leaders appreciate the importance of soldierly identity in the same cause. The Prussian military would, like the Weimar theater, learn to exploit this strange tension between feeling and function, expression and extreme control.

—University of Oklahoma

Notes

[1] Geertz refers here to the theatricality of the traditional Bali state but his discussion of the semiotics of power has much broader implications for the study of social institutions, including the military.

[2] See, for example, Gillian Russell's analysis of the reciprocity between the theatricality of the political and military arenas and the politics of the theater in Georgian England.

[3] Carl August entered the Prussian army in September 1787 and was quickly made a General Major, left the army at the end of 1793, and reentered it in 1798 as a General Lieutenant (Klauß 68, 74–75). As a grandnephew of Frederick II, he also had dynastic ties to the Prussian throne. Nonetheless Weimar's relationship to the Prussian army was as ambivalent as it was close. Weimar had had its own standing troops since the seventeenth century (Scharf 306). Carl August had been deeply troubled when in 1778–79 Prussia insisted on recruiting his subjects to fight in the War of Bavarian Succession. In the wake of this affair Carl August became involved in an alliance of smaller states called the League of Princes in order to create a buffer against Prussian domination (Schmidt 208–9; Tümmler 27–29).

[4] As head of Weimar's war commission in the 1780s Goethe had struggled to rein in Carl August's enthusiastic military spending (Klauß 36, Henning 241). When he became theater director, Goethe in turn had to accept a quite modest annual court subsidy of 7,000 talers, which the Duke temporarily cut back in early 1793 because of military expenses (Flemming 109; Carlson 75).

[5] Carl August began looking for ways to reform the theater at a time when Prussia was involved in a power struggle over Poland with Austria. Goethe wrote to the duke on 6 February 1790: "Daß Sie sich, unter den gegenwärtigen Umständen, noch mit der mechanischsten aller Wissenschaften dem deutschen Theater abgeben mögen, läßt uns andere Verehrer der Irene hoffen daß diese stille Schöne noch eine Zeitlang regieren wird" [That you can occupy yourself in these troubled times with the most mechanical of all branches of knowledge, the German theater, allows us other patrons of Peace (Irene) to hope that this quiet goddess will remain long on her throne; WA 4.9: 172–73/Carlson 55].

[6] Schiller was an important intellectual friend beginning in 1794. He actively collaborated in the theater from his move to Weimar at the end of 1799 until

his death in 1805. It also should be mentioned that, beginning in 1797, the theater was administered by a commission, consisting initially of Franz Kirms, Georg Lebrecht von Luck, and Goethe himself.
[7] While Wilhelm consistently encounters gaps between his ideals and the realities of the German stage, this early fragment approaches the dream of the national theater with much less irony than does Goethe's revised version of the novel, *Wilhelm Meisters Lehrjahre*.
[8] This incident also appears in the *Lehrjahre* (MA 5; bk. 4, ch. 4–5), but the earlier novel places greater emphasis on Wilhelm's role as commander, including a description of the strange figure he cuts with his great weapon belt, sabre, and two pistols (MA 2.2: 276–77; bk. 5, ch. 14).
[9] Foreigners made up more than twenty-five percent of Frederick's army at the end of the Seven Years' War in 1763; by the end of Frederick's life in 1786 foreigners outnumbered natives by two to one (Rothenberg 17).
[10] This despite the fact that in the initial years of transformation the new recruits were indeed short on training and in some cases ideologically opposed to discipline and drill (Rothenberg 99).
[11] "The increasing hatred toward France cannot obscure the fact that it simultaneously served as a model" (Latzel 85). This tendency to mirror the foe is a common phenomenon in war. According to Martin van Creveld, "war represents perhaps the most imitative activity known to man" (qtd. in Ehrenreich 137).
[12] As Larkin has discussed, problems of perception emerge in many different facets as a central, organizing theme in Goethe's war narratives (121–42).
[13] Goethe actually cut these lines from the speech that was recited in the theater (Oellers 96). Nevertheless, in a letter to Schiller of 18 March 1799, Goethe identifies a trajectory in the trilogy from politics to "das reinmenschliche" [the purely human; MA 8.1: 687].
[14] See his letters to Reichardt of 28 February 1790 and to Knebel of 5 October 1791. In December of 1795 Goethe even asked to be relieved of his position but Carl August politely turned him down (Carlson 56, 70–71, 85).
[15] Aurelie appears in *Theatralische Sendung*, but only in the *Lehrjahre* is it clear that her style of acting is an error rather than a worthy sacrifice for the nation.
[16] While I have followed Schwind's reconstruction of this incident, it should be noted that Schwind diverges from Witkowski's 1935 interpretation of these documents. Schwind takes the memorandum signed by Goethe to be the initial decision handed down by the commission and the second, undated document to be a response to Deny's appeal to the duke. Witkowski treats the second document as part of the initial decision and speculates that it reflects the opinion of Kirms because of its concern with revenue (Witkowski 87).

Works Cited

Biedrzynski, Effi. *Goethes Weimar. Das Lexikon der Personen und Schauplätze.* Rev. ed. Zurich: Artemis and Winkler, 1993.

Borchmeyer, Dieter. "'Dem Naturalism in der Kunst offen und ehrlich den Krieg zu erklären ....' Zu Goethes und Schillers Bühnenreform." *Unser Commercium. Goethes und Schillers Literaturpolitik.* Eds. Wilfred Barner, Eberhard Lämmert, and Norbert Oellers. Stuttgart: Cotta, 1984. 351–70.

Carlson, Marvin. *Goethe and the Weimar Theatre.* Ithaca: Cornell UP, 1978.

Craig, Gordon. *The Politics of the Prussian Army 1640–1945.* London: Clarendon-Oxford, 1955.

Ehrenreich, Barbara. *Blood Rites: Origins and History of the Passion of War.* New York: Holt, 1997.

Fisher, Richard. "'Dichter' and 'Geschichte': Goethe's *Campagne in Frankreich.*" *Goethe Yearbook* 4 (1988): 235–74.

Flemming, Willi. *Goethe und das Theater seiner Zeit.* Stuttgart: Kohlhammer, 1968.

Geertz, Clifford. *Negara: The Theater State in Nineteenth-Century Bali.* Princeton: Princeton UP, 1980.

Genast, Eduard. *Aus Weimars klassischer und nachklassischer Zeit. Erinnerungen eines alten Schauspielers.* Ed. Robert Kohlrausch. Stuttgart: Lutz, 1905.

Haswell, Jock. *Citizen Armies.* London: Peter Davies, 1973.

Henning, Hans. "Die Entwicklung Weimars in der Zeit der Emanzipation des Bürgertums und im Jahrhundert Goethes: 1750–1830." *Geschichte der Stadt Weimar.* Weimar: Hermann Böhlaus Nachfolger, 1976. 230–337.

Hinck, Walter. *Goethe — Mann des Theaters.* Göttingen: Vandenhoeck und Ruprecht, 1982.

Hinderer, Walter, ed. *Friedrich von Schiller. Wallenstein.* Trans. Jeanne Willson. New York: Continuum, 1991. 8–251.

Jarrell, Randall, trans. *Johann Wolfgang von Goethe. Faust.* New York: Farrar, Straus, and Giroux, 1976.

Köpke, Wulf. "Nachwort." Johann Wolfgang von Goethe, *Wilhelm Meisters theatralische Sendung.* Ed. Wulf Köpke. Stuttgart: Reclam, 1986. 365–87.

Klauß, Jochen. *Carl August von Sachsen-Weimar-Eisenach: Fürst und Mensch. Sieben Versuche einer Annäherung.* Weimar: Klassikerstätten zu Weimar, 1991.

Kuczynski, Jürgen. "Der Alltag des Soldaten (1650–1810)." Wette 68–75.

Larkin, Edward T. *War in Goethe's Writings: Representation and Assessment.* Lewiston, NY: Mellen, 1992.

Latzel, Klaus. "'Schlachtbank' oder 'Feld der Ehre'? Der Beginn des Einstellungswandels gegenüber Krieg und Tod, 1756–1815." Wette 76–92.

Linder, Jutta. *Ästhetische Erziehung. Goethe und das Weimarer Hoftheater.* Bonn: Bouvier, 1990.

Marwitz, Ulrich. "Die Grundlagen deutscher militärischer Tradition im Zeitalter des Absolutismus." *Tradition in deutschen Streitkräften bis 1945.* Eds. Gustav-Adolf Caspar, Ulrich Marwitz, and Hans-Martin Ottmer. Bonn: E. Mittler, 1965. 19–65.

Oellers, Norbert. "Die Heiterkeit der Kunst. Goethe variiert Schiller." *Edition als Wissenschaft. Festschrift für Hans Zeller.* Eds. Gunter Martens and Winfried Woesler. Tübingen: Niemeyer, 1991. 92–103.

Paret, Peter. *Understanding War. Essays on Clausewitz and the History of Military Power.* Princeton: Princeton UP, 1992.

Rothenberg, Gunther E. *The Art of Warfare in the Age of Napoleon.* Bloomington: Indiana UP, 1980.

Russell, Gillian. *The Theatres of War: Performance, Politics, and Society 1793–1815.* Oxford: Clarendon-Oxford, 1995.

Saine, Thomas P. "Goethe's Novel, *Campagne in Frankreich*." *Goethe's Narrative Fiction: The Irvine Symposium.* Ed. William J. Lillyman. New York: de Gruyter, 1983. 193–223.

Scharf, Isolde. "Militär." *Weimar: Lexikon zur Stadtgeschichte.* Eds. Gitta Günther, Wolfram Huschke, and Walter Steiner. Weimar: Hermann Böhlaus Nachfolger, 1993. 306–7.

Scharnhorst, Gerhard von. *Ausgewählte militärische Schriften.* Eds. Hansjürgen Usczeck and Christa Gudzent. Berlin: Militärverlag der Deutschen Demokratischen Republik, 1986.

Schmidt, Georg. "Goethes politisches Denken." *Goethe Jahrbuch* 21 (1995): 197–212.

Schwind, Klaus. "'Man lache nicht!' Goethes theatrale Spielverbote. Über die schauspielerischen Unkosten des autonomen Kunstbegriffs." *Internationales Archiv für Sozialgeschichte der deutschen Literatur* 21.2 (1996): 66–112.

Tümmler, Hans. *Goethe als Staatsmann.* Göttingen: Musterschmidt, 1976.

Wette, Wolfram, ed. *Der Krieg des kleinen Mannes. Eine Militärgeschichte von unten.* Munich: Piper, 1992.

Witkowski, Georg. "Neue Urkunden zu Goethes Theaterleitung." *Jahrbuch der Sammlung Kippenberg* 10 (1935): 49–117.

6

Susan E. Gustafson

From Werther to Amazons:
Cross-Dressing and Male-Male Desire

Goethe was into cross-dressing. His cultural performances, ranging from flaunting a Werther costume upon his arrival in Weimar to essayistic revelations about cross-dressing men on Roman stages in the *Italienische Reise* (Italian Journey, publ. in full 1826) to the almost obsessive return in his literary and dramatic works to images of Amazons dressed as men, all point both to Goethe's interest in performances of gender and sexuality and to his contribution to such culture and identity-forming theatricality in Weimar. At the same time Goethe figures prominently both as a personality and in terms of his literary works in the "crossing culture" of eighteenth-century Weimar. Men who were attracted to men in eighteenth-century Weimar found a discourse and model for the theatricality of their desire in Goethe and his works. In other words, Goethe and Weimar converge at a moment of "category crisis," that is, cross-dressing and the male-male desire it illustrates in eighteenth-century Weimar reflect a challenge to identities, a transgressing of categories of sexual identification and orientation, and a traversing of a "borderline that becomes permeable, that permits of border crossings from one category to the next" (Garber 16). Cross-dressing — Goethe style — hints at an underlying coding of male-male desire in Weimar that relies on images of Goethe and Goethean images.

Cross-dressing in Weimar provided a means for expressing male-male desire, of subverting heterosexual borders in a society that condemned homosexuality.[1] It is important to note that male-male desire or sodomy, as it was usually referred to then, was an egregious offense throughout Europe in the eighteenth century. In Germany, France, Holland, and England, the penalty prescribed was usually death.[2] Indeed, until 1794 sodomy was punishable by death in Prussia. After 1794 the penalty was mitigated and the legal paragraphs concerning sodomy read:

> Sodomiterei und andere dergleichen unnatürliche Sünden, welche wegen ihrer Abscheulichkeit nicht genannt werden können, erfordern eine gänzliche Vertilgung des Andenkens [...]. Es soll daher ein solcher Verbrecher, nachdem er eine ein- oder mehrjährige Zuchthausstrafe mit Willkommen und Abschied ausgestanden hat, aus dem Orte seines Aufenthaltes, wo sein Laster bekannt geworden ist, auf immer verbannt werden. (Qtd. in Pruys 44)

> [Sodomy and other such unnatural sins, which, because of their horrific character cannot be named, demand a complete eradication from memory (...). Such a criminal should, after serving one or several years of penal servitude and after his crime has been made known, (...) be banned forever from his place of sojourn.]

In addition to legal restrictions, Goethe himself notes that even the *subject* (barring the actual activity) of same-sex desire was, for eighteenth-century Weimar, "eine Materie von der sich kaum reden, geschweige schreiben läßt" [a matter about which can hardly be spoken, let alone written; letter to Carl August, 29 December 1787, WA 4.8: 315]. For these reasons, overt public references by men to their attraction for other men would have been unimaginable. The only safe communication of male-male desire would have been through encoded discourses and performances. But of that, according to Derks, there is little evidence. He, for instance, insists that the difficulty of being a homosexual in eighteenth-century Germany was compounded by the fact that homosexuality was largely not discursively encoded (106). In his view, without specific codes men had little or no means to signal partners of like orientation. Derks does demonstrate, however, that some terms suggestive of male-male love were in use in Germany in the eighteenth and nineteenth centuries such as "heiliger Päderast" [holy pederast; 61–62], "warme Brüder" [warm brothers; 92–94], and "florenzen" [literally to act like someone from Florence; 25]. In this essay I intend to illustrate the beginnings of a discursive coding of male-male desire in Weimar through cross-dressing activities related to the figure and literary works of Goethe.

Before concentrating on the role of cross-dressing in Weimar specifically it seems appropriate to remember that, as Garber illustrates, cross-dressing disrupts and calls attention to "cultural, social, or aesthetic dissonances" (16). It highlights a cultural-wide primal scene (389) in which amorphous boundaries between identities (man/woman, male/female, masculine/feminine, heterosexual/homosexual) are articulated and simultaneously disrupted, questioned, and transgressed. Cross-dressers challenge the notion of stable sexual and gender identities. Cross-dressing is both an individual and cultural event. It has various meanings depending on who is cross-dressing, how, and in what historical or aesthetic context. Indeed, although cross-dressers seem in modern times more often "straight" than gay (Garber 131 — and we must wonder if those categories can even be invoked in this way?!), the act of cross-dressing destabilizes normative notions about sexual identity and orientation. Equally important is the fact that the

> history of transvestism and the history of homosexuality constantly intersect and intertwine, both willingly and unwillingly. They cannot simply be disentangled. But what is also clear is that neither can simply be transhistorically "decoded" as a sign for the other. (Garber 131)[3]

What Garber accentuates here is the uniqueness of cross-dressing and its implications for our understanding of sexual identities within different historical eras. Cross-dressing by Goethe and other men in Weimar cannot be assumed to mean the same thing as cross-dressing by Dustin Hoffman in *Tootsie*, Madonna in *Express Yourself*, Rose Sélavy (Marcel Duchamp) in a portrait by Man Ray, or by drag performers on a college campus or in a New York City club.

Even within the eighteenth century, cross-dressing is a highly nuanced and site-specific activity. The cross-dressing of Anne Bonny and Mary Read as male pirates is significantly distinct from the accounts in actress Charlotte Charke's autobiography of her adoption of male clothing, both onstage and off. In the one instance, cross-dressing (and thereby assuming male privilege) facilitates criminal behavior, in the other it allows a woman to move as freely in English society as any man of her station. Each of these crossing activities is distinguished as well from that of Chevalier d'Eon de Beaumont whose crossing became a matter of tremendous social importance in England and France — sparking debates, generating bets, and instigating court proceedings over the issue of sexual ambiguity. What each of these examples illustrates is that regardless of whether one examines different historical periods or different events within the same era, specific historical and cultural contexts must be taken into consideration when evaluating the significance of cross-dressing acts.

As one might expect, cross-dressing in "Goethe's Weimar" is unique to the city itself. What is perhaps most striking from a contemporary point of view is that crossing-dressing in Weimar (at least that associated with Goethe and his works) appears to have been largely manifested in the swapping of clothes between men — and not in the activity of men wearing women's clothing. In contrast, there is, as we shall see, some evidence of women cross-dressing as men in Weimar (specifically as Werther). In addition, Goethe's literary works are filled with men dressing as, identifying with, and desiring other men. We also find numerous examples of women crossing as men — for example in *Wilhelm Meisters Lehrjahre* (Wilhelm Meister's Apprenticeship, 1795–96) — but not of men dressing as women.[4] I do not mean to imply here that cross-dressing as we think of it today occurred only in literature and not in the city of Weimar, but the evidence available to date suggests that some of Weimar's men expressed their love for men by "crossing" as other men. The cultural and historical specificity of "crossing and cross-dressing" in Weimar distinguishes it from other forms of cross-dressing which entail more overt challenges to notions of gender fixity. Crossing in Weimar, as we shall see, contests normative heterosexuality and constitutes a space allowing for the expression of male-male desire. At any rate exchanging one's clothes with another man or dressing as a male literary hero and thereby expressing both identification with and desire for other men emerges as at least one significant cross-dressing activity in Weimar. And it is precisely this type of crossing that is intricately conjoined to Goethe and Goethean images in Weimar's coding of male-male desire. In order to explicate the complexity of the coding of male same-sex desire in Weimar, I will review initially the positioning of Goethe within a discourse of same-sex desire by the men around him.

Epistolary evidence indicates an almost overwhelming adulation of Goethe by male intellectuals in and near Weimar. Pruys (85–86) records the following exchanges: Sprickman wrote to Boie on 18 July 1776: "In Goethe bin ich verliebt [...]" [I am in love with Goethe]; Wieland to Merck on 27 August 1778: "Ich hätte Goethe vor Liebe fressen mögen" [I loved Goethe so much I could have devoured him]; Gleim to Jakobi on 21 November 1781: "Alle meine Freunde waren sterblich in den Engel Goethe verliebt" [All of my friends were mortally in love with the angel Goethe]; and finally Gleim to Herder on 6 April 1784: "Ich lieb ihn aber doch, wie man die Mädchen liebt [...]" [I love him indeed as one loves girls].[5] For these men, Goethe was an object of male desire and was himself, sexually, of an inexplicable, double nature: "nur in der Liebe ist er nicht rein und dazu nicht wirklich groß genug. Er hat zuviele Mischungen in sich, die verwirren [...]" [Only in love he is not pure and in that really not great enough. He has too many mixes in himself, which confuse; Schlosser to Jakobi, 31 October 1779]. For his contemporaries, Goethe is, as Lenz wrote to Lavater, a real "Mignon." Lenz's association of Goethe with Mignon, who is a girl/boy figure of sexual and gender amorphousness, implies Goethe's bisexuality — a sexuality that ensures, if not Goethe's exclusively "homosexual" tendencies, at least the possibility of his desire for both women and men.

At the same time that Goethe was loved by the male intellectuals who surrounded him and sought him out in Weimar, he was also Weimar's master of masquerade and cross-dressing. Indeed, one of his principal duties upon arrival in Weimar in 1775 was the organization and production of masquerades, balls, and theater productions. Goethe was purportedly Weimar's maître de plaisir (Ludwig 143). Conversely, Weimar-Eisenach was, for Goethe, "immer ein Schauplatz, um zu versuchen, wie einem die Weltrolle zu Gesichte stünde" [always a stage to try out how a world role might suit one; letter to Merck, 22 January 1776, WA 4.3: 21]. Throughout this period Goethe was engaged in and produced various forms of cross-dressing and performance. Although he often referred later to his duties as court poet and masquerade organizer as "Dienste der Eitelkeit" [services of vanity; letter to Lavater, 19 February 1781, WA 4.5: 56) and as "Zerstreuung" [diversion] and "Vertrödeln der Zeit" [dawdling away of time; letter to Charlotte von Stein, 14 January 1782, WA 4.5: 251], he also acknowledges how much energy he devotes to the fashioning and producing of these events (letters to Knebel, 2 and 26 February 1782, WA 4.5: 256, 272) and that they allow him to do some good "indem man zu scherzen scheint" [while appearing to jest; letter to Charlotte von Stein, 14 January 1782, WA 4.5: 251]. All in all, it is evident that Goethe had a tremendous influence on the masquerading activities in Weimar.

In fact, Goethe had literally arrived in Weimar sporting a "Werther-Uniform." Wearing the Werther clothing was "crossing" (in the sense of challenging identities) to the extent that Goethe was posing as the fictional male hero of his novel. Following in Goethe's sartorial theatricality, the whole world of Weimar was transfixed by and wore the famous Werther costume. Balls and masquerades were full of the Weimar elite, including some women (who were then crossing in the modern sense of transgressing gender delimitations), flaunting their *Werthertracht*.

> Das Wertherkostüm bestand aus hohen Stulpenstiefeln mit Kappe, gelben ledernen Beinkleidern, gelber Weste und blauen Frack; dazu trug man den Hals und das Haar frei, was bei der älteren Generation besonders Mißfallen erregte. Selbst unter den Damen sah man die "Emanzipierten" mit Werthertracht, Weste und Frack, dem berüchtigten "caraco." (Friedell 325)
>
> [The Werther costume consisted of high-top boots with toe-caps, yellow leather trousers, a yellow vest and a blue coat, in addition the neck and hair were free, which roused particular disapproval on the part of the older generation. Even among the women one saw the "emancipated" in Werther costume, vest and coat, the notorious "caraco."]

The older generation in Weimar found the Werther costume provocative and particularly inflammatory (see Klauß 34). Contemporaries referred to this as Weimar's "wild period" or "the rollicking time in Weimar" (Friedenthal 215). Others were not so thrilled. Voß insists: "In Weimar geht es erschrecklich zu" [Things in Weimar are appalling; qtd. in Friedenthal 220]. The donning of the Werther costume signaled a shift in sensibilities which underscored a gap between generations in Weimar. Goethe and his friends wore it to flaunt their freedom and to accentuate their identification with a social outsider like Werther. Dressing as Werther represented a crossing of boundaries between generations, a dissolution of the borders established between acceptable social and class behavior and the more bohemian actions of young men and women — young Werthers all — who scoffed at the more rigid values of their elders.

The fad of wearing a Werther costume is also connected subtly to male bonding and the establishment of codes of male-male desire in Weimar. The assumption of Werther clothing implies an identification with Werther — a fictional character who exhibits a certain kind of male desire. Werther is in love with himself being in love. His own feelings and desires are his sole focus: "Auch halte ich mein Herzchen wie ein krankes Kind; jeder Wille wird ihm gestattet" [I treat my heart like a sick child and gratify its every fancy; 13 May, MA 2.2: 353]. Moreover, in one of his very first letters Werther reveals that what he really desires is to love like another man:

> Wie reizend es war, wenn er von ihrer Gestalt, von ihrem Körper sprach [...]. Ich hab' in meinem Leben die dringende Begierde und das heiße, sehnliche Verlangen nicht in dieser Reinheit gesehen, ja wohl kann ich sagen, in dieser Reinheit nicht gedacht und geträumt. Schelte mich nicht, wenn ich dir sage, daß bei der Erinnerung dieser Unschuld und Wahrheit

> mir die innerste Seele glüht, und daß mich das Bild dieser Treue und Zärtlichkeit überall verfolgt, und daß ich, wie selbst davon entzündet, lechze und schmachte. (MA 2.2: 361)

> [How charming it was when he spoke of her figure, her body (…). Never in my life have I seen or imagined in this purity such intense desire or such ardent affections. Do not scold me if I say that the mere recollection of this innocence and truth burn in my very soul. That this image of fidelity and tenderness haunts me everywhere; and that I consume myself in longing, and desire, as though kindled by the flame. (SE 11: 13)]

Werther envies this man's ability to express his desire. He foregrounds a man's identification with and desire for a certain kind of male desire and for a discourse of desire. And finally, he is charmed by the *man* who can speak so compellingly about his desire — an admission that indicates clearly Werther's desire for the man who can desire so well.

While Werther's affections (as related in Goethe's novel) appear to be largely directed toward Lotte, his desire to desire *like* another man and his desire for a desiring man both evince the possibility of his desire for the desire *of* another man. Indeed, the dominant heterosexual discourse of the novel should not confuse us given the fact that heterosexual norms were socially mandated in eighteenth-century Germany and overt effusions of male-male desire were not tolerated. Moreover, Goethe's own discourses on love during this period are permeated with a mix of homosexual and heterosexual sentiments and insinuations. In a letter to J. C. and Charlotte Kestner, for instance, Goethe couches his description of his own longings for Carl August within a discourse of heterosexual reproduction:

> Der Herzog mit dem ich nun schon an die 9 Monate in der wahrsten und innigsten Seelen Verbindung stehe, hat mich endlich auch an seine Geschäfte gebunden, aus unsrer Liebschaft ist eine Ehe entstanden. (9 July 1776; WA 4.3: 8).

> [The duke, with whom I have stood now for nine months in the truest and innermost spiritual connection, has finally bound me to his affairs as well. From our love a marriage has arisen.]

Should there be any doubt about the male-male desire underlying Goethe's "Werther discourse," he dispels it in a letter to Friedrich Leopold Graf zu Stolberg on 26 October 1775, in which he reveals his love for him and the Werther discourse it invokes:

O Bruder! Nennbaare aber unendliche Gefühle durchwühlen mich — und wie ich dich liebe fühlst du da ich unter alten Linden in dem Augenblick dein Gedencke. Das Erbärmliche liegen am Staube, Friz! und das Winden der Würmer ich schwöre dir bei meinem Herzen! Wenn das nicht Kindergelall und Gerassel ist der Werther und all das Gezeug! (WA 4.2: 203)

[O Brother! Expressible but infinite feelings burrow through me and how much I love you, you feel in that I think of you under the old lindens in this moment. Pitiful lying in the dust! and the twisting of worms, I swear to you by my heart! If that isn't the childlike babbling and rattling of Werther and all that stuff.]

Goethe's love for Stolberg bubbles out in the form of a Werther discourse — that is, in an effusive language of sentiment that Goethe relates to the kind of writing Werther constructs in his letters. The donning of a Werther costume and the miming of Werther's speech entail a further overt iteration of Werther's (read Goethe's) desire for another man's desire. Goethe's letter to Stolberg reveals as well that he was not reluctant to express his affections for other men in his letters or to hint at the connection between Werther discourse and his same-sex sentiments.[6] He employs his Werther discourse and costuming in order to encode his desire for men.

In this context, Friedenthal's intimation that Weimar boys began to speak the language of *Götz von Berlichingen* (1773) takes on new meaning since this play provides yet another early paradigm of male-male desire and identification (216). It is not at all surprising that Weimar youth masquerading as Werther also appropriated the speech of Götz, for the knight's language and performance is one of homosocial and male-male bonding. In the play, the boy Georg, who idolizes Götz, is driven to mimic him. In fact, Georg first arrives onstage bearing armor and ready to accompany Götz into the next male fray. He admits to Götz how he donned another knight's armor, borrowed his father's sword, and practiced hours of fictional battles. Georg's initiation into the homosocial order of knights commences with a masquerade of men — his emulation of his father, the other knight, and Götz. Like Georg, the monk, Martin, is also enamored of Götz's knightly trappings. And just as the boy desires to be like the knight he adores, Martin wants to be Götz as well. As he gazes admiringly at Götz he exclaims: "Wollte Gott meine Schultern fühlten sich Kraft den Harnisch zu ertragen, und mein Arm die Stärke, einen Feind vom Pferd zu stechen" [Would to God my shoulders could feel the power to bear armor and my arm the strength to strike my enemy from his horse; MA 1.1: 554/SE 7: 6]. Ultimately, Martin discloses his love for Götz's armor and for Götz himself (MA 1.1: 555). The play portrays how young boys and men masquerade as knights and adore knighthood resulting not only in their *identification* with men, but also in their *desire* for men. The language which these men speak, the theatricality they engage in, incites a language of male-male desire. Indeed, Götz's love of Weislingen comes to the fore when he speaks of the times when they "noch beisammen schliefen und miteinander herumzogen" [still slept and wandered around together; MA 1.1: 564/SE 7: 14] and when he reminds Weislingen of his more than brotherly status:

> Freilich, wenn ich wieder so bedenke, wie wir Liebs und Leids zusammen trugen, einander alles waren, und wie ich damals wähnte, so sollt's unser ganzes Leben sein! War das nicht all mein Trost, wie mir diese Hand weggeschossen ward [...] und du mein pflegtest, und mehr als Bruder für mich sorgtest? Ich hoffte, Adelbert wird künftig meine rechte Hand sein. (MA 1.1: 565)

> [True, now that I think about it, how we bore everything together, both love and loss, were everything to each other, and how I supposed it would be so our whole life long. Was that not my only comfort when this hand was shot away (...) and you attended me, showed more care than a brother. I hoped that Adelbert would be my right hand in the future. (SE 7: 11)]

Speaking the language of *Götz von Berlichingen* would necessarily entail invoking codes of homosocial bonding and male-male desire (see Krimmer in this volume).

The elite young men of Weimar blurred the boundaries between life and literature, between individual identity and literary subjectivity in establishing both discourses and performances of male-male desire. Not only did they mimic the costuming and discourses of Werther and Götz, they also acted out the roles of Crugantino and Basko (from Goethe's *Claudine von Villa Bella*, 1775) during a trip to the Weimar countryside. There they swapped clothes and masqueraded as lower class ruffians:

> Nach Tisch rammelten sich Crugantino und Basko, nachdem wir vorher unsre Imagination spazieren geritten hatten wies seyn möchte wenn wir Spitzbuben und Vagabunden wären, und um das natürlich vorzustellen, die Kleider gewechselt hatten. Kraus war auch gekommen und sah in Bertuchs weissen Tressenrocke und einer alten Perroucke des Wildmeisters

wie ein verdorbener Landschreiber, Einsiedel in meinem Frack mit blauen Krägelgen wie ein verspielt Bürschgen, und ich in Kalbs blauem Rock mit gelben Knöpfen, rothem Kragen und vertrotteltem Kreuz und Schnurrbart wie ein Capital-Spitzbube aus. (Goethe to Carl August, 25 December 1775, WA 4.3: 12)

[After the meal Crugantino and Basko scuffled with each other after we had previously imagined, how it would be if we were rogues and vagabonds, and had, in order to portray that naturally, changed clothes. Kraus had also come and looked like a depraved clerk in Bertuch's white, braided (military) coat and the gamekeeper's old wig, Einsiedel looked like a frolicsome rascal in my coat with a little blue collar, and I looked like a first-rate rogue in Kalb's blue coat with a red collar and tassled back and moustache.]

Goethe's letter about the cross-dressing activities of Carl August's friends in Weimar is stunning in its elaborate description of the clothing the men wore, their exchange of clothes, the cross-classing and identifying it stages, and the bawdy behavior it recounts. Moreover, several terms Goethe deploys in his description evoke intriguing sexual innuendoes. According to Grimm's *Deutsches Wörterbuch*, "sich rammeln" stems from the vocabulary of hunters and from the Middle Ages onward refers principally to the rutting of animals: "zufrühest ist das Wort [rammeln] aus viehzüchter- und jägerkreisen, wo es die begattung von thieren bezeichnet" [in its earliest meaning the word comes from animal breeders' and hunters' circles and signifies the copulation of animals; DW 8: 77]. A more secondary meaning alludes to having sex with questionable women, especially whores. Finally, it denotes the less common meaning of scuffling or tussling with someone in a jocular manner (DW 8: 78). Each of these meanings is invoked by Goethe's letter. Moreover, the tassled waist of Kalb's coat, his "Kreuz," also evokes critical anatomical associations. "Kreuz" is the German term for the small of the back and a euphemism for the anus (DW 5: 2185).[7] Even if Goethe merely meant to insinuate that he and his friends were simply tramping around in each others clothes, his letter evokes sexual intimations associated with cross-dressing, cross-classing, and homosexual activity. In this passage we see the sexual proclivities of the Weimar boys converging with and emerging within the activity of cross-dressing.

In each case cited so far, cross-dressing and cross-identifying by young men in eighteenth-century Weimar was associated with men desiring men. It is also striking that Goethe's literary works provided at least some of the material across which, through which, and around which young men alluded to their desire for other men and their identification with fictional male, homosexual subjectivities. The male-oriented men of Weimar appear to have been establishing their identities at least in part through the re-enactment or performance of the fictional characters of Goethe's literary works — anchoring their evocation of male-male desire in the imaginary subjectivities of Crugantino, Basko, Götz, and Werther.

Goethe's male literary heroes were integrated into a nascent discourse and performance of male-male desire in Weimar. Clearly, Goethe and his literary works reflected something significant about the attraction between men in Weimar. Werther, Crugantino, Basko, and Götz provided sexual models. By parading as these Goethean figures the men in Weimar *fictionalized* their own desire, gave fiction a reality, and wove reality, literature, and performance together into a powerful paradigm of male-male desire. In this manner, fiction appears to have become a unique medium for expressing certain sexual realities and simultaneously for undoing the fiction of normative heterosexuality. Subsequently, the reality of male-male desire finds an avenue of expression through fictional performances or performances of fictions. While I do not want to claim that fiction simply reflects reality here or vice versa, the Weimar focus on literary models of male-male desire suggests at the very least that Goethe's admirers were reading his works for potential images and codes of that "scandalous" desire. And they were finding them, indicating that Goethe's treatments of cross-dressing and male-male desire in his literary works might provide additional key information about the coding of male-male desire in Weimar.

I would like to turn to Goethe's *Wilhelm Meisters Lehrjahre,* for it is there that we find his most overt and complicated literary treatment of cross-dressing and male-male desire. Wilhelm, the main character, is obsessed with clothing and dressing up. He glorifies the life of the actor and specifically the "Kleider, Rüstungen und Waffen" [costumes, suits of armor, and weapons; MA 5: 58; bk. 1, ch. 15/SE 9: 31] various characters get to don. Much attention is devoted to the clothing worn by the women Wilhelm falls in love with, to Mignon's dressing up as a boy (MA 5: 205), to Wilhelm's Hamlet costume (MA 5: 321), to his masquerade as the count (MA 5: 188–89), and to the attire of numerous cross-dressed women. The baroness, for example, loves to disguise herself "und kam, um die Gesellschaft zu überraschen, bald als Bauernmädchen, bald als Page, bald als Jägerbursche zum Vorschein" [and was always appearing, in order to surprise everybody, as a peasant girl, or a page boy, or a huntsman; MA 5: 186; bk. 3, ch. 10/SE 9:

110]. Wilhelm, on the other hand, fetishizes Mariane's male attire (see also MacLeod 397):

> Wie oft ist mirs geschehen, daß ich abwesend von ihr, in Gedanken an sie verloren, ein Buch, ein Kleid oder sonst etwas berührte, und glaubte ihre Hand zu fühlen, so ganz war ich mit ihrer Gegenwart umkleidet. (MA 5: 72; bk. 1, ch. 17).
>
> [How often has it happened that, being away from her, or lost in thoughts of her, I touched a book or some garment, and thought it was her hand I felt, so absorbed was I in her presence. (SE 9: 39)]

From the clothing of others, Wilhelm turns his attention to his own clothing: "Er fing nun an über seine Kleidung nachzudenken" [He began to think about his clothes; MA 5: 208; bk. 4, ch. 2/SE 9: 123]. In fact, costuming is so important in *Wilhelm Meisters Lehrjahre* that when Felix and Mignon barely escape death by fire, Wilhelm struggles to keep his attention on them and "nicht an die Kleider und was er sonst verloren haben konnte" [not on the clothes and what he might have lost; MA 5: 332; bk. 5, ch. 13/SE 9: 201].

Dressing up is an obsession that Wilhelm traces back to his youth and his early love of theater. He and his friends were constantly disguising themselves as hunters, soldiers and knights:

> Einen Teil meiner jungen Gesellen sah ich nun wohlgerüstet, die übrigen wurden nach und nach, doch geringer, ausstaffiert, und es kam ein stattliches Korps zusammen. Wir marschierten in Höfen und Gärten, schlugen uns brav auf die Schilde und auf die Köpfe; es gab manche Mißhelligkeit, die aber bald beigelegt war. (MA 5: 26; bk. 1, ch. 7)
>
> [Some of my young comrades were now well armed, the rest were gradually, though not quite so elaborately, equipped, and soon we were a respectable army. We marched into courtyards and gardens, knocking against each other's shields and heads. (SE 9: 11)]

As in *Götz von Berlichingen*, Goethe describes here the early socialization and bonding of boys masquerading as knights. It is this sport, according to Wilhelm, that is inextricably conjoined to his reading of early novels and his keen interest in "Ritterideen" [notions of knighthood]. Knights, knighthood, and knightly escapades function as ciphers for male-male bonding and are models emulated by boys who grow up to desire men. Historical, literary, and dramatic men provide the heroic templates for the social and sexual development of male-desiring men.

In Wilhelm's case, Torquato Tasso's *Jerusalem Delivered* becomes his most favored work and one whose scenes he repeats constantly to himself. In particular, Wilhelm stresses the importance of the literary models Tasso's poem presents to him: "Ich wollte Tancreden und Reinalden spielen, und fand dazu zwei Rüstungen ganz bereit, die ich schon gefertigt hatte" [I wanted to play both Tancred and Rinaldo, and found two suits of armor that I had made which were quite suitable for these characters; MA 5: 27; bk. 1, ch. 7/SE 9: 12]. Wilhelm desires to be like the greatest of knights. He adopts them as soldierly models and plays them in a theater of his own making. Goethe reveals here the importance of literary paradigms for male bonding and the development of male-desiring subjectivities. Tasso's Tancred and Rinaldo serve as Wilhelm's male models in the way that Werther, Götz, Crugantino, and Basko did for the young Weimar elite. Crossing as literary figures allows these men (including the fictional man, Wilhelm) to establish a stable sense of their own male subjectivity and desire for other men.

But beyond male masquerade, Wilhelm's fascination with Tasso's *Jerusalem Delivered* also reveals a homosexual subtext of male bonding and cross-dressing which parallels that of the cross-dressing Weimar elite. Playing hunters, soldiers, and knights is conjoined in Wilhelm's memory with his love of Tasso's poem. Specifically, he reveals that he was enamoured above all by the description in *Jerusalem Delivered* of Clorinda:

> Besonders fesselte mich Chlorinde mit ihrem ganzen Tun und Lassen. Die Mannweiblichkeit, die ruhige Fülle ihres Daseins, taten mehr Wirkung auf den Geist, der sich zu entwickeln anfing, als die gemachten Reize Armidens, ob ich gleich ihren Garten nicht verachtete. (MA 5: 26–27; bk. 1, ch. 7)
>
> [Especially Clorinda, in all that she did, fascinated me. Her masculinity-femininity, the serenefulness of her being had a stronger effect on my developing mind than the artificial charms of Armida, however much I was captivated by her "Bower of Bliss." (SE 9: 11)[8]]

With his young developing mind, Wilhelm is most affected by the masculine-femininity of Clorinda and rejects the "Bower of Bliss" with all its sexual innuendoes offered by the thoroughly feminine Armida. Clorinda, in contrast, is depicted as particularly seductive because of her "Mannweiblichkeit." She evinces a masculinity which Wilhelm finds compelling. It is true that Goethe evokes for us a sense of oscillation between subjective masculinity and femininity in describing Clorinda in terms of "Mannweiblichkeit" (MacLeod 398). However, given the context of masquerading and cross-identifying that Wilhelm associates with Clorinda, I would suggest that the term actually functions within this text to concomitantly mask and reveal the male-male desire Clorinda encodes.

Furthermore we must keep in mind that Tasso's Clorinda is portrayed in *Jerusalem Delivered* as a woman who has "altogether disprized the feminine nature and its usages" (Canto Two, # 39). Clorinda is, indeed, the knightly man Wilhelm aspires to be:

> While yet immature with childish hand she tightened and loosened the bit of a warhorse; she managed spear and sword, and in the palestra hardened her limbs and trained them to the race course. Through mountain path or forest thereafter she followed the tracks of the fierce lion and bear; she followed the wars. (Canto Two, #40)

Just like Tancred and Rinaldo, Clorinda carves her victories on the bodies of the men who oppose her in war:

> Not far off is Clorinda [...]. She thrusts her sword into Berlingher's breast to the heart's core where life is lodged; and that stroke made so full a journey to find it that bloodily it issued from his back. Then she wounds Albin where first our nourishment is taken, and cleaves his face for Gallus. (Canto Nine, #68)

Wilhelm's fascination with Clorinda underscores his desire for knightly valor and for the hyper-masculinity such warriors represent. Clorinda is, indeed, characterized by Arsetes as having relinquished all femininity and womanliness: "You grew, and daring and valorous in arms you overcame your sex, and very nature" (Canto Twelve, #38). Wilhelm is enamoured of a "woman" who has completely overcome her sex, that is, a "woman" who figures as a "man." Here, as in *Werther* and in Goethe's letter to Carl August, a discourse of presumed heterosexual love reveals a subtext of male-male desire.

Conversely, Armida is the totally feminine woman Wilhelm passes over. She deploys "every feminine art" (Canto Four, #25). Her enchanting ways capture Rinaldo, who loses himself in the "mirrors of her limpid eyes" (Canto Sixteen, #20) and can only be saved from his plight by two fierce knights who force him to gaze upon himself in a shining shield,

> in which is mirrored for him what manner of man he is become, and how much adorned with delicate elegance: he breathes forth all perfumed, his hair and mantle wanton; and his sword, he sees his sword, (not to speak of other things)

> made effeminate at his side by too much luxury; it is so trimmed that it seems a useless ornament, not the fierce instrument of war. (Canto Sixteen, #30)

In both instances the women function in Tasso's poem as objects of desire and mirrors of subjectivity (they determine what kind of men the men become). In each case, objects of desire and identification collapse into one. Wilhelm desires Clorinda and wants to be like her. She represents the desired male self. Armida represents the female object of desire and threatens the hyper-masculine Rinaldo with effeminacy for he sees himself in his female object of desire. The secret of the cipher "Clorinda" is that *she* is really a *he*. Wilhelm's fascination with Clorinda, the fact that he chooses her, clearly foregrounds his desire for and identification with other men.

Goethe accentuates in these passages the significant influence that masquerading literary male models have on the developing male subject and male-male desire. The parallels with the experiences of Goethe and his Weimar friends are quite intriguing. Wilhelm's account of his own subjective development provides a literary "key" to the function of cross-dressing in eighteenth-century Weimar. Not only does Wilhelm reiterate the connection between masquerading as male, literary heroes and the emergence of male-male desire, the novel itself points out how homosexual codes can underlie and emerge in a text that seems to be exclusively concerned with normative heterosexuality.

In this context Wilhelm's fetishization of clothing in *Apprenticeship* takes on new significance. While he does not cross-dress himself, he is attracted almost exclusively to cross-dressing women. Wilhelm is less fascinated by the women themselves than by their masculine costuming. Mariane is a case in point. She is described from the very beginning of the novel as "das weibliche Offizierchen" [the young (female) officer; MA 5: 9; bk. 1, ch. 1/SE 9: 1]. As in the case of Clorinda, it is the masculinity that Mariane evokes which stimulates Wilhelm's desire. Indeed, in his first encounter with her he embraces not *her*, but her soldierly *uniform*:

> Wilhelm trat herein. Mit welcher Lebhaftigkeit flog sie ihm entgegen! mit welchem Entzücken umschlang er die rote Uniform! drückte das weiße Atlaswestchen an seine Brust! (MA 5: 11; bk. 1, ch. 1)
>
> [Wilhelm entered the room. How eagerly she rushed towards him! And how passionately he embraced that red uniform and white satin vest. (SE 9: 2; see also MacLeod).]

Wilhelm does not celebrate Mariane's sexual ambiguity here, but her uniform — that which makes her a soldier — that which codes her as male and desired. He does not bask in sexual ambivalence and confusion when he takes Mariane's uniform into his arms, but in the hyper-masculinity which he longs for and with which he hopes to identify (compare MacLeod 397). Like Clorinda, Mariane symbolizes an underlying male object of sexual desire and identification cloaked beneath a discourse of heterosexual attraction.

The same cross-dressing trope is repeated when Wilhelm first meets the woman he refers to as "the beautiful Amazon." She also signifies the male object that Wilhelm desires and his attention is fixed on her masculine dress. "Er glaubte nie etwas edleres noch liebenswürdigeres gesehen zu haben. Ein weiter Mannsüberrock verbarg ihm ihre Gestalt" [He thought he had never seen anything more beautiful or noble. Her figure was concealed beneath a man's loose overcoat; MA 5: 224; bk. 4, ch. 6/SE 9: 134]. While Wilhelm ostensibly desires the beautiful Amazon, his attention is turned almost exclusively to her coat. He notes that her form is concealed from him, leaving only the man's coat as an object for his desire. In fact, when the beautiful Amazon offers him her coat, Wilhelm is thoroughly taken aback, he was "nun, als der Überrock fiel, von ihrer schönen Gestalt überrascht" [was now, once the greatcoat was off, amazed at the beauty of her figure; MA 5: 226; bk. 4, ch. 6/SE 9: 135]. This moment of charged heterosexual attraction dissipates quickly as Wilhelm focuses on the man's coat and he loses his power of speech:

> Sie trat näher herzu, und legte den Rock sanft über ihn hin. In diesem Augenblicke, da er den Mund öffnen und einige Worte des Dankes stammeln wollte, wirkte der lebhafte Eindruck ihrer Gegenwart so sonderbar auf seine schon angegriffenen Sinne, daß es ihm auf einmal vorkam, als sei ihr Haupt mit Strahlen umgeben, und über ihr ganzes Bild verbreitete sich nach und nach ein glänzendes Licht [...]. Die Heilige verschwand vor den Augen des Hinsinkenden. (MA 5: 226; bk. 4, ch. 6)

> [She came up and gently put the coat over him. When he opened his mouth to murmur some words of thanks, the vivid impression of her presence had the strangest effect on his impaired senses. Her head seemed to be surrounded by shafts of light and there was a glow spreading across her whole appearance (...). So the saint disappeared from his fainting sight. (SE 9: 135)]

While this passage might appear to underscore Wilhelm's desire for a beautiful woman, it must also be read within the context of its multiple allusions to codes of male-male desire. First of all, Wilhelm only refers here to the effect on him of the beautiful Amazon's *presence* — he does not specifically suggest that it is her femininity or female body which attracts him. Second, he is clearly drawn to her "man's coat." His sense of his own masculinity, his sensual stimulation and comfort is intricately conjoined to the masculine dress she proffers him:

> Dieser lag, in seinen warmen Überrock [given him by her] gehüllt, ruhig auf der Bahre. Eine elektrische Wärme schien aus der feinen Wolle in seinen Körper überzugehen; genug er fühlte sich in die behaglichste Empfindung versetzt. (MA 5: 226; bk. 4, ch. 7)

> [He lay quiet on his bier, wrapped in the warm overcoat. Electric warmth seemed to be penetrating his body from the fine wool, and he felt transported into a state of extreme comfort. (SE 9: 135)]

Moreover, as in his childhood Wilhelm becomes obsessed with the clothing of the male object he desires and with his desire to wear it himself:

> Mit der größten Sorgfalt für dieses Gewand war das lebhafteste Verlangen verbunden, sich damit zu bekleiden. Sobald er aufstand, warf er es über, und sorgte den ganzen Tag, es möchte durch einen Flecken, oder auf sonst eine Weise beschädigt werden. (MA 5: 233; bk. 4, ch. 9)

> [The care he took of this garment he combined with a passionate desire to wear it; and whenever he got up from his bed, he hung it over his shoulder, fearing all day that he might get a spot on it, or in some way damage it. (SE 9: 139)]

It is the coat which assures Wilhelm that the vision of male desire really did appear before him:

> Oft kam ihm die Geschichte wie ein Traum vor, und er würde sie für ein Märchen gehalten haben, wenn nicht das Kleid zurück geblieben wäre, das ihm die Gewißheit der Erscheinung versicherte. (MA 5: 233; bk. 4, ch. 9)

> [At times the whole incident seemed a dream, and he would have considered it a fantasy if the coat were not still there to assure him of the reality of the apparition. (SE 9: 139)]

The man's coat left to Wilhelm attests to the fleeting appearance of a space for male-male desire.

Finally, Wilhelm connects the vision of the manly dressed Amazon incontrovertibly to his childhood memories of male bonding and the cross-dressing codes of male-male desire. And as in his youth, Wilhelm is engaged in a constant reiteration of the sexually charged moments he perceives in these events and codes:

> Unaufhörlich rief er sich jene Begebenheit zurück, welche einen unauslöschlichen Eindruck auf sein Gemüt gemacht hatte. Er sah die schöne Amazone reitend aus den Büschen hervorkommen, sie näherte ihm [...]. Er sah das umhüllende Kleid von ihren Schultern fallen; ihr Gesicht, ihre Gestalt glänzend verschwinden. Alle seine Jugendträume knüpften sich an dieses Bild. Er glaubte nunmehr die edle heldenmütige Chlorinde mit eignen Augen gesehen zu haben. (MA 5: 233; bk. 4, ch. 9)

> [Time and again he recalled the incident which had left such an indelible impression on his mind. He saw the lovely Amazon riding out of the bushes, saw her coming towards him (...). He saw the coat falling from her shoulders, her face and figure disappearing in a blaze of light. All his youthful visions returned to his mind and associated themselves with this image. He now thought he had seen the heroic Clorinda with his own eyes. (SE 9: 139)]

As opposed to his earlier account in which the Amazon's form appears to Wilhelm as she relinquishes the man's coat to him, here Wilhelm remarks that her form and her face disappear as he obtains the coat. All that remains for Wilhelm is the cloak of his desire and the fantasy of the heroic "man," Clorinda. The fact that the female form disappears in Wilhelm's imagined reiteration of the encounter with Clorinda underscores "her" signification of the knightly, soldierly object of desire which fascinates him. Wilhelm rediscovers the male object of his desire in the fantasy of the beautiful Amazon — in his "own" Clorinda — in the code of manly dress. Wilhelm grasps the male-male code of desire evinced in the masquerading of his childhood and in his encounter with the beautiful Amazon and repeats the pleasurable scene ad infinitum in his imagination. Indeed, these are the codes that operated for the young Weimar elite masquerading as Werther, Götz, Crugantino, and Basko.

Of course, Wilhelm eventually marries his beautiful Amazon. The story runs its expected heterosexual course. And while it is true that the more overt discourse on heterosexuality dominates the novel, it is also true that sites of male-male desire assert themselves throughout the novel. Given the manner in which Goethe describes how Wilhelm's childhood sexual experiences and feelings meld with his contemporary ones throughout the novel, it is clear that he is not indicating a structure of sexual development that begins with a homosexual or polymorphously perverse phase that is later replaced by "normal" heterosexual longings (see MacLeod and Tobin). Rather he is demonstrating how the primal same-sex desires experienced early in childhood by a man like Wilhelm persist into adulthood and are the present and driving forces underlying his sexual experiences as an adult. Moreover, male-male desire, although suppressed by a dominant social injunction to heterosexuality, seems to find at least one form of expression between the heterosexual lines (so to speak) of various literary productions by Goethe. And finally, what we perceive in *Wilhelm Meisters Lehrjahre* is more evidence of the deployment of fiction in Weimar in the encoding and suggestive performances of male-male desire.

In eighteenth-century Weimar the beginnings of a discursive coding of male-male desire was forming. Goethe's literary and epistolary representations of specific cross-dressings provide us with at least one indicator of the struggle to encode the longing of men for men in spite of the suffocating discourse of heterosexual normativity. As Garber suggests, Goethe and his literary works serve to establish categories of crisis or spaces of signification, in fact, within the dominant discourse of heterosexuality that allow for the emergence, expression and performance of male-male desire. We have seen how the young, male Weimar elite appropriated Goethe's literary figures for their own performances and codings of their sexual inclinations. By concentrating on the trope of cross-dressing and masquerade, I have been able to trace some of the "queer" spaces — both discursive and performative — manifest in Weimar culture of the eighteenth century. I suspect as we learn more about the beginnings of same-sex codings in the eighteenth century, in Germany, and in Weimar in particular, that we will find ever more evidence of these kinds of discursive struggles. Moreover, the codes of male-male attraction formed in Weimar and especially their pervasiveness in several different cultural performances is most important because it indicates the simultaneous existence of divergent discourses and the persistence of the discourse and performance of male-male love in Weimar, despite the overwhelming social ascendance of normative heterosexuality.

—University of Rochester

Notes

[1] Throughout this essay I try to use the term male-male desire to describe the attraction encoded in the eighteenth and nineteenth centuries in Weimar to avoid anachronistically applying modern terms such as "homosexual" and "gay" or "queer." In a few select cases I have used these terms, if I felt that they captured an essential meaning not expressed by the term "male-male desire" or in accord with their use by other scholars I cite.

[2] Scholars often stress how few cases of conviction for "sodomy" are on record. See, for example, Hull (36) and Derks (10) who mention the conspicuous absence of court records of trials against sodomites in the German states of the eighteenth century. Derks searched in vain for trial records: "Der einzige Strafprozeß von symptomatischem Wert, der um den bedeutenden deutschen Komponisten Johannes Rosenmüller, fällt bereits ins 17. Jahrhundert; ein zweiter Prozeß um den Rechtsanwalt Franz Desgouttes von 1817 ist in der Hauptsache ein Mordprozeß. Ein dritter Fall, der des Berliner Schauspielers Albert Wurm, endete mit einem Freispruch. Weiteres Material war nicht zu finden" [The only trial of symptomatic worth — that of the important German composer Johannes Rosenmüller — occurred in the seventeenth century; a second trial — that of the lawyer Franz Desgouttes in 1817 — was essentially a murder trial. A third case, that of the Berlin actor Albert Wurm, ended in acquittal. Further material could not be found; Derks 10]. Rey (129) recounts that seven sodomites were burned to death in France between 1715 and 1781. Moreover, police records provide evidence of 20,000–40,000 sodomites the police held under surveillance at one time or another between 1725 and 1780. However, penalties were being relaxed and many of the culprits brought in were simply released (Rey 144). An exception to such leniency appears to be Holland where waves of round-ups occurred in 1730 and 1764 (van der Meer 189), resulting in six to eight hundred prosecutions.

[3] Weeks writes similarly about sexual identity (and not specifically cross-dressing) that "sexual meanings and identities are historical constructs. A human identity is not a given in any particular historical situation but is the product of different social interactions, of the play of power, and sometimes of random choices" (108).

[4] The only place Goethe mentions men crossing as women is in his account of the "Römische Carneval" [Roman Carnival, 1789] in the *Italienische Reise*. His analysis of Roman cross-dressing returns almost compulsively to those moments which underscore the male performers' masculinity. Goethe demonstrates how the male actor's costume is subverted by his body and voice which refuse to be masked. Their cross-dressing accentuates their inner masculinity as their deep voices and beards continually betray them. This is im-

portant in the context of this essay, because it suggests the consistency of Goethe's view of the function of cross-dressing, that is, that it allows for a space for male-male desire.

[5] I am taking the position in this essay that eighteenth-century sentimentalism constitutes expressions of male-male desire. Traditionally, scholarship has suppressed the homoeroticism of these letters, insisting that their effusive expressions of love between men indicated a "style" of expression in the eighteenth-century, not homoerotic content. More recent scholarship in gay and lesbian studies and research on the Age of Goethe by feminists and gender theorists have challenged the traditional view of sentimentalism in ways that are parallel to the way I do in this essay. See, for example, the essays by Richter and Pfeiffer in Kuzniar's *Outing Goethe*.

[6] Compare Tobin who argues that the *Briefe aus der Schweiz* (Letters from Switzerland, 1808, consisting of letters from Werther's youth) include a homosexually charged description of Werther's friend Ferdinand's body while he bathes in a lake (104).

[7] Goethe often asserts the equivalence of clothing and bodies — as for instance in his *Briefe aus der Schweiz* — in which he notes: "Ein kleiner Schuh sieht gut aus, und wir rufen: welch ein schöner kleiner Fuß! ein schmaler Schnürleib hat etwas Elegantes, und wir preisen die schöne Taille" [A little shoe looks good and we call out: what a beautiful little foot! a snug corset has something elegant about it, and we praise the beautiful waist; MA 1.19: 218].

[8] Note that I have altered the available translation by translating "Mannweiblichkeit" as "masculinity-femininity" instead of "almost masculine femininity."

Works Cited

Derks, Paul. *Die Schande der heiligen Päderastie: Homosexualität und Öffentlichkeit in der deutschen Literatur, 1750–1850*. Berlin: Verlag Rosa Winkel, 1990.

Friedell, Egon. *Kulturgeschichte der Neuzeit*. Vol. 2. Munich: C. H. Beck, 1928.

Friedenthal, Richard. *Goethe, sein Leben und seine Zeit*. Munich: Piper, 1963.

Garber, Marjorie. *Vested Interests: Cross-Dressing and Cultural Anxiety*. New York: Routledge, 1992.

Gilman, Sander. "Goethe's Touch: Touching, Seeing, and Sexuality." *Inscribing the Other*. Lincoln: U of Nebraska P, 1991. 29–49.

Grimm, Jacob and Wilhelm Grimm. *Deutsches Wörterbuch*. 33 vols. Leipzig: Verlag von S. Hirzel, 1854–1960. (= DW)

Gustafson, Susan E. "Male Desire in Goethe's *Götz von Berlichingen.*" *Outing Goethe and His Age.* Ed. Alice Kuzniar. Stanford: Stanford UP, 1996. 111–24.

Hull, Isabel V. *Sexuality, State and Civil Society in Germany 1700–1815.* Ithaca: Cornell UP, 1996.

Klauß, Jochen. *Alltag im "klassischen" Weimar 1750–1850.* Weimar: Nationale Forschungs- und Gedenkstätte der klassischen deutschen Literatur, 1990.

Kuzniar, Alice, ed. *Outing Goethe and His Age.* Stanford: Stanford UP, 1996.

Ludwig, Emil. *Goethe, Geschichte eines Menschen.* Stuttgart and Berlin: Cotta, 1920.

MacLeod, Catriona. "Pedagogy and Androgyny in *Wilhelm Meisters Lehrjahre.*" *Modern Language Notes* 108.3 (1993): 389–426.

Meer, Theo van der. "Tribades on Trial: Female Same-Sex Offenders in Late Eighteenth-Century Amsterdam." *Forbidden History. The State, Society and the Regulation of Sexuality in Modern Europe.* Ed. John C. Fout. Chicago and London: U of Chicago P, 1992. 189–210.

Pfeiffer, Joachim. "Friendship and Gender: The Aesthetic Construction of Subjectivity in Kleist." *Outing Goethe and His Age.* Ed. Alice Kuzniar. Stanford: Stanford UP, 1996. 215–27.

Pruys, Karl Hugo. *Die Liebkosungen des Tigers. Eine erotische Goethe Biographie.* Berlin: edition q, 1997.

Rey, Michel. "Police and Sodomy in Eighteenth-Century Paris: From Sin to Disorder." *Journal of Homosexuality* 16 (1988): 129–46.

Richter, Simon. "Winckelmann's Progeny: Homosocial Networking in the Eighteenth Century." *Outing Goethe and His Age.* Ed. Alice Kuzniar. Stanford: Stanford UP, 1996. 33–46.

Steakley, James D. "Sodomy in Enlightenment Prussia: From Execution to Suicide." *Male Homosexuality in Renaissance and Enlightenment Europe.* Eds. Kent Gerard and Gert Hekma. New York and London: Harrington Park P, 1988. 163–76.

Tasso, Torquato. *Jerusalem Delivered.* Ed. and trans. Ralph Nash. Detroit: Wayne State UP, 1987.

Tobin, Robert D. "In and Against Nature: Goethe on Homosexuality and Heterotextuality." *Outing Goethe and His Age.* Ed. Alice Kuzniar. Stanford: Stanford UP, 1996. 94–110.

Weeks, Jeffrey. "Inverts, Perverts, and Mary Annes: Male Prostitutes and the Regulation of Homosexuality in England in the Nineteenth and Early Twentieth Centuries." *Journal of Homosexuality* 6 (1980–81): 113–34.

WOMEN IN WEIMAR

7

ELISABETH KRIMMER

Sartorial Transgressions:
Re-Dressing Class and Gender Hierarchies in
Masquerades and Travesties

Some Preliminary Contradictions

THE IDEA OF HAVING TO COMBINE Cultural Studies and Goethe's Weimar is enough to make a scholar's hair stand on end, no matter whether that scholar be an aficionado of Cultural Studies or of Goethe. For everything Cultural Studies stands for seems to be blatantly contradicted by everything eighteenth-century Weimar has come to symbolize. If Cultural Studies champions the marginalized and oppressed (see During 7; Wallace 122; Johnson 76), Weimar accommodated the elite of the elite. Where Cultural Studies is famous for Raymond Williams's definition of culture as a "whole way of life" that abstains from an artificial separation of literature from other life-practices as well as from the traditional low- versus high-culture differentiation (see During 2; Storey 1), Weimar is synonymous with the autonomy of Culture with a capital C. While Cultural Studies is interested in how categories such as race and gender are socially constructed (see De Lauretis 77; Wallace 126), Weimar Culture was seen as giving expression to a transhistorical essence of something universally valid or "allgemeinmenschlich" [common to all human beings]. How can such obvious contradictions be reconciled? And even more difficult: how can they be reconciled without the complete renunciation of the traditional methods and contents of literary studies?

Cultural Studies defines culture as a site of "continual struggle over meaning, in which subordinate groups attempt to resist the imposition of meanings which bear the interests of dominant groups" (Storey 3;

see Johnson). On the one hand, this means that wherever there is hegemony, there also is resistance (see During; Hall). On the other hand, it means that the hegemonic system itself is not a unified and consistent whole, but consists of multiple, ever shifting, and sometimes even internally contradictory forces. In this essay I focus on both the resistance to and inconsistencies within the new ideology that resulted from the renegotiation of traditional class and gender hierarchies in the eighteenth century.

The first part of my essay, the analysis of the masquerades in Weimar, is primarily concerned with the class aspect of these social shifts. It is informed by Gebauer's thesis that the epistemological model that regarded the social position of an individual as a quality of his body — inherited by birth and immutable — was replaced by a new model in which social rank and personal achievement became interdependent. In the old model, clothing, as an outward sign of an innate quality, functioned as a mediating element between the body and the social rank of a person. The masquerade can be interpreted as an intermediary stage between the old and the new model. For the wearing of a costume temporarily eliminated dress as social marker and thus disassociated body and social rank. Thus, the masked ball created an artificial space where social equality could be practiced. But, as the analysis will show, the assimilation of nobility and bourgeoisie that characterized such balls was not only predicated on the careful containment of sartorial transgressions but also on the exclusion of the third estate.

The following reading of cross-dressing both on the Weimar stage and in texts by Weimar authors is concerned with women's position in the social hierarchy. My reading is based on research by Claudia Honegger and Thomas Laqueur. Both scholars assume that the French Revolution and its demands for freedom and equality of all put pressure on the traditional gender hierarchy. But as the social power structure did not change, man's unaccounted mastery over woman needed to be legitimized within this new framework. Eventually, the justification for woman's subordination was provided by an essentialist discourse that linked biology and destiny. By instituting biology as the foundation of the social order, women's inferiority came to be located in her body (see Honegger; Laqueur) and women's physical constitution accounted for their supposed intellectual deficiency (see Becker-Cantarino 247; Bovenschen 138–49; Cocalis "Vormund"; Hausen; Lange, *Weiber* 421). Among the proponents of this model of "Geschlechtscharakter" [gender-specific character] are such well-known writers as Friedrich Schiller (see Bovenschen 220–23), Wilhelm von Humboldt (see *Über den Geschlechtsunterschied und dessen Einfluß auf die organische Natur*

[On the Difference Between the Sexes and Its Impact on Organic Nature, 1795]) and Johann Gottlieb Fichte (see *Grundriß des Familienrechts* [Outline of Family Law, 1796]). But no matter how common this model may have been, there was resistance to it. My analysis of a drama by Charlotte von Stein will demonstrate that the alleged interdependence between sex and gender, that is, between the biological facts and the social implications with which they are linked, did not remain uncontested.

The thread that ties together the discussion of the making of the bourgeois and the creation of the "natural" woman is the focus on the body and its clothing. It is in the discussion of everyday dress codes, carnivalesque costumes, and transvestite outfits, where the runs and rips in the fabric of ideology will become visible.

Dress For Success: Masquerades in Weimar

In the late eighteenth century, visitors to Weimar were usually struck by its smallness and poverty. The city with its roughly 6,000 inhabitants (6,120 in 1785, Eberhardt 4), far off the major trade routes, was characterized by a stark contrast between its squalid streets and its domineering castle. Herder speaks of an "unseliges Mittelding zwischen Hofstadt und Dorf" [unfortunate mixture of residence and village; qtd. in Eberhardt 6] and Madame de Staël flatly declares: "Weimar n'est pas une petite ville, mais un grand chateau" [Weimar is not a little town, but a great castle; qtd. in Kühn, *Weimar* 24]. As laid out in this architectural structure, class distinctions were still very rigid in Weimar during Carl August's reign. Bruford speaks of an "estate society in which class privileges were taken seriously and protected by law as well as by custom" (403). Such privileges manifested themselves in a wide variety of social practices, ranging from the difficulties that Goethe's nomination to the Council caused to the seating plan of the Weimar theater, where middle class and nobility were strictly separated.

Another way to make social distinctions visible was the dress code. As late as 1778 a sumptuary law was decreed by Carl August. It demanded that cotton dresses be stamped by the police before use so as to help distinguish the rank of the wearer (Bruford 61). But while dress and class distinctions were reinforced strictly in public life, artificial spaces were created where such distinctions were consciously confused. One such space which eliminated dress as a social marker, thus allowing for the playful fusion of aristocracy and middle-class, was the masked ball.

Masked balls, or "Redouten," as they were called, took place every week or fortnight in Anton Hauptmann's "Redoutenhaus" which also served as a temporary home for theatrical performances after the old theater in the ducal palace Wilhelmsburg had been destroyed by fire in 1774. Due to the enormous popularity of the balls (between 200 and 400 participants), however, this estate soon proved too small. In 1779, Carl August therefore commissioned Hauptmann with the construction of a new "Redouten- und Komödienhaus," whose inaugural festivities took place on 7 January 1780. Not only the increasing number of balls (up to fifteen per winter) but also their financial profitability attest to the continued fascination with the redoubt. When the new building needed to be altered in 1798, the entire renovation was paid for by income generated by such masked balls. It seems reasonable to attribute at least part of the attractiveness of the masked ball to the fact that it allowed for an unproblematic intermingling of nobility and bourgeoisie (see Barth 110). This fusion could be associated with what Terry Castle defines as the very principle of the masquerade, namely "systematic anarchy" (5). In Weimar, however, the stress needs to be on systematic, rather than on anarchy. In fact, every attempt was made to assure that whatever anarchy there was, it better be a systematic one. And who could have been more apt to systematize anarchy than Goethe? In 1798 on the occasion of the reopening after the renovation, Goethe crafted a "Redoutenordnung" [rules for the redoubts] in which everything — including the order and duration of every kind of dance — was laid down.[1] Most careful attention was devoted to the question of whom to admit and whom to exclude, thereby establishing a strict dichotomy of those on the inside and those on the outside. After all, the word "redoubt" comes from military terminology and originally meant casemate, that is, the small opening in the wall of a fortress or battleship from where one's position is defended in case of an attack. Thus, in order to prevent intruders from entering the fortress of social privilege, access to the redoubt was strictly controlled. Subscribers to the balls could be asked to unmask before entering in order to assure that the identity of the masked person corresponded to the name on the subscription ticket. But once a person was inside, the revelation of one's true identity was taboo: unmasking in the ballroom was strictly prohibited. In fact, the Weimar native Karl Lyncker mentions in his memoirs that the greatest pleasure at the masquerades consisted in the attempt to keep up one's anonymity as long as possible (Lyncker 27).

But while this deliberate effort to prevent social identification by removing sartorial markers certainly demonstrates the eagerness of both the nobility and the bourgeoisie to find a space where they could communicate without facing the usual restrictions and sanctions, the impact of the redoubts on Weimar's daily life remains questionable. The crucial question of social anthropology, that is, the question whether "symbolic rituals of disorder function within a culture as safety valves that reaffirm the status quo by exorcising social tensions, or are subversive events that explicitly threaten the prevailing order" (Castle 88) remains unanswered. In unveiling the theatricality of social identity, masquerades demonstrate that social status is not anchored in qualities inherent in and inseparable from the body (as was characteristic of earlier models of domination; see Gebauer). Clothes make the man, to speak with Gottfried Keller, not the other way around. But one must concede that the effects of such knowledge of the arbitrariness of signs on everyday social interaction can only be surmised. Furthermore, the newly achieved community of nobility and bourgeoisie was predicated on the exclusion of the third estate. Goethe emphasized that subscription tickets were valid for family members only; the servants and subordinates of subscribers were not to be admitted. Not surprisingly, the bourgeois author of the "rules for the redoubts" defended the rights of his own class by denying those of another. Even the maid who delivered a letter had to deposit her package at the entrance. The few servants who were admitted for the greater convenience of the guests were not allowed to wear masks. Where Goethe did allow the wearing of masks, as for the musicians, he also determined the precise nature of the costume, in this instance that of slaves (see Satori-Neumann 54).

While the exclusion of the third estate obviously served the purpose of facilitating the coming together of nobility and bourgeoisie, it also had an almost uncanny side-effect. For in addition to lavish, exotic costumes, the preferred masks at such balls were the clothes of the common people. However, the fact that Carl August and Goethe dressed as peasants (see Kühn, *Weimar* 87) while others came as chimney-sweeps and the like (see Lyncker 27), is less a return of the repressed than a retreat to a neutral ground that releases the participants from openly defying the social order by having a bourgeois wear the clothes of a nobleman or vice versa. The alternative to such a union on neutral ground, that still allowed for an individual choice of costume, was the carnival procession, a much more work-intensive enterprise. While donning the clothes of peasants almost automatically guarantees that all transgression remains contained within its strictly demarcated limits (that is, that the costume of a bourgeois not pertain to a social rank above that of one of the noblemen present), the carnival procession needed to be carefully orchestrated. And again, Goethe was entrusted with such orchestration and made sure that the costumes retained traits of the established social distinctions. When Goethe wore the costume of a medieval knight, Carl August appeared as emperor.

It seems that, even though the transgression implied in the donning of a costume was encouraged by the very institution of the masked ball, it was also understood that this transgression remain limited. Diligent planning of every detail of the ball kept in check the tendency of the costume to lay bare the theatricality of the social order by exposing the arbitrariness of its outward signs. However, the fact that one went to such great pains to control sartorial transgressions suggests that the power of clothes should not be underestimated. Rather, it was the sensitivity to such signs of power and a combined strategy of gradual assimilation and self-censored 'moderate' transgression, as displayed in Goethe's orchestration of the masked ball, that at least partly accounts for the social ascendancy of the bourgeois in the eighteenth century. That the masquerade played an important part in this process is also suggested by the fact that it went out of fashion when social equality became more concrete, as Johann Friedrich Reichardt reports from revolutionary France: "Maskeraden sind itzt in Frankreich verboten. Mein Demokrat sagt: man bedarf itzt des Hofmittels nicht mehr, einmal zum Spaß allgemeine Gleichheit einzuführen" [Masquerades are now prohibited in France. My democrat says that the courtly method of introducing general equality just for fun is no longer necessary; qtd. in Geitner 181].[2]

According to Reichardt, the French Revolution did away with masquerades. Weimar, on the contrary, continued this tradition well into the nineteenth century. Goethe's diary mentions redoubts and preparations for a masked procession as late as 1818. The masquerades were, of course, not the only kind of entertainment available in Weimar. At least equally important was the theater. But whereas the masks at the ball were part of a larger process of restructuring class hierarchies, theatrical costumes served the primary purpose of redefining gender roles.[3]

Transvestite Theater: Witches and Lovely Boys

The theater in Weimar had a long tradition of cross-dressed casting.[4] All female roles were performed by men up to Duke Johann Wilhelm (1554–73). Johannes Veltheim (1640–93) is known as the first principal to engage female actors (Schrickel 14), but cross-gendered performances were still to be found after his time. We know of men who portrayed women and of women who portrayed men. But while the typical material for a male-to-female performance was a wicked and/or old woman, the female-to-male cross-dresser usually played an adolescent boy.

Examples of the first variety are Siegmund von Seckendorf whose portrayal of the wicked landlady Fullmer in Cumberland's *Der Westindier* (The West Indian, translated by Bode) was generally admired (see Lyncker 63), or Johann Joachim Christoph Bode playing the title-role in *Die Gouvernante* (The Governess, adapted by Bode from a play attributed to Nivelle de la Chaussee) on 31 July 1779. Another example that illustrates this model is Friedrich Schiller's adaptation of *Macbeth*, in which the witches were played by men. What are we to make of this practice? The limited scope of character available for such performances seems to indicate that a reading that understands the detachment of a woman's social gender from her biological body as a subversive act is inappropriate here. Rather, the male witch, far from undermining gender stereotypes, functions as a warning signal. Where a character who defies traditional female stereotypes by being neither lovely nor well-meaning jeopardizes her femininity to the point of renouncing her gender altogether, the female spectator learns that she had better hold on to "feminine" virtue and beauty (or youth for that matter).

The dynamic of female-to-male performances was different. Rather than middle-aged men playing old witches, young attractive women played young boys. This was probably due to casting difficulties. For many plays which were popular at the time demanded an almost entirely male cast. Thus, every young female actress portrayed one or the other peasant boy or page in plays such as Goethe's *Großkophta* (Malcolmi as the boy Jäck), Goethe's *Götz von Berlichingen* (Sophie Teller as gypsy boy) or Goethe's *Stella* (Louise Becker as Karl).[5] But although these performances made no lasting impression on the audience, other female-to-male performances were remembered as outstanding. Karoline Jagemann (1777–1848), Weimar's leading actress during Goethe's tenure as director of the Weimar theater, won one of her greatest successes as the male god of elves Oberon in Paul Wranitzky's opera *Oberon* (1797). Jagemann's biographer reports that her Oberon was enthusiastically received by the press wherever she performed (Bamberg 195). Although Jagemann only occasionally starred in breeches roles — other examples are her portrayal of Gustel in *Der Alchimist* and of Sextus in Mozart's *Titus* — Christiane Neumann came to be identified with them. The Weimar actor Eduard Genast writes, "selbst Knabenrollen spielte sie mit einer Vollendung, daß sie ein ganzes Publikum über ihr Geschlecht täuschen konnte" [Even breeches roles she played with such perfection that she could deceive the whole audience about her gender; Genast 49]. She played the role of Jakob in *Alte und neue*

Zeit (Old and New Time), Walter Tell in Friedrich Schiller's *Wilhelm Tell*, a boy in Schiller's *Don Carlos*, the title-role of J. Engel's *Der Edelknabe* (The Noble Boy) on 2 February 1787 as well as prince Arthur in William Shakespeare's *Life and Death of King John* on 20 November 1791. The fascination that her performances aroused is manifest in Goethe's admiration for her. He speaks of the "miraculous impact" of her play (qtd. in Schrickel 90), and Genast reports that, while Goethe made general suggestions when he came to see rehearsals, the only person to receive his special attention was Christiane Neumann (48). It seems to me that Goethe's attraction to the young actress is inseparable from her association with breeches roles. Even the poem "Euphrosyne" (1799), which Goethe wrote after her untimely death, includes a reference to this fact: "Knabe schien ich, ein rührendes Kind, du nanntest mich Arthur" [A boy seemed I, a sweet child, you called me Arthur; MA 4.2: 749]. How then are we to understand this fascination with the male impersonator? For to assume that Goethe derived some form of postmodern pleasure from the fact that the performance of gender on stage uncovered the performative nature of gender itself is unlikely. Given the fact that at the time of these performances, Christiane Neumann was an adolescent girl who is generally described as very slim, it is also unlikely that her breeches could accentuate her "feminine" features, thus accounting for the popularity of her performance. One might therefore speculate whether Goethe's fascination with Christiane Neumann can be found in a dynamic of homosexual desire where the disguise of the actor on stage allows for the disguise of the spectator's desire because "love for — or cathexis onto a boy turns out to be love for or cathexis onto a woman, after all" (Garber 175).[6]

But while all statements concerning an economy of desire must remain speculation, an analysis of the economy of power is more clearcut. Interestingly, all examples of male impersonation are not only portrayals of boys, that is, not yet men, but of boys of lower class status: peasants, gypsies, servants. This restriction of actresses to the portrayal of powerless male adolescents allowed for the containment of an otherwise possible female assumption of male power on stage. For after all, the eighteenth century believed in the theater as an educational tool which could bring about a transformation of its audience, as exemplified in Kant's words:

> denn dadurch daß Menschen diese Rollen spielen, werden zuletzt die Tugenden, deren Schein sie eine geraume Zeit hindurch gekünstelt haben, nach und nach wohl wirklich erweckt, und gehen in die Gesinnung über. (Qtd. in Laermann 150)

[For when people play roles, the virtues, whose semblance they assume for a considerable time, may little by little be aroused in reality, and become part of their way of thinking.]

It seems that this otherwise desirable transformation of appearance into reality was a rather frightening possibility if applied to gender roles. It is therefore not surprising that women who wanted to assume the prerogatives of men could not do so on stage but were relegated to the realm of literary imagination. Thus, it is in a play by Charlotte von Stein, which was not published during her lifetime, that the transvestite boy is replaced by the transvestite man.

Officer and Lady: Charlotte von Stein's *Ein neues Freiheitssystem oder Verschwörungen gegen die Liebe* (A New System of Freedom, or the Conspiracies Against Love, 1798 and 1867)

Charlotte von Stein (1742–1827) can be considered a member of the cultural and social elite of Weimar. The daughter of Duke Konstantin's major-domo von Schardt became a lady-in-waiting at Anna Amalia's court in 1757 and married Duke Carl August's equerry Josias von Stein in 1764. She participated in the activities of the court and entertained a close friendship with Duchess Luise throughout her life. But even though Stein enjoyed the privileges of nobility, she was keenly aware of the discrimination from which women suffered. In her letters she expresses indignation about the fact that, even though many of the "thousands of little daily chores" of women's daily life require more strength of mind than the work of the genius, it is the latter who reaps all honor and reward while women's work counts for nothing.[7] She also draws a connection between women's domestic chores and the lack of women artists. Because few women find the time to write at all, and because, even among men, it takes countless authors to produce a few good ones, only an increase in the number of women writers could result in more female talents.[8] Furthermore, Stein often points out the gender-bias implied in Schiller's and Goethe's works.[9] Her drama *Dido* (1794) has recently been read as a rejection of Goethe's concept of the Eternally Feminine as expressed in *Iphigenie auf Tauris* (Iphigenia in Tauris, 1787; see Bohm 46; Lange, "Episch/Dramatisch" 343–45), or, more radically, as questioning the "humanistic discourse and the social construction of love" (Cocalis, "Acts" 89) as well as the myth of masculinity and femininity in general (Kord, "Image" 59).

Charlotte von Stein's situation was paradoxical in that she was marginalized as a woman and yet privileged as a member of the aristocracy. The reception history of her work adds yet another paradox. Susanne Kord points out that, in spite of numerous biographies and articles about Stein as Goethe's lover, Goethe's friend, Goethe's muse, and so on, practically no information about her work as writer is available (Kord, "Image" 53–55; *Name* 147–50). The focus on Goethe has gone to such extremes that those dramas that cannot be construed as allusions to him were not handed down at all.[10] Thus, Charlotte von Stein's prose comedy *Ein neues Freiheitssystem oder Verschwörungen gegen die Liebe* (A New System of Freedom, or the Conspiracies against Love), which she wrote in 1798, first appeared in print in 1867. It was edited by Stein's great-grandson Freiherr Felix von Stein, who revised the play significantly (see Kord, "Image" 59). Although Felix von Stein's changes are extensive, Charlotte von Stein's witty style is still clearly visible.

The title of the play refers to the extravagant philosophical tenets of Daval, one of the protagonists. Daval, lord of the manor in Buchdorf, devotes his life to waging war on love which, for him, is equivalent to tyranny. He has even prevented the marriage between his friend Avelos and his own sister Menonda by forging letters. When the play begins, Daval has engaged Avelos to kidnap two actresses whom he needs for his private theater in Buchdorf. His friend Avelos, however, kidnaps the wrong ladies: Theodora, niece of a major from Warsaw, and her cousin Menonda, his own lost lover. But Daval's intended victims, the actresses Luitgarde and Florine, are also on their way to Daval's castle. Finally, all are united at the castle, including young sergeant Montrose who came to rescue the ladies, and the stage is set for a happy ending. Menonda and Avelos are reunited, Theodora and Montrose confess their love for each other, and even Daval is teamed up with Luitgarde.

Disguises and intrigues are ever-present in this play. But all intrigues go wrong, and all logical deductions that bring them about are flawed. While the characters Ogon, Dodus, and Aratus in Stein's *Dido* are examples of intellectuals in the service of the wrong cause, *Ein neues Freiheitssystem* demonstrates how eloquent argumentation can prove the most absurd points.[11] The most striking example of reason gone awry is Daval himself. In forcing others to do what he thinks is good for them, he becomes a living refutation of his own professed advocacy of freedom. In fact, Daval's philosophy wreaks havoc wherever it is applied. Even his horse succumbs to his "new philosophical method of riding" (14) and suffers from colic. It seems that in Stein's play the powers of the male mind cannot be trusted. The more educated a man is, and the higher his social position, the more absurd and confused is his reasoning. In contrast, the socially inferior servants in the play are characterized by their firm hold on reality and common sense. Repeatedly, the servant Peter points out to his master Avelos that he has kidnapped the wrong ladies, but Avelos does not listen to him. Conrad, the major's servant, is the only one who knows where the abducted ladies are hidden. And Daval's coachman understands perfectly well why his master's horse is sick. But whenever he, or the others, try to intervene, they fail. This is not the case with their female counterparts. Whenever the maid Susette or the actress Luitgarde try to rectify the situation, they manage. While the socially respected Menonda and Theodora are resigned and accept their fate, the maid Susette and the actress Luitgarde foil the men's scheme (Kord, "Image" 61). Thus, when the young officer Montrose, upon learning about the abduction, threatens to kill the perpetrator, Susette resolves immediately to take action in order to prevent a disaster. She dons Montrose's clothes and gives the real Montrose wrong directions to the castle. Thereupon she goes to the castle herself and claims to be Montrose. With great ease, she succeeds in imitating Montrose's martial behavior and flowery language with his "parrot-like references to Greek mythology" (Kord, "Image" 61). It is no surprise that the uniform suffices to transform her into an officer, as — according to the major — Montrose, himself a feminine youth, relies on the uniform for his manhood.[12] That Susette, the copy, is more convincing than the original from which the copy is taken, is proven when Montrose, who finally found the castle, cannot persuade Daval's servant Friedrich that he truly is himself.[13] Friedrich flatly refuses to let him enter. All that is left to Montrose is to make do with the vacant part, so that he, as the major says, is "zur Kammerjungfer avanciert" [promoted to the position of maid; 29].

Meanwhile, Susette, who — still in her disguise — tries to gain entry to her mistresses' room, is equally not admitted at first because the ladies think that she is really Montrose pretending to be Susette. Susette, however, manages to convince Theodora that she is truly Susette:

> THEODORA: Erst die Parole, daß du Susette bist. — Was für eine Heilige hängt zu Hause über meinem Schreibtische?
> SUSETTE: Das hab' ich rein vergessen. Da sehen Sie doch, daß ich Susette bin, die immer alles vergißt, selbst die Heiligen.
> MENONDA: Der Beweis ist untrüglich. (21)

> [THEODORA: First the password, that you really are Susette. — Which saint hangs above my desk at home?
> SUSETTE: I've completely forgotten. There you see that I am Susette, who forgets everything, even the saints.
> MENONDA: This is unmistakable proof.]

Obviously, the maid Susette changes her role easily. She possesses the greatest flexibility in the game of ever-changing identities. But her superiority is only temporary. The obligatory happy ending that the genre demands enforces the reinstitution of the original order, and Susette must return the uniform. In spite of that, I want to argue that her victory was not a superficial one. For not only did Susette prove that a woman can "ihren Mann stehen" [hold her own], her actions also question the numerous marriages at the end of the play.[14] When Susette returns Montrose's uniform unwillingly, the major comments that women are always crazy about uniforms (29). Suddenly, the common heterosexual interpretation of this statement according to which women always want to marry a man becomes questionable. Actually, it seems more likely that they want the power and privileges connected with being a man.

Furthermore, Susette is not the only one to master the game of uniforms and gender identities. Luitgarde and Florine, who, as actresses, have professionalized the donning of other characters, change clothes and roles several times. They come to Daval's castle in male disguise, as Harlekin and Scapin, and explain their cross-dressing as a necessary precaution for women who travel alone. Daval, however, who for a while lived in an inn next to where they stayed and who heard male voices in their room, has doubts about their virtuousness. But Luitgarde and Florine convince him that there were no lovers but rather that they themselves played the part of lovers. Unlike Daval, the reader is not fooled, having already learned that there were male officers present. Thus, in a remarkable coup, Luitgarde manages to convince Daval of her morality by pretending that she pretended to be an officer. In substituting a supposed performance for an authentic body, she succeeds in eliminating the presence of the real man in her inn. She maintains the appearance of innocence and eventually achieves financial security by marrying Daval, and she does so by convincing him that his philosophy of the tyranny of love is of innermost concern to her, too. Clearly, Daval's philosophy is no match for Luitgarde's wit and performative skills.

In Stein's comedy, mimicry proves to be a superior strategic weapon for women (Kord, "Image" 61). By imitating men, women salvage a situation that was created (and wrecked) by male reasoning which is itself shown to be inherently flawed. Consequently, Susette becomes Montrose in order to prevent the latter from spoiling everything, and Luitgarde pretends to correspond to Daval's ideal in order to get what she wants. The deception succeeds as neither body, nor voice, nor handwriting guarantee authenticity. Montrose's own face looks like that of a girl. Susette's and Luitgarde's voices are thought to be men's voices, and Daval can easily forge the handwriting of his sister. All these examples of cross-dressing and mimicry demonstrate that in Stein's play a person's identity is not a derivative of the body but the result of a complex interplay between individual and society. In insisting that identity, and therefore gender identity, is not established through one's body, but constructed through performance, Stein refuses a model that institutes biology as the foundation of social order. In her play, power is not an innate quality. Rather, power comes from pants. It is therefore appropriate to claim that Stein's comedy undoes the work of ideology which exercises its power by turning "what was in fact political, partial and open to change into something seemingly natural, universal and eternal" (During 6).

But the fascination that Stein's play holds for modern readers is not just based on its de-essentializing quality. It is rather predicated on *how* Stein achieves this. For the fact that mimicry plays such an important role, that is, that women overcome men by imitating them, points to a strategy that Judith Butler has described as "subversive repetition": "a repetition of the law which is not its consolidation but its displacement" (30). In depicting women who parody men, Stein encourages her readers to regard men themselves as parodies of masculinity, thus questioning the concepts of masculinity and femininity themselves. The fact that this is not frightening but entertaining is due to the genre. For the threat that is latent if identity is conceived of as "a normative ideal rather than a descriptive feature of experience" (Butler 16) is defused by the genre of comedy and its seemingly harmonious resolution of a happy ending. Instead of a dreaded loss of self, one encounters the playful cunning of the weak.

Goethe's Ideas

It is interesting to compare Stein's portrayal of cross-dressed characters with Goethe's views on the matter, expressed in his essay "Frauenrollen auf dem römischen Theater von Männern gespielt" (Women's Parts Played by Men in the Roman Theater), published 1788 in the *Teutscher Merkur* (German Mercury, 1773–89).[15] Surprisingly, this text also lays bare the arbitrariness of the body-gender-connection, but while Stein does so intentionally, Goethe achieves the same effect rather against his will.

Goethe's essay was inspired by a visit to the theater in Rome. On 3 January 1788, Goethe saw a performance of Goldoni's *La Locandiera*, given by an exclusively male cast due to the papal ban on women on the stage. Goethe, who himself had produced this play in Weimar in 1777, enjoyed the performance exceedingly. But as the pleasure that he took in it seemed to be somewhat embarrassing to him, he set about explaining its origin. Whereas in Stein's play all cross-dressers are taken for real, the spectator Goethe stresses in his account that he is never deceived but always aware that he is watching cross-dressed men, not women. He goes on to explain that it is precisely this awareness that accounts for the pleasure, in that it reminds the spectator of the self-reflectivity of art. The fact that one sees an imitation of a woman, not a real woman, demonstrates that art itself is concerned with imitation. In watching cross-dressers, one becomes conscious of, not absorbed in, the theatrical illusion. Thus far, Goethe and Marjorie Garber would seem to agree. For Garber also claims that the transvestite contains the essence of theatricality which consists of the substitution of one signifier by another (40). But unlike Garber, of course, Goethe assumes that there is a "thing" to which the sign refers, that is, that art does imitate nature. However, as he himself admits, the term "imitation" is slippery and the relationship between a sign and that to which it refers is complicated. For Goethe art does not just imitate a thing as it is, but it intends to capture its "wahres Wesen" [true essence], and that is why a young male actor can portray a woman much better than a female actor can. As he explains:

> Der Jüngling hat die Eigenheiten des weiblichen Geschlechts in ihrem Wesen und Betragen studiert [...] er spielt nicht sich selbst, sondern eine dritte und eigentlich fremde Natur. Wir lernen diese dadurch nur desto besser kennen, weil sie jemand beobachtet, jemand überdacht hat, und uns nicht die Sache, sondern das Resultat der Sache vorgestellt wird. (Qtd. in Ferris 49)
>
> [The young man has studied the characteristics of the female sex in its essence and bearing (...) he does not portray himself but a third nature actually foreign to him. We come to know this nature even better because someone else has observed it, reflected on it, and presents us not with the thing itself but with the result of the thing. (Trans. Ferris 49)]

Thus, true femininity is best presented by a man. But what is true femininity? In order to form an idea, one must abstract from the empirical object. But abstraction endangers the stable connection between the idea and the object, as Goethe explains in a letter to Sömmerring:

> Die Idee kann mir sehr bequem sein, ich kann andern zeigen, daß sie es Ihnen auch sein werde: aber es läßt sich nach meiner Vorstellung nur sehr schwer, und vielleicht gar nicht beweisen, daß sie wirklich mit den Objekten übereinkommen und mit ihnen zusammentreffen müsse. (GA 19: 244–45)
>
> [The idea can be very handy for me, I can demonstrate to others that it will be handy for them as well: but it is, in my opinion, only with great difficulties, or maybe not at all, possible to prove that it really corresponds to objects and necessarily converges with them.]

In short, according to Goethe's logic, one can represent "true femininity," but whether true femininity has anything to do with women, one does not know. And while the idea of "true femininity" presupposes the existence of a body-gender connection, the fact that femininity can be severed from the body of woman contradicts it. Thus, the idea of the Eternally Feminine is revealed as a normative ideal rather than a natural entity. And so Goethe himself admits in a conversation with Eckermann:

> Meine Idee von den Frauen ist nicht von den Erscheinungen der Wirklichkeit abstrahiert, sondern sie ist mir angeboren, oder in mir entstanden, Gott weiß wie! Meine dargestellten Frauencharaktere sind daher auch alle gut wegkommen; sie sind alle besser, als sie in der Wirklichkeit anzutreffen sind. (22 October 1822; qtd. in Kühn, *Frauen* 213)
>
> [My idea of women is not abstracted from the appearances of reality but is rather innate, or it developed within me God knows how! My female characters therefore all come off well; they are all better than one would find them in reality.]

It is against this background that we must understand Goethe's remark to Charlotte von Stein, "ein Weib soll ihre Weiblichkeit nicht ausziehen wollen" [a woman should not want to shed her femininity; letter to Stein, 21 September 1785, GA 18: 874]. And keeping this in mind, it makes sense to read Goethe's own works as an attempt to prevent women from wanting to strip themselves of their femininity.[16] But the fact that the imperative of "nicht wollen sollen" [you should not want to] had to stand in wherever female stereotypes could not be sustained "naturally" shows that the closely woven fabric of biology and gender — in spite of its success — also had its rips and tears. The continual effort to mend these rips and tears forms an integral part of the cultural products that we associate with Weimar Classicism.

Conclusion

The social practices of the masked ball, the theater, and literature are an integral part of the discourse on power and the meaning of the body. Clothing functions as a mediating element between the two. Even though this discourse affected the definition of both class and gender hierarchies, the implications for these categories are diametrically opposed. The Weimar masquerade achieved an assimilation of nobility and bourgeoisie through the elimination of nobility and bourgeoisie by means of the, at least partial, elimination of the social legibility of clothing. The Weimar theater, on the contrary, whose use of cross-dressing seems destined to question a stable definition of gender, did not undo gender stereotypes, but rather reinforced them by means of its casting decisions. It was left to Charlotte von Stein to challenge the model that legitimizes women's social discrimination with a reference to the body. But due to her own precarious position as a woman writer, Stein's text was largely ignored by her contemporaries as well as by literary scholars. Rediscovering her text, however, does not only add one more new voice to the already established ones, it also alters our understanding of already familiar texts. Reading Goethe against Stein allows us to detect the inconsistencies and blind spots in Goethe's remarks about gender until we understand that Cultural Studies and Weimar are not so contradictory after all.

—University of Missouri at Columbia

Notes

[1] "Die Redoute geht um sieben Uhr an. Man tanzt Menuets bis halb Acht, bis 8 Uhr Dreher, dann fängt ein Englischer an [...]" [The redoubt begins at seven. Minuet is to be danced until half past seven, country waltz till eight, then the English dance begins (...); qtd. in Satori-Neumann 50]. For a dis-

cussion of the rules of the redoubts, see Satori-Neumann; Weichberger 58–60; Barth 109–110.

[2] J. F. Reichardt was Goethe's favorite composer. He also set to music some of Goethe's texts.

[3] Even though the primary concern was gender, sparse remarks indicate that class issues were at stake as well. Because they indicate social status, Carl August found it "simply not fitting that contemporary military uniforms, court costumes, court pages' and lackeys' liveries are worn. There are orders already in existence against the wearing of pieces of military costume on stage" (to Goethe; qtd. in Carlson 189). On the relationship between Goethe, the military, and the Weimar theater see Karin Schutjer's essay in this volume.

[4] For a history of the Weimar theater see Meßner, Sichardt, Schrickel, Kindermann.

[5] Other examples are Schiller's *Don Carlos* (Christiane Neumann and Malcolmi as boys), Schiller's *Wallenstein's Camp* (Malcolmi as peasant boy), Schiller's *Wilhelm Tell* (Corona Becker as Walter Tell).

[6] I do not intend to "out" Goethe. For an analysis of the complex interrelation of homosexuality and heterosexuality in Goethe's works see Tobin, who claims that Goethe's "positive understanding of homosexuality rests in large part on his belief that it points to heterosexuality" (109) and Gustafson's analysis of *Götz von Berlichingen,* in which she claims that homosexual desire in the play is ultimately frustrated and replaced by compulsory bonds with women.

[7] "Und man glaubt nicht, wie zu so viel tausend kleinen Geschäften des Lebens, die wir besorgen müssen, mehr Geisteskraft muß aufgewendet werden, die uns für nichts angerechnet wird, als die eines Genies, das Ehre und Ruhm einerntet" [It seems incredible how much more spiritual energy must be spent on so many thousands of little daily chores, which we accomplish and which count for nothing, than on a work of genius which is rewarded with honor and fame; qtd. in Düntzer 1: 18].

[8] "Ich glaube, daß wenn ebenso viel Frauen Schriftsteller wären, als Männer es sind, und wir nicht durch so tausend Kleinigkeiten in unserer Haushaltung herabgestimmt würden, man vielleicht auch einige gute darunter finden würde; denn wie wenige gute gibt es nicht unter den Autoren ohne Zahl" [I think that if as many women were writers as are men, and if we were not dragged down by a thousand trifles of our household work, one would perhaps also find some good women authors among them; for how few good ones are there among the countless male authors; qtd. in Düntzer 2: 99].

[9] For example, when she mentions to her friend Charlotte von Schiller that, even though Schiller may praise women in his poem "Die Würde der Frauen" (Dignity of Women), he has clandestinely reintroduced man as paragon of all virtue (see Düntzer 1: 30). Furthermore, her poem "An den Mond" (To the

Moon) and her play *Dido* can both be read as responses to and refutations of Goethe's "An den Mond" and *Iphigenie auf Tauris*.

[10] Kord assumes that one comedy is lost and that von Stein probably authored *Die Probe* (The Trial) which is also lost. See Kord, "Image" 54.

[11] An example for this is a monologue in which a gambler, who has just lost all his money, elaborates on the beneficent and virtuous nature of gambling: "ZWEITER SPIELER: Alter Freund, betrachte einmal die Sache mit ruhigem Blut. Was für Tugenden bringt das Spiel nicht alle in Übung? — Die Geduld, wenn die Karte nicht einschlägt; die Ausdauer, wenn man ein Blatt forciert; die Mäßigkeit, wenn man mit einem kleinen Gewinn nach Hause geht; die Bescheidenheit, wenn andere mehr Glück haben — ERSTER SPIELER: Und die Barmherzigkeit, wenn man einen, den die Glücksgöttin vor die Thür gesezt hat, mit nach Hause nimmt." [SECOND GAMBLER: Now dear friend, consider this matter calmly. All the virtues that you develop when you gamble? — Patience, when your card does not take the trick. Endurance, when you try to push your color. Moderation, when you go home with a small prize; modesty, if others are luckier than you. FIRST GAMBLER: And compassion, if you take somebody home with you whom the goddess of luck has just kicked out; 5].

[12] "MAJOR: Junker, Du siehst selbst noch wie ein Frauenzimmer aus. MONTROSE: Aber meine Uniform straft mein Gesicht lügen." [MAJOR: Junker, you look like a woman yourself. MONTROSE: But my uniform gives the lie to my face; 4].

[13] "FRIEDRICH: Ein für allemal, ich melde seinen Fähndrich Montrose nicht. — Er ist schon einmal da und ich will mich nicht zum Narren haben lassen. CONRAD: Aber ich sag' ihm ja, es giebt nur einen Fähndrich Montrose und das ist mein Herr und eben angekommen. FRIEDRICH: Dann ist sein Geist schneller gereist als er. Dem kann er gleich die Jacke ausklopfen. CONRAD: Himmlischer Vater, mir graust, wenn ich den Geist noch extra bedienen müßte." [FRIEDRICH: Once and for all, I won't announce his sergeant Montrose. — He is already here and I don't want to make a fool of myself. CONRAD: But I tell him, there is only one sergeant Montrose and that is my master, and just arrived. FRIEDRICH: Then his spirit has traveled faster than he. He can go ahead and beat the dust out of his jacket. CONRAD: Heavenly father, I dread having to wait on the spirit as well; 26].

[14] See also Kord who questions the validity of the obligatory happy ending and claims that, beneath the surface, "the spectator has been encouraged to ridicule the posturing of male superiority" (Kord, *Image* 62).

[15] For a discussion of cross-dressing in Goethe's fictional works see Susan Gustafson's essay in this volume.

[16] See Kittler who claims that by the end of the eighteenth century the arousal of wishes had become the central means of socialization (41).

Works Cited

Bamberg, Eduard von, ed. *Die Erinnerungen der Karoline Jagemann*. Dresden: Sybillen-Verlag, 1926.

Barth, Ilse-Marie. *Literarisches Weimar: Kultur/Literatur/Sozialstruktur im 16.-20. Jahrhundert*. Stuttgart: Metzler, 1971.

Becker-Cantarino, Barbara. "(Sozial)geschichte der Frau in Deutschland 1500–1800. Ein Forschungsbericht." *Die Frau von der Reformation zur Romantik. Die Situation der Frau vor dem Hintergrund der Literatur- und Sozialgeschichte*. Ed. Barbara Becker-Cantarino. Bonn: Bouvier, 1980. 243–80.

Bohm, Arnd. "Charlotte von Stein's *Dido, Ein Trauerspiel*." *Colloquia Germanica* 22 (1989): 38–52.

Bovenschen, Silvia. *Die imaginierte Weiblichkeit: Exemplarische Untersuchungen zu kulturgeschichtlichen und literarischen Präsentationsformen des Weiblichen*. Frankfurt a. M.: Suhrkamp, 1979.

Bruford, W. H. *Culture and Society in Classical Weimar 1775–1806*. Cambridge: Cambridge UP, 1962.

Butler, Judith. *Gender Trouble: Feminism and the Subversion of Identity*. New York: Routledge, 1990.

Carlson, Marvin. *Goethe and the Weimar Theatre*. Ithaca: Cornell UP, 1978.

Castle, Terry. *Masquerade and Civilization: The Carnivalesque in Eighteenth-Century English Culture and Fiction*. Stanford: Stanford UP, 1986.

Cocalis, Susan. "Acts of Omission: The Classical Dramas of Caroline von Wolzogen and Charlotte von Stein." *Thalia's Daughters: German Women Dramatists from the Eighteenth Century to the Present*. Eds. Susan Cocalis and Ferrel Rose. Tübingen: Francke, 1996. 77–98.

———. "Der Vormund will Vormund sein: Zur Problematik der weiblichen Unmündigkeit im 18. Jahrhundert." *Gestaltet und Gestaltend: Frauen in der deutschen Literatur*. Ed. Marianne Burkhard. Amsterdam: Rodopi, 1980. 33–57.

De Lauretis, Teresa. "Upping the Anti [sic] in Feminist Theory." *The Cultural Studies Reader*. Ed. Simon During. New York: Routledge, 1993. 74–89.

Düntzer, Heinrich. *Charlotte von Stein, Goethes Freundin: Ein Lebensbild mit Benutzung der Familienpapiere entworfen*. 2 vols. Stuttgart: Cotta, 1874.

During, Simon. "Introduction." *The Cultural Studies Reader*. Ed. Simon During. New York: Routledge, 1993. 1–25.

Eberhardt, Hans. *Weimar zur Goethezeit: Gesellschafts- und Wirtschaftsstruktur.* Weimar: Stadtmuseum Weimar, 1980.

Ferris, Lesley. "The Legacy of Goethe's Mimetic Stance." *Crossing the Stage: Controversies on Cross-Dressing.* Ed. Lesley Ferris. New York: Routledge, 1993.

Fichte, Johann Gottlieb. "Erster Anfang des Naturrechts: Grundriß des Familienrechts." *Johann Gottlieb Fichtes sämtliche Werke.* Berlin: Veit and Comp, 1845. 3: 304–68.

Garber, Marjorie. *Vested Interests: Cross-Dressing and Cultural Anxiety.* New York: Routledge, 1992.

Gebauer, Gunter. "Ausdruck und Einbildung: Zur symbolischen Funktion des Körpers." *Die Wiederkehr des Körpers.* Eds. Dieter Kamper and Christoph Wulf. Frankfurt a. M.: Suhrkamp, 1982. 313–29.

Geitner, Ursula. "Die eigentlichen Enragées ihres Geschlechts: Aufklärung, Französische Revolution und Weiblichkeit." *Grenzgängerinnen: Revolutionäre Frauen im 18. und 19. Jahrhundert. Weibliche Wirklichkeit und männliche Phantasien.* Eds. Helga Grubitzsch et. al. Düsseldorf: Schwann, 1985. 181–217.

Genast, Eduard. *Aus Weimars klassischer und nachklassischer Zeit: Erinnerungen eines alten Schauspielers.* Ed. Robert Kohlrausch. Stuttgart: R. Lutz, 1905.

Gustafson, Susan E. "Male Desire in Goethe's *Götz von Berlichingen.*" *Outing Goethe and His Age.* Ed. Alice A. Kuzniar. Stanford: Stanford UP, 1996. 111–24.

Hall, Stuart. "Encoding, Decoding." *The Cultural Studies Reader.* Ed. Simon During. London: Routledge, 1993. 90–103.

Hausen, Karin. "Die Polarisierung der Geschlechtscharaktere — Eine Spiegelung der Dissoziation von Erwerbs- und Familienleben." *Sozialgeschichte der Familie in der Neuzeit Europas.* Ed. Werner Conze. Stuttgart: Ernst Klett, 1976. 363–93.

Honegger, Claudia. *Die Ordnung der Geschlechter: Die Wissenschaften vom Menschen und das Weib 1750–1850.* Munich: dtv, 1996.

Humboldt, Wilhelm von. "Über den Geschlechtsunterschied und dessen Einfluß auf die organische Natur." *Werke.* Stuttgart: J. G. Cotta, 1960. 1: 268–95.

Jagemann, Karoline. *Die Erinnerungen der Karoline Jagemann.* Ed. Eduard von Bamberg. Dresden: Sybillen-Verlag, 1926.

Johnson, Richard. "What is Cultural Studies Anyway?" *What is Cultural Studies? A Reader.* Ed. John Storey. London: Arnold, 1996. 75–114.

Kindermann, Heinz. *Theatergeschichte Europas: Von der Aufklärung zur Romantik.* Vol. 5. Salzburg: Otto Müller, 1962.

Kittler, Friedrich A. "Über die Sozialisation Wilhelm Meisters." *Dichtung als Sozialisationsspiel: Studien zu Goethe und Gottfried Keller*. Eds. Gerhard Kaiser and Friedrich A. Kittler. Göttingen: Vandenhoeck and Ruprecht, 1978. 13–115.

Klauß, Jochen. *Alltag im "klassischen" Weimar 1750–1850*. Weimar: Nationale Forschungs- und Gedenkstätte der klassischen deutschen Literatur, 1990.

Kord, Susanne. "Not in Goethe's Image. The Playwright Charlotte von Stein." *Thalia's Daughters. German Women Dramatists from the Eighteenth Century to the Present*. Eds. Susan L. Cocalis and Ferrel Rose. Tübingen: Francke, 1996. 53–75.

———. *Sich einen Namen machen: Anonymität und weibliche Autorschaft 1700–1900*. Stuttgart: Metzler, 1996.

Kühn, Paul. *Die Frauen um Goethe*. Vol. 1. Leipzig: Klinkhardt and Biermann, 1911.

———. *Weimar*. Leipzig: Klinkhardt and Biermann, n.d.

Laermann, Klaus. "Die riskante Person in der moralischen Anstalt. Zur Darstellung der Schauspielerin in deutschen Theaterzeitschriften des späten 18. Jahrhunderts." *Die Schauspielerin: Zur Kulturgeschichte der weiblichen Bühnenkunst*. Ed. Renate Möhrmann. Frankfurt a. M.: Insel, 1989. 127–53.

Lange, Sigrid. "Über epische und dramatische Dichtung Weimarer Autorinnen: Überlegungen zu Geschlechterspezifika in der Poetologie." *Zeitschrift für Germanistik* 1/2 (1991): 341–51.

———, ed. *Ob die Weiber Menschen sind: Geschlechterdebatten um 1800*. Leipzig: Reclam, 1992.

Laqueur, Thomas. *Making Sex: Gender Constructions from the Greeks to Freud*. Cambridge: Harvard UP, 1990.

Lyncker, Karl Freiherr von. *Am Weimarischen Hofe unter Amalien und Carl August*. Ed. Marie Scheller. Berlin: E. Mittler, 1912.

MacLeod, Catriona. "Pedagogy and Androgyny in *Wilhelm Meisters Lehrjahre*." *Modern Language Notes* 108 (1993): 389–426.

Meßner, Paul. *Das Deutsche Nationaltheater Weimar: Ein Abriß seiner Geschichte von den Anfängen bis Februar 1945*. Weimar: Stadtmuseum Weimar, 1988.

Satori-Neumann, Bruno. "Goethe und die Einrichtung der Weimarischen Redouten." *Festgabe der Gesellschaft für Deutsche Literatur zum siebzigsten Geburtstag ihres Vorsitzenden Max Herrmann*. Langensalza: Julius Beltz, 1935. 47–60.

Schrickel, Leonhard. *Geschichte des Weimarer Theaters von seinen Anfängen bis heute*. Weimar: Pauses Verlag, 1928.

Sichardt, Gisela. *Das Weimarer Liebhabertheater unter Goethes Leitung: Beiträge zu Bühne, Dekoration und Kostüm unter Berücksichtigung der Entwicklung Goethes zum späteren Theaterleiter.* Weimar: Arion, 1957.

Stein, Charlotte von. *Ein neues Freiheitssystem: Lustspiel in vier Akten: Nach einem Lustspiel gleichen Namens aus dem Nachlaß der Frau Charlotte von Stein, geb. von Schardt neu bearbeitet von Felix Freiherrn von Stein-Kochberg. Deutsche Schaubühne* 8.10 and 8.11 (1867): 1–31.

Storey, John. "Cultural Studies: An Introduction." *What is Cultural Studies? A Reader.* Ed. John Storey. London: Arnold, 1996. 1–13.

Tobin, Robert D. "In and Against Nature: Goethe on Homosexuality and Heterosexuality." *Outing Goethe and His Age.* Ed. Alice A. Kuzniar. Stanford: Stanford UP, 1996. 94–110.

Wallace, Michele. "Negative Images: Towards a Black Feminist Cultural Criticism." *The Cultural Studies Reader.* Ed. Simon During. London: Routledge, 1993. 118–31.

Weichberger, Alexander. *Goethe und das Komödienhaus in Weimar 1779–1825: Ein Beitrag zur Theaterbaugeschichte.* Leipzig: Leopold Voß, 1928.

West, Cornel. "The New Cultural Politics of Difference." *The Cultural Studies Reader.* Ed. Simon During. London: Routledge, 1993. 203–17.

Wilson, Daniel W. "Amazon, Agitator, Allegory: Political and Gender Cross(-Dress)ing in Goethe's *Egmont.*" *Outing Goethe and His Age.* Ed. Alice A. Kuzniar. Stanford: Stanford UP, 1996. 125–46.

8

Linda Dietrick

Women Writers and the Authorization of Literary Practice

In late eighteenth-century Germany, the literary elite responded to the unprecedented expansion of the market for *belles lettres* (Schön, *Verlust* 43–44) with intensive reflections on their product (aesthetic texts), its consumers (readers and buyers), and its producers (writers). The proliferation of all three was reflected in theorizing about what constitutes value in literary art, what constitutes appropriate consumption or reading behavior, and what constitutes a professional poet as opposed to a dilettante. Certain of these theories took hold around 1800 and prevailed into the twentieth century. Essentially, they claimed that: (1) great art is autonomous, universally and timelessly valid in itself, without significant regard to its socio-historical or biographical context; (2) to read well is to appreciate texts as aesthetic wholes rather than as sources of information, moral guidance, or emotional gratification; and (3) the poet is defined neither by technical ability, commercial success nor social recognition, but by an imputed "calling" to mediate secularized transcendence.[1] These successful theories have been preserved as part of the same set of literary biographies and works the canonization of which they were designed to ensure. And so we tend to read them as descriptive rather than as the rhetorical texts that they were (Kord, *Namen* 41).

As rhetoric they represent an exercise of symbolic power in a specific, historical social context, that is, in a *market* or *field* as Pierre Bourdieu defines it (*Language and Symbolic Power* 43–65, 163–70; see also Moi). In this more broadly defined market, public discourse is part of a process, a contest over the distribution of various forms of resources or social *capital*— economic capital to be sure, but also cultural capital (for example, education), symbolic capital (for example, prestige), and linguistic capital. The latter entails an ability to produce discourse appropriate to the social field or market — the ability to join the conversation, as it were. In its most powerful form as linguistic authority, it entails the ability to set the terms of reference that are recognized within the field as legitimate. The exercise of linguistic authority in turn feeds back into individual practices by shaping what Bourdieu calls the *habitus*. The habitus is the set of inculcated dispositions that strongly incline persons to interact with the social field in ways felt to be appropriate or congruent. Linguistic habitus, for example, is the predisposition shared by persons of similar background, socialization, etc. to use language in a certain way. But the habitus does not fully determine *practice*; actual practices depend as well on individuals' responses to shifting conditions in the particular market where they are positioned. Practices can thus be analyzed in terms of processes rather than rigid determinants (see MacLeod in this volume for display practices). Nevertheless, there will always be dominant groups, and those that acquire linguistic dominance or authority will exercise a symbolic power that, from within the social field, is essentially invisible, for it rests upon a value system that all participants have come to see as legitimate or natural. In other words, the dominated are at least to some degree complicit in their own oppression.

Bourdieu's cultural model offers a useful approach to the study of the participation of women — which was considerable — in the late eighteenth-century literary market. The subject has long been problematic, because women, a dominated group in the larger economy of bourgeois society, lost the struggle for legitimate authority over the literary market. With the institutionalization of classical aesthetics in the nineteenth century, many of the things they valued in literary works, in reading, and in writing no longer counted, and to the extent that the classical aesthetic criteria persist, they still do not count. At the same time, feminist efforts to recover their forgotten practices often come up against their partial or complete complicity in the rules of the game that excluded them. But if one studies their texts, including their unpublished ones, not as discrete aesthetic units but as instances of literary practice arising out of the relationship between a specific habitus and a specific social context, then they matter again. As complex textual negotiations of that relationship, they reflect issues that still concern us today.

The literary economy circa 1800 was embedded in a context of more fundamental socio-economic shifts that have been extensively described.[2] The emergence in Germany of a bourgeoisie as a cultural (though still not political) force is closely connected with the emergence of a public sphere in which educated laypersons could participate. Within the new bourgeois model of the family, women became more strictly limited to the private, domestic sphere, though they might now be expected to enter it voluntarily, by way of marriage based on love. Bourgeois men were generally employed outside the home as civil servants to states controlled by the nobility. Spurred by the moral and educational ideals of the Enlightenment, middle class women acquired the skills and the desire to read extensively, and by the late eighteenth century the vast majority of the reading public for *belles lettres* was, in fact, women. In genres like the romantic novel and the family drama, they found the relational world they knew enjoyably reflected and expanded beyond the limited worlds they knew (Schön, "Weibliches Lesen" 22–28). For a few women, this literary culture offered opportunities to secure an independent income from writing, though they had still to rely on the good will of male mentors. These very small gains were met with a reaction: a series of publications in the 1790s that defined women's traditional gender roles in terms of innate, polarized character traits. These traits included, for example, male rationality, aggressiveness, and independence vs. female emotionality, gentleness, and dependence. These appeared complementary in theory, but were hierarchical in practice: women were deemed to be destined by nature only for the relational and emotional tasks of wifedom, motherhood and domesticity.[3]

While there are no simple explanations for this public exercise of linguistic authority, it was clearly a reaction to perceived threat. Though invisible and unmeasurable in monetary terms, the sheer labor and the emotional support provided by women in the home was essential to the smooth functioning of the bourgeois economy. Women's improved education could be viewed as cultural capital only so long as it did not detract from women's material value to the household or bring them into unwanted competition in the same fields. As writers, they competed for shares of a market that was still developing and where the principle of intellectual property was just beginning to become accepted (Bosse 79–98). Moreover, insofar as women were perceived as undisciplined consumers of literature, their pleasure was enviable but suspect, for this too might prevent the cheerful carrying out of their domestic duties (see Schön, *Verlust* 46–49, 107–12; "Weibliches Lesen" 28–34). Finally, one cannot fail to connect the intensity of male reactions to the threat of female equality with German responses to the French Revolution. In Germany (as in France), its emancipatory impulses were rejected as entailing an intolerable level of social chaos.

The wave of polemics on the character of the sexes coincides, most remarkably in the 1790s, with the wave of classicist theorizations about literary practice, and not surprisingly, many of the aesthetic writings are gender-coded. The character polarities attributed to the genders are mapped onto the definitions of art vs. non-art, appropriate vs. inappropriate literary consumption, and professional poets vs. dilettantes. In fact, it is often difficult for a modern reader to distinguish between the anthropological, the moral-pedagogical and the aesthetic arguments. For example, in "Über Anmut und Würde" (On Grace and Nobility, 1793), Schiller ascribes to women the quality of grace as an expression of sensuousness or Kantian inclination, while to men he ascribes the quality of nobility as an expression of moral reasoning or Kantian duty. Schiller's moral and aesthetic ideal is, of course, meant to be a synthesis of these apparently equal complementarities. But with women, the ideal manifests itself not in creative works, but in character: the "beautiful soul" acts virtuously and beautifully out of inclination, without consciousness of also following the rational dictates of duty. In other words, women can at best embody the ideal, but unless they are prepared to lose something of their femininity, they cannot actively, consciously, and rationally set about to create it (Schiller, NA 20: 287–89; see Bovenschen 251–53 and Goodman and Waldstein 14–16).

In another essay of 1793 published in the same journal, Schiller makes clear his rejection of the emotionality and sensuality he finds in genres favored by women:

> Die schmelzenden Affekte, die bloß zärtlichen Rührungen, gehören zum Gebiet des *Angenehmen*, mit dem die schöne Kunst nichts zu thun hat. Sie ergötzen bloß den Sinn durch Auflösung oder Erschlaffung, und beziehen sich bloß auf den äußern, nicht auf den innern Zustand des Menschen. Viele unsrer Romane und Trauerspiele, besonders der sogenannten *Dramen* (Mitteldinge zwischen Lustspiel und Trauerspiel) und der beliebten Familiengemählde gehören in diese Klasse. Sie bewirken bloß Ausleerungen des Thränensacks und eine wollüstige Erleichterung der Gefäße; aber der Geist geht leer aus, und die edlere Kraft im Menschen wird ganz und gar nicht dadurch gestärkt. ("Über das Pathetische" [On the Pathetic, 1793], NA 20: 199; Schiller's emphases)
>
> [The melting emotions, the merely tender feelings, belong to the realm of the agreeable, with which fine art has nothing to do. They merely delight the senses through release and relaxation and relate only to the outward, not the inner state of the person. Many of our novels and tragedies, especially the so-

called *Dramas* (something in between comedy and tragedy) and the popular "family portraits," belong in this category. They merely effect an emptying of the tear ducts and a sensual relieving of the bodily vessels; but the mind goes away empty, and the nobler powers in humanity are not in the least strengthened.]

The same suspicion toward undisciplined pleasure is manifest in contemporary warnings about the consequences of excessive reading and in other attempts to prescribe correct reading behavior. Schiller's vocabulary of the body also parallels that of the anti-masturbation polemics of the age (Richter 118; Kern and Kern 93–94). He goes on to describe the "bis ins thierische gehende" [even animalistic] expression of pleasure on the faces of concert-goers and concludes that this is

> zum deutlichen Beweise, daß die Sinne schwelgen, der Geist aber oder das Princip der Freyheit im Menschen der Gewalt des sinnlichen Eindrucks zum Raube wird. Alle diese Rührungen sage ich, sind durch einen edeln und männlichen Geschmack von der Kunst ausgeschlossen, weil sie bloß allein dem *Sinne* gefallen, mit dem die Kunst nichts zu verkehren hat. (NA 20: 200; Schiller's emphasis)
>
> [evident proof that the senses may revel, but the mind or the principle of freedom in humanity has fallen prey to the violence of sensuous impression. All of these feelings, I say, are excluded from art by noble and manly taste, because they only please the *senses*, with which art has no dealings.]

This passage is difficult to harmonize with Schiller's sustained dialectical attempts to incorporate the sensual aspect of art into his classical aesthetics. Here, it has no place, and by definition, "manly" taste is unlikely to be exercised by either women artists or women consumers of art.

Goethe's and Schiller's correspondence, notes, and schemata from the late 1790s on the subject of dilettantism reflect a similar concern to discipline pleasure in literary practice. Although the aesthetic treatise they planned was never published, the project is significant because it attempts to define classicist practice in terms of what it is not, namely unprofessional, unauthorized production and inappropriate modes of consumption. It is evident from their correspondence that the two men's ideas on the subject developed in large part out of their interactions with women writers whose works Schiller published in his journals, particularly Karoline von Wolzogen (Charlotte Schiller's sister), Sophie Mereau, Amalie von Imhoff (later Helvig; Charlotte von Stein's niece), and Louise Brachmann. The salient characteristic of a dilettante, according to the schematic outline arising out of their discussions in May 1799, is a failure to distinguish between the work of art and its effect:

> Weil der Dilettant seinen Beruf zum Selbstproducieren erst aus den Wirkungen der Kunstwerke auf sich empfängt, so verwechselt er diese Wirkungen mit den objektiven Ursachen und Motiven, und meint nun den Empfindungszustand in den er versetzt ist auch produktiv und praktisch zu machen, wie wenn man mit dem Geruch einer Blume die Blume selbst hervorzubringen gedächte. Das an das Gefühl sprechende, die lezte Wirkung aller poetischen Organisationen, welche aber den Aufwand der ganzen Kunst selbst voraussezt, sieht der Dilettant als das Wesen derselben an, und will [es] damit selbst hervorbringen. (NA 21: 60)

> [Because the dilettante only derives the conception of his calling to produce art himself from the effects of works of art upon him, he confuses these effects with the objective causes and motives, and then thinks he can make the emotional state into which he has been put productive and practical as well, as if from the scent of a flower one could produce the flower itself. The dilettante regards that which speaks to the emotions, the final effect of all poetic structures which in turn presupposes the whole artistic effort, as the essence of art, and thus wishes to produce (it) himself.]

What this rhetoric does is to split literary practice into rigidly opposed functions. Artistic technique and effort are sharply distinguished from their enjoyment; the objective practice of art seems to preclude its subjective reception; writing has nothing to do with reading. In other words, artist and work are lifted out of their social context, literate Weimar society around 1800. The reception of a work by actual, historical consumers, as well as the response of the producers to that specific market, appear to play no role in determining artistic value; they are mere side-effects. Yet the rhetoric which here attempts to decontextualize the artwork, to construct it as an autonomous essence, is itself reacting to and participating in a specific historical and social context. As Cocalis has argued ("Acts of Omission" 80–81), Schiller's and Goethe's hierarchical distinction between the productive and the "merely" receptive functions in literary practice matches the contemporary polarization of gender roles, thus implying the exclusion of women from literary production a priori (see C. Bürger, "'Dilettantism der Weiber'" and Becker-Cantarino, "Goethe as a Critic of Literary Women"; see also Schulte-Sasse 101–12). Or to put it somewhat differently, the equation of woman writer and dilettante depends on a historical linkage between two parallel forms of decontextualizing, essentializing rhetoric.

A key concept in Goethe's and Schiller's discussion is the dilettante's imputed "Inkorrigibilität" (Goethe to Schiller, 22 June 1799, Seidel 2: 228). "Incorrigibility" implies that the dilettante's bad qualities are permanent, impervious to education, that is, to any social inputs. At the same time, the term reflects the two men's personal interest in controlling what those social inputs should be. Of Karoline von Wolzogen and her novel *Agnes von Lilien* (Agnes of the Lilies, 1796), which Schiller had seen fit, after working with her on revisions, to publish anonymously in *Die Horen*, Goethe writes that "eine solche Natur, wenn sie einer Kunstbildung fähig gewesen wäre, etwas Unvergleichliches hätte hervorbringen müssen" [if a nature like hers had been capable of an artistic education, it could have produced something incomparable; letter to Schiller, 3 February 1798, Seidel 2: 40]. Earlier in the same letter, Goethe records his reaction to a poem Schiller had sent him, "Die Kapelle im Wald. Idylle" (The Chapel in the Forest. Idyll). Its author was Louise Brachmann, but Schiller had told him only that this was "ein neuer Poet" [a new (male) poet]. Goethe observes:

> ein beinahe weibliches Talent, hübsche jugendliche Ansichten der Welt, ein freundliches, ruhiges, sittliches Gefühl. Wäre es nun den Deutschen möglich, sich zu bilden, und eine solche Person lernte, was doch zu lernen ist, in Absicht auf innere und äußere Form des Gedichts, so könnte daraus was recht Gutes entstehen. (Seidel 2: 39; see also 2: 35 and commentary 3: 311)
>
> [an almost feminine talent, attractive youthful views of the world, a friendly, calm, morally upright sensibility. Now if it were only possible for the Germans to educate themselves, and a person like this would learn what needs to be learned in respect to the inward and outward form of the poem, then something quite good might come of it.]

Male writers are clearly held to be educable, whereas there is a strong implication that "femininity" — "a nature like" Wolzogen's, "an almost feminine talent" — is a quality that precludes or resists artistic education (see Lange 101–3).

In May 1799 Amalie von Imhoff (1776–1831) seems to have become a prime example for Goethe and Schiller of feminine incorrigibility. Precisely when they were working together in Jena on their plans for a treatise on dilettantism, she came to discuss with them her epic poem "Die Schwestern von Lesbos" (The Sisters of Lesbos) as a contribution to Schiller's *Musenalmanach* (Almanac of Muses, 1796–1800; see Steiger 4: 32, 41–43). In March, Schiller had expressed pleasure on reading the poem, adding: "Es ist überaus zart und rein entwickelt, mit einfachen Mitteln und ungemeiner Anmutigkeit" [It is most delicately and purely developed, with simple means and uncommon gracefulness]. Goethe had replied: "Es soll mir recht lieb sein, wenn unsere Frauenzimmer, die so ein hübsches Talent haben, auch wirklich avancieren" [I shall be quite pleased if our ladies, who have such an attractive talent, really do make progress; 19 and 20 March, Seidel 2: 208]. Goethe read the text on 1 April and was generally positive about it in a letter to Meyer, but on 10 May, after a week of theorizing with Schiller about dilettantism, he wrote to Meyer that the manuscript needed major revisions, adding: "Recht sonderbar ist es was die Frauenzimmer durchaus in der Kunst Undulistinnen sind" [It is quite strange what thorough undulists (one of Goethe's synonyms for dilettantes) women are in art; Steiger 4: 41; see NA 21: 367].

Goethe's and Schiller's meeting on 13 May with Imhoff (Charlotte von Stein and possibly also Karoline von Wolzogen were present) went very badly. Goethe wrote to Meyer that the situation was so delicate and complicated that he preferred to discuss it personally (14 May 1799, WA 14: 93; see Steiger 4: 42). The incident seems to have created a serious crisis in the Weimar circle of friends. At the meeting, it appears that Schiller made Imhoff an offer, probably an honorarium well below what she thought her work was worth, which she declined, and Schiller seems to have misunderstood her no as a rejection of his personal sponsorship. She wrote to Schiller three days later to the effect that she stood by her decision, but had never meant him to take it that way. Her letter (NA 38.1: 86–87) is a remarkable performance of humility and defiance. Here is a characteristic example:

> Ich bin vielleicht zu offen und grade, doch leugne ich nicht, daß ich nie gefürchtet habe, durch diese Eigenschaften die Achtung oder das Zutrauen meines edlen Freundes zu verscherzen, welche tausendmal mehr Werth in meinen Augen haben, als selbst der Ruhm, von ihm beschützt zu werden.
>
> [Perhaps I am too open and direct, however I do not deny that I have never feared that I might lose, as a result of these qualities, the respect and trust of my noble friend (Schiller), which are a thousand times more valuable in my eyes than even the fame of being his protégé.]

Imhoff does not risk alienating her influential friend, but neither does she grovel. Apparently a bargain was struck: after his return to Weimar, Goethe grudgingly took on the task of correcting the "Gravamina" [grave errors] in her text (letter to Schiller, 29 May 1799, Seidel 2: 214), and Schiller replied:

> Ich begreife wohl, daß Ihnen das Gedicht unserer Dilettantin immer weniger Freude machen mag, je näher Sie es betrachten. Denn auch darin zeigt sich der Dilettantism besonders, daß er, weil er aus einem falschen Prinzip ausgeht, nichts hervorbringen kann, das nicht im ganzen falsch ist, also auch keine wesentliche Hilfe zuläßt. Mein Trost ist, daß wir bei diesem Werke den dilettantischen Ursprung ja ankündigen dürfen und daß wir, indem wir eine Toleranz dafür beweisen, bloß eine Humanität zeigen, ohne unser Urteil zu kompromitieren. (31 May 1799, Seidel 2: 214–15)

> [I can certainly understand that the poem of our dilettante should give you less and less pleasure the more you look at it. For dilettantism is especially manifest in this also, that, because it starts from a false principle, it cannot produce anything that is not false as a whole, and so it will also not admit of help in any essential way. My consolation is that in the case of this work we may announce its dilettante origin and that, by showing tolerance for it, we merely demonstrate humaneness without compromising our judgment.]

Imhoff's "Sisters of Lesbos" is about a peaceful matriarchy, in which a woman renounces her claim to a man, but does so from a position of legal power and out of love for her sister. Emotional and relational subject matter (romantic and sisterly love, female friendship) is presented in the technically demanding form of elevated hexameters (see Lange 115–21). In other words, aesthetically suspect themes like female political power and emotionality are tempered by the aesthetically correct theme of feminine renunciation and by controlled classical form. Thus both author and text accept, but only partially, the discipline of male cultural and aesthetic authority. Imhoff's resistance is carefully encoded, but it is resistance nonetheless. What makes her "incorrigible" in the eyes of her mentors is precisely what makes her interesting. Her literary practice reflects the complexity of discursive negotiations over the authorization to participate in a market whose value system was still unstable. And it is only by re-contextualizing Imhoff's work in the historically specific social field of late eighteenth-century Weimar that one can rediscover its value today.

Goethe and Schiller never made their dilettantism project public, and for all their private fulminations about female dilettantes, during the same period they did a great deal to get them into print. They mentored or helped publish the work of at least eight women. In addition to Wolzogen, Mereau, Imhoff and Brachmann, these included Friederike Brun, Elisa von der Recke, Charlotte von Stein, and Charlotte Schiller. All but Stein appeared in Schiller's own journals *Neue Thalia* (New Thalia, 1792–93), *Horen*, and the *Musenalmanach*. Attributed in the table of contents to "A. v. I.," Imhoff's "Sisters of Lesbos" fills most of the final issue of the *Musenalmanach*, though Schiller also printed here his "Lied von der Glocke" (The Song of the Bell, 1799), with its German version of the "angel in the house." If one took into account all of the women who were published individually or in other periodicals of the time, one would have a remarkable record of participation by women in the literary market as producers, not just as its primary consumers. That they frequently published anonymously and pseudonymously is, admittedly, a major and symptomatic problem. But pseudonyms were often feminine or decodable by acquaintances (that is, by those most likely to pass judgment), which suggests again that the rigid role prescriptions had not yet fully taken hold (Kord, *Namen* 53–54, 93–95).

It is probably true that, as Christa Bürger has argued, Schiller and Goethe were prepared to let women writers occupy a certain middle ground between "high" art and "lower" forms because women's literary practice could play an intermediary role in promoting public appreciation of classical literature ("Dilettantism der Weiber" 31). But it is also evident that material considerations were at work. In particular Schiller, who was not financially secure until shortly before his death in 1805, needed the income from his periodicals to support his growing family, and to judge from his correspondence, he was often desperate for material — desperate enough, it seems, to accept it from dilettantes. As a salaried official of the Weimar state Goethe was much better situated, but he was not above writing for the market with *Herrmann und Dorothea*, which he published in Vieweg's *Taschenbuch für 1798* in return for a record honorarium (Engelsing 128). Classical literature, as we sometimes forget, was rarely profitable and did not enjoy wide circulation until well into the nineteenth century (Ward 128–34). It did not yet command the market in either the financial sense or in Bourdieu's sense of a social field. What did command the market were still those popular forms of literature favored by a mainly female public. And so one could say that in terms of their own literary practice,

Goethe and Schiller were themselves compelled to occupy a middle ground, as their rather two-faced dealings with women writers attest.

In the Weimar circle, literary women like Imhoff were of course well aware of the aesthetic standards Goethe and Schiller were attempting to set, just as they were aware of the new gender characterizations. But their sense of authorization to participate in the literary market, their sense of what appropriate practice might entail for them, varied considerably. Charlotte Schiller, née von Lengefeld (1766–1826) and Charlotte von Stein (1742–1827) provide some interesting further examples. Their close friendship linked Jena and Weimar in the same years as Goethe's and Schiller's did, and well beyond. Only Stein's letters to Charlotte Schiller appear to have survived, but one can often get a feel for the latter's concerns from the replies, and a number of Charlotte Schiller's other letters and writings are extant. Both women wrote and translated *belles lettres*. Charlotte von Stein was the author of four or possibly five dramas (Kord, "Not in Goethe's Image" 54), only one of which was published, anonymously, with Friedrich Schiller's help, in her lifetime.[4] Charlotte Schiller's posthumous papers held at the Goethe and Schiller Archive in Weimar contain numerous poems as well as stories, dramas, and essays. Some of this material was published in 1860 by Ludwig Urlichs in collaboration with Schiller's daughter Emilie von Gleichen-Rußwurm (Urlichs 1: iii–iv and 3–156). However, two of the stories in her papers had already been published anonymously in the Ungers's periodical *Flora* in 1800,[5] and two others had appeared anonymously in their *Journal der Romane* (Journal of Novels, 1801).[6] Moreover, the five poems which Schiller published in the 1798 and 1799 editions of the *Musenalmanach* under the name "Louise ***" were most likely written by her.[7]

That Friedrich Schiller's wife, of all people, wrote for publication has remained little known. There is no question that she, like other wives in the period (for example, Friederike Unger, Dorothea Schlegel, and Caroline Schlegel), did so as a contribution to the income of a struggling household. That this was often kept quiet — certainly the case with Friedrich and Charlotte Schiller — is an indicator of the habitus of married women. Their sense of what was appropriate in their social context meant that writing for money might be a form of loving support for a spouse, but it could never be competition for his efforts to establish himself publicly and professionally as a writer. Nevertheless, the fact that Charlotte Schiller wrote at all, despite the domestic burdens of a frequently ill husband and, eventually, four children, suggests that she actively sought and found the authorization to write where she could. In March 1801 she wrote from Weimar to Friedrich Schiller in Jena:

> Damit doch jemand im Hause die Feder führt, bin ich auch mit meiner angefangnen Geschichte beschäftigt, die vielleicht doch so wird, daß man sie brauchen kann. Ich gehe streng zu wercke und lasse mir nichts hingehen, und so wollen wir sehen was heraus kommt. (Fielitz 3: 141)
>
> [So that at least someone in the house will be wielding a pen, I am also busy with my story that I have started, which will perhaps turn out to be something usable. I am going sternly to work and not letting anything get past me, and so we'll see what comes of it.]

She authorizes herself by referring to her diligence and discipline in the domestic space while he is outside of it. She takes care to leave the judgment about the value of her literary work open, though she does not explicitly turn over that prerogative to Friedrich.

She and Stein had shared each other's literary lives since at least the early nineties. On 25 February 1792, Stein wrote to her: "Ihr Kunstwerck sieht lustig aus, aber hat nichts vom griechischen Stil, ich habe leider nichts wieder gemacht; lauter unpoetische Geschäfte nehmen mir meine Zeit" [Your work of art looks delightful, though it has nothing of the Greek style, unfortunately I have once again not done anything; nothing but unpoetic business keeps taking up my time; GSA 83/1856].[8] This struggle to be actively creative despite domestic cares remained a constant theme. Stein only began writing dramas (aside from the early *Rino*) after the death of her ailing husband in 1794. Freed of domestic responsibility, she found in writing a source of immense pleasure, as she expressed to her son Fritz in 1798:

> Ich schreibe eine Komödie, denn je älter man wird, je lustiger muß man sich das Leben lassen vorkommen. Ich glaube beinahe, sie wird nicht schlecht.
>
> Dieses Stück soll aber in's Publikum kommen, doch ohne meinen Namen. Die Wolzogen treibt mich ordentlich dazu und beschreibt mir ihre selige Empfindung und neue Begeisterung, wenn sie recht viele Louisdor für ihre Werke aufgezählt auf dem Tisch liegen sieht. Bei den meisten Theatern bekommt man 8 Louisdor für eine gute Komödie im Manuskript, auf 10 Theatern hat man also 80 Louisdor [...].
>
> Ich hätte also doch ein Mittel von Erwerb, wenn uns die Franzosen verjagten oder die Gebrüder Stein Bankerott machten. (Quoted in Bode, *Charlotte von Stein* 404–5; Stein's characteristic orthography is obviously normalized)

[I am writing a comedy, for the older you get, the merrier you must let life seem to you. I almost think it won't turn out badly.

This play should get to the public, though without my name. (Karoline von) Wolzogen is really pressing me to do it and describes to me her blissful feeling and new enthusiasm whenever she sees lots of *Louisdor* for her works counted out on the table. At most theaters you get 8 *Louisdor* for a good comedy in manuscript, so at 10 theaters you have 80 *Louisdor* (…).

I would thus have a way to make a living if the French chased us out or the brothers Stein went bankrupt.]

She speaks equivocally about the quality of her creation, concedes the role of real breadwinner to her sons, and jokes about merely hypothetical situations where an income of her own might be important. But these qualifiers so typical of women's linguistic habitus do not fully disguise the self-esteem and sheer joy she derives from her writing. She is quite open about being motivated to write comedy by the pleasures of its reception, and to give that pleasure to an audience, for money if not for fame, represents to her a legitimate goal.

On 15 February 1797 she had written positively to Charlotte Schiller about another woman's work which had appeared anonymously in the *Horen*:

Frl. Goechhauß hat mir gesagt daß Agnes Lilien von der Wolzogen wäre; ein Moment muß ich sagen hab ichs einmahl gedacht, aber weil mein Lologen so treuhertzig unwissend beim Manuscript that, so glaubte ich, wie ichs gedruckt las es sey von der Kalben; denn mir wars als müste es eine Frau geschrieben haben. Ich habe es damahls im Manuscript sehr flüchtig überlesen, und gar nicht die Schönheiten so bemerkt wie ich mir sie jetz drinn unterstreiche; Es findet bei der Lesewelt einen auserordentlichen Beyfall, und ich habe es schon dreymahl gelesen […]. Ich habe vorhin die Lesewelt genennt, den die Critiker kan ich nicht gut leiden, mir deucht das Gefühl wäre der beste Criticus, mit Knebel habe ich mich letz drüber gezanckt der mir Verse die mich gerührt hatten, herunter setzte, und mir sie recht abgeschmackt vorlas und ich habe sie ihm aus die Hände gerißen. (GSA 83/1856; see Urlichs 2: 320–21)

[Fräulein Göchhausen told me that Agnes Lilien was by (your sister Karoline) Wolzogen. For a moment, I must say, I once thought that was so, but because my Lologen [Stein's name for Charlotte Schiller] acted so innocent and unknowing with the manuscript I thought, when I read it in print, it was by

> (Charlotte von) Kalb, for to me it was as if a woman had to have written it. At the time when it was in manuscript I read it over very quickly and did not at all notice the beauties such as I am underlining now. In the reading world it is receiving extraordinary acclaim, and I have already read it three times (...). I mentioned the reading world, for I cannot much stand the critics, I think that feeling is the best critic, I had an argument about it recently with Knebel, who criticized some verses that had touched me and read them aloud to me in a quite fatuous way and I tore them out of his hands.]

From her reference to the argument with her friend Knebel one can see her awareness of two competing modes of literary reception: that of the critics, and the subjective response she has to certain works, especially those by women. But she is able to legitimate both women's writing and her own mode of reception by referring to the novel's acclaim in the "reading world," which she counts here as the final arbiter. Moreover, in a letter to her only a month before, Friedrich Schiller himself had seemed to place his critical imprimatur on her own tragedy *Dido*. He praised "die Lebendigkeit [...], womit sich eine zarte und edle weibliche Natur [...] darin gezeichnet hat" [the liveliness with which a delicate and noble feminine nature (...) is drawn in it; letter to Stein of 2 January 1797, Ebers and Kahlert 172–73, quoted and trans. Goodman 91–92]. So she had no reason to believe that the literary practice she valued was not valid (Cocalis, "Acts" 80; Dietrick 123).

In early 1799 Stein wrote to Charlotte Schiller about the latest *Musenalmanach*, which had just appeared:

> Ich habe noch nicht mit Muße drinn lesen können, den ich besitz ihn nicht selbst, aber von der Herzogin bekomm ich ihn noch, von Schillern, Lollogen, und Goethe, habe ich mir nur geschwind etwas ausgesucht, das Glück vom Schiller finde ich sehr schön; Goethes elegie auf die B. hat mich sehr intereßirt doch ist mir etwas dunkel drin, [...] und mein Lollogen beneide ich ein wenig daß ich nicht auch so etwas artiges machen kan. (GSA 83/1856, see Urlichs 2: 332)

> [I have not yet been able to read in it at leisure, for I do not possess it myself, but I will still get it back from the duchess, I just quickly picked out something by Schiller, Lologen, and Goethe, "Das Glück" (Happiness) by Schiller I find very beautiful; Goethe's elegy to B. (to Christiane Becker, i.e., "Euphrosyne") interested me very much, though I find it somewhat obscure, (...) and I envy my Lologen a little that I cannot also make something so charming.]

For Stein, the poems published under the name Louise *** place her friend on the same artistic footing as her male company and call for the same appreciative acknowledgment. Charlotte Schiller was in turn a faithful supporter of Stein's literary practice, often interceding for her with Friedrich to help find publishing opportunities. Both women were keenly interested in and almost always expressed positive judgments about the work of other women writers.

In the Weimar of the 1790s, there was still room for negotiation over the values that were at stake in the literary market. Within limits, women felt that they had a say in the matter, that they were authorized to speak. Because they were close to the men whose cultural authority eventually prevailed, their record has survived, and we can reconstruct at least in part what they valued in their own practice. The scholarly recovery of their writings and voices for the present demands that process of reconstruction. Literary studies need to draw on the methods of social history and sociology to re-situate them in their own time and place, for it is the invisibility of that context in the dominant aesthetic, philosophical and anthropological discourses of their time that has enforced their marginalization. To evaluate them against the ostensibly universal standards of classical aesthetics is to apply criteria that from the outset devalued and trivialized their literary practice. Once those criteria became institutionalized or "legitimate," to speak with Bourdieu (138–40), they exercised symbolic power by virtue of their apparent detachment from all social determinants, by virtue of the misrecognition of the political forces and processes that made them into the only legitimate way of talking about literary value. Fortunately, we can begin to see this now. "Weimar" has ceased to be a timeless symbol of Olympian intellectual achievement and become instead a material locale with a richly layered history of social relationships and conflicts. There, in the classicist period that made the town famous, literary women like Amalie von Imhoff, Charlotte von Stein, and Charlotte Schiller were central participants.

—University of Winnipeg, Canada

Notes

[1] What I have outlined is called in German scholarship the *Autonomieästhetik*, the aesthetics of autonomy, for which I will use the less awkward term "classical aesthetics." See for example, Peter Bürger, *Zur Kritik der idealistischen Ästhetik* and Christa Bürger, "Philosophische Ästhetik und Populärästhetik."

[2] See, for example, Hausen; Frevert 9–21; Blackwell and Zantop 21–30; Becker-Cantarino, *Der lange Weg* 48–65 and 149–200.

[3] In addition to Hausen, see Becker-Cantarino, "Gender Censorship"; Bovenschen 220–45; Cocalis, "Vormund" 46–55; Dotzler; Duden; Hoffmann; Kord, *Namen* 36–46 and 77–85; and Rasch.

[4] Recent critical treatments of Stein's plays, especially her "Anti-*Iphigenie*," *Dido*, include Bohm; Cocalis, "Acts"; Dietrick; Goodman; Kord, *Ein Blick* 181–85 and "Not in Goethe's Image"; and Lange 104–12.

[5] A note signed by Emilia Gleichen on the first page of the manuscript of "Rosalie" (GSA 83/1636) states that it appears as "Die Nonne. Eine Erzählung" (The Nun. A Tale) in the March 1800 issue of *Flora*, 163–222; a similar note on the manuscript of "Die neue Pamela" (The New Pamela; GSA 83/1637) states that it appears in the *Flora* of May 1800, 81–157.

[6] According to the afterword by the so-called Saxo Bibliophilus to the 1927 reprint of Charlotte Schiller's "Der Prozeß. Eine Erzählung" (The Trial. A Tale), the piece originally appeared in the fourth issue of the *Journal der Romane* 1801, while "Autun und Manon. Eine Erzählung" (Autun und Manon. A Tale) appeared in the third. Gallas and Runge confirm the latter (151), indicating it is on pages 217–338. Based on his reading of Friedrich Schiller's correspondence, Saxo Bibliophilus claims the stories are translations, but it is not clear to me that they are.

[7] Louise was Charlotte Schiller's actual first name. Some sources attribute the poems to Louise Brachmann (see Brinker-Gabler et al 39), but in the 1797 edition of the *Horen* (published June 1798) Friedrich Schiller uses the cryptonym "L." for Brachmann poems which he had discussed with Goethe in their correspondence of 3 and 6 February 1798 (Seidel 2: 39–40).

[8] Quotations from Stein's letters to Charlotte Schiller are from the manuscripts in the Goethe and Schiller Archive (cited as GSA 83/1856), but I will also give the location in Urlichs's heavily edited, linguistically normalized, and occasionally inaccurate edition, which omits this passage from the letter in 2: 285. I would like to thank the Weimar Classics Foundation for its generous support of my research on Charlotte Schiller and Charlotte von Stein at the archive.

Works Cited

Becker-Cantarino, Barbara. *Der lange Weg zur Mündigkeit: Frau und Literatur in Deutschland (1500–1800)*. Stuttgart: Metzler, 1987.

———. "'Gender Censorship': On Literary Production in German Romanticism." *Women in German Yearbook* 11 (1995): 81–97.

———. "Goethe as a Critic of Literary Women." *Goethe as a Critic of Literature*. Eds. Karl J. Fink and Max L. Baeumer. Lanham: UP of America, 1984. 160–81.

Blackwell, Jeannine, and Susanne Zantop. "Trivial Pursuits? An Introduction to German Women's Writing from the Middle Ages to 1830." *Bitter Healing: German Women Writers 1700–1830*. Eds. Blackwell and Zantop. Lincoln: U of Nebraska P, 1990. 9–50.

Bode, Wilhelm. *Charlotte von Stein*. Berlin: E. Mittler, 1910.

Bohm, Arnd. "Charlotte von Stein's *Dido, Ein Trauerspiel*." *Colloquia Germanica* 22 (1989): 38–52.

Bosse, Heinrich. *Autorschaft ist Werkherrschaft: Über die Entstehung des Urheberrechts aus dem Geist der Goethezeit*. Paderborn: Schöningh, 1981.

Bourdieu, Pierre. *Language and Symbolic Power*. Trans. Gino Raymond and Matthew Adamson. Ed. and introd. John B. Thompson. Cambridge, MA: Harvard UP, 1993.

Bovenschen, Silvia. *Die imaginierte Weiblichkeit: Exemplarische Untersuchungen zu kulturgeschichtlichen und literarischen Präsentationsformen des Weiblichen*. Frankfurt a. M.: Suhrkamp, 1979.

Brinker-Gabler, Gisela, Karola Ludwig, and Angela Wöffen, eds. *Lexikon deutschsprachiger Schriftstellerinnen 1800–1945*. Munich: dtv, 1986.

Bürger, Christa. "'Dilettantism der Weiber.'" In *Leben Schreiben. Die Klassik, die Romantik und der Ort der Frauen*. Stuttgart: Metzler, 1990. 19–31.

———. "Philosophische Ästhetik und Populärästhetik: Vorläufige Überlegungen zu den Ungleichzeitigkeiten im Prozeß der Institutionalisierung der Kunstautonomie." *Zum Funktionswandel der Literatur*. Ed. Peter Bürger. Frankfurt a. M.: Suhrkamp, 1983. 107–26.

Bürger, Peter. *Zur Kritik der idealistischen Ästhetik*. Frankfurt a. M.: Suhrkamp, 1983.

Cocalis, Susan L. "Acts of Omission: The Classical Dramas of Caroline von Wolzogen and Charlotte von Stein." *Thalia's Daughters: German Women Dramatists from the Eighteenth Century to the Present*. Eds. Susan L. Cocalis and Ferrel Rose. Tübingen: Francke, 1996. 77–98.

———. "Der Vormund will Vormund sein: Zur Problematik der weiblichen Unmündigkeit im 18. Jahrhundert." *Gestaltet und Gestaltend: Frauen in der deutschen Literatur*. Ed. Marianne Burkhard. Amsterdam: Rodopi, 1980. 33–55.

———, and Ferrel Rose, eds., in collaboration with Karin Obermeier. *Thalia's Daughters: German Women Dramatists from the Eighteenth Century to the Present*. Tübingen: Francke, 1996.

Dawson, Ruth. "'And This Shield is Called — Self-Reliance': Emerging Feminist Consciousness in the Late Eighteenth Century." *German Women in the Eighteenth and Nineteenth Centuries: A Social and Literary History*. Eds. Ruth-Ellen B. Joeres and Mary Jo Maynes. Bloomington: Indiana UP, 1986. 157–74.

Dietrick, Linda. "Woman's State: Charlotte von Stein's Dido. Ein Trauerspiel and the Aesthetics of Weimar Classicism." *Verleiblichungen: Literatur- und kulturgeschichtliche Studien über Strategien, Formen und Funktionen der Verleiblichung in Texten von der Frühzeit bis zum Cyberspace*. Eds. Burkhardt Krause and Ulrich Scheck. St. Ingbert: Röhrig Universitätsverlag, 1996. 111–31.

Dotzler, Bernhard. "'Seht doch wie ihr vor Eifer schäumet...' Zum männlichen Diskurs über Weiblichkeit um 1800." *JDSG* 30 (1986): 339–82.

Duden, Barbara. "Das schöne Eigentum: Zur Herausbildung des bürgerlichen Frauenbildes an der Wende vom 18. zum 19. Jahrhundert." *Kursbuch* 47 (1977): 125–40.

Ebers, Johann Jakob Heinrich, and August Kahlert, eds. *Briefe von Goethe und dessen Mutter an Friedrich Freiherrn von Stein. Mit Beilagen*. Leipzig: Weidmann, 1846.

Engelsing, Rolf. "Wieviel verdienten die Klassiker?" *Neue Rundschau* 87 (1976): 124–36.

Fielitz, Wilhelm, ed. *Briefwechsel zwischen Schiller und Lotte 1788–1805*. 3 vols. 5th ed. Stuttgart and Berlin: Cotta, 1905.

Frevert, Ute. *Women in German History: From Bourgeois Emancipation to Sexual Liberation*. Trans. Stuart McKinnon-Evans et al. New York: Berg, 1989.

Gallas, Helga, and Anita Runge. *Romane und Erzählungen deutscher Schriftstellerinnen um 1800: Eine Bibliographie mit Standortnachweisen*. Stuttgart: Metzler, 1993.

Goodman, Katherine R. "The Sign Speaks: Charlotte von Stein's Matinees." *In the Shadow of Olympus: German Women Writers Around 1800*. Eds. Katherine R. Goodman and Edith Waldstein. Albany: SUNY P, 1992. 71–93.

———, and Edith Waldstein, eds. *In the Shadow of Olympus: German Women Writers Around 1800*. Albany: SUNY P, 1992.

Hausen, Karin. "Family and Role-Division: The Polarization of Sexual Stereotypes in the Nineteenth Century — An Aspect of the Dissociation of Work and Family Life." Trans. Cathleen Catt. *The German Family.* Eds. Richard J. Evans and W. R. Lee. London: Croom Helm, 1981. 51–83.

Helvig, Amalie, née von Imhoff. "Die Schwestern von Lesbos." *Musenalmanach* 5 (1800): 1–182.

Hoffmann, Volker. "Elisa und Robert oder das Weib und der Mann, wie sie sein sollten. Anmerkungen zur Geschlechtercharakteristik der Goethezeit." *Klassik und Moderne: Die Weimarer Klassik als historisches Ereignis und Herausforderung im kulturgeschichtlichen Prozeß.* Eds. Karl Richter and Jörg Schönert. Stuttgart: Metzler, 1983. 80–97.

Kern, Bärbel and Horst Kern. *Madame Doctorin Schlözer. Ein Frauenleben in den Widersprüchen der Aufklärung.* Munich: C. H. Beck, 1988.

Kord, Susanne. *Ein Blick hinter die Kulissen: Deutschsprachige Dramatikerinnen im 18. und 19. Jahrhundert.* Stuttgart: Metzler, 1992.

———. "Not in Goethe's Image: Charlotte von Stein's Dramas." *Thalia's Daughters: German Women Dramatists from the Eighteenth Century to the Present.* Eds. Susan L. Cocalis and Ferrel Rose. Tübingen: Francke, 1996. 53–75.

———. *Sich einen Namen machen: Anonymität und weibliche Autorschaft 1700–1900.* Stuttgart: Metzler, 1996.

Lange, Sigrid. *Spiegelgeschichten. Geschlechter und Poetiken in der Frauenliteratur um 1800.* Frankfurt a. M.: Ulrike Helmer, 1995.

Moi, Toril. "Appropriating Bourdieu: Feminist Theory and Pierre Bourdieu's Sociology of Culture." *NLH* 22 (1991): 1017–49.

Rasch, William. "*Mensch, Bürger, Weib*: Gender and the Limitations of Late Eighteenth-Century Neohumanist Discourse." *German Quarterly* 66 (1993): 20–33.

Richter, Simon. "The Ins and Outs of Intimacy: Gender, Epistolary Culture, and the Public Sphere." *German Quarterly* 69 (1996): 111–24.

Schiller, Charlotte. Nachlaß: Werkmanuskripte. GSA. Bestand Schiller 83/1552–1682.

———. *Der Prozeß. Eine Erzählung.* Berlin: J. G. Preuß, 1927.

Schiller, Friedrich, ed. *Die Horen. Eine Monatsschrift.* Tübingen 1795–97. Rpt. Darmstadt: fotokop, 1959.

———, ed. *Musenalmanach für das Jahr ... [1796, 1797, 1798, 1799, 1800].* 5 vols. Neustrelitz: Michaelis, 1796 and Tübingen: Cotta, 1797–1800. Rpt. Leipzig: Insel, 1980.

———, ed. *Neue Thalia.* Leipzig 1792–93. Rpt. Hildesheim: Olms, 1977.

Schön, Erich. *Der Verlust der Sinnlichkeit, oder die Verwandlungen des Lesers. Mentalitätswandel um 1800*. Stuttgart: Klett-Cotta, 1987.

———. "Weibliches Lesen: Romanleserinnen im späten 18. Jahrhundert." *Untersuchungen zum Roman von Frauen um 1800*. Eds. Helga Gallas and Magdalene Heuser. Tübingen: Niemeyer, 1990. 21–40.

Schulte-Sasse, Jochen. *Die Kritik an der Trivialliteratur seit der Aufklärung*. Munich: W. Fink, 1971.

Seidel, Siegfried, ed. *Der Briefwechsel zwischen Schiller und Goethe*. 3 vols. Munich: C. H. Beck, 1984.

Steiger, Robert. *Goethes Leben von Tag zu Tag. Eine dokumentarische Chronik*. Vol. 4. Zurich: Artemis, 1982.

Stein, Charlotte von. Briefe an Charlotte Schiller. GSA. Bestand Schiller 83/1856.

———. Briefe an Charlotte Schiller. Urlichs 2: 252–359.

Urlichs, Ludwig, ed. *Charlotte Schiller und ihre Freunde*. 3 vols. Stuttgart: Cotta, 1860–65.

Ward, Albert. *Book Production, Fiction and the German Reading Public 1740–1800*. Oxford: Oxford UP, 1974.

9

SUSANNE KORD

The Hunchback of Weimar: Louise von Göchhausen and the Weimar Grotesque

Conflicting Evidence: Göchhausen in Scholarship

ALTHOUGH THERE IS VERY LITTLE literature on Louise von Göchhausen (a biographical novel, a scholarly article that treats her together with two other authors, and an encyclopedic entry), she emerges as a fairly contradictory character in literary history. Uncontested facts about her are rare: Louise Ernestine Christiane Juliane von Göchhausen was born in 1752 in Eisenach into an aristocratic family and became Duchess Anna Amalia's lady-in-waiting in 1783. She was famous and respected for her wit and intelligence and kept an avid correspondence with many figures connected with the court, among them Goethe, Wieland, Herder, the author and composer Friedrich Hildebrand von Einsiedel (1750–1828), chamberlain Karl Friedrich von Seckendorff (1744–1785), the philologist and archaeologist Karl August Böttiger (1760–1835), the journalist and critic Johann Heinrich Merck (1741–91), and Carl Ludwig von Knebel (1744–1834), who served as Prince Constantin's tutor from 1774 until 1780. Although some of these letters were written on Anna Amalia's behalf (invitations to court functions and the like), the personal tone and the flippant forms of address she used indicate that much of her correspondence was also personal in nature. She called Goethe "Hätschelhans" [pampered boy; in letters to his mother] and "Bestes Geheimderäthchen" [dearest little Privy Councillor; to his face], his mother "Gute, liebe, Herzens Mutter" [good, dear mother of my heart], Wieland "Liebster bester Freund" [dearest best friend] and "Papa Wieland." Perhaps more indicative in an age that so heavily employed sentimental discourse in epistolary writing, she committed indiscretions in her writing that seem either extraordinarily careless or extraordinarily courageous, given her position as lady-in-waiting and appointed guardian of court etiquette. Her letters were enthusiastically received: Goethe and Wieland both greatly admired her epistolary style; Wieland claimed that her letters would do honor to the greatest author. She accompanied Anna Amalia to Tiefurt every summer, on her journeys to the Rhine (1778) and to Italy (1788–90), and on her flight from Napoleonic troops (1806). She was active on the amateur stage, where she took over a great deal of the organization and acted occasionally, and served as co-editor to the *Tiefurter Journal* (Tiefurt Journal, 1781–84), to which she also contributed. For ten years, she was the center of a literary salon, aptly titled "Freundschaftsloge" [Friendship Lodge, 1790–1800], which included Goethe and Wieland. Her written works consist of her letters edited by Werner Deetjen in 1923; of letters from Italy to Wieland cited in Seuffert, 1890; her travel diary during the Italian journey (handwritten manuscript in the Goethe and Schiller Archive); descriptions of her Italian travels in Bertuch's *Journal des Luxus und der Moden*; and various publications in the *Tiefurt Journal*, which are difficult to ascribe to her because contributions to the journal were anonymous. She died in Weimar in 1807, only a few months after Anna Amalia.[1]

Given the scarcity of sources about her, there are a startling number of contradictory descriptions of her, which can, to some extent, be attributed to the fact that Göchhausen received contradictory treatment by contemporaries, including people who knew her personally. Most of these contradictions concern one of four components of her character: her body, her name, her position, and her work. These multiple contradictions are worth investigating, not in an attempt to arrive at an authoritative biographical truth, but in an attempt to examine what these different readings reveal about our investigative behavior. To anticipate here one of my conclusions: I view defining Weimar as "Goethe's" Weimar, as classical Weimar, as a conditioned response that is necessarily limited in its perception of deviating artforms, particularly of those that existed side by side with the dominant aesthetics then being developed by Goethe and Schiller, the Weimar "greats." That *any* research on non-dominant artforms in "Goethe's" Weimar will face mostly conflicting evidence is indicative of a history of scholarly neglect and disinterest and the scarcity of source materials, but that is not all. Recurring contradictions in scholarship tell us something about the subject of research as well as the researcher: about the subject because they indicate that "truth" is not recoverable for these authors, about the researcher because these contradictory accounts demonstrate the scholar's view of non-classical aesthetics in Weimar as a contradiction *in terms*, as incompatible with "Goethe's" Weimar.

Hunchback or Beauty?

One of the first remarks made in any secondary work on Göchhausen, Lange's excepted, is that she was tiny and had a hunchback. Her deformity is usually viewed in direct relation either to her position at court or to her character: Göchhausen's biographers are quick to philosophize that she was blessed with wit, humor, and intelligence *as compensation for* her deformity[2] or to marvel at the fact that she attained and kept her position as lady-in-waiting *despite* her outward appearance.[3] This position seemed to imply and demand a certain bodily stature (tall and stately, perhaps) that stands in equal contradiction to Göchhausen's small size and disfigurement as well as to her intentional flippancy concerning court etiquette. Contradictory accounts with regard to her outward appearance permeate written accounts and drawings, paintings and sculptures: while written accounts tend to emphasize her deformity, the hunchback vanishes in paintings and sculptures. Goethe drew her twice, once in profile (1780; Fig. 1), showing an erect head ending in a frilly neckdress that might or might not camouflage a hunchback, and once in 1776–77. This earlier drawing (Fig. 2) shows Göchhausen full-figure, sitting at her desk, leaning forward slightly; and although the picture does emphasize her small stature, her hunchback again gets lost: the viewer, not knowing of Göchhausen's deformity, would be more likely to take the small protrusion on her back for a scarf than a hunchback. Other visual representations employ similar means: she appears hunched over, intent on her work, her deformity camouflaged by her hair (Kraus's famous painting of 1795; Fig. 3, detail Fig. 4) or a hat (Schütz's painting of the visit in the Villa d'Este; Fig. 5); some representations omit it altogether (one silhouette, artist unknown; Fig. 6). In all pictures, she appears as undeniably attractive by conventional standards, certainly a far cry from the usual descriptions of her as "ugly" and "misshapen."

The delicacy with which Göchhausen's deformity is treated in contemporary visual representations should not be viewed as an indication that contemporaries were more hesitant than later scholars to point it out. In one of the last issues of the *Tiefurt Journal* (46, 1784) appeared "An Anecdote" attributed to Einsiedel and unquestionably directed at Louise von Göchhausen,[4] who was apparently frequently the butt of jokes because of her disfigurement. In this anecdote, a lady experiences a swelling of the throat and neck (such as might have been occasioned by the position in which Göchhausen was constantly forced to hold her neck):

> Durch eine ungewöhnliche Wendung eines wenig polien Schnupfens bekam eine Dame einen etwas aufgeschwollenen Hals, ohngeachtet die Ärzte einmüthig versicherten, dieser vorübergehenden kleinen Unzierde in wenig Tagen abhelfen zu können; so schwebte dennoch die Dame in der Furcht: daß sie einen Kropf bekommen werde, und überredete sich allmälig: daß sie würklich einen habe.
> Das folgende Consilium medicum ist daher abgefaßt worden, die Dame ist völlig geneßen, und hat ihre eigenthümliche Schönheit wieder erlangt. (*Journal* 331)

[Through an unusual turn in a case of the pollinary sniffles, a lady acquired a somewhat swollen throat. Despite the unanimous assurances of doctors to the effect that they would be able to cure this temporary and negligible unseemliness in a few days, the lady feared that she would get a goiter, and finally persuaded herself that she did indeed already have one.
The following Medical Council was therefore composed; the lady has recovered completely and regained her former peculiar beauty.]

The "Consilium medicum" identifies four sources as the cause of the illness:

- "aufgethürmte Kopf Decorationen, und hauptsächlich stolzes Empor-Recken des Halses" [towering head decorations, and primarily the proud craning of the neck; *Journal* 331] — Göchhausen was known to camouflage her deformity by wearing large hats and keeping her head and neck as straight as possible;
- "wenn Reichthum und Überfluß an Geschmeide und Edelgesteinen die Patientinnen verleitet hat, ihre Hälse zur Ungebühr damit zu behängen" [when riches and an abundance of jewelry and diamonds have seduced the patients to hang an overabundance of such around their necks; 331] — as lady-in-waiting, Göchhausen received many gifts of jewels and was obliged to wear them at court functions;
- "wenn sie durch übermüthiges Trachten und Streben nach Weisheit und Wissenschaft ihr Haupt und das darinn befindliche Gehirn dergestallt überladen und beschwert haben: daß

der Hals, als die Stütze und der Pfeiler des Hauptes, solche Last nicht zu tragen vermag" [when (women) have, through wanton strife and pursuit of wisdom and knowledge, overburdened and over-charged their heads and the brains inside to such an extent that the neck, as the support and pillar of the head, can no longer bear such a burden; 331–32] — Göchhausen was well-read in literature and many scientific fields and known for her intelligence; and

- "wenn sie, durch Convenienz, durch Politik, oder andere Zufälligkeiten genöthiget worden sind: witzige Spott- und Stichel-Reden, Medisancen, Persiflages und dergleichen, welche eben ihren Zungen entschlüpfen wollten, zu unterdrücken und gleichsam in der Geburth zu ersticken; als wodurch der Hals, wegen Schwierigkeit des Herabschlingens, auf eine gewaltsame Weise gedrängt, und ausgedehnt wird" [when they, through considerations of convenience or politics or other coincidences, are obliged to suppress and, as it were, throttle at birth, the witty sarcasms and taunts, evil gossip, satires and the like, which were just about to escape their tongues; this difficulty of swallowing causes the throat to forcibly press and expand; 332] — Göchhausen was as infamous for her sharp tongue and her satirical gifts as known for her ability to "swallow" her comments when courtly etiquette demanded:

In case of incurability, the "Consilium medicum" encourages the afflicted to view the deformity not as an evil, but rather as a distinguishing mark of beauty: in what could be a direct allusion to Göchhausen's deformity, the author claims that "das Gewundene, Geschlungene, Gewölbte, Convexe and Concave [ist] allein schön, und das Attribut idealischer Vollkommenheit; ein gerad-liniger Hals sollte daher mit gutem Fug und Recht ein Gänse-Hals, und keines Weges ein Schwanen-Hals genennt werden" [the wound, twisted, vaulted, convex, and concave alone is beautiful, and the attribute of ideal perfection; a straight neck should therefore justifiably be called a goose-neck, and never a swan's neck; 332].

What appears as biographical "truth" in scholarly accounts on Göchhausen is here presented as open to interpretation: like beauty, deformity is in the eye of the beholder. Rather than seeing Göchhausen as ugly and rachitic, one could re-view her as a "Schönheit," if perhaps an "eigenthümliche Schönheit" [peculiar beauty], a feat accomplished in this piece and in contemporary art representing her. These strange contradictions do not stop at accounts of her physical appearance, but permeate views of her self-image as well: in other words, there are contradictory views of Göchhausen's view of herself (since she herself never mentioned her deformity in letters, she cannot be consulted for her own view). To name just one example: according to Deneke, Göchhausen hated mirrors and avoided them where she could (21); according to Biedrzynski, she acted on the amateur stage "sicher und gelöst" [with self-confidence and ease; 122]. In other words: while Göchhausen could not stand to look at herself, she did not object to others looking at her. Although there is no way to establish to what extent these visions are grounded in biographical fact (Deneke may have invented Göchhausen's aversion to mirrors, which is not corroborated in any other source), this particular contradiction can perhaps be read as a commentary on her position at court (see below).

Gnome or Heroine?

As is the case for many eighteenth-century women authors, there is a plethora of names for Göchhausen, a fact that can be read as an indication for both her position in contemporary Weimar and her status in current literary criticism. Wieland called her his "Gnomide," Goethe his "Kauz" [odd fish], possibly affectionately. The Counts of Stolberg perhaps more maliciously named her "Thusnelda," supposedly in reference (deference?) to her "wehrhafte[s] Mund- und Schreibwerk" [her armored tongue and pen; qtd. in Biedrzynski 121]. Anna Amalia transformed this nickname to the diminutive "Thuselchen." Göchhausen herself signed her letters with variations on her birth-name: frequently, like most eighteenth-century women authors, with her first name and abbreviated last name ("Louise G."), using mere initials ("L. G." or simply, perhaps grandly: "G."), or — more rarely — with her full name or abbreviated first name ("L. Goechhausen").

There can be no question that all names given her by others refer, in some form, to her body stature and her deformity: Wieland's "Gnomide" does so explicitly; the Stolbergs's "Thusnelda" (which became, incidentally, the name by which she is most often referred to in scholarship) indirectly. "Thusnelda" clearly evokes the physical type represented in the Thusnelda of Germanic lore, Arminius's heroic wife: tall, stately, blond, and valiant, she towers over her minions and strikes fear in the hearts of her enemies. Conversely, Anna Amalia's "Thuselchen" is an attempt to remove this stature from Göchhausen and reinstate to her the small, harmless, and diminutive: "Thuselchen" could be a child's nickname, perhaps a reference to her physique or perhaps (as is implied in some accounts; see Deneke 51–62 and 102–3; Biedrzynski 121) an allusion to Anna Amalia's maternal feelings towards Göchhausen. More than each of the names says about contemporary perceptions of Göchhausen's body or her writing, all these names together constitute what can be seen as *the* single defining characteristic of contemporary women authors: the namelessness that expresses itself in the constant process of exchangeable (nick)naming. What's in a name is identity ("Goethe"), what's in many names is *exchangeable* identities: each name evokes one personality to the exclusion of all others. In this reading, the famous question posed by the former slave and abolitionist "Sojourner Truth" (alias "Isabella Baumfree," alias "Isabella van Wagener," alias "…", ca. 1797–1883): "Ain't I a Woman?" could easily be answered negatively: she is *not* a woman or *not necessarily* a woman in contexts in which other identities are read into the foreground (nobody, black, slave, pilgrim, abolitionist), each of which could be expressed in her various names. As a slave, she bore the names of whatever family owned her at the time, and she underwent a period of "namelessness" before she named herself "Sojourner Truth," thereby defining herself as pilgrim and abolitionist.[5] Similarly, Göchhausen can be read and has been read as different historical and authorial identities, each of which corresponds to a name: as the diminutive child, as the malicious gnome, or, somewhat ironically, as the mighty author wielding her pen the way the Germanic hero wields his sword. Rather than reading her names as a mere expression of already established views, it can be assumed that, to some extent, her identities both as a court-personality and as an author were and continue to be established by these names.

Courtly Lady or Court Jester?

Interpretations of Göchhausen's position at Anna Amalia's court frequently hinge upon the implications inherent in Wieland's nickname "Gnomide": the "gnome" does not exclusively describe her physical stature, but, more important, an attitude attributed to her — her "Gnomiden-Geist," as it is frequently referred to in the literature (for example, Suphan's introduction to the *Journal* xviii-xix). Göchhausen's "gnome spirit" manifests itself in untiring, though usually unintellectual activity such as her secretarial work for the *Journal*,[6] but also in malicious satire and mockery.[7] For both sides of her character, researchers have found ample evidence in her writing: she served not only as editor and secretary to the *Journal*, but also as Goethe's part-time secretary;[8] and she entered the annals of literary history because her handwritten copy of Goethe's *Urfaust* (Original Faust) was found among her effects. The satirical side of her writing is amply recorded in her letters. Among the many eminently quotable examples are her ironic depictions of Duke Carl August, whom she calls her "Landespapa" [daddy of the country; letter to Merck, 2 March 1787, Deetjen 64]; her burlesque occasional poetry written to Goethe's mother;[9] her ironic account of the "concert" given by Tiefurt farm animals in honor of the Prussian Queen-Mother's visit in 1804 (letter to Böttiger, 5 July 1804, Deetjen 132–35); her allusions to body functions (letter to Goethe, 17 July 1795, Deetjen 124–25); and her viciously witty characterizations of talkative courtiers (letter to Knebel, 14 October 1782, Deetjen 52). One typical example of her style is her letter to Knebel of 13 October 1783, in which she accuses him of not writing:

> Ehrenhalber müßen Sie gestorben seyn, mein lieber Knebel, um sich wegen des langen Stillschweigens gegen mich auf eine gute Art zu entschuldigen. Wenigstens habe ich Ihnen vor der Reise drey Briefe geschrieben und keinen Laut vernommen. Unterdessen bin ich bekandermaßen 6 Wochen in Braunschweich gewesen; hätte ich einen Brief von Ihnen gefunden, so wüsten Sie jezt alles und hättens in der ersten Wärme der lebendigen Darstellung genossen; — jezt ists vorbey, [...]
>
> Doch nichts mehr; da Sie hoffendlich todt sind und keine Briefe mehr zerreisen können, so ists gefährlich, weil gewiß Ihrer vornehmen, gelehrten und berühmten Freunde wegen Ihre Correspondenz gedruckt wird.
>
> Auch noch Ihren Schatten mit Freundschaft zugethan bin ich Ihre
> Louise G. (Deetjen 55–56)

[By rights, dear Knebel, you must have died to excuse with any decency your long silence towards me. At any rate, I wrote you three letters before my journey and I have not heard a word. In the meantime, as everyone knows, I have spent six weeks in Brunswick; if I had found a letter from you there, you would know everything now and you would have been able to hear it all in the first warmth and enjoyment of relating recent experience. But now it's over, (...).

But no more; since it is to be hoped that you are dead and incapable of tearing up letters, this is dangerous, since your

correspondence will undoubtedly be printed because of your noble, erudite and famous friends.
 Ever in affectionate friendship, even towards your shadow, I remain
Louise G.]

The image of the gnome combined with the liberties she took in her writing (jester's license?) led her biographers to read her as a court jester, as "Hofdame" [lady-in-waiting] turned "Hofnarr" [court jester] (Deneke 226, Deetjen's introduction 8 and 11, Biedrzynski 121–22). As in the images and imaginings of her body and in the act of naming, we are presented with a split image in which "Hofdame" describes her title while "Hofnarr" outlines her function at court. An integral part of the image of Göchhausen as court jester is the frequent assertion that Göchhausen took jokes about her deformity with equanimity and humor (see Biedrzynski 121; Deetjen's introduction 11–12). Like any good fool, Göchhausen joined in the laughter at her own expense. Finally, the aforementioned contradiction between Göchhausen's aversion to mirrors and her self-confident performances on the stage of the *Liebhabertheater* [amateur theater] could be read as part of the court jester image: like court jesters, Louise von Göchhausen is viewed not as being "there" for her own benefit, but for the entertainment of others, not to see herself, but to be seen by others.

Prosaic Chronicler or Spirited Narrator?

In Sigrid Lange's essay "Italienreisen," one finds the following description of Göchhausen's diary of her Italian journey (1788–90):

> Göchhausens gesamtes, 86 Doppelseiten füllendes Reisetagebuch liest sich [...] nüchtern, knapp, korrekt. Sie hält Orte, Daten, Personen — immer mit vollständigem Titel aufgeführt — akribisch fest, beschrieben werden in immer gleichen sprachlichen Wendungen Wetter, Wegverhältnisse und zumeist mangelhafter Gasthauskomfort, fürstliche Empfänge stehen gleichrangig neben Belanglosigkeiten [...]. Die Eindrücke aus Italien scheinen eher einem durchschnittlichen Reiseführer als eigener Anschauung entnommen zu sein. Urteile über Landschaften und Kunsteindrücke fallen formelhaft: "sehr artig", "mittelmäßig", "interessant". Land und Leute werden aus der Distanz wahrgenommen, die die Etikette ohnehin vorschreibt [...]. Kaum einmal findet man eine persönliche Stimmung wiedergegeben, die Verfasserin tritt hinter ihren Text weitge-

hend zurück [...]. Sowieso wäre Louise von Göchhausen, wie sie gelegentlich durchblicken läßt, lieber zu Hause geblieben. (Lange, "Italienreisen" 22–23)[10]

[Göchhausen's complete travelogue, filling eighty-six double pages, comes across as dry, sparse, and correct. She records places, dates, persons — always listed with their complete titles — minutely; she describes, in ever-identical turns of phrase, the weather, the conditions of the roads, and mostly uncomfortable inns; royal receptions receive equal weight with irrelevancies (...). Her impressions of Italy seem taken from a mediocre traveler's guide rather than from her own observation. Her judgments of landscapes and artistic impressions are formulaic: "very nice," "mediocre," "interesting." The country and its people are perceived from the distance prescribed by etiquette (...). Hardly ever does one encounter a personal mood; for the most part, the author removes herself from the text (...). In any case, as Louise von Göchhausen occasionally gives us to understand, she would much rather have stayed at home.]

What Lange describes here is not a journey but its refutation. Göchhausen's listlessness expresses itself everywhere in her "clichéd" and bored descriptions of everything "we saw" (25; 29) and in her steadfast refusal to enter any personal impressions into her travelogue. In this view, Göchhausen identified exclusively with her role as lady-in-waiting and felt uncomfortable in any other; the only thing that made the Italian journey at all bearable to her was that it transferred her courtly space to Italy (34), giving her the opportunity to continue to play her part there. Göchhausen in Italy "'sieht' nichts" ["sees" nothing; 37], merely biding her time until the order was given to return to her sheltered space in Weimar.

The same journey reads very differently, however, in Göchhausen's letters, for example in this letter to Knebel of 25 October 1788.

[Ich] kan [...] das Schicksal nicht genug preißen, daß es einen so hellen Sonnenblick auf mein Leben warf, als bis jetzt die Reise nach Italien für mich gewesen ist.

Was dieses Land für den Künstler seyn muß, ist unaussprechlich, wer es aber auch nicht ist, findet noch immer reichen Genuß in der Menge großer Gegenstände, die einem auf allen Schritten umgeben und der herrlichen Natur, die iezt, zum zweytenmal verjüngt, in aller Fülle einer unglaublichen Vegetation hervortritt. O könte ich Ihnen einen Blick ins Coliseo erkaufen! wie es so groß in seiner Zerstörung da steht, die Fülle der Lorbeern, Zipressen, Pinyen, die aus allen Steinritzen hervordrängen und es vorzüglich in dieser Jahreszeit zum größten und zugleich mahlerischsten Anblick machen, wo keine Imagination hinreicht [...].

Daß die alte Mutter Natur dieses Land mit all seinen herrlichen Gaben und Früchten beynahe 300 Meilen weit von Weimar wech legte, war gar nicht freundschaftlich von ihr gehandelt. (Deetjen 69)

[I cannot praise fate enough for bestowing such a bright ray of sunshine onto my life as the journey to Italy has proven for me so far.

What this country must mean for artists is unthinkable. But even those who are not artists will still find rich enjoyment in the multitude of great monuments which surround one everywhere, and in glorious nature which now, rejuvenated again, emerges in the full richness of an incredible vegetation. O that I could buy you one glance at the Coliseum, as it stands there, great in its destruction; the richness of laurel, cypresses, pines pushing outward from every crevice in the stone, making the Coliseum, especially at this time of the year, the most superb and simultaneously the most picturesque sight possible — no imagination is equal to the task (...).
That old Mother Nature situated this country, with all its wonderful gifts and fruits, nearly three hundred miles away from Weimar, was truly an unkind deed of her.]

Of the seventy-nine letters republished in Deetjen's 1923 edition, twenty were written in Italy; all contain concrete, elaborate, loving, dynamic, and ardently enthusiastic descriptions of Italy, its landscape, people, customs, museums, art, and music. Clearly, her Italian journey, as described in her letters, must be considered the most momentous event in Göchhausen's life: she is consistently and unabashedly exuberant in her descriptions of the country and its people and enjoyed her many unusual experiences to the fullest (among them the ascent of Mount Vesuvius while it was erupting; see her letter to Wieland from Naples, 25 August 1789, Deetjen 105–6). In many of her letters, Göchhausen intimates, rather than describes, a heartfelt tribute to the indescribable. There is no evidence that she missed Weimar or even her beloved Tiefurt — on the contrary, many of her letters avow a more intense *joie de vivre* than she had ever experienced in Weimar.

Es scheint überhaupt, man muß nach Italien und vorzüglich nach Neapel reißen, um einen Begriff von Sommer Tagen und Nächten zu bekommen, ich glaube, hier scheinen die Originale von der Sonne und dem Mond, die uns zuweilen besuchen. (Letter to Wieland, 25 August 1789, Deetjen 105–6)

[It seems that one has to travel to Italy and especially to Naples to get an idea of summer days and nights: I think it is here that the originals of the sun and moon shine who visit us occasionally.]

Months before she left Italy, she mourned her loss in anticipation:

Ach, liebster Freund, wie sehr weiß ich, wie sehr fühle ich, wozu Sie so wohlmeinend mich vorbereiten. O könte man auch vergessen, was man verlassen muß! ich schäme mich beynahe zu sagen, wie sehr mein Herz an diesem Lande, an diesen Menschen hängt; und doch wozu soll ich Ihnen verschweigen [...]. Einen der schwersten Abschiede aus Italien habe ich schon genommen — aber noch nicht überstanten [...]. (Letter to Wieland, 17 November 1789, Deetjen 114–15)[11]

[Oh, dearest friend, how well I know, how strongly I feel that for which you in your kindness are preparing me! Oh that one could also forget that which one must leave! I am almost ashamed to admit how much my heart is attached to this country and to these people, but why should I hide this from you (...). I have already said one of my most difficult goodbyes from Italy, but I have not yet gotten over it (...).]

What is one to conclude from these contradictory impressions of the same Italian journey? Lange professed herself unaware of the existence of Göchhausen's published letters ("Italienreisen" 29) and did not include them in the discussion; her reading of the travelogue is therefore necessarily one-sided, but, I believe, essentially correct. Short of discrediting Lange's work, the interpreter is left with the unpalatable option of declaring one version of Göchhausen's travel impressions, both recorded by herself, as the "correct" account and ignoring the other. The choice in this case is complicated by the fact that both genres in question, diary and letters, are not easily attributable to either the public or the private sphere. As is well known, eighteenth-century letters were a semi-public forum; however, what makes it difficult to read Göchhausen's letters in that context is that most of them were written to close friends and contain not so much a description of her Italian journey as a testimony of the ineradicable impression her journey left on her. Equally obviously, the supposedly private diary form could be considered more public, in the event, that is — and based on Lange's depiction of this "dry, sparse, correct" account, one could speculate that this may have been the case — that Anna Amalia ordered her to keep this diary as a record of *her* Italian journey. I believe that the biographical "facts" as we "know" them do not permit a valuation of one account over the other: like Göchhausen's varying body images, her multiple names, and her fluctuating position at the court of Weimar, the diametrically opposed accounts of her Italian journey (or her renunciation of that journey) must be considered yet another irreconcilable contradiction in the maze of conflicting views that make up Göchhausen's image in scholarship today.

The Body in the Mirror: Theories of the Grotesque

Beyond the lack of source materials, such irreconcilable differences in interpretation point to a methodological flaw in the investigation: an inability to read Göchhausen in the context of Weimar Classicism. I would therefore like to suggest an alternative context: that of the "Weimar Grotesque." Theories of the grotesque seem more applicable here because they refer extensively to the body[12] and because they allow for contradictions that apparently cannot be adequately interpreted in the classical context. The grotesque, in most theories, tends to incorporate these contradictions: "By the word [is] understood not only something playfully gay and carelessly fantastic, but also something ominous and sinister in the face of a world totally different from the familiar one" (Kayser 21). This incorporation of opposites has already been noted by two scholars of the grotesque who were Louise von Göchhausen's contemporaries: her "Papa" Wieland and Carl Friedrich Flögel (1729–88), whose major work on the grotesque, *Geschichte des Groteskekomischen* (History of the Grotesque-Comic, 1788), appeared the year Göchhausen set out for Italy. Wieland differentiated between three kinds of caricature: "true" caricatures (in which painters portray exactly what they see), "exaggerated" caricatures (in which painters exaggerate that which they see), and "grotesque" caricatures (in which painters do not work from nature, but purely from their own imagination; "Unterredungen" 374). This means that the grotesque is by definition that part of the painting that does not exist in nature: art is no longer imitation of nature (which would mean that by mimetic definitions, the grotesque cannot be considered art). According to Wieland, a definition of the grotesque cannot merely be arrived at by a glance at the painting, but must also consider its effect on the viewer: the viewer's reaction (amusement, disgust, surprise, etc.) produces the grotesque; he or she smiles at the deformations presented in the picture, but is appalled by the monstrous elements because they represent the dissolution of his or her reality (Kayser 31). The grotesque, in other words, is transferred from the artist's "wild imagination" (Wieland's term) to that of the viewer: it is, literally, in the eye of the beholder. It is the viewer who provides the "mirror" in which the grotesque comes into being (the implication being that in "nature," everything continues to be fine). The grotesque, then, describes three distinct phases in the creation of the work of "art": the artist's creative attitude (which Wieland, based on the premise that the artist was not working from nature, considered "dreamlike"); the work of art itself (its contents and structures), and its effect on the beholder (Kayser 180). Flögel, one of the major contemporary theorists of the grotesque, defined the grotesque in a similar manner. Although he sees it as occasioned by and expressed in the work of art, he situates the grotesque primarily in two realms, in the imagination of the artist and in the reception of the work of art, that is, in the imagination of the viewer (*Groteskekomisches* 3).

Another important aspect of the grotesque, and one that it shares with classical art, is its concentration on the body. Figuring prominently in all discussions of the grotesque, from Flögel to Bakhtin and beyond, is the idea of incorporating contradictions into the same painting or representation and the prominence of two body parts: the hunchback and the mouth. In Flögel's description of the masks used in grotesque theater in ancient Greece, all masks had "übertriebene Züge, ein gräßliches oder lächerliches Ansehn, und einen großen aufgesperrten Mund, als wenn sie die Zuschauer verschlingen wollten" [exaggerated features, a horrifying or ridiculous demeanor, and a huge gaping mouth, as if they were about to devour the audience; *Groteskekomisches* 6]. Most of these masks featured not one facial expression, but two: "eine von den Augenbrauen auf der Larve [war] gerunzelt, und die andre glatt [...]. Man findet auf verschiednen geschnittnen Steinen Larven mit solchen doppelten Gesichtern" [one eyebrow on the mask was furrowed, the other smooth. Masks with such two-fold faces can be found on many carved stones; 8]. In later years, he casts the court jester as the star of grotesque representations and lists the court jester's hunchback as his sole qualification: "Ja, die häßlichsten Zwerge, rachitische Ungeheuer, krumm und schief gewachsene Menschen sind oft als Hofnarren gebraucht worden" [Indeed, the ugliest dwarves, rachitically deformed monsters, people with crooked and lop-sided bodies have often been employed as court jesters; *Hofnarren* 6]. Reversing Wieland's position that the grotesque never occurs in nature, the hunchback in this discussion is "naturally" grotesque.[13] Similarly, if more elegantly, Bakhtin defines the physical grotesque as "that which protrudes from the body, all that seeks to go out beyond the body's confines."[14] Equally prominent in Bakhtin's discussion of the physical grotesque is the gaping mouth as "related to the lower stratum": the mouth as the gate leading into the body's underworld (*Rabelais* 325).

I contend that these theories can help us arrive at a more differentiated interpretation of Louise von Göchhausen where classical theories have failed. Re-reading Louise von Göchhausen in the light of these theories would mean abandoning the search for biographical "truth" in favor of an investigation of ways of reading. Such an approach would recognize the multiple contradictions in her reception (her various names and bodies, the opposing viewpoints of her position at court and her writing) as a product of conscientious scholarship, but at the same time — to the extent that the result of the investigation is already in the eye of the beholder — also as a result of the viewers' "wild imagination"; ultimately, then, as having little to do with the original herself.[15] That approach would view all endeavors to arrive at "biographical truth" or one dominant interpretation as an attempt to heal or prevent the dissolution of our reality illustrated in the grotesque. Because in Göchhausen's case, as is the case with most eighteenth-century women authors, there is little "biographical truth" left to investigate, we must rely on multiple mirrors creating diverse interpretations, so that valuation of one interpretation over another becomes difficult, if not impossible.

It is possible, however, to re-evaluate the classical position from the viewpoint of the grotesque, because the classical position limits our view of what can or cannot occur in "nature" and establishes a context in which the grotesque cannot be considered anything but an aberration. The grotesque is a sign of a world out of synch; it belongs in the world of dissolution and estrangement (Kayser 43), a world that, from the viewpoint of high or classical art, can only be considered unclassical, or anti-classical. It is little wonder that Goethe, the classicist ever in search of aesthetic categories that center on the work of art and its structure while ignoring its reception, "pursues the grotesque, wherever he finds it, with his hatred,"[16] and that he became the one to strike the deathblow to the grotesque during *his* Italian journey (Kayser 180). If the grotesque is indeed in the eye of the beholder, Goethe's drawings of Göchhausen begin to make sense: Goethe, drawing Göchhausen's hunchback, "sees" nothing. In drawing Göchhausen, Goethe transforms her into a "classical" body. The bodily canon, according to Bakhtin, presents "a finished, completed, strictly limited body, which is shown from the outside as something individual. That which protrudes, bulges, sprouts, or branches off (when a body transgresses its limits [...]) is eliminated, hidden, or moderated" (*Rabelais* 320). More importantly, "the body of the new canon is merely one body; no signs of duality have been left. It is self-sufficient and speaks in its name alone" (*Rabelais* 321).

Clearly, interpretations that have sought to transform Göchhausen into a classical body, into one individual body with one name, cannot contend with the many contradictions beyond suppressing them to arrive at this interpretation. Göchhausen is multiple bodies (she can be dissected into her "hunchback" and into her "big mouth" or "sharp tongue," as secondary literature has it); she is multiple names (Louise-Gnomide-Thusnelda-Thuselchen), each indicating a different position (courtly lady and court jester) and a different style of writing (boring stylized chronicle and spirited and dynamic narrative).

A more discerning way of reading Göchhausen can perhaps be suggested by Diego Velásquez's painting *Las Meninas*: charming ladies-in-waiting surround the lovely princess, the reflection in the mirror (one of Velásquez's favorite motifs) shows the royal parents seated in state, and in the foreground of the picture, two additional ladies-in-waiting, shockingly deformed and misshapen, contest the idyllic scene (see Kayser's description, 18). Velásquez's painting, which depicts the classical norm side by side with the grotesque, suggests a modified reading of the grotesque vis-à-vis the classical, one that has been taken up by some post-Bakhtinian scholars. In this interpretation, the grotesque is seen not so much as opposite or opposed to the classical (a reading that clearly emphasizes the aberrant qualities inherent in the grotesque), but rather as an artform that incorporates both affinity and antagonism, that embodies both the normative and the abnormal (see, for example, Kayser 21; Harpham; Stallybrass and White). The grotesque in this view is "formed through a process of hybridization or inmixing of binary opposites, particularly of high and low, such that there is a heterodox merging of elements usually perceived as incompatible" (Stallybrass and White 44). Harpham calls this "the taboo compromise" (9) and claims that it represents a confusion of hierarchies in the work of art which then, presumably, would be mirrored in the viewer. I would agree that "cultural categories of high and low [...] are never entirely separable" (Stallybrass and White 2), and consider the distinction made here — between the grotesque as opposed to the classical norm and the grotesque as incorporating both the classical and the anti-classical — a vital aspect of a differentiated reading of grotesque artforms. Nonetheless, I would contend that such distinctions are completely irrelevant from the classical viewpoint, precisely because the classical, in its insistence on being and remaining the dominant artform, rejects infiltrations and "compromises" no less vigorously than it would more encompassing or direct challenges to its authority. As long as our aesthetics are affected by the classical, I believe that an assessment of the grotesque in general and Göchhausen's work in particular entails the reader's initial willingness to permit the complete dissolution of the classical world; in other words, to read the grotesque as a direct challenge to and negation of classical doctrine. For this reason, my interpretation of Göchhausen's writing in the following tends towards a reading of the grotesque as the anti-classical (although I believe that Göchhausen's own creative attitude was much closer to the "taboo compromise" of classical and anti-classical that Harpham describes).

Another reason why I would contend that the more radical view of the grotesque as the anti-classical is initially more useful is that I am not convinced that theories of the grotesque that subscribe to the hybridization or compromise theory, as discussed by Harpham and Stallybrass and White, always lead to an open-minded re-assessment of non-canonized literature, particularly women's. It seems to me that where women's literature is concerned, a denunciation of the high-low dichotomy in the service of grotesque theory does not necessarily entail relinquishing familiar paradigms of good-bad literature, as Harpham's judgmental remarks on Emily Brontë's "bad" writing demonstrate (105). I believe that the interpretive stance called for in a discussion of *women's* grotesque literature is, to adapt Flögel's term, yet another variation of grotesque theory, the *Groteskefeministisches*. I view this interpretive stance as one that not only "takes the marginal [...] as the type" (Harpham 22), one that not only views the socially peripheral as the symbolically central (Babcock, qtd. in Stallybrass and White 20), but one that also insists on gender as a central category in this interpretive enterprise and refuses once again to de-centralize, de-emphasize, or de-grade women's literature in interpretations of grotesque art.

"Hell Bruegel in a Magic Dress": Göchhausen Writing the Grotesque

Indications that Göchhausen was familiar with theories of the grotesque and saw some of her own writing in that light abound in her work. The two most obvious facets in her writing that indicate this are first, her frequent incorporation of a "world out of synch" into her work (by creating contradictory interpretations of the same event, as she may have done in case of her Italian journey; by mixing genres, styles, and moods, or by creating contradictory or confusing paradigms within the same piece); and second, her frequent employment of grotesque body imagery. Because Göchhausen's writing defies traditional literary analysis even in terms of genre definition (for example, it would be almost impossible clearly to designate most of her texts as either epistolary, or autobiographical, or fictional), I would like to set aside these distinctions for the purposes of this essay and instead take her two main methodologies of writing as my point of departure.

Göchhausen wrote at least four congratulatory poems to Goethe's mother, three on the occasion of her birthday, which happened to coincide with carnival. In each of these poems, the grotesque rears its head in the depiction of sorrow or, in some cases, horror intruding into the carnivalesque celebration:

> Am Tage, wo kein Mensch sich freut,
> Sich jeder das Haupt mit Asche bestreut,
> Nach Tanz und Schmause nicht mehr fragt,
> Für seine Sünden am Finger nagt,
> Und künftig den Freuden der Welt entsagt; —
> An diesem Tag war's viel gewagt,
> Daß dich deine Mutter, so nöthig es war,
> Der Kirche zum Troz, zur Welt gebahr;
> Weil in der ganzen Christenheit
> Bey dieser büßenden heiligen Zeit
> Solch einen Actum der Fröhlichkeit
> Sogar die Polizey verbeut.
> Es wäre demnach ungewiß,
> Ob nicht deine Geburt ein Ärgerniß
> Zu jener Zeit schon gewesen ist? —
> Und ob auch jetzt, nimmt man es scharf,
> Sich eine gute Christin drob freuen darf? (*Journal* 162)[17]

> [On the day, when nobody feels glad and vivacious,
> When everyone covers his head with ashes,
> When nobody cares about the dance and the feast,
> But instead bites his nails and remembers his sins
> And renounces all future joys on this earth:
> On this very day, your mother gave birth
> To you, driven by necessity
> Thus daring the Church defiantly,
> Because in all of Christianity

Such a joyous act is forbidden by law
In this holy time of atonement and awe.
Thus, one may ask, if one's nature is pensive:
Whether your birth was not rather offensive,
And whether, aside from all merriment and mirth,
Good Christians should rejoice on the day of your birth?]

Whether a birthday is indeed an occasion to celebrate is further drawn into question by considerations that normally do not enter into congratulatory notes: considerations of the child's mother[18] and the newborn herself.

Bescheiden und sittsam, wie's jedem gefällt,
Betrattst du die Laufbahn der büßenden Welt:
Man sah in dir nicht die mindeste Spur
Von Freude, — du wimmertest lediglich nur
Und stelltest dich ächzend und wehmütig an,
Als hättst du schon Böses die Fülle gethan. (*Journal* 163)

[Just as we like it, so modest and shy,
You entered the path of this world full of sighs,
Not the least trace of joy was in you detected,
You just whined and groaned and generally acted
As if you had, even before life begins,
Committed an overabundance of sins.]

The grotesque in this instance is represented by a distortion in the mirror, showing not the grown-up Frau Aja, but the new-born, whose image is further removed from the traditional identification of infancy and innocence: the infant in this mirror is guilty by implication, a fitting parallel to the mother's "guilt" in bearing her child during the day of the fast and in direct opposition to church doctrine, and to the general ironic mood of atonement permeating the entire poem. In a very similar fashion, Göchhausen undercuts the congratulatory message in other poems by pointing to the contrast between the celebratory mood and the horrors of carnival (see letter to Frau Rath Goethe, 19 Februar 1784, Deetjen 59–60), by citing the devil's intervention as an excuse for why she does not send a gift (same letter, Deetjen 63–64), or — in lieu of wishing the birthday child the traditional "alles Gute" — by *un*wishing her all the horrors implied in her scenario:

> So nimm doch meine Wünsche an:
> Krieg, Pestilentz und theuere Zeit,
> Kopf, Zahnweh, Schneiden in den Leib,
> Und alles, womit Pandora die Erde
> An Uebeln in ihren Griesgram beschwerde,
> Sey fern von Dir! [...]
> Auch Höllenprögel in Magischen Gewand
> Wünscht Dir Thusnelda mit Herz und mit Hand!
> (Letter to Frau Rath Goethe, Christmas 1778, Deetjen 19)

> [Please accept my wish demure:
> May war, pestilence, and expenditure,
> Headaches, toothaches, stomachaches and worse,
> And everything that Pandora's curse
> And her grouchiness inflicted on this Earth
> Be far from you! (...).
> And a Hell Bruegel in a Magic dress
> Wishes you Thusnelda with a kiss and caress.]

That "Thusnelda" (this is one of the rare times that Göchhausen employs that name for herself) knew that she was writing within paradigms of the grotesque is indicated in her reference to "Höllenprögel": it was that same "Höllenbreugel" — intended is probably either Pieter Bruegel the Elder (1525/30–69), or Pieter Bruegel the Younger (1564?-1638) — whom Wieland considered a "master of the grotesque" ("Unterredungen" 374; see also Kayser 32). Based on this reference, one could assume that Göchhausen was familiar with Wieland's treatise and consciously adopted Bruegel's style — the grotesque style — "in a magic dress": clothed in a different medium, that of poetry instead of painting.

Whereas these poems employ body images indirectly (in references to birth, labor pains, and physical diseases), the following letter on the occasion of Knebel's birthday evokes a set of grotesque body images more directly, in the implied-yet-denied depictions of the drooling, filthy, long-nailed, spitting slob:

> An den heutigen festlichen Tage wünschen auch wir ein kleines Zeichen von unsern Antheil an demselben, Ihnen dar zu bringen. Da nun die Erhaltung alles deßen, was zu Ihrer werthen Person gehört, uns ganz besonders intereßiret, so erfolgt hier 1) Eine Serviette; bey Tisch, wo die Zerlegung der Speisen zuweilen Schwürigkeiten für Ihnen zu haben scheint,

sich die Finger bequemer abwischen zu können und Ihre Wäsche zu schonen.

2) Eine Scheere, als ein Mittel, Ihre Nägel auch noch anders, als mit den Zähnen, in Schranken zu halten.

Da uns aber zugleich das feine ameublement und besonders die kostbaren Fuß-Teppiche unserer Gebieterin pflichtschuldigst am Herzen liegt, so erfolgt

3) Ein Spuck-Näpfchen, welches Sie ganz bequem bey jeder Gelegenheit bey sich führen können. (Letter to Knebel from Göchhausen and von Wolfskeel, 30 November 1793, Deetjen 123)

[On the occasion of today's festivity, we wish to offer you a small token of our affectionate regard. Since the preservation of all that pertains to your worthy person is of particular interest to us, we send you 1) a napkin, so that at table, where the carving up of food seems, at times, to hold particular difficulties for you, you can more comfortably wipe your fingers and spare your shirts.

2) A pair of scissors, as a means to subdue your nails by other means than by employing your teeth.

Since simultaneously the fine furniture and especially the precious carpetry of our employer are of particular and dutiful concern to us, we send you

3) A spittoon, which you can comfortably carry with you on every occasion.]

Much of Göchhausen's grotesque writing centers on "unmentionable" subjects: physical diseases, physical grossness, birth, death, labor, and body discharge like spit or blood are brought into the foreground. Particular emphasis is placed on grotesquely elongated or protruding bodies or body parts (Knebel's fingernails) and on bodies in pain. One example of the grotesque body is her "Lied eines Gefangenen" (Song of a Prisoner), which employs a number of bizarre contrasts: the theme (a prisoner bemoaning his captivity) stands in stark contrast to the style (a folk-song à la Herder); the beautiful May landscape is contrasted with the prisoner's depressing surroundings. In his dungeon, the prisoner contemplates his own transformation into a grotesque body in captivity:

Ach die Haare meines Hauptes
Reichen schon zur Ferse mir.

Und die Haare meines Kinnes
Könnten wohl mein Tischtuch seyn

> Und die Nägel meiner Hände
> Mir ein scharfes Messer seyn. (*Journal* [32] 263)[19]

> [Woe, the hair upon my head
> Reaches down upon my feet.
>
> And the beard upon my chin
> Could well serve as a tablecloth,
> And the nails upon my hands
> As a sharp knife, by my troth!]

As in the letter to Knebel, the grotesque body is not merely grotesque by virtue of its visual representation, but in the reader's imagination, which is invoked through the implication of body *function* (in both cases, the consumption of food). This truly Bakhtinian body (a body that "seeks to go out beyond the body's confines") remains the object of tragic contemplation until the captive is rescued: first in his own imagination, then in the "reality" of the poem. The manner of the rescue itself and the stark contrast between the highly tragic prisoner's lament and the fantastically nonsensical outcome could in itself be considered grotesque: the prisoner fantasizes about his lover sending him a bird to provide him with food; the food contains a file for the bars at his window; and the king, upon overhearing the prisoner fantasize in this manner, decides to release him. But more important, this ending is grotesque in the sense that it ostentatiously attempts to reinstate "reality." As in Göchhausen's letters, the grotesque body is examined and contemplated before the world is brought back "into synch" in ways that could well be read as Harpham's "taboo compromise": the genuine congratulatory endings in letters to Frau Aja, the fact that the letter to Knebel masquerades as a *preventive* measure against the grotesque image evoked, and the prisoner's freedom fantasy reinstate the classical world-view, but not until the reader is made aware of what an immense tour de force it takes to do so.

Bodies in pain enter into Göchhausen's writing particularly in metaphorical form. A case in point is her poem "Die zwey Linden" (The Two Linden Trees), which she may have patterned after Werther's wrath about the destruction of the trees in the clergyman's courtyard. The poem describes the felling of two linden trees in the following manner:

> Sie liegen nun, und ihre Kronen nieder
> In Staub, und von dem Fall

Krächzt im dumpfen Wiederhall
Ihre Mutter, die Erde, wieder.
Getrennt sind ihre Glieder
Von Stamm und Wurzeln — und nun, —
Weil rothes Blut nicht fließt, kein Stöhnen,
Kein Zucken folgt, — so wähnen
Die Verderber kein Übels zu thun.
[...]
Sie sahen nicht wie die Mutter Erde
Seit langem her, mit liebender Beschwerde
Diese Lieblinge ihres Schooßes gepflegt,
An ihren Busen sie gelegt,
Lebenskraft daraus zu trinken,
[...]
Also manche des Hofes wähnen,
Wo Blut nicht fließt, kein Stöhnen,
Kein Zucken folgt; da sey
Kein Unrecht, alles einerley.
(*Journal* [15] 124–25; original in Göchhausen's handwriting;
   see note to 124 on 376–77)

[They lie, their crowns in dust, and from their fall
Their mother, Earth, reverberates in agony.
Their limbs are torn from stem and root, and yet —
Because there flows no blood, because no groans
And no convulsions follow, the destroyers
Think they have done no evil.
(...)
They did not see how Mother Earth, for long
With loving care caressed these darlings of her womb,
How she offered them her breasts
To nourish them with vital energy,
(...)
As do these villains, some at court maintain:
That where no blood flows, where no groans
And no convulsions are discernible, there is
No Evil, no injustice has been done, and
All is immaterial.]

The bodies in this poem transcend traditional metaphorical usage both in their intensity and thematically, in their evocation of unmentionable body parts and functions: birth, nursing, breasts, the womb, death, blood, convulsions. These physical manifestations are not evoked merely to transmit or intensify the poem's obvious message, which is essentially Werther's. Instead, the poem establishes a paradigm between the grotesque and the world-in-synch: just as the commission of an act of brutality necessitates *un*imagining the suffering body, the survival of the world-in-synch entails the willful suppression of the Grotesque and other non-classical discourses (here represented by the body imagery).

A World Out of Synch: The Grotesque and Classicism

Re-reading Louise von Göchhausen in light of the grotesque, that is, as a grotesque biographical figure and as an artist of the grotesque, is suggested by many facets of her work: her themes (carnival, body imagery, frequent emphasis on unmentionable body parts and functions) and methodologies (her disregard of the compatibility of literary genres, styles, themes, and mood). Such an act of reading is also productive in the sense that suppression of contradictory aspects in her work or biography is no longer necessary. Instead, these aspects could be mined for their commentary on both Göchhausen's work and our reading behavior. By portraying the grotesque and offering classical resolutions, Göchhausen, I would contend, does not merely vindicate classical theories over the grotesque or submit to the prevailing aesthetic norm. Instead, she points to her own awareness of this norm as well as aspects in her own personality and work that differ, and provides the reader with an impetus to re-evaluate literary doctrines which have, to a large extent, shaped our reading behavior. Read as manifestations of the grotesque, the contradictions in her work could be read as a sign that her world was out of synch, that she intentionally did not portray a trustworthy, reliable universe. Our efforts to read Weimar as such a universe, as classical Weimar, have in effect rendered us unable to read anything radically deviating from this doctrine with any kind of understanding or pleasure.

Reading Göchhausen in light of the grotesque also demands a re-(e)valuation of "truth" (biographical or aesthetic) versus "fantasy." Such an act of reading would assume that Göchhausen did not work from life but from imagination — unlike other Weimar women authors, who have recently gained critical acclaim as astute observers and caricaturists of Weimar life (for example, Charlotte von Stein, whose complete plays appeared as a facsimile reprint in 1998; see also Kord, "Not in Goethe's Image"; Bohm; Goodman; Dietrick). Göchhausen's work is not mimetic, but fantastic and demands a readership that is not bent on the search for eternal truths, but capable of mirroring and reproducing the grotesque aspects in her work without dismissing them as contradictions or aberrations. Such a readership has been denied her since the ascendancy of Weimar Classicism. Early sources concentrate on her life and do not even perceive her as an author, and there had been *no* scholarly work on her until Lange's essay in 1995. What little research there is indicates clearly both the extent to which we perceive the classical as the only permissible aesthetics in reading Weimar and the extent to which we are unable to comprehend other aesthetic forms. Read against this background, that of classical Weimar, the dismissal or distortion of Göchhausen as an author is understandable: unlike the work of other authors, Göchhausen's writing is not a "body of work" — no such unity and correlation can be attributed to her writing. Unlike classical works (at least as described in classical aesthetics), Göchhausen's work is not a work per se, but intricately connected with her character, her position, her names, and her creative attitudes; it is not self-sufficient, but dependent on the reader's receptive disposition. To read Göchhausen the way she undoubtedly deserves to be read would entail more research into her imagination (that is, archival research), but also, perhaps more important, an investigation into our own. It would entail an abandonment of the classical world-view, of that world that insists on being and remaining clean, aesthetic, well-balanced, and in synch, the world that depends for its survival and predominance on the eradication of all other artistic attitudes (witness, for example, Goethe's vehement derision of Early Romantic theories).[20] To re-read Louise von Göchhausen, it is necessary, to take our cue from Bakhtin once more, to develop a dialogic imagination: read as examples of "multi-voiced" discourse, the apparent contradictions in her work can be interpreted as the author's determination not to value one view over the other, as a conscious avoidance of assigning to either the classical or the grotesque the status of "truth" (see also Harpham's discussion of the grotesque as a "compromise" between high/ideal and low/degenerate art; 9–10). The reader who succeeds in mirroring this creative attitude in his or her own imagination would perhaps come to understand Louise von Göchhausen as one of the most fantastic and imaginative figures in the history of Weimar.

—Georgetown University

Notes

I would like to thank Friederike Eigler and James Harding for their critical reading of this article and their helpful comments, Francisco LaRubia-Prado and Simon Richter for help with secondary sources, and the Goethe-Museum Düsseldorf, the Stiftung Weimarer Klassik, and the Verlagsgruppe Koehler/Mittler for their kind permission to reprint representations of Göchhausen.

[1] For biographical information on Göchhausen, see Deneke; Deetjen, "Einleitung" 1–15, and Biedrzynski 121–23. My tentative biography of Göchhausen consists of instances on which all of these sources agree; nonetheless, I would consider some of this information unreliable because of the Goethe-centrism inherent in early Weimar scholarship and because of the fictional nature of the most extensive of these three sources (Deneke). Although Deneke's novel corresponds precisely to scholarly accounts of Göchhausen's life, including quotations from her letters, remarks by other people about her, and innumerable small details, it is to be assumed that some poetic license was employed in the relation of Göchhausen's life.

[2] "Die Gestalt der Göchhausen war klein, mager und verwachsen, aber gleichsam als Entschädigung dafür hatte ihr die Natur eine leichte Auffassungsgabe, ein scharfes Beobachtungsvermögen und einen klaren Verstand gegeben, dazu einen köstlichen Humor [...]. Im Grunde war sie liebenswürdig, gemütvoll und begeisterungsfähig" [Göchhausen's body was small, thin and deformed, but as if in compensation, Nature provided her with a facile apprehension, a sharp ability to observe and clear thinking, and in addition a delicious sense of humor (...). At bottom, she was lovable, tender-hearted and enthusiastic; Deetjen, "Einleitung" 1]. See also Bruford: "The lady-in-waiting was Thusnelda von Göchhausen [sic], now twenty-three, whose lively mind enabled her to bear with cheerfulness the burden of her misshapen body" (*Culture and Society* 69).

[3] "Eine Hofdame, entgegen den üblichen Erwartungen nicht anmutig und wohlgestalt, sondern von körperlicher Kümmerlichkeit: klein, häßlich, rachitisch verwachsen" [A lady-in-waiting, in contrast to the usual expectations not graceful and shapely, but physically wretched: small, ugly, rachitically deformed; Biedrzynski 121].

[4] See Eduard von der Hellen's annotation to *Journal* 331: "Fräulein von Göchhausen, auf die sich ohne Frage diese Neckerei bezieht, wird unter 1–4 recht launig charakterisirt" [Fräulein von Göchhausen, to whom this banter unquestionably refers, is merrily characterized in 1–4; *Journal* 392].

⁵ See Haraway; on names as pertaining to German women and authorship, anonymity and pseudonymity, see Kord, *Sich einen Namen machen,* and Hahn.

⁶ Attributing the editorship to Einsiedel, Suphan delegates her to the status of secretary: "als Secretär stand ihm [...] die 'Gnomide' Göchhausen zur Seite; sie schickte sich ausgezeichnet zu der Stellung mit ihrer 'mobilen' Feder" [the "gnomide" Göchhausen assisted him as secretary; with her "mobile" pen, she was excellently suited for this task; xiii].

⁷ In his introduction to Göchhausen's letters, Deetjen places particular emphasis on her sense of humor, "der nur vielfach in Ironie, Spötterei und satirische Schärfe ausartete" [that only too often degenerated into irony, mockery and satirical sharpness; 1].

⁸ See, among others, Deetjen, "Einleitung" 6; Deneke 123, 131, 135–36. All of these instances are corroborated in other literature or Göchhausen's letters.

⁹ See letters to Frau Rath Goethe of February 1782, *Journal* 162–63; also 19 February 1784 and 19 February 1785, Deetjen 59–60 and 63–64; Christmas 1778, Deetjen 19.

¹⁰ The diary Lange describes here is an unpublished manuscript in the GSA to which I have not had access. For that reason alone, my statements and conclusions in the following concern less Göchhausen's writing per se but rather the contradictory ways in which it can be and has been interpreted. Until more archival research has been done, my statements about the diary in particular will necessarily remain speculative.

¹¹ Göchhausen left Italy in May 1790, more than six months after this letter was written. The anticipated pain of leaving Italy is an occasional topic even in earlier letters: "Liebster Hofrath, was soll aus Ihrer Thusel werden, wenn es dereinst heißen wird, anstat von Ischia nach Neapel: von Weimar nach Tiefurth!" [Dearest Privy Councilor, what will become of your Thusel when, one day, it'll have to be "from Weimar to Tiefurt" instead of "from Ischia to Naples"! Letter to Wieland, 11 August 1789, qtd. in Seuffert 554].

¹² Of the extensive secondary and methodological literature on the body in literature and aesthetics, theories of the grotesque are generally the only sources that deal directly with deformities. Other works that do not address this topic but that I found methodologically useful include the studies by Grosz, Althoff, and Hart Nibbrig as well as the anthologies by Terry and Urla, Kamper and Wulf.

¹³ "Menschen mit Buckeln [...] sind wandelnde grotesk-komische Geschöpfe, welche nur copirt werden zu brauchen" [Hunchbacks (...) are walking grotesque-comic characters which need only be copied; Ebeling 410–11].

¹⁴ *Rabelais* 316. I would like to emphasize here that I am not reading Bakhtin historically (although there are excellent arguments against appropriating his work out of context; see Eigler), but rather as a theorist of the grotesque, meaning, among other things, that I do not wish to relate the Renaissance

grotesque to the Weimar grotesque I propose here. Bakhtin's *Rabelais* in particular is commonly de-historicized into a purely theoretical study; that is, it is not read predominantly as a study of a Renaissance author (produced in Stalinist Russia), but as one of the first extensive studies of the non-classical body and the grotesque in general.

[15] Naturally, I am not excepting my own work from this charge.

[16] Kayser 47. This is obviously directed at the Goethe of Göchhausen's time, not at the late Goethe of the *West-östlicher Divan* (West-Eastern Divan, 1819) and *Faust II* (1832).

[17] This poem is not attributed to Göchhausen by the editors of the 1892 edition of the *Journal*, but was clearly written by her on the occasion of Frau Aja's birthday 1782, as the verbatim correspondences with her poem for Frau Aja's birthday 1784 indicate (Deetjen 59–60).

[18] "Denn *erstlich* war deiner Mutter Schmerz/ Doch warlich kein üppiger Carnavals Scherz" [Since firstly, your mother's pain at birth/ Was certainly not part of Carnival's mirth! *Journal* 163].

[19] Original in Göchhausen's handwriting, see editor's note to 262, 386. Since all contributions to the journal were anonymous, there is some doubt as to the attribution of this poem. In general, the 1892 editors of the *Journal* attribute a work to a certain author if the original exists in his or her handwriting. In Göchhausen's case, this method is complicated by the fact that Göchhausen served as secretary to the journal and may have copied works by others which were subsequently lost in the original. Poems that are here discussed that were tentatively attributed to Göchhausen as probably, but not certainly authored by her include this one and "Die zwey Linden" (The Two Linden Trees). Although I cannot dispel these uncertainties, I have chosen to assume Göchhausen as the author in both cases, for the following reasons: both works exist *only* in Göchhausen's handwriting; both works correspond to her style and predilection of themes in other works; and all other attributions of works to her by the editors were, as far as my research was able to confirm, accurate with one exception: the mistaken attribution of one of her works to another author (see editor's note to 162 on 378–79).

[20] For this reason, I do not find Harpham's interpretation of the grotesque as the sign of a "paradigm crisis," which he views as "the interval of the grotesque writ large," applicable to classical Weimar, in which the classical had just established itself as the dominant paradigm. The moment "when enough anomalies have emerged to discredit an old explanatory paradigm or model, and to make it impossible to continue adhering to it, but before the general acceptance of a new paradigm" (17) can perhaps be better used to describe our own challenges in reading Weimar than contemporary classical ("Goethe's") Weimar itself. See especially Harpham 179–80.

Works Cited

Althoff, Gabriele. *Weiblichkeit als Kunst: Die Geschichte eines kulturellen Deutungsmusters*. Stuttgart: Metzler, 1991.

Bakhtin, Mikhail. *The Dialogic Imagination. Four Essays*. Trans. Caryl Emerson and Michael Holquist. Austin: U Texas P, 1981.

———. *Rabelais and His World*. Trans. Helene Iswolsky. Cambridge: MIT P, 1968.

Bauer, Dale M., and Susan Jaret McKinstry, eds. *Feminism, Bakhtin, and the Dialogic*. Albany: SUNY P, 1991.

Biedrzynski, Effi. *Goethes Weimar: Das Lexikon der Personen und Schauplätze*. 3rd ed. Zurich: Artemis and Winkler, 1994.

Bohm, Arnd. "Charlotte von Stein's Dido, Ein Trauerspiel." *Colloquia Germanica* 22 (1989): 38–52.

Borchert, Angela. "Grotesque." *The Feminist Encyclopedia of German Literature*. Eds. Friederike Eigler and Susanne Kord. Westport: Greenwood P, 1997. 221–23.

Bruford, Walter Horace. *Culture and Society in Classical Weimar 1775–1806*. Cambridge: Cambridge UP, 1962.

———. *Deutsche Kultur der Goethezeit*. Konstanz: Athenaion, 1965.

Burkhardt, C. A. H. "Das Tiefurter Journal: Eine literarhistorische Studie." *Grenzboten* 34 (1871): 1–19.

Burns, Rob, ed. *German Cultural Studies: An Introduction*. Oxford and New York: Oxford UP, 1995.

Deetjen, Werner, ed. *Die Göchhausen: Briefe einer Hofdame aus dem klassischen Weimar*. Berlin: E. Mittler, 1923.

Deneke, Toni. *Das Fräulein Göchhausen*. Weimar: G. Kiepenheuer, 1962.

Dietrick, Linda. "Woman's State: Charlotte von Stein's Dido. Ein Trauerspiel and the Aesthetics of Weimar Classicism." *Verleiblichungen: Literatur- und kulturgeschichtliche Studien über Strategien, Formen und Funktionen der Verleiblichung in Texten von der Frühzeit bis zum Cyberspace*. Eds. Burkhardt Krause and Ulrich Schenk. St. Ingbert: Röhrig, 1996. 111–31.

Ebeling, Friedrich W. *Floegels Geschichte des Grotesk-Komischen, bearbeitet, erweitert und bis auf die neueste Zeit fortgeführt*. 4th ed. Leipzig: H. Barsdorf, 1887.

Eigler, Friederike. "Feminist Criticism and Bakhtin's Dialogic Principle: Making the Transition from Theory to Textual Analysis." *Women in German Yearbook* 11 (1995): 189–203.

Femmel, Gerhard, ed. *Corpus der Goethezeichnungen.* 7 vols. Leipzig: E. A. Seemann, 1958–73.

Flögel, Karl Friedrich. *Geschichte der Hofnarren.* Liegnitz and Leipzig: David Siegert, 1789.

———. *Geschichte des Groteskekomischen. Ein Beitrag zur Geschichte der Menschheit.* Liegnitz and Leipzig: David Siegert, 1788.

Goodman, Katherine R. "The Sign Speaks: Charlotte von Stein's Matinees." *In the Shadow of Olympus: German Women Writers Around 1800.* Eds. Katherine Goodman and Edith Waldstein. Albany, NY: SUNY P, 1992. 71–93, 226–27, 243–44.

Grosz, Elizabeth. *Volatile Bodies: Toward a Corporeal Feminism.* Bloomington and Indianapolis: Indiana UP, 1994.

Hahn, Barbara. *Unter falschem Namen. Von der schwierigen Autorschaft der Frauen.* Frankfurt a. M.: Suhrkamp, 1991.

Haraway, Donna. "Ecce Homo, Ain't (Ar'n't) I a Woman, and Inappropriate(d) Others: The Human in a Post-Humanist Landscape." *Feminists Theorize the Political.* Eds. Judith Butler and Jean W. Scott. New York: Routledge, 1992. 86–100.

Harpham, Geoffrey Galt. *On the Grotesque: Strategies of Contradiction in Art and Literature.* Princeton: Princeton UP, 1982.

Hart Nibbrig, Christian L. *Die Auferstehung des Körpers im Text.* Frankfurt a. M.: Suhrkamp, 1985.

Das Journal von Tiefurt. Mit einer Einleitung von Bernhard Suphan. Ed. Eduard von der Hellen. Weimar: Goethe-Gesellschaft, 1892.

Kamper, Dietmar, and Christoph Wulf, eds. *Die Wiederkehr des Körpers.* Frankfurt a. M.: Suhrkamp, 1982.

———, eds. *Das Schwinden der Sinne.* Frankfurt a. M.: Suhrkamp, 1984.

Kayser, Wolfgang. *The Grotesque in Art and Literature.* Trans. Ulrich Weisstein. New York: Columbia UP, 1981.

Kiceluk, Stephanie. "Made in His Image: Frankenstein's Daughters." *The Female Body: Figures, Styles, Speculations.* Ed. Laurence Goldstein. Ann Arbor: U of Michigan P, 1991. 204–20.

Kord, Susanne. "Not in Goethe's Image: The Playwright Charlotte von Stein." *Thalia's Daughters: German Women Dramatists From the Eighteenth Century to the Present.* Eds. Susan Cocalis and Ferrel Rose. Tübingen: Francke/Narr, 1996. 53–75.

———. *Sich einen Namen machen: Anonymität und weibliche Autorschaft, 1700–1900.* Stuttgart: Metzler, 1996.

Lange, Sigrid. "Italienreisen: Paradigmen in der Kunst des Symbolisierens aus der Sicht Luise von Göchhausens und Henriette von Egloffsteins." *Spie-*

gelgeschichten: Geschlechter und Poetiken in der Frauenliteratur um 1800. Frankfurt a. M.: Ulrike Helmer, 1995. 21–41.

———. "Über epische und dramatische Dichtung Weimarer Autorinnen: Überlegungen zu Geschlechterspezifika in der Poetologie." *Zeitschrift für Germanistik* 1/2 (1991): 341–51.

Russo, Mary. "Female Grotesques: Carnival and Theory." *Feminist Studies/Critical Studies.* Ed. Teresa de Lauretis. Bloomington: Indiana UP, 1986. 126–41.

Seuffert, Bernhard. "Der Herzogin Anna Amalia Reise nach Italien. In Briefen ihrer Begleiter." *Preußische Jahrbücher* 65 (1890): 535–65.

Stallybrass, Peter, and Allon White. *The Politics and Poetics of Transgression.* Ithaca: Cornell UP, 1995.

Stein, Charlotte von. *Dramen. Gesamtausgabe.* Ed. Susanne Kord. Hildesheim: Georg Olms, 1998.

Terry, Jennifer, and Jacqueline Urla, eds. *Deviant Bodies: Critical Perspectives on Difference in Science and Popular Culture.* Bloomington and Indianapolis: Indiana UP, 1995.

Wieland, Christoph Martin. "Unterredungen mit dem Pfarrer von ***." *C. M. Wielands Sämmtliche Werke.* Vol. 30. Leipzig: Georg Joachim Göschen, 1797. 310–82.

Fig. 1: Louise von Göchhausen.
Pencil drawing by Johann Wolfgang von Goethe, circa 1780
(courtesy of Stiftung Weimarer Klassik/Museen).

Fig. 2: Louise von Göchhausen.
Pencil drawing by Johann Wolfgang von Goethe, circa 1776–77
(courtesy of Goethe-Museum Düsseldorf).

Fig. 3: Georg Melchior Kraus, "Tafelrunde bei Anna Amalia" (Roundtable at Anna Amalia's). Watercolor, 1795 (in Effi Biedrzynski, Goethes Weimar 111).

Fig. 4: Georg Melchior Kraus, "Tafelrunde bei Anna Amalia" (Roundtable at Anna Amalia's), detail. Watercolor, 1795 (in Effi Biedrzynski, Goethes Weimar *111).*

Fig. 5: Johann Georg Schütz, "Besuch in der Villa d'Este" (Visit to the Villa d'Este). Watercolor, n.d. Louise von Göchhausen is seated at the center (courtesy of Verlagsgruppe Koehler/Mittler).

*Fig. 6: Louise von Göchhausen (left) in the Weimar park.
Silhouette, artist unknown, n.d. (courtesy of Stiftung
Weimarer Klassik/Museen).*

Wrapping Up the Weimar Myth

10

STEPHANIE HAMMER

Creation and Constipation: Don Carlos and Schiller's Blocked Passage to Weimar

> "Displacement from behind forwards; excrement becomes aliment; the shameful substance which has to be concealed turns into a secret which enriches the world."
> — Freud, "Character and Anal Eroticism" (in Ronell, "Le Sujet Suppositaire" 113)

> "Forgive my returning to this lewd orifice. Tis my muse will have it so."
> — Beckett 80

Layer 1

TWO DAYS AFTER HIS ARRIVAL in Berlin, quintessential twentieth-century novelist and dramatist Samuel Beckett has this to say about Germany and the state of his own writing:

> The trip is being a failure. Germany is horrible. Money is scarce. I am tired all the time [...]. And not the ghost of a book beginning. The physical mess is trivial beside the intellectual mess. I do not care and I don't know whether they are connected or not. It has turned out to be a journey *from*, and not to, as I knew it was, before I began it. (Qtd. in Knowlson 227)

Beckett's letter to Mary Manning in 1937 presents to our view a familiar, modernist portrait of the artist as both blocked and broke. Beckett conflates physical and mental suffering and piles on top of those two pains the equally unpleasant psychological awareness that his planned journey through Germany has proved to be, not an artistic quest *toward* an aesthetic goal, but rather an ineffectual, juvenile escape *from* something unnamable that cannot be left behind. A few weeks later, however, during this same ill-fated German journey, Beckett successfully purges his frustration through an aptly chosen set of metaphors:

> My next work shall be on rice paper wound about a spool, with a perforated line every six inches and on sale in Boots. The length of each chapter will be carefully calculated to suit with the average free motion. And with every copy a free sample of some laxative to promote sales, The Beckett Bowel Books, Jesus in farto. Issued in imperishable tissue [...]. All edges disinfected. 1000 wipes of clean fun. Also in Braille for anal pruritics. All Sturm and no Drang. (Qtd. in Knowlson 231)

Through the enema of humor — the act of "sending in" punning word play (Ronell, "Le Sujet Suppositaire" 129) — Beckett is able to eventually flush out the blocks to his creativity. In this manner, Beckett uses his own artistic quirks as the medication which brings on his cure — the renewed ability to write. Unlike Freud's Rat Man, Beckett is at once analyst and analysand; through the enabling mechanism of his own defecatory imagination, he is able to break through his own blocks, and create an art of unspeakables and unspeakable fun.

James Knowlson, Beckett's biographer, interjects a tantalizing observation, noting that, along the way, the author found time to visit Weimar where he made careful and detailed notes concerning Goethe's and Schiller's houses. The last piece of information fascinates and frustrates the Weimar scholar with questions that cannot be answered. Did visiting Weimar accelerate or slow Beckett's recovery? And how might the visit to Weimar have contributed to his subversive vision of art as exuberant, plentiful, pre-Romantic anal jouissance — "all Sturm and no Drang"?

A very different story of blockage and travel *from* inflects the narrative of the anally obsessed Rat Man, Freud's famous patient. Here compulsion, not creation, is the matter at hand, and the result is not art, but the fulfillment of one's duty as soldier and citizen. Mistakenly convinced that he owes money to another officer who refuses payment, the young lieutenant boards a train going in the wrong direction; as a result, he finds himself on an ass-backwards excursion, from which he constantly and vainly strives to eject himself:

> In this way he had struggled through from station to station, till he had reached one at which it had seemed to him impossible to get out because he had relatives living there. He then determined to travel through to Vienna, to look up his friend there and lay the whole matter before him [...]. When he had arrived in Vienna however, he had failed to find his friend at the restaurant at which he had counted on meeting him. (Freud, "Rat Man" 17)

Rat Man frantically attempts to reach the post office to pay off his debt and to make things right, but he is unable to arrive at his destination. He is repeatedly blocked by his own compulsions, till he purges his troubles successfully, not with the missing friend mentioned above (whom he reaches too late, and who gives him an explanation of his actions disappointingly similar to his own), but rather to Dr. Freud himself. The young man is eventually cured; psychoanalysis clears the roadblocks to his mental health, and the rat punishment which triggered the appearance of the illness is explained and also cleared away.

Arguably, Beckett and the distraught lieutenant have little in common other than the obvious — an interest in the anus and what comes out (Beckett) versus what goes in (Rat Man). They are dramatically different in most other respects: the one an author and the other a military man, the one an angry artist and the other a faithful son; the one Irish, the other Austrian; one long-lived, the other dead prematurely in battle. But their anally directed circuits through Austro-Germany (in particular, Beckett's passage through Weimar), their internal psychological obstacles, and their concern with cash provoke intriguing questions about the author and the authorial transit to be considered here: Friedrich Schiller and his crucial, career-making move to Weimar.

Thus, I will use Beckett — and behind him the furtive but equally important figure of Freud's Rat Man — as a proctological instrument to explore, excavate, and diagnose passages from the textual body we know as Schiller's, extracted from the time period that includes the Weimar journey. Accordingly, I will bring to the foreground texts usually left in the background when discussing Schiller's oeuvre — namely his private correspondence: the hidden, intimate performances of identity which he enacted behind the more public presentations of drama, lyric, essay, and history.

Significantly, behinds find a prominent place in the cultural work of the Enlightenment which was continually obsessed with backsides as political and social metaphors.[1] In *Candide*, the buttocks of the innocent literally furnish the nourishment of the wicked, and in earlier writers such as Swift, and in visual artists such as Hogarth, the underbelly of the body politic refers always to the anus. Throughout this period, cultural practitioners employed the bottom in an attempt to get to the bottom of social injustice and an untenable state of political affairs. At the same time, essayistic and dialogic investigations of nation, of natural right and natural law went hand in hand with speculations about the physiological and psychological nature of both the child and the (male) citizen, as well as the mechanics of the human body, the categorization of sexual behaviors, and the anatomy of the state. Odd and sometimes monstrous generic innovations characterized eighteenth-century writing, and the bourgeois tragedy, the critique, the travelogue, the pornographic and epistolary novels, the *Declaration of Independence* and the proceedings of the sodomy trials in England may be seen as only a few examples of the long and short forms through which such discussions ran their course.

Piled upon the mass of texts, pictures, and scandals which passed through the eighteenth century, Beckett's and Rat Man's concern with the anal looks familiar to us indeed, but it does not, at least at first glance, seem to have anything to do with Schiller. Indeed, Schiller's writing lacks the visceral attention to the body that marks the more cosmopolitan work of his mentor-rival Goethe and the more overtly queer sensibilities of his almost coeval Kleist. But the fact that the body is missing discursively in Schiller's plays is noteworthy; absence of the physical at the site dedicated to the display of bodies — namely in the theater — indicates the degree to which the body is contested, repressed territory for the dramatist. Further, while the overly scatological does not taint the pages of his work, the imperfect repressions of such problematic identities as masculinity, nation, and the child certainly do. Moreover, the notion of the backside in the more general sense of the back — of that which is concealed, of that which is turned around — in the form of the dirty secrets of the body politic and of the citizen infiltrates every play he wrote. These agonistic sensibilities are particularly prominent in the transitional play *Don Karlos* (Don Carlos, 1785–87) with which Schiller struggled and which he reworked in four different phases.

Layer 2

The creation of *Don Carlos* would appear to function in Schiller's own career as his ticket to Weimar. His reading of the prose version of Act 1 for Duke Carl August (December 1784), marks the first, important step toward making a permanent move there (von Wiese 240).[2] *Don*

Carlos was, then, profoundly motivated by a desired transit to Weimar — a utopian space which would endow the struggling playwright with all the things he lacked and needed: economic and psychological safety guaranteed by a good, providing father figure (Carl August replacing Carl Eugen's role as bad, withholding surrogate father), artistic freedom and friendship (the venue of the Weimar theater and the active support of Goethe), and intellectual legitimacy (a university post at nearby Jena).

Schiller's intention to get to Weimar is evident from the exuberant pronouncement he makes in the *Rheinische Thalia* (Rhineland Thalia, 1785) shortly after the meeting with Carl August:

> Wie teur ist mir der jetzige Augenblick, wo ich es laut und öffentlich sagen darf, daß *Carl August*, der edelste von Deutschlands Fürsten und der gefühlvolle Freund der Musen, jetzt auch der meinige sein will, daß *Er* mir erlaubt hat, *Ihm* anzugehören. (*Schillers Dramen 2*, 539; Schiller's emphasis)

> [How dear to me is the present moment when I may loudly and openly proclaim that *Carl August*, the noblest of Germany's princes and the sympathetic friend of the muses now wishes to be one of mine, that *he* has permitted me to belong to *him*.]

The elegant sentimentality of the passage shows us a Schiller already very much on the make, already hard at work creating the persona of flattering protégé. This passage also indicates how well Schiller understood that the shrewd marketing of *Don Carlos* to Carl August could make his own story as well as that of the Spanish prince into a successful one. At once resume and passport, the play could ensure Schiller's passage to a new identity and a greatly improved self-narration. No longer the Swabian provincial, Schiller could hope to become a Weimar cosmopolitan: a man who had literally and figuratively arrived.

Significantly, the play bears witness to many other passages in Schiller's career — formally from prose to verse, from the bourgeois to the classically inspired tragedy, from Storm and Stress to Classicism, from young to mature writer, and from a critique of unbridled individualism to a resigned and selfless nationalism which takes the place of all other love attachments. But most important, the play was conceived and written during a complicated and tortuous passage from Mannheim to Weimar/Jena. Schiller voyaged jaggedly from Mannheim to Dresden to Leipzig to Hamburg in a set of geographic maneuvers that oddly prefigures those of Beckett and Rat Man. Like the former, he wandered from city to city and was broke most of the time. Like the latter, he vacillated frenetically from place to place, unable to get to the person and destination he desired most. And, like both of them, Schiller's state of mind matched his physical movement and economic circumstances. The troubled transition was not only geographical and artistic, but psychological as well, as the aptly named Charles Passage reminds us; he terms this period of Schiller's life a "crisis" — from which Schiller was never to recover altogether (Passage 63–66).

Reading backwards, we can be struck by the adolescent emotionalism of Schiller's letters to his intimate friends. In stark contrast to the language of the *Rheinische Thalia,* these resonate both with the Beckettian obsession with getting away *from* at any cost and with the Rat Man's grammar of discombobulated thoughts and truncated sentences (see Freud, "Rat Man" 12). A turning point letter to Körner begins, stops, and recommences after a parenthetical interruption; even his letters can not proceed straight from beginning to end. The letter invokes a disturbance, framed as at once outside and inside — as phenomenon and as a physical attack, as an onset of symptoms:

> Hier bin ich neulich durch einen unvermuteten Besuch unterbrochen worden, und diese zwölf Tage ist eine Revolution mit mir und in mir vorgegangen, die dem gegenwärtigen Briefe mehr Wichtigkeit gibt, als ich mir habe träumen lassen […]. Ich kann nicht mehr in Mannheim bleiben […]. Ich kann nicht mehr hierbleiben. Zwölf Tage habe ich's in meinem Herzen herumgetragen wie den Entschluß, aus der Welt zu gehn. (Letter to Körner, 22 February 1785, *Briefwechsel* 36)

> [Here I was recently interrupted by an unexpected visit, and during these twelve days a revolution has occurred in me and with me that has endowed this present letter with more significance than I had allowed myself to imagine (…). I cannot stay in Mannheim any longer (…). I cannot stay here any longer. For twelve days I have carried it (the decision) around in my heart, like the decision to leave this world.]

Linked to this desperation is still another preoccupation — that of getting to Weimar:

> Außerdem verlangt es meine gegenwärtige Konnexion mit dem guten Herzog von Weimar, daß ich selbst dahin gehe und persönlich für mich negoziere, so armselig ich mich auch sonst bei solcherlei Geschäften benehme. (36)

> [In addition, my present connection with the good Duke of Weimar necessitates my going there myself and negotiating for

myself, albeit that I conduct myself miserably in such affairs as a rule.]

Here, abruptly, the language of commerce injects itself. Schiller's letter is clearly motivated by the desire to use the credit he has already established with the duke to — in the discourse of Bank of America — elevate his credit limit and gain more financial power.

But what commodity is being credited and symbolically traded here? It is — at least in this letter — the writer himself who emerges as the goods in question. Small wonder then that the prospect of buying and selling himself arouses disgust in the young writer. Thus, for Schiller, the hermeneutics of credit bears none of the transcendent markings of Adam Müller's theories. Rather, such interactions inaugurate a terrible and traumatic splitting of his own subjectivity: making him at once a thing — a literal object of exchange — and an unwilling salesman, or worse yet, a prostitute — an individual who sells himself or herself for the pleasure of others (a suggestion already hinted at in Schiller's concluding remark in the *Rheinische Thalia* that he now "belongs" to Carl August).

Clearly, Schiller despises such negotiations; the Frenchified verb marks his entry into enemy, foreign, feminine, corrupt territory where he must make himself an object of exchange. Yet, his letter indicates his full recognition that such business deals are inevitable if he is to survive; the impersonal "es verlangt" [it demands] signals his awareness of this necessity. The Latinate "Connexion" and not "Freundschaft" [friendship] is — regrettably — what counts here. And money matters also, although Schiller clearly resents this fact.

Schiller's subsequent letters to friends during this period all betray such a double, vacillating perspective. Schiller represses questions of money as much as he can, claiming to each correspondent the importance of the particular friend, expressing longing and delight for whichever place he will be going to visit, but behind it all lies the concern with Weimar and with the duke, and the not quite spoken anxiety of making something concrete happen. Frequently, passionate homosocial attachment on the heroic friendship model — in particular to Körner and Huber — goes hand in hand with questions of artistic inspiration, a stated desire for a home, and the unwilling, resentful pursuit of filthy lucre, and of the duke himself as the means to that end.

This aggravated sense of the importance of money appears elsewhere in Schiller's early work, as the tortured attacks on capital in *Die Räuber* (The Robbers, 1781) and of both bourgeois and aristocratic *arrivisme* in *Kabale und Liebe* (Intrigue and Love, 1784) make plain. The letters from this period share the early theatrical view, articulating an ambivalence toward money heavily infiltrated by what Max Weber would call a Puritan stance. Near the end of *The Protestant Ethic and the Spirit of Capitalism*, Weber observes that this mode of thinking is particularly problematic vis-à-vis artistic production:

> We should call attention to the fact that the toleration of pleasure in cultural goods, which contributed to purely aesthetic or athletic enjoyment, certainly always ran up against one characteristic limitation: they must not cost anything. Man is only a trustee of the goods which have come to him through God's grace [...]. The idea of a man's duty to his possessions, to which he subordinates himself as an obedient steward, or even as an acquisitive machine, bears with chilling weight on his life. The greater the possessions the heavier, if the ascetic attitude toward life stands the test, the feeling of responsibility for them, for holding them undiminished for the glory of God and increasing them by restless effort. (Weber 170)

Such a view places the artist in a complicated relation to the acquisition of money, as Schiller's attitude painfully exemplifies. The Puritan view of work insists on its nature as "calling" (Weber 181) with the paradoxical result that material acquisition becomes more not less important as the mark of rational and virtuous economic life (not wasteful, not profligate). These views are absorbed into ambivalence. Schiller considers himself an artist and wants to make art, but not for money and prestige, both of which he needs in order to make art, although attempting to obtain these goods prostitutes him, taints his German, and blocks his creative output.

Schiller's ambivalence toward a means of employment in which calling and business are messily intermeshed is clear in such comments as the following, which dates from January 1784: "Mein Clima ist das Theater, in dem ich lebe und webe, und meine Leidenschaft ist glücklicherweise auch mein Amt" [My climate is the theater in which I live and move, and my passion is happily also my employment; qtd. in von Wiese 222]. In the original German the interplay in the young playwright's mind between the official and the religious is very strong. The turn of phrase "leben und weben" plays on the Christian profession of faith, "in Ihm leben, weben und sind wir," [living in Him, we move and are], while "Amt" [office] stresses the official, bureaucratic function of the author's work.

Not surprisingly, the production of the manuscript of *Don Carlos* is at once dirtied and backed up by such negotiations. Tacked on to Schiller's expression of worldly concern in the letters is the awareness of *Don Carlos* as a burden, a chaotic mess, a left-over remnant which will not be cleaned away, and which adheres, piles up on top of the new and improved work which Schiller was trying to create out of the subject matter. "Noch sehe ich die chaotische Maße des übrigen Karlos mit Kleinmut und Schrecken an" [Still I contemplate the chaotic mass of the remaining Karlos with despondency and terror; letter to Huber, 5 October 1785, *Schillers Briefe* 86].

Layer 3

Fittingly, the play itself, so labored upon during this period, is about obstructions and obstacles, about that which can never come to the surface; about secrets and infiltrations, perverse loves and family romances gone awry; about the failure of fatherhood and fatherland — all of which can never be revealed and which does painfully leak out nonetheless. Three secrets combine and cohere at the beginning of *Don Carlos* — the secret of rebellion, the secret of the son's incestuous love for the mother, and the deepest secret of all: a traumatic experience involving the father. Although *Don Carlos* is a drama rather than a novel, it is narrative and not exposition which drives the work — making it an internal drama of telling.[3]

Act 1, scene 2 regresses through layers of reminiscence toward the recollection of a traumatic incident from the past. The Infante, an apt title, connoting innocence and a childishness bordering on the babyish, is a manchild who must do without — a deprivation that makes itself felt in a halting set of speeches which outline a baffling array of desires: for a mother who is and is not his mother, for a friend who is and is not really a friend, for a father who is and is not a father. In the space of a few minutes we learn that the present clash of agendas between the two friends — Posa's intention to win Carlos's support for the Flanders campaign, and Carlos's hopes to win Posa's in the amorous pursuit of the queen — replays in more overtly political terms the equally politicized homosocial dynamics of a much earlier relation. During their childhood Posa sought power and affection from the greater social worlds of male interaction and accomplishment, while Carlos wanted exclusive love from one person, Posa himself. The object of adulation is now changed — from masculine stand in for father to feminine stand in for mother (since the queen is in fact his contemporary). But the primacy of this earlier relation becomes clear when Carlos relates the crisis that it inaugurated. And even as he invokes these memories, he becomes enthralled by them — becoming in his own mind's eye not the hero which Posa hoped to find in the present, but an abject victim of violence:

> Im Angesicht des ganzen Hofgesindes,
> das mitleidsvoll im Kreise stand, ward sie
> auf Sklavenart an deinem Karl vollzogen.
> [...]
> ich weinte nicht. Mein königliches Blut
> floß schändlich unter unbarmherz'gen Streichen;
> ich sah auf dich und weinte nicht. (NA 6: 20; 1.2.277–84)

> [In view of all the members of the court,
> Who stood in sympathetic circle round me,
> Revenge was taken on me like a slave.
> (...)
> I did not cry. Although my royal blood
> Flowed basely under unrelenting blows,
> I looked at you and did not cry. (*Plays* 112)]

The tale of the shuttlecock is shocking — both in its brutality and the odd lack of emotional affect with which it is delivered, ending, not with agony, but with the disconnected fiscal language of pay-back; according to Carlos, Posa declares, "Ich will bezahlen, wenn du König bist!" [I will repay you when you are king! NA 6: 20; 1.2.292] — a response which again marks the unhappy correlation between bodies and money suggested in Schiller's correspondence. Carlos's disjointed relating of the tale *as though he were still there* as well as his emotional disconnection from the event point together to the event's status as traumatic moment.[4] For the trauma victim, to tell is to literally relive all over again, but to live in traumatic terms of an experience which is at once unapproachable and intimate (Kristeva 6), where pieces of vision and sensation stand in for the lost terror of the entire event.[5] There is in Carlos's narration little sense of the heroic, although he would clearly have it read in those terms; rather, the emphasis is, despite him, on being at once humiliated and annihilated (as Kristeva notes about Celine's writing, "there is no glory in this suffering"; 147). Ironies abound: Carlos's princely identity is reduced to a fluidity which shamefully leaks away into nothing; he claims he could control his tears but not the "tears" in his skin opened by the punitive strokes of the father, who is completely disembodied and invisible.

The unseen and unseeable nature of the king indicates the degree to which repression is operative in Carlos's traumatized memory.[6] To look the father and the state in the face is also to recognize and to acknowledge; to look is to assume command of the gaze and of one's feelings for the father, in particular feelings of hatred for one who stands between the son and the fulfillment of his sexual desire. This is a key feature of the goal in Freud's treatment of the Rat Man, behind whose adulation of his departed father lies hatred and fear. But it is precisely his hatred for the father that Don Carlos most wants to deny. Posa asks him pointedly if he hates his father, to which the prince responds with a frightened denial that literally foreshadows our current slang expression "Don't take me there!":

> Nein! Ach nein!
> Ich hasse meinen Vater nicht — doch Schauer
> und Missethäters Bangigkeit ergreifen
> bei den zwo fürchterlichen Sylben mich.
> [...]
> O Gott!
> hier fühl ich, daß ich bitter werde — Weg —
> weg, weg von dieser Stelle. (NA 6: 23; 1.2.344–59)

> [No! Oh no!
> I do not hate my father — but such fear
> And sinner's apprehension seizes me
> At the mere mention of his fearful name.
> (...)
> My God!
> I feel that I am becoming bitter so —
> Away — away from here. (*Plays* 114)]

This uncannily precocious picture of child abuse, which culminates in a nightmare scene of public spectacle is resonant; it is the most important scene in the play, although/because it is a scene which we never see directly. The public display of the prince's back (the horror of the memory suggests obliquely that more than the back has been revealed to the throng) is the formative, albeit completely disruptive, moment of his identity. Interestingly, a similar traumatic event inaugurates the illness of Rat Man: "When he was very small [...] he had done something naughty, for which his father had given him a beating" (Freud, "Rat Man" 46). Like Freud's patient, the consistently fearful military man, Carlos behaves ever after in the hold of the trauma. And like him, Carlos is at once a shell-shocked victim of a castrating father-figure and an idolater of idealized men, also seen as father, even as he simultaneously quests to compensate for the lost source-site of the mother, which alone holds out the hope of sanctuary from the angry kingdom of the fathers. With characteristic simplicity and naiveté, Carlos informs Posa "Ich brauche Liebe" [I need love; NA 6: 20; 1.2.298]. But under such circumstances, love, and the desire which drives it, cannot do their work either. If the father cannot be hated outright, then it is the circuitous affections of male love, or the symbolically incestuous promise of mother love toward which Carlos turns.[7] The unorthodox and politically tangled emotional relationships of the play suggest, indeed, that there is no desire other than a queer desire. Desire in *Don Carlos* is literally deviant (Dollimore 104), in so far as it is continually forced into unusual paths, thwarted, blocked, resorting to hidden and forbidden channels of entry and expression, looking for some body, any body, in the words of Beckett, to "rub up against" (Beckett 56).[8]

The result of such thwarted love is always betrayal or renunciation but never fulfillment.[9] Carlos learns again to do without, as he did as a child. Like the Rat Man, he travels a psychic route which eternally loops back on itself — ending, not in cure, but in premature obliteration.[10] "Ausgestorben in meinem Busen ist die Natur" [The voice of nature has totally departed from my breast; NA 6: 337; 4.11.6250–51], Carlos tells the queen near the end of the play, and there is, it seems, no other possibility for desire but to die. But he cannot do his duty either, and dies a blocked man of rebellion — a revolution which remains purely internal.

Layer 4

Like the unauthorized *eros* which it heartbreakingly displays, Schiller's play demarcates a Spain which is itself a curious place. Rigid and regimented, this Spain looks more like the modern state under Franco than the baroque Spain of the Golden Age that Schiller was ostensibly describing. Lacking any quality that could possibly be misconstrued as Mediterranean, Schiller's Spain displays the Catholic militarism of the Jesuits but eschews the emotionalism, sensuality, and profound interest in the aesthetic which governed the cultural work of artists such as Calderón, Velásquez, and Cervantes. This Spain is not only doctrinaire but so spare that the French queen feels surprisingly constrained and out of place. In this sense, Schiller's Spain manifests all the qualities that will contribute to the stereotype of what is *Prussian*.

Read one way, the world of *Don Carlos* is clearly Schiller's Germany — the Fatherland which does not yet exist, but which dreams of itself as a nation of Enlightenment principles even as the fractured remnants of the *Reich* operate on a ducal system as antiquated as the system which governs that of King Philip — where provincialism and rigidity prevail, despite the efforts of the most enthusiastic artists and intellectuals. When Posa declares his time has not yet come, is it not place rather than time that is the problem? Finished in 1787, Schiller's play fairly bristles with the frustration of a revolutionary wave which is *now* but is not *here*. In this light, both Posa's and Carlos's inability to physically get to Flanders marks the larger inability of Schiller's Germans to get to the place where revolution happens.[11]

But, read autobiographically, Schiller's Spain represents not only Germany in general — a national dream space of the future — but also specifically the place that Schiller was trying so desperately to get away from, namely Mannheim which his letters describe as a prison from which he plans a criminal escape.[12] From this point of view, Flanders is not only the place where revolution happens, but the place where Schiller's own private revolution, the "innere Revolution" [inner revolution] he writes of in the letter to Körner, can find free expression in the realm of economic safety. Flanders becomes, according to this schema, a projection of the hoped-for Weimar.

Such a reading gives us some insight into the strange character of Don Carlos the dreamer, queer mother-lover and homosocial drop-out; the prince who does not speak or act like a prince, the traumatized son who can remember but who cannot get over. In his final meeting with the queen, Posa requests Elizabeth's undying affection for Carlos. But the terms of this request are surprising and would seem to reveal yet another dimension to this play about suppression and repression:

> Gehört die süße Harmonie, die in
> dem Saitenspiele schlummert, seinem Käufer,
> der es mit taubem Ohr bewacht? Er hat
> das Recht erkauft, in Trümmern es zu schlagen,
> doch nicht die Kunst, dem Silberton zu rufen
> und in des Liedes Wonne zu zerschmelzen. (NA 6: 272;
>   4.24.5158–63)

> [And does the lovely harmony that sleeps
> Within the lyre (the play of strings) belong to one who buys
> It and who guards it with deaf ears? He has
> Bought up the right to smash it into pieces,
> But not the art to summon silvery tones
> And melt away into the song's delight. (*Plays* 262)]

Significantly, the play reports yet another unseen drama of blows meted out on an innocent victim — wherein an all-powerful buyer shatters the orphic stringed instrument, to which he has purchased complete rights. Art survives, just barely and only momentarily, as the sound leaks out of the destroyed body. This artistic utterance complements the traumatized memory of Carlos, and aligns the hero with the production of art in a violent marketplace to which the instrument belongs and by which it is enthralled and shattered. Read as a series of autobiographical displacements, the smashed lute stands in for Carlos standing in for Schiller,[13] who emerges as the traumatized bourgeois producer of German art, a commodified (and therefore reified) humiliated son of a patriarchal market moving into capitalism. In such a system the artist, like Carlos, is always relegated to the status of child — to be tolerated, trained, disciplined, and punished but never to achieve full majority, never to be home, never to be safe.

Such a reading of the play is supported by Schiller himself, who used a variation on the same metaphor invoked in the play when he assured Körner in February 1785, "In Ihrem Zirkel, will ich froher und inniger in meine Laute greifen" [In your circle, I will more happily and more ardently touch my lute; *Briefwechsel* 37]. But his comment a few lines earlier is even more to the point: "Mein Herz und meine Musen mußten zu gleicher Zeit der Notwendigkeit unterliegen" [My heart and my muses had to succumb to necessity at the same time; 37].

Beckett understood the paradoxical nature of this kind of necessity full well. The 1955 novel *Molloy* opens with the portrait of the artist as a resentful, childish invalid which postfigures that of the physically wrecked Schiller trying to eject the rest of *Demetrius* (1805), his last play, from his dying body:

> There's this man who comes every week. [...] He gives me money and takes away the pages. So many pages, so much money [...]. What I'd like to do now is to speak of the things that are left, say my goodbyes, finish dying. They don't want that. Yes, there's more than one apparently [...]. Yet I don't work for money. For what then? (7)

Seen from this point of view, Schiller's *Don Carlos* and the texts around it function as a repressed, traumatized autobiography — *Don Carlos* is possibly Schiller's most confessional work — where fundamental anxieties leak out, and as a docudrama and dramatic case-study of the author's agonized quest for legitimacy and for solvency.[14] The concern with cash, the resentment against negotiations mark Schiller's unwilling move into the emerging space of commodified literature, what Horkheimer and Adorno have called the "culture industry." Within this framework the writer in Anglo-Europe would have two salient choices — to become a best-selling celebrity, salon guest, and man about town who schmoozes with the powerful and famous (Goethe's choice), or to become an academic, who schmoozes too, but differently, for he must seem not to write *for* money, and yet to write *to obtain* money all the same.[15]

Seen in this light, the consistent scholarly preferences for Goethe over Schiller (in *Germanistik* and elsewhere) points to an intriguing discursive repression — namely the denial of the historical connection between Schiller's cultural positioning and our own. His predicament reveals the fundament of our predicament — that of the academic intellectual who would be, and can never be, free of the concerns of enterprise. Like Schiller, academic humanists also write, think, and teach for a market, no matter how displaced, and no matter how small, while they survive in such a market precisely by appearing to concentrate on the authenticity of their "calling."

Layer 5

Don Carlos never gets to Flanders, Rat Man cannot reach the post office, and Beckett does not uncover the inspiration he hoped to find during his trip to Germany. Like these frustrated travelers, Schiller never quite arrives in Weimar, for the Weimar he finds proves to be a more intense variation on the Mannheim he had left. Weimar as described in Schiller's letters emerges as something of a corporate community,[16] and in its constituency, far more like a creative consortium than a gentlemen's club. The group which Schiller depicts resembles an enterprise not unlike DC Comics, where free-lance creative men (and a few women) all jockey for position in a sometime cooperation, sometime competition with the editors-in-chief. The editor-in-chief here is clearly Goethe, whose birthday Schiller and others in Weimar celebrate at Goethe's house in 1787, while the author himself is still in Italy — an odd prefiguration of the ubiquitous celebrity parties of our time, held for authors, movie stars, rock personalities, and other guests of honor who rarely show up.[17] Schiller attends the party, at once resentful and hopeful — wondering, with some justification, what actual good it will do (letter to Körner, 29 August 1787, *Briefwechsel* 59–61). And, as he pursues the doubtful fellowship of the Herders and the ever-absent Goethe, he is repeatedly unable to win the attention of the Duke, and spends a full two months trying to gain an audience with him.

Against this personal history, Weimar already looks a bit like Klassik, Inc. — as Schiller's descriptions of it make clear. His first letter to Körner from Weimar specifically describes an arrival which contains all manner of frustrations, a journey fraught with obstacles and the more painful problem of self-marketing:

> Vorgestern abend kam ich hier an. [...] In Naumburg, hatte ich das Unglück, den Herzog von Weimar um eine Stunde im Posthause zu verfehlen, wo er mir beinah die Pferde weggenommen hat. Was hätte ich nicht um diesen glüklichen Zufall gegeben! Jetzt ist er in Potsdam und man weiß noch nicht wie bald er zurückkommen wird. [...] Die Erwartung, der mancherlei Dinge, die sich mir hier in den Weg werfen werden, hat meine ganze Besinnungskraft eingenommen [...]. Überhaupt wißt ihr, daß ich bald von den Dingen, die mich umgeben und nahe angehen, betäubt werde. [...] die vielerlei Verhältniße, in die ich mich hier zerteilen muß, in deren jedem ich doch ganz gegenwärtig sein muß, erschröckt mein Mut und läßt mich die Einschränkung meines Wesens fühlen. (Letter to Körner, 23 July 1787, *Briefwechsel* 50)
>
> [I arrived here two nights ago. (...) In Naumburg I had the misfortune to miss the Duke of Weimar by an hour at the post house, where he, like me, changed horses. What I wouldn't have given for such a fortuitous chance! Now he is in Potsdam, and as of yet, no one knows how soon he will return. (...) The expectation of the many things which will throw themselves in my way has captured my consciousness (...). As things stand, you know that I soon become stupefied by the things which surround and nearly concern me. (...) The many sorts of relationships into which I must apportion myself, in each one of which, however, I must be fully present terrifies my spirit and causes me to feel the limitation of my being.]

Like the Rat Man in the restaurant, Schiller literally arrives in Weimar too late — narrowly missing his hoped-for patron along the way. He now finds himself stuck in an uncertain position waiting for Carl August to return while having to struggle to make ends meet in the meantime. Moreover, from the moment he arrives in Weimar, he understands that the dirty business of "negozieren" for money and position, for legitimacy, for "Connexion" as opposed to "Freundschaft" [friendship] have not ceased. Rather, these transactional processes have redoubled, and the stakes are higher. Significantly, the opportunities for advancement strike Schiller not as positive but as negative; these possibilities resemble literal obstacles thrown in his artistic path. These "things" throw him psychologically off course by triggering unwelcome thoughts and feelings — the painful awareness of inner obstacles, unspoken but powerful constrictions which block him even more.

The confession to Körner eerily predicts Schiller's future in Weimar. The obstacles seem to only accrue as time passes, and almost two years later Schiller writes in similar fashion about yet another thing lying in the way — Goethe himself:

> Dieser Mensch, dieser Goethe ist mir einmal im Wege, und er erinnert mich so oft, daß das Schicksal mich hart behandelt hat. Wie leicht war *sein* Geist von seinem Schicksal getragen, und wie muß *ich* bis auf diese Minute kämpfen! (Letter to Körner, 9 March 1789, *Briefwechsel* 109)
>
> [This person, this Goethe is just in my way; and he so often reminds me that fate has treated me harshly. How easily was *his* genius carried by fate and how, until this very minute, must *I* still fight! (Qtd. in Ronell, *Dictations* 56)]

Throughout Schiller's career in Weimar, outside "things" (including his famous friendship) will remind the author of increasingly heavy interior burdens, as an accumulating mass of psychological pressures will mold Schiller's art into an ever more static classicism. The physical manifestations of this distress will literally crush the life out of him in his mid-forties. Schiller's *Kampf* [struggle], like that of Don Carlos, never expresses itself directly and therefore never ends; the struggle stops only with his untimely death.

Thus, *Don Carlos* is a testament to both horror and finance — family trauma and the traumatic experience of creating art for a marketplace which consumes and destroys the artist, even as it makes his career. From this point of view, Weimar's Schiller emerges, not as the ethereal idealist partner to Goethe's virile realist, but as a powerful and powerfully repressed prototype of one sort of modern artist, upon whom layers of resentful and withdrawn male visionaries load up their melancholy lineage. Blocked intellectuals who are aggravated priests of an increasingly hard-to-market high culture, they are frustrated men of feeling who vacillate between hating to sell and feeling utterly compelled to market themselves — from Victor Hugo to Dostoevsky and Kafka, to Thomas Wolfe and J. D. Salinger, to Peter Handke, Heiner Müller, and beyond. Neither altogether obedient sons of the state nor rebellious producers of scatological jouissance, these authors circulate within the stopped up interstices between the Rat Man's therapy and Beckett's curative theatrics.

And Schiller's Weimar? Against this reading of Schiller, the murky outlines of a different city appear — an urban space, not of classical statuary, but of crooked, narrow streets where struggling cultural practitioners hide out in the studies of their constricted houses, barricaded against the realities of a burgeoning culture industry, whose mechanisms we are only now beginning to glimpse:

> So viele Familien, ebensoviele abgesonderte Schneckenhäuser, aus denen der Eigentümer kaum herausgeht, um sich zu sonnen [...]. Jetzt gehe ich sehr wenig aus. (Letter to Körner, 10 September 1787, *Briefwechsel* 61)
>
> [So many families, ever so many isolated snail shells, from which the inhabitant barely comes out to sun himself (...). I go out very seldom now.]

Schiller's choice of words fleetingly makes a connection which psychoanalysis would have leapt upon: the Weimar citizen as snail, a shelled worm. Worms, Freud tells us, resemble rats, turds, phallic remnants, bills of money, or chthonic children (Freud, "Rat Man" 52–53).

Schiller's brief depiction of the worm citizens of Weimar aptly summarizes his own concerns with money, with blockage, and with dirty secrets. *Don Carlos* and Schiller's uncertain passage to success as a writer reveal the backside of the resplendent, seemingly pristine Weimar we know and admire. Equally important, Schiller's struggle to write and survive psychologically and financially as an artist displays a pile of unhappy concerns in which we are still enmeshed as critics and as writers, which block us, which build up within our own discourse about the Weimar greats, and which implicate us in the perpetuation of their myth.

—University of California at Riverside

Notes

This essay has undergone several transformations thanks to the input of the participants at the Center for Ideas and Society seminar on male love in the eighteenth century (University of California, Riverside, spring 1996). George Haggerty, Carole Fabricant, Linda Tomko, and Richard Godbeer made particularly useful suggestions. Thanks also to John Ganim and Robert Gross who read penultimate drafts, and to Burkhard Henke for editorial suggestions. From its inception, this project has been actively supported and encouraged by Gail Hart, to whom this essay is dedicated with love and appreciation.

[1] Laura Gergorian, discussion of work in progress, Spring 1996, Center for Ideas and Society.

[2] This meeting was facilitated by Charlotte von Kalb (von Wiese 224).

[3] With some reason, Wieland called the work a "dramatic novel"; see von Wiese 246.

[4] Feminist psychiatrist Judith Herman notes "traumatized people relive the traumatic event as though it were continually recurring in the present [...]. It is as though time stops at the moment of trauma" (Herman 37).

[5] This description in terms of sensation and a few vivid images are constitutive of traumatic memory, according to Herman (38).

[6] "The trauma, instead of being forgotten, is deprived of its affective cathexis; so that what remains is nothing but its ideational content, which is perfectly colourless and is judged to be unimportant" (Freud, "Rat Man" 38).

[7] Benno von Wiese suggests that this relationship may reflect the tensions of the troubled passion between Schiller and Charlotte von Kalb (226–27) — a passion blocked effectively by the fact that she was, albeit unhappily, married.

[8] The erotic circuits of the play continually go in perverse directions, marking eros as queer in the double sense of being either unusual and/or displaying homo- or otherized sexuality. Curious charges of desire inform the relations between Carlos and Posa but also those between Posa and the king, Posa and the queen, Eboli and Carlos, and even Eboli and the queen.

[9] In this sense, the play clearly derives from bourgeois tragedy traditions in which "sexual yearnings are inherently illicit" (Gustafson 112). Here the state replaces the family, and *Don Carlos* gestures toward "disciplining" and normalizing desire through enlisting it as duty to the fatherland, rather than the *father*. But desire sublimated into duty doesn't fare well either, and while the notion of "Staatsliebe" [state love] will eventually culminate in the heterosexual father-hero of *Wilhelm Tell* (1804), it remains deeply problematic for Schiller up through *Die Jungfrau von Orleans* (The Maid of Orleans, 1801).

[10] Freud's final footnote to the Rat Man case study suggests a tragic dimension to the therapy, for the patient has been cured only to be killed: "Like so many other young men of value and promise, he perished in the Great War" (Freud, "Rat Man" 81).

[11] Occasional writings composed ten years later bear out such a reading of *Don Carlos* (see Sauder 224). Schiller critiques both his historical moment and his homeland when he observes in a letter to Johann Süvern in 1800: "Unsere Tragödie, wenn wir eine hätten, hat mit der Ohnmacht, der Schlafheit, der Charakterlosigkeit des Zeitgeistes [...] zu ringen" [Our tragedy, if we had one, must wrestle with the impotence, the slackness, and the characterlessness of the spirit of the times; qtd. in Sauder 224].

[12] Benno von Wiese hints fleetingly at such a reading when he notes the psychological similarities between Carlos and Schiller during his Mannheim stay (von Wiese 247). See also Friedrich Kittler's intriguing reading of the play as a displaced description of the Karlsschule in terms of discipline and psychiatry. Kittler's analysis suggests to me that *Don Carlos* represents several layers of traumatic experiences in Schiller's own life — originating perhaps with traumatic experiences in his own home as a child.

[13] Schiller made a direct and visceral connection between himself and his creation early on, writing to Reinwald in 1783 that Carlos had Hamlet's soul but that his "*pulse*" comes from "me" (qtd. in von Wiese 247–48).

[14] Such a reading of the play is supported by the valuable stylistic analysis of Arnd Bohm who notes a recurring obsession with property exchanges and with problems of giving, taking, and earning. Bohm's reading suggests once again *Don Carlos*'s deep indebtedness to such homosocial/mercantilist bourgeois tragedies as *The London Merchant* (see my analysis in *The Sublime Crime*), but while Bohm sees the play as a shoring up of mercantilist values, I tend to see it rather as what Alan Sinfield calls an ideological "fault-line story" (4) where notions of gender, libidinal economy, power relations, and modes of artistic production all break down.

[15] Thus, in the ubiquitous Goethe-Schiller pair we can see the template for a powerful bifurcation of male cultural work (in Anglo-Europe and the United States) which seeks to join the figure of the bestselling, virile literary businessman with his effete, professorial, and/or spiritual partner even as it sets the two apart. Contested and complicated versions of this already problematic binary may be seen in such couples as: Byron/Shelley, Sartre/Camus, Washington/Du Bois, Hemingway/Fitzgerald, and even McCartney/Lennon.

[16] A preliminary reading suggests that the letters are ironic and bitterly parodistic, indicating the leakage of yet another of Schiller's repressed interests, namely satire, theorized later in *Über Naive und Sentimentalische Dichtung* (On Naïve and Reflective Poetry, 1795–96).

[17] One can also see that the various Goethe properties were already in the process of being transformed to the authorial shrines that they now are.

Works Cited

Beckett, Samuel. *Three Novels*. New York: Grove, 1955.

Bohm, Arnd. "'Ich will den Käufer nicht betrügen': Give and Take in Schiller's *Don Carlos*." *Seminar* 27.3 (1991): 203-18.

Burns, Rob, ed. *German Cultural Studies: an introduction*. Oxford: Oxford UP, 1995.

Dollimore, Jonathan. *Sexual Dissidence: Augustine to Wilde, Freud to Foucault*. Oxford: Clarendon, 1991.

Freud, Sigmund. "The 'Rat Man'." *Three Case Histories*. Introd. Philip Rieff. New York: Collier, 1993 [1963]. 1-81.

Grey, Margaret E. "Beckett Backwards and Forwards: The Rhetoric of Retraction in *Molloy*." *French Forum* 19:2 (1994): 161-74.

Gustafson, Susan E. "Male Desire in Goethe's *Götz von Berlichingen*." *Outing Goethe and His Age*. Ed. Alice Kuzniar. Stanford: Stanford UP, 1996. 111-24.

Hammer, Stephanie. "Schiller, Time and Again." *German Quarterly* (1994): 153-72.

———. *The Sublime Crime: Fascination, Failure, and Form in the Literature of the Enlightenment*. Carbondale: Southern Illinois UP, 1994.

Herman, Judith Lewis. *Trauma and Recovery*. New York: Harper Collins, 1992.

Horkheimer, Max and Theodor W. Adorno. *Dialektik der Aufklärung. Philosophische Fragmente*. Frankfurt a. M.: Fischer, 1991.

Kittler, Friedrich. "Carlos als Karlsschüler." *Unser Commercium: Goethes und Schillers Literaturpolitik*. Eds. Wilfried Barner et al. Stuttgart: Cotta, 1984. 241-74.

Knowlson, James. *Damned to Fame: The Life of Samuel Beckett*. New York: Simon and Schuster, 1996.

Kristeva, Julia. *Powers of Horror: An Essay on Abjection*. New York: Columbia UP, 1982.

Kuzniar, Alice, ed. *Outing Goethe and His Age*. Stanford: Stanford UP, 1996.

Passage, Charles. *Friedrich Schiller*. New York: Ungar, 1975.

Ronell, Avital. *Dictations: On Haunted Writing*. Bloomington: Indiana UP, 1986.

———. "Le Sujet Suppositaire: Freud and Rat Man." *On Puns: The Foundation of Letters*. Ed. Jonathan Culler. Oxford: Basil Blackwell, 1988. 115-39.

Sauder, Gerhard. "Die Jungfrau von Orleans." *Schillers Dramen: Neue Interpretationen*. Ed. Walter Hinderer. Stuttgart: Reclam, 1979. 217–41.

Schiller, Friedrich. *Briefwechsel zwischen Schiller und Körner*. Ed. Klaus Berghahn. Munich: Winkler, 1973.

———. *Don Carlos*. In *Plays*. Ed. Walter Hinderer. Trans. A. Leslie and Jeanne R. Wilson. New York: Continuum, 1983. 103–303.

———. *Schillers Briefe*. Eds. Erwin Streitfeld and Viktor Žmegac. Königstein/Ts: Athenäum, 1983.

———. *Schillers Dramen 2*. Ed. Herbert Kraft. Frankfurt a. M.: Insel, 1966.

Sharpe, Lesley. *Friedrich Schiller: Drama, Thought, Politics*. Cambridge: Cambridge UP, 1991.

Sinfield, Alan. *Cultural Politics: Queer Reading*. Philadelphia: U of Pennsylvania P, 1994.

Weber, Max. *The Protestant Ethic and the Spirit of Capitalism*. New York: Scribners, 1958.

Wiese, Benno von. *Friedrich Schiller*. Stuttgart: J. B. Metzler, 1959.

11

W. DANIEL WILSON

Skeletons in Goethe's Closet:
Human Rights, Protest, and
The Myth of Political Liberality

ONLY ONE SIDE OF THE HISTORY of political Weimar during the classical period has been written — the sunny side. The other side remains largely in the shadows to this day. The significance of this neglect is not merely antiquarian — it is not merely that one of Germany's greatest poets, Goethe, was a minister of state, or, more accurately, one of the four members of the Privy Council, the inner circle of advisers to Duke Carl August. It goes beyond the consequences for a questionable Goethe cult to the course of political culture in Germany to this day, for Goethe and Weimar are two of the central political icons in German culture. My working hypothesis is that the usual portrayal of classical Weimar as a refuge of benevolent authoritarianism, of "enlightened" absolutism, is based on little more than the Weimar government's support of writers, and the government's and intellectuals' capitalizing on this support, but that it ignores the real political dynamic of the duchy. Furthermore, this valorization of Weimar paternalism is an indispensable pillar of the legitimation of authoritarian government in Germany — of the notion that all good things are passed down from on high, from a generous but strong ruler unencumbered by annoying democratic institutions. Any examples of Weimar suppression of free speech or denial of fundamental human rights had to be swept under the rug, since the ideology of authoritarian government holds that such rights are guaranteed by the benevolence of the monarch.

Though the history of this whitewashing is largely unwritten, I have presented evidence for it during the Weimar Republic and Nazi years, arguing that the inception of modern research on Duke Carl August and his government from the 1920s to the 1940s was guided by a notion of the duke as a paradigmatically enlightened ruler who became a substitute for Frederick the Great in the eyes of historians seeking such a model strong ruler. I have shown (see also "Tabuzonen") how this conception guided the research that emerged during these years, paradigmatically embodied in Carl August's political correspondence edited starting around 1930 by Willy Andreas and Hans Tümmler. The image of Carl August that emerges from this edition is one of an early proponent of a strengthened *Reich*, a precursor to Bismarck and Hitler. Opposition and the suppression of opposition had no place in this hagiography. Most significantly, documents that reveal the use of informants during the period of the French Revolution were carefully excluded from this edition; though the collection contains only a selection of documents, the editors do not follow their own principle of selection when it comes to these cases. For example, in a couple of letters, passages are omitted in which the duke writes about these informants — whom he calls a "Maulwurfsgeschlecht" [race of moles] —, but the usual summary of such omitted passages is absent. As a result, unsuspecting scholars have used this important edition uncritically, as they have historical studies by the editors, and have cultivated the image of an unbelievably liberal monarchy that coincided with arguably the greatest flowering of German culture.

This image, however, did not originate in modern scholarship, but was carefully cultivated in classical Weimar itself. The key figure here is, again, Goethe, but he was not the first. When the duke's mother, the Duchess Anna Amalia, brought Christoph Martin Wieland, one of the most important writers of the day, to Weimar to be the tutor of the fifteen-year-old Prince Carl August in 1772, she reaped accolades in the world of German intellectuals, who throughout the eighteenth century had clung to the notion that their own influence on monarchs was the key to social and political progress. They also yearned for a prince who would provide them with the material support that they needed in an age in which they could not live from their writings. These strivings of intellectuals combine several strands of thought: the ancient notion of the philosopher's influence on the king, transformed, in the new, bureaucratized state into the ideal that Wolfgang Martens has recently called the "patriotic minister"; the idea that in their works writers could hold up a mirror to monarchs (the *Fürstenspiegel*) and thus improve the lot of society — a tradition in which Wieland himself was firmly anchored (see Wilson, "Intellekt" and "Wieland's *Diogenes*"); and notions of patronage inspired by the ancient Maecenas heritage and frustrated

11 • SKELETONS IN GOETHE'S CLOSET: THE MYTH OF LIBERALITY

by minor German princes, the Prussian king, and later by the Emperor Joseph II. Three years after Wieland's triumphant entry into Weimar, the duke turned eighteen and succeeded his mother, and when, in 1776, he appointed the young and famous (or infamous) middle-class writer Johann Wolfgang Goethe to his Privy Council, his place as an enlightened prince was firmly established among liberal opinion-makers in Germany. Even before the duke had time to change public policy, he was wildly praised by intellectuals outside of Weimar as "wise and enlightened."[1] Thus, his reputation was initially based not on any particular reforms or other accomplishments of the young duke, but on such appointments, which were, in the eyes of an eagerly believing public, obviously the mark of an ideal ruler. Bringing Johann Gottfried Herder to Weimar as the leading religious authority in the duchy the same year as Goethe was merely icing on the cake. To be sure, other writers flocked to Weimar and expected to scoop up their share of the icing; almost all had to leave hungry. But these disappointments did little to shake the liberal reputation of the duchy.

Undoubtedly, Goethe, the duke, and the other two members of the council did institute several reforms that improved the general situation in Weimar — although these reforms can easily be exaggerated, and usually are. They are all social and particularly economic reforms, not political. However, none of them materially improved the lot of the vast majority of the population or touched the most serious problem of the century, social inequality. They always avoided infringing the interests of the duke or the nobility, and the notion of relinquishing any part of this power was taboo before the Congress of Vienna. In the familiar deference to benevolent authoritarian government, both writers of Goethe's day and scholars in subsequent periods have praised this reform activity to the skies. Much of this praise parrots public relations work by the Weimar government itself. The theme of my work, human rights, was not addressed in public discourse (except in such celebrated cases as the dismissal of Johann Gottlieb Fichte as Jena professor). In modern scholarship, it has automatically been assumed — without much evidence — that such a benevolent ruler must have allowed free expression of ideas. Of course, it was also an unspoken tenet of faith that no one in Weimar really wanted to test their (presumed) right to free speech, since everybody was basically happy on their little island of liberality under their paternalist ruler and his enlightened council. Opposition simply did not exist — this is the consensus —, but it would have been allowed if it had existed.[2]

Some published evidence, and a couple of episodes that became known even during the classical period, should have refuted this rosy picture. It was known, for example, that two professors at the University of Jena (Johann Gottlieb Fichte and Lorenz Oken) were dismissed for reasons of their publicly expressed opinions. However, through ingenious interpretation of the documents, these incidents were minimized — in essence, the blame was laid at the feet of the victims themselves, who are to this day accused of being hotheads. This tradition had its beginnings in the Privy Council itself, where the mental balance of such opponents was regularly called into question (Goethe, *Amtliche Schriften* 1: 243; 2.2: 581, 954, 959, 963).

More important, crucial documents relating to such cases have remained unpublished or, if they were published, were ignored. They relate mainly to behind-the-scenes intimidation of oppositional figures, through the most ingenious methods. Some relevant documents were published in the nineteenth and early twentieth centuries, but they were mostly neglected during and after the Second World War.[3] In East Germany, there were early attempts to extend the Marxist critique of feudalism and absolutism to include Goethe and classical Weimar, and in this project there were a few hints of the suppression of free speech in classical Weimar and of civil unrest (see some of the documents contained in Holtzhauer). This trend was, understandably, ignored in West Germany, and in the GDR itself it was quickly marginalized as the communist party began to realize the ideological potential of claiming Goethe as a harbinger of socialism. More important, however, documents published in the monumental edition of Goethe's official writings from his work in the Council should have provided material for a critical view. However, this edition remains one of the least noticed in Goethe research, and scholars have misunderstood what it represents: it is only an edition of Goethe's official *writings*. It does *not* include those documents by others that refer to Goethe's official activities when they do not result in a document written by Goethe. Just as important, in the case of the first volume, covering the period when Goethe was most active in the Council (1776–86), the edition does not contain the more than eleven thousand documents to which he merely put his initials to indicate that he had participated in the decision, without adding anything to the text. Goethe's *Amtliche Schriften* (Official Writings), in other words, represent only a small fraction of his official *activities* in the period 1776–85.

In this venue, I can only sketch out some of the conclusions from about five months of full-time research in the Thuringian State Archive in Weimar (the material is presented in full detail in my book, *Das Goethe-Tabu*). Most important, there was much more opposition and political criticism in Weimar than was previously suspected. I should stress that the cases I have studied are only the documented ones, that is, those that came to the attention of the Privy Council as the result of appeals or other extraordinary measures. Most of but not all these protests took place during the French Revolution. And it is surely significant that protest during the Revolutionary period increased exponentially as the French armies approached — the threat of a French occupation in 1792 freed up the voices of grievance on issues that were not "imported" by the French, but rather were demonstrably present before the Revolution. For example, in Eisenach, which lay most directly in the path of the French troops, anonymous handwritten flyers were found that threatened the Weimar authorities with the wrath of the French general Custine if they did not redress grievances against feudal dues.[4] Several cases of citizens protesting undue taxation in public inns are documented — again, not in the capital, but in outlying villages, where protest was deemed safer. Even a local official of the Ducal government was accused of reminding the peasants of their ancient rights vis-à-vis the nobility.[5] Finally, there are dark references to "Unruhen" [violent protests]. One of the best-documented (but totally unknown) cases is a 1793 full-scale uprising of textile workers in the town of Apolda. The impoverished workers burned down the house of one factory owner and drove all the others out of town; the entrepreneurs fled to Weimar, where they pleaded for (and received) military support.[6] But this unrest did not begin only with the French Revolution; even earlier, there were disturbances in Apolda every few years, notably in 1784, when Goethe was involved in such matters.[7] This rebellion lends a particular poignancy to Goethe's well-known contrast, in a 1779 letter, between the starving textile workers in Apolda and the lofty verses of King Thoas in *Iphigenie auf Tauris*. As he writes to Charlotte von Stein on 6 March: "Hier will das Drama gar nicht fort, es ist verflucht, der König von Thoas soll reden als wenn kein Strumpfwürcker in Apolde hungerte" [Here (in Apolda) my play is not getting written at all; damn it all, King Thoas is supposed to speak as if the textile workers in Apolda were not starving; *Briefe* 1: 264]. Goethe's image of workers and peasants who were perhaps poor, but certainly docile, is shattered by such documents. Furthermore, it can be shown that some of Goethe's literary works that are usually tagged responses to the French Revolution are *also* responses to unrest in Saxe-Weimar itself.

The other important conclusion that can be drawn from this material is that — not surprisingly — organized groups had much more forceful forms of opposition than individuals, who were fairly easily intimidated by the government. This difference maps onto a significant socially stratified pattern of protest. The best organized protests came from the peasants, who had long since cherished powerful solidarity in conflicts with the state. Most often, this protest took legal forms, particularly petitions to the duke appealing a government infringement on written rights, particularly regarding feudal dues and service. The government responded to this form of protest mainly by criminalizing it. If the government unilaterally declared that the protest or appeal was inappropriate, it punished the local lawyer who had been called on by the largely illiterate peasants to write up their petition in the proper legalese and in the appropriately floral handwriting. Punishment of the lawyer effectively ended the peasants' chances of serious protest. Violent opposition then sometimes resulted.

The only other significantly organized groups were the student secret societies, which were something of a special case because all secret societies — the only real potential for organized opposition among intellectuals in eighteenth-century Germany — were suppressed by German governments. Other intellectuals were effectively isolated by the lack of a unified urban literary culture in this period and were co-opted by their dependence on the state for their livelihood. As a result, the Weimar government had no difficulty intimidating such pesky nonconformists. One of the easiest ways of doing so was surveillance, which had a chilling effect on dissent. Although surveillance was also carried out in villages — local officials were instructed to report immediately any suspect activity or too-free speech, especially in taverns, where peasants could be infected by political protest[8] — it was most notoriously deployed against students and professors in Jena, where it took on much more modern forms. The most important minister of the 1790s, Christian Gottlob Voigt, maintained a small army of paid informers among students and teachers at the university and among the local populace. Occasionally in Goethe's published official writings, there are vague hints at such sources, but the extent of it is not clear from those "Privat-Nachrichten" or "eingezogene Nachrichten" [private reports; *Amtliche Schriften* 2: 242–43]. In letters, Voigt boasts that he has a collection of informants' documents several fingers thick. I have been able to find only one such document that has survived.[9] Goethe's involvement in the hiring of such informants is clear in at least one letter that was published both in the Weimar edition of Goethe's works and in official writings, when that letter is seen in the context of the other documents.[10]

Surveillance seems to have been very effective in forestalling dissent among intellectuals. But the government also carried out direct intimidation. This generally meant private pressure from a member of the

Privy Council, usually Voigt. A consistent practice of intimidation becomes clear in the hirings of Jena professors. The façade of liberality at the university contributed materially to the welfare of the duchy because of the number of students it drew to Jena, thus enriching the local economy. The government was thus concerned to maintain at all costs this façade of liberality, so it appointed some of the stars in the world of learning to professorships. However, the documents reveal that it was made clear to these professors before they even came to Jena that they were to avoid political discourse altogether. Thus, the first stirrings of German Romanticism, at the University of Jena, took place in an atmosphere of censorship and intimidation — which makes the Romantics' turn from political progressivism to a purely philosophical and literary project (under the influence of Fichte) seem all too understandable. Furthermore, Herder's abrupt transformation from a proponent to an opponent of the French Revolution came about not because of the execution of the French king, as had been previously thought, but under pressure from several Weimar government officials and even Charlotte von Stein and the duchess.

The dynamics of the public sphere are essential to understanding these tactics. The government apparently felt no qualms about punishing peasants and other non-intellectual types, since it did not fear any repercussions from those with no access to the press. Thus, we find myriad cases of political protest from the lower classes resulting in imprisonment or other classical punishment. With intellectuals, the situation was much more risky for the government. Punishment was almost always avoided because it could create a public-relations scandal, and the government relied on intimidation and the resultant self-censorship of cowed intellectuals. This system failed in only two cases when professors proved too resistant to intimidation and had to be dismissed (Fichte and Oken). In general, professors responded to this pressure by avoiding political topics and simultaneously claiming that they were teaching at Germany's most liberal university. In a typical psychological maneuver, they convinced themselves of the liberality of their government without ever summoning up the courage to test it. Instead they concentrated on developing the "inward" project of German idealist philosophy and avoided collision with the authorities.

The result of these tactics and counter-tactics is, in a sense, paradoxical. Although organized peasants suffered the most consistent punishment, they also mounted the most sustained protest. By contrast, the intellectuals proved ridiculously easy to control. Punishment was generally avoided in their case, since surveillance and relatively low-level intimidation proved to be sufficient to the task of forestalling opposition. Of course, the political culture referred to earlier proved to be the key in this dynamic. Intellectuals were able to convince themselves that their government was "enlightened," and thus they made their peace with the authoritarian but supposedly benevolent state. They learned to live with the illusion that Germany needed no reform from below, through representation of the populace, but rather could transform itself "from above," through the happy influence of intellectuals on the absolutist ruler. Goethe and the other ministers took on this role of benevolently influential advisers in Weimar and became the political alibi for other intellectuals in the duchy, who were able to live with the idea that reform was slowly but surely being carried out. The result was that the intellectuals cheerfully participated in the Weimar government's campaign to convince the reading public and posterity that Weimar citizens lived in the most liberal state imaginable under the circumstances, in a land guided by the rule of law.

The Weimar government's treatment of fundamental issues of free speech and other human rights thus takes on crucial importance in assessing the gap between claim and reality. I am not mapping these concepts onto the eighteenth century from an anachronistic modern perspective. A very strong discourse of the Enlightenment — even before the Revolution — demanded fundamental human rights (see Bödeker, also the other essays in the volume edited by Birtsch; Klippel). I want to end with an example of broader infringement of human rights as defined in this period, before the classical liberal rights such as free speech gained widespread currency. I am referring to the notion that Weimar treated its citizens strictly in adherence to legal principle and the rights of the citizens to due process, and clearly defined punishment. This issue is of crucial historical importance because "enlightened" absolutism, primarily in Prussia, is credited with the birth or at least conception of the "Rechtsstaat," the state based on laws and legal rights. And it was of supreme significance to contemporaries, for whom "Willkür" [arbitrariness] in the treatment of citizens was the primary point of criticism of "enlightened" absolutism. Of course, historians do not attempt to claim that this period saw the full-blown modern state founded on law, in which executive power is limited by laws passed by a legislature and carried out by an independent judiciary (exceptions such as the celebrated case of the miller of Sanssouci only point at the absence of such guarantees otherwise, and were blown out of all proportion by contemporary publicists for Frederick).[11] However, these rulers certainly laid claim to treating their citizens in clear conformity with written laws and principles, even if those principles were not guaranteed by a balance of power. Judging by the archival material in which such principles are appealed to, Weimar took great pride in following them. In most cases, the government probably did so, but not always, thus demonstrating the fundamental arbitrariness of absolutist respect for legality and due process.

The case in point is particularly interesting to an American audience. Schoolchildren here to this day learn about those nasty "Hessian mercenaries" whom the British king rented from German princes to fight against the patriotic Americans. It is well known that Hesse was not the only German principality to lease its human capital — mainly peasants — to the British; a half dozen others played the same game. It was never known, however, that Weimar provided perhaps a few dozen of such soldiers. Carl August refused early on to provide an entire battalion of troops,[12] probably because he did not have enough peasants to do so, but probably also because this practice was universally loathed and publicly criticized in Germany. Thus, sending a whole contingent would have been the death-knell for Weimar claims to liberality, just when Goethe had joined the government. Nor were "normal" citizens sent from Weimar. Instead, the government sold off prison inmates who were deemed incorrigible (even if there was no real evidence that they were) to a Hanover officer who was explicitly in the market for "recruits" for the American war.[13] Since these men were criminals who were presumably sentenced by a court, such transactions might not seem particularly repugnant. But we have to remember the Weimar government's claim to strict legal practices, which were undeniably violated here. For example, the punishment for theft was clearly defined in Weimar law (Schmidt 2: 163–184). But when a thief was sold as a mercenary for the American war, his punishment was changed, potentially transformed into a death penalty (about forty-two per cent of mercenary soldiers who were sent to America never returned; of those, over half were killed or died of disease; see Smith iii-v). Because such deals clearly would infringe on the rights of its citizens, the Weimar government at first went to great pains to send to America only those prisoners who agreed to go. The principle of shipping them only with their free consent was explicitly stated by the duke.[14] However, a few years later this principle quietly disappeared: now the prisoners were no longer even asked whether they wished to fight in America instead of completing their jail term.[15] After the war, Prussia took up the slack for England. There is evidence that by this time, the Weimar jail had been practically emptied by such deals.[16] Obviously, the government had found the temptation too great to dispose of its undesirables in this way, without their consent. The temptation was partly financial: the price per head had risen from five reichstalers at the beginning to ten, in some cases even thirty or forty reichstalers for particularly tall "recruits."[17] The government not only reaped these premiums, but also saved a certain amount of money on incarceration costs – although these were not as high as might be imagined, partly because the prisoners only received warm meals three times a week and otherwise lived on bread and water. The costs for a typical thief in prison for six years were sixty-eight reichstalers;[18] add to that the five reichstalers premium from the so called "recruitment" and the savings are not particularly high. The Weimar government liked to complain about how poor the duchy was, and modern historians echo such laments when they insist how little could be done to better the life of the ordinary people. But a look at the private finances of the duke reveals that money was theoretically available to guarantee citizens' rights: in a single year, which cost between eleven and twelve talers for the incarceration of a prisoner, the duke lost over one thousand talers gambling, including three hundred and forty-five talers, on a single unfortunate evening, to Charlotte von Stein's husband. This one evening's loss amounted to more than the yearly salary of the average Jena professor, of which Weimar paid only a part. In the same year — the last year of the American War of Independence — the duke spent over 4,600 talers for gifts of money and objects for the nobility and other princes.[19] Of course, such expenses were considered necessary to represent the power and status of the prince. But Weimar was not financially dependent on this human waste disposal.

Goethe was involved in almost all of these transactions, because they took place while he was an active member of the Council. Because the documents contain only Goethe's initials indicating his assent to the decisions, none of them are contained in the edition of his official writings. As director of the war commission, Goethe was in fact more deeply involved in these deals than the other privy councillors. And yet the scholars who have written on Goethe as "minister of war," though they are almost certain to have seen these documents, passed over the entire phenomenon in silence.[20] And those critics who have dealt with the question of Goethe's attitude toward America and the War of Independence had no inkling of these goings-on. America and the principle of freedom that it represented for Goethe found their way into minor literary works and his autobiography — in fact, in *Das Neueste von Plundersweilern* (The Latest from Trashville, 1781) he even criticized the selling of soldiers to the British, although in a very opaque passage and referring of course to Hesse, not Weimar (MA 2.1: 7–12). So a full understanding of these literary passages, and of the contradictions in Goethe's life, depends on this unpublished archival evidence from his political career.

I want to end with a double plea: not to exaggerate the gravity of Weimar repression, but also not to underestimate the significance of these phenomena. I do not want to make Weimar out to be a reign of terror, as my work has been caricatured. And there is no doubt that the Weimar government's efforts to live up to its public image did result in practices more liberal than in many other German principalities. My conclusion is partly that classical Weimar was not *as* liberal as was claimed either by its own stewards or by modern scholars who take these claims at face value, simply because these claims depended on suppression of evidence to the contrary. However, I would suggest that we keep these practices in mind when discussing all aspects of classical Weimar. The entire Weimar culture examined in this volume — literature, theatre, music, art, and so on — cannot be divorced from its underpinnings, the feudal and absolutist system that relied on surveillance, intimidation, violation of fundamental rights, punishment of dissidents, and "public relations" for its existence and for its subsequent reputation. The lofty edifice of classical *Humanität* — humanity and culture — rests, at best, on a shaky political foundation. As a corollary, I would urge a moratorium on mobilizing Goethe for the democratic cause, a trend that threatens to rear its head on the coincidence of his two hundred and fiftieth birthday and the fiftieth birthday of a viable German democracy in 1999. The myth of Goethe the democrat does great violence to his central political tenets. Instead, Germans would do well to end the neglect of their truly democratic institutions — in this case, an alternative heritage with which they can more properly identify: the previously silenced culture of political protest and opposition under the noses of the cultural elite in Weimar.

—University of California at Berkeley

Notes

[1] Johann Georg Zimmermann in a letter from Hanover to Charlotte von Stein, 29 December 1775, less than four months after Carl August's accession to power, qtd. in Bode 159.

[2] This tendency is most pronounced in the work of the most important scholar of the duke's government and of the minister Goethe, Hans Tümmler (see Wilson, "Tabuzonen"); Tümmler's work has remained hugely influential and has been taken over uncritically by many scholars, notably the popular introduction to classical Weimar by Dieter Borchmeyer.

³ With respect to published documents, I am referring mainly to those in Diezmann (70–71) and, for Fichte's dismissal, Houben. Houben's researches in archives would have been directly relevant to Tümmler's portrayal of the Fichte dismissal (see Wilson, "Tabuzonen" 426–28). Tümmler knew of Houben's work before 1949 (ibid., 437), but ignored it in his study of Fichte's dismissal.
⁴ Johann Carl Salomo Thon to Christian Gottlob Voigt, Eisenach, 11 December 1792, Thuringian State Archive, Weimar, ThHStAW J 344, fol. 1–3, here 3r (this correspondence comes from Voigt's papers).
⁵ Voigt to Carl August, 21 December 1792, ThHStAW A 442a, fol. 126–27, here 126v. See also the numerous other documents relating to this official (Johann Friedrich Schwabhäuser, 1740–99, the "Amtmann" in Allstedt) in A 442a, B 2742, and B 2766.
⁶ Voigt to Carl August, 16 June 1793, ThHStAW A 442a, fol. 381–82, here 382r, as well as subsequent letters; see B 5718.
⁷ ThHStAW B 5711, fol. 144ff.
⁸ See copy of the letter from Carl August to the Privy Council, Breslau, 21 August 1790, ThHStAW B 5333, fol. 1, and other documents in this file.
⁹ The enclosure to the letter from Voigt to Carl August, 14 July 1792, ThHStAW A 442a, fol. 77, 83–86. The enclosure (fol. 78) has no signature or date, but Voigt wrote in pencil at the bottom: "D. Skerman" and noted that he received it on 6 July.
¹⁰ Goethe to Voigt, 10 September 1792, *Amtliche Schriften* 2: 299 (the letter had already been published in the Weimar Edition); on the context of this letter see Wilson, "Tabuzonen" 433. In her commentary, Helma Dahl remarks that this is an "interesting" document that makes us regret the loss of so many confidential official communications by Goethe (*Amtliche Schriften* 3: 97); Goethe had a tendency to destroy letters from his politically sensitive correspondence.
¹¹ See the useful corrective by Karl Biedermann in the second half of the nineteenth century (93–94 — here also a good portrayal of "enlightened" despots' intrusion into judicial matters is to be found).
¹² Carl August to Philip Ernst Graf zu Schaumburg-Lippe, 3 December 1777, draft initialed by Carl August, Fritsch, and Schnauß, ThHStAW B 36568, fol. 2r.
¹³ The cases are documented in the files ThHStAW B 36557, 36568, 36569, 36598, 36599, 36603, 36605, 36606, 36618, and 36619.
¹⁴ "Actum" [protocol] of the Weimar government, 21 June 1777, signed by Chancery Secretary Friedrich Christian Tripplin; also present were Government Chancellor Achatius Ludwig Carl Schmid, Privy Government Councillors Wilhelm Emanuel Gottlieb Hetzer and Johann Friedrich Kobe von Koppenfels, and Government Councillor Johann Ludwig Eckart. ThHStAW B 36569, fol. 5r.

[15] The duke and his Privy Council later inquired whether prisoners were available, and no longer asked whether they were willing to serve. Carl August to the Weimar government, 29 August 1780, scribe's copy with the duke's signature, ThHStAW H 1586, fol. 1r. Since this is the *Mundum*, that is, the scribe's fair copy, only the duke's signature is present (the councillors' initials are only on the draft, which is missing in this case). However, all councillors present on the day of the Council meeting (which is always identical with the date on the scribe's copy) took part in the decision, and Goethe was present on 29 August (*Amtliche Schriften* 1: lxxiv).

[16] This can be surmised from the fact that a few years earlier, there had been ten prisoners in the Weimar jail, whereas in 1786 there were only four, and only one of these was deemed fit for military service. Prison Inspector Johann Gottfried Premsler to the Weimar government, 29 November 1786, ThHStAW H 1597, fol. 13.

[17] Rittmeister von Göchhausen to Government Councillor Traugott Lebrecht Schwabe, Osterburg, 1 October 1786, ThHStAW H 1597, fol. 12. This letter contains greetings to Fritsch, Schnauß, and Goethe.

[18] See Premsler's accounting, 19 April 1781, ThHStAW H 1586, fol. 18r.

[19] See the ducal "Schatulle" [privy purse] for the year 1 October 1782 to 1 October 1783, ThHStAW A 1107, fol. 11r, "Serenissimi Spielgelder," as well as for 1782–83, ThHStAW A 1107, fol. 31v. For Goethe's accounting of Jena professors' salaries in 1785 see *Amtliche Schriften* 1: 364–68.

[20] Hans Bürgin used files in close proximity to the ones revealing the sale of prisoners, but never mentions them (see esp. 152–58); it is practically impossible that Hans Wahl, director of the State Archive, did not know of these files when writing his study.

Works Cited

Andreas, Willy, and Hans Tümmler, eds. *Politischer Briefwechsel des Herzogs und Großherzogs Carl August von Weimar*. 3 vols. Stuttgart: Deutsche Verlags-Anstalt, 1954–1973.

Biedermann, Karl. *Deutschland im 18. Jahrhundert: Ausgabe in einem Band*. Ed. Wolfgang Emmerich. Frankfurt a. M.: Ullstein, 1979.

Birtsch, Günter, ed. *Grund- und Freiheitsrechte im Wandel von Gesellschaft und Geschichte: Beiträge zur Geschichte der Grund- und Freiheitsrechte vom Ausgang des Mittelalters bis zur Revolution von 1848*. Göttingen: Vandenhoeck und Ruprecht, 1981.

Bode, Wilhelm, ed. *Goethe in vertraulichen Briefen seiner Zeitgenossen 1749–1803*. Berlin: E. Mittler, 1918.

Bödeker, Hans Erich. "Menschenrechte im deutschen publizistischen Diskurs vor 1789." *Grund- und Freiheitsrechte von der ständischen zur spätbürger-*

lichen Gesellschaft. Ed. Günter Birtsch. Göttingen: Vandenhoeck and Ruprecht, 1987. 392–433.

Borchmeyer, Dieter. *Weimarer Klassik. Portrait einer Epoche.* Weinheim: Beltz Athenäum, 1994. [First edition: *Die Weimarer Klassik: Eine Einführung.* 2 vols. Königstein/Ts.: Athenäum, 1980.]

Bürgin, Hans. *Der Minister Goethe vor der römischen Reise: Seine Tätigkeit in der Wegebau- und Kriegskommission.* Weimar: Hermann Böhlau, 1933.

Diezmann, August, ed. *Aus Weimars Glanzzeit. Ungedruckte Briefe von und über Goethe und Schiller, nebst einer Auswahl ungedruckter vertraulicher Schreiben von Goethes Collegen, Geh. Rath v. Voigt.* Leipzig: Hartung, 1855.

Goethe, Johann Wolfgang. *Amtliche Schriften. Veröffentlichung des Staatsarchivs Weimar.* [Vols. 1–4:] *Goethes Tätigkeit im Geheimen Consilium.* Vol. 1 ed. Willy Flach, vols. 2–4 ed. Helma Dahl. Weimar: Hermann Böhlau, 1950–1987.

———. *Goethes Briefe und Briefe an Goethe.* Hamburger Ausgabe. Eds. Karl Robert Mandelkow et al. 6 vols. 4th ed. Munich: dtv, 1988.

Holtzhauer, Helmut. *Goethe-Museum: Werk, Leben und Zeit Goethes in Dokumenten.* Berlin and Weimar: Aufbau, 1969.

Houben, Heinrich Hubert. *Verbotene Literatur von der klassischen Zeit bis zur Gegenwart.* Vol. 2. Dresden: Rauch, 1928.

Klippel, Diethelm. *Politische Freiheit und Freiheitsrechte im deutschen Naturrecht des 18. Jahrhunderts.* Paderborn: Schöningh, 1976.

Martens, Wolfgang. *Der patriotische Minister: Fürstendiener in der Literatur der Aufklärungszeit.* Weimar: Böhlau, 1996.

Schmidt, Johannes. *Aeltere und neuere Gesetze, Ordnungen und Circular-Befehle für das Fürstenthum Weimar und für die Jenaische Landes-Portion bis zum Ende des Jahres 1799 in einem alphabetischen wörtlichen Auszug gebracht.* 9 vols. and 2 suppl. vols. Jena: n.p., 1800–1805, 1805–1819.

Smith, Clifford Neal. *Muster Rolls and Prisoner-of-War Lists in American Archival Collections Pertaining to the German Mercenary Troops Who Served with the British Forces During the American Revolution.* McNeal, AZ: Westland, 1976.

Wahl, Hans. "Vom Kriegskommissar Goethe und seinen Soldaten." *Goethe-Kalender auf das Jahr 1942.* Ed. Frankfurter Goethe-Museum [pref. Ernst Beutler]. Leipzig: Dieterich, 1941. 1–68.

Wilson, W. Daniel. *Das Goethe-Tabu: Protest und Menschenrechte im klassischen Weimar.* Munich: dtv, 1999.

———. "Intellekt und Herrschaft. Wielands *Goldner Spiegel*, Joseph II. und das Ideal eines kritischen Mäzenats im aufgeklärten Absolutismus." *Modern Language Notes* 99 (1984): 479–502.

———. "Tabuzonen um Goethe und seinen Herzog. Heutige Folgen nationalsozialistischer Absolutismuskonzeptionen." *Deutsche Vierteljahrsschrift für Literaturwissenschaft und Geistesgeschichte* 70 (1996): 394–442.

———. "Wieland's *Diogenes* and the Emancipation of the Critical Intellectual." *Christoph Martin Wieland: North American Scholarly Contributions on the Occasion of the 250th Anniversary of his Birth*. Ed. Hansjörg Schelle. Tübingen: Niemeyer, 1984. 149–79.

12

GERT THEILE

*The Weimar Myth:
From City of the Arts to Global Village*

Memory Museum

IF WE ACCEPT PHILOSOPHER Karl Friedrich Forberg's metaphor of cities as "Hospitäler der Menschheit" [hospitals of humankind],[1] then we must see Weimar after 1800 as having gained the rank of a national and patriotic health spa. Innovative nineteenth-century literary and arts movements connected with names such as Poe, de Quincey, and Baudelaire created artificial paradises to which Germany offered its own dream in stone: Weimar as city of the arts. This tiny place both mimics the national political situation and replicates in miniature national cultural claims; the spiritual greatness staged within its walls serves as balsam for the phantom pains of what Helmuth Plessner called the "verspätete Nation" [belated nation].

Anna Amalia, Duchess of Saxe-Weimar, established her court of muses in the enlightened absolutist tradition of the sovereign as patron. She thus enabled her muses, Goethe and Schiller, to rescue to "another shore" in the lifeboat of aesthetic culture the most valuable items from aboard the proud ship of courtly civilization, wrecked by the storm of the French Revolution (Borchmeyer 475). As a bourgeois version of courtly culture, the Weimar court of muses indeed embodied national cultural identity at the close of the eighteenth century, both because of the political division of Germany and the concomitant change in public mood to subordinate the desire for a political nation state to the concept of a national culture. The aesthetic program of Weimar Classicism evolved into a small center of cultural imperialism (as evidenced by the *Xenien* dispute), so that after the turn of the century it was in vogue to pay one's literary compliments at the house on the Frauenplan square, with sometimes comical results (see Henke in this volume). This has not least of all to do with the person of Goethe (more on this later) who stood as deity, or better, as founder, of the temple of the German spirit.

Typical German intellectual tendencies are reflected in the cultural life of Weimar: a mixture of courtly-aristocratic attitudes and competitive bourgeois perfectionism, crowned with the laurels of the poet-monarch and ennobled through the categorical imperative of state reformism. The corresponding ideological correctives developed during the nineteenth century in cosmopolitan Munich and Prussian Berlin. Notwithstanding attempts to create a Weimar-Prussian synthesis, over time, the political weight of Prussia dominated; thus, for example, Wilhelm von Humboldt's neoclassically oriented ideals of bourgeois cultivation and education were given concrete structures in the form of the humanistic gymnasium as a prerequisite for university study.

But it seemed the post-Hegelian age wanted a cultural and political consensus: an unfathomable "Weltinnenraum" (Rilke's notion of the cosmos inside oneself) gained success abroad through the likes of Hoffmann and Tieck. Goethe, who later in his life learned a thing or two from Romanticism (see Zabka), had already become an icon of German cultural *gravitas* to such an extent that critics like Georg Gottfried Gervinus (1805–71) or Friedrich Theodor Vischer (1807–87) were unable to show any sympathy for "the very serious jests" of his late works (see Mandelkow). The division in Goethe's reception between the oeuvre and the man already exists at this point. The playful artifice of an ironic muse falls by the wayside after 1800, for the politicized generation of the new century repudiates that and aspires toward certainty. Rising nationalism writes its own newly canonical books. Rather than flights of fancy or explorations of the twilight zone, the new marching route, drawn up after the anti-Napoleonic wars of liberation by a militarily demobilized German intelligentsia, becomes a path towards a national cultural consciousness. In spite of all the political indifference of classical Weimar and Goethe's defense of the incommensurability of culture, young German literary scholars traveled this new route not only looking out for keystones to top the monumental arches of the newly awakened nation of culture, but also — as Ortega y Gasset put it — "wie der Vogel Strauß entschlossen alle Steine der Goetheschen Lebenslandschaft [zu] verschlucken, als wären es Rosen" [determined like an ostrich to swallow every pebble in the landscape of Goethe's life, as if they were all roses; 188].

And so a phenomenon of the provinces, endowed with national historical meaning, becomes a perpetual passion play. Ascendant historicism finally satisfied the nation's inner need for tangible representations of the past. In the nineteenth century, historiography, linked with the care of historical landmarks and monuments, becomes the

> narrative Gerüst von bürgerlicher Gesellschaft und Nationalstaatlichkeit. Als säkularisierte Mythologie stiftet sie [die Geschichtsschreibung] den politischen Kräften der Moderne ihre kulturelle Legitimität. Das Geschichtsbuch ersetzt den Kirchenkalender, das Denkmal, den Reliquienkult. (Wyss 191; see also Berghahn)

> [narrative framework of bourgeois society and the nation state. This secularized mythology gives cultural legitimacy to the political forces of modernity. The history book has replaced the church calendar, monuments, reliquaries.]

The constitutive phase of the Spirit of Weimar, that is, the cultural and political consolidation of the memorabilia of the late eighteenth century, was precisely coincident with the melding of idealism and historicism. A kind of commemorative heroism was thus introduced, which — despite all of its Schinkel-inspired provinciality — turned the arts town of Weimar into a haphazard museum of memories. The museum-like doll house ambience demanded constant devotion as a way of life; the poets' citadel was proclaimed the pilgrimage destination for the non-unified nation. In Weimar we are concerned with the archaeological evidence along the German national road to destiny, for Weimar is the memory-made-stone of the German culture nation that tries to compensate for its own political nullity and the "vollendeten Verlust des Himmels" [consummate loss of salvation; Jean Paul] with a world and poetic theology able to be seen only through a German lens (Timm 9–11, 50–78).

The metaphors of memory made valid by scholars are completely present, spatially as well as temporally, in the phenomenon of Weimar (see Assmann). The codification of memory contained in signifying image formulas and the ordering of these images into specifically structured spaces leads to buildings as symbols of memory, the temple and the library (14). Now one really could talk of carrying coals to Newcastle (or rather Goethe to Weimar) if one wanted to strain the memory symbolism with more than references to the Weimar situation, the poets' memorials, the Anna Amalia Library, or the Goethe and Schiller Archive. The memory metaphor of the library, says Assmann, is only one step away from that of the book (19); we will take this step literally and cross the threshold into Weimar. In the midst of carefully honored "great authors" and their so-called classic editions of up to one hundred and fifty volumes, the mass of literature on Weimar, and the antlike collecting urges of generations, another metaphor of memory comes to mind: the notion of the gods' book of ages which symbolizes absolute memory as a totalizing book (19). The completeness and hermeticism of the text, however, stands always in opposition to the "Unvollständigkeit und Unendlichkeit der Interpretation" [incomplete and infinite nature of interpretation; 19]. This leads to temporal metaphors of memory and gives us a cognizant glimpse of the results of Weimar-inspired service to the intellect that Goethe scholars — "watchdogs of the primal text," says Arno Schmidt — have been directing for nearly two hundred years.

Forgetting and remembering are also the psychological columns supporting the eschatological edifice built around German poetry of the Age of Goethe: exhibited in this place is a politically legitimating story of salvation of this folk of poets and philosophers (see Assmann 22–31). The story, rooted in Winckelmann's paradoxical formula — "durch Nachahmung unnachahmlich" [inimitable through imitation] — defined the German search for identity as a path toward the self and its socio-cultural tardiness as difference with respect to other nations. Classical Weimar is the most important aspect of the post-Goethean consciousness of the history of the German special path. And thus it follows when, for example, Wilhelm Scherer's popular nineteenth-century literary history posits a lineage that leads from the Meistersinger at the Wartburg to Luther's table talks and from the "Era of Frederick the Great" (and it is well-known that he cared nothing for German literature) to classical Weimar. The poetic phenomenon of Weimar becomes a heroic national highpoint; the year of Goethe's death the culminating caesura marking all the literature that follows as nothing but a coda to the Goethean artistic period (see Scherer 527–28, 614).

Goethe in Weimar — like Luther at the Wartburg castle or Frederick II at Sanssouci — becomes the tradition-laden essence of the German cultural landscape even to this day. Only this notion appears more modern than the aura of the reformer in flight: self-consciously grounded and poetically sanctioned, the Weimar god is available for continuous reception. Face to face with the poet's body lying in state, longtime Goethe admirer Luise Seidler can thus interpret his life work as gospel: "So schön wie sein ganzes Leben war" [As beautiful as was his life; 56]. Halo and crown — as both sacred and secular attributes — unite to become the poet's laurels in the place of aristocratic cynicism and laisser-faire attitudes in matters of faith. Goethe and Weimar — great places, great faces — Germany's Mount Rushmore as Parnassus: with its characteristic small-town look, it lies there, nestled in the mountains of Central Germany.

Distance and Taking Leave with a Grin

"Kein Reich von dieser Welt, vielmehr das Imaginarium einer Kontinentalisierung alles Großen aus Geschichte und Gegenwart durch den Geist: 'Geist der Goethezeit'" [No earthly realm, rather an imaginary continentalization of all that is spiritually great from the past and the present: this is the "Spirit of the Age of Goethe"], is how Hermann Timm defines H. A. Korff's label for a literary epoch which has become synonymous with this German cultural empire of the mind and spirit (191). But the question about just why this Spirit of Weimar — the Age of Goethe — went on to become the spirit of the age, and then why this spirit of the age is able to perform atemporally, loosed from its temporal bonds, disengaged from the time span of Goethe's contemporaries, points to the indissoluble interweaving of Goethe and Weimar. We speak of Goethe's Weimar, or Goethestadt Weimar, whenever the place is meant, not the person. The life and work of national author Goethe are, at least partially, separate from Weimar. But Weimar is never separate from Goethe.

Weimar's renaissance depended on the mythology of humanist values found in an Humboldtian high culture (though already made common by association with the middle class and militarism), and this despite the discreditation — even spiritually — of the imperial German idea around 1918. It was then also the political concerns of the Weimar Republic that served to bestow value once again upon Weimar.[2]

Weimar without Goethe simply does not exist in the world's cultural consciousness. The town's myth depends first of all on Goethe's own original being, this bourgeois poet who literarily and poetically opened up whole new realms of feeling and thinking at the dawn of the modern era, simply because he made his home here. On the other hand, that many famous Germans happened to live in Weimar for a long time, "dafür kann man billigerweise Weimar selbst nicht verantwortlich machen" [is not by virtue of Weimar itself]; that it was not some "Fabrik berühmter Leute" [factory for producing famous people] had become clear to everyone shortly after Goethe's death (Laube 143).

Schiller's historically ambitious works provide a better point of departure for patriotic-eschatological fantasies than do the — supposed — indifference and incommensurable privy-councillor-small-mindedness of that house on the Frauenplan. But scolding Goethe for his politics (see also W. Daniel Wilson's essay in this volume) is soon forgotten and in the medium term it is precisely his stylized existence which predestined him to become the founding figure of a national cultural heritage. Practiced unapproachability and neohellenic self-dramatization, as well as a multifaceted artistic nature not only provide Goethe's aura with its incomprehensibility and enigmatic nature, but also allow him to rise above the crowd of his contemporaries. Korff's formulaic equation of essence and time can be understood then only as the descriptive consequence of a sensational coincidence of national-political expectations of salvation and charismatic form, while the fusion of personal and local mythology characterizes the need to assign transcendental feelings to a place. The promised land of the enlightened nation is called cultural landscape — externally it is a political patchwork, but internally a paradise. Goethe, who was well aware of the extraordinary times in which he lived, and who was also well known for his knack of making historical judgments about "experiencing the here and now," said appropriately that this was an epoch that would not soon return (see Schulz).

Since we are looking here at Goethe's mythic-structural meaning for Weimar, rather than examining the undisputed epoch-making achievements of Goethe, we can turn to other similar small towns as counter examples: Jena, important philosophical center of German idealism and meeting place of Early Romantic philosophy and literature, and Richard Wagner's Bayreuth, national site of cultic devotion and of dramatic festivals. Jena has never represented itself nationally or internationally as a mythic cultural landscape; reasons for this lie both in a transcendental philosophical attitude that remained distant from the people even in its formulaic, aphoristic manner, as well as in its continuously changing cast of characters. In times of semi-religious disorientation, neither ironic jokesters nor philosophical radicals make very good founding personalities.

Bayreuth gets a bit closer to the phenomenon of "Iphigenia's village," as Hans Mayer observes in his book *Richard Wagner and Bayreuth*: "Vergleichbar ist eine Formel, die Wagner und Bayreuth zusammenschließt, in ihrer historischen Tragweite *höchstens* mit der Parallelformel 'Goethe und Weimar'" [One can compare the historical consequences of a formula that includes Wagner and Bayreuth *at most* with the parallel formula of Goethe and Weimar; 21, my emphasis]. But he then immediately adds the following reservation.

> Goethe hat keine Nachfolge begründet oder auch nur begründen wollen. Die letzten Jahrzehnte seines Lebens wurden immer planvoller stilisiert als Gegensatz einer "inkommensurablen" Subjektivität zu einer Außenwelt, die als Welt schlechthin genommen werden mochte, da das Weimar Goethes, *wie man es am Frauenplan befand*, ohnehin eine Welt bedeutete. Weltbürger und Weimaraner. (Mayer 21–22; my emphasis)

> [Goethe did not produce any disciples and did not want to. The last decades of his life were systematically stylized as the antithesis of an 'incommensurable' subjectivity to an outside world that wanted to be taken seriously as a world, since Goethe's Weimar, *as it existed at the Frauenplan*, was a world of its own anyway. World citizen and Weimarian.]

Though Mayer's observations about the similarity of the symbiotic relationships of place and artist are quite fitting, his conclusions about the lack of consequences of Goethean incommensurability are completely false.

Goethe's continuously propagated self-diagnosis was that his own star would have followed its prescribed path anyway and he would likewise have acted in accord with the rules which governed him regardless. In short, by favoring the notion of entelechy he blurred the difference between being and appearance he was subject to his whole life. Ortega y Gasset's unnoticed observation at the hundredth anniversary of Goethe's death (and current Cultural Studies work has only confirmed this) is correct: all philology is at the same time Goethe philology. Goethe of all people created an unparalleled succession. His early modern (actually Romantic) realization about the impossibility of individual expression and his attempts to find signs which are capable of "formulating the indistinguishability of meaning as a problem of form able to integrate itself into a potential of meaning for the work" (Wellbery 24), lead him to just the sort of poetry-and-truth methodology that Wellbery, among others, sees at work in modern authors like Beckett and Borges. Thus the question, productive for the poetic work of art, of just who is speaking — Goethe or I; or "Borges or I" (see Borges 47 and Hörisch 117–48) — helps the poet gain a unique status like Shakespeare, Dante, or Cervantes. This conditional existence situates Goethe, as an Olympian with a bourgeois address, in a nonbourgeois, classicized interior space (see Schlaffer 1). This is a notion that extends particular local constraints to the cosmos inside oneself (Rilke's "Weltinnenraum"), and thus empowers spiritual worldliness: the world as village, and that is *his* world, which is also *a* world. This conditional existence also naturally incurs a conditional context as the reception-historical by-product of this poetic introspection. In Weimar, then, begins the process of fabricating imaginations, since no one knows what true genius is supposed to be. To each his own Goethe. Eckermann is the first to make his own living off Goethe,[3] a process that continues to this day.

Naturally Goethe's own introspection is successful as national culture; not by chance does Scherer cite in his literary history the poet's epigram in the context of an anecdote about Goethe's stay in the Lutherite atmosphere at the Wartburg. It reflects the prince-poet alliance as well as the turn toward the interior self:

> Klein ist unter den Fürsten Germaniens freilich der meine;
> Kurz und schmal ist sein Land; mäßig nur, was er vermag.
> Aber so wende nach innen, so wende nach außen die Kräfte
> Jeder; da wär' es ein Fest, Deutscher mit Deutschen zu sein.
> (Qtd. in Scherer 528)

> [Among the German princes mine is surely lowly;
> His land is small and slight; modest his abilities.
> But each should turn inward, and thus expose outwardly his
>   strengths;
> That would be a festival, to be a German among Germans.]

Today's reader might well smirk at the upright local patriotism here, though one can also see this culturally based national consciousness in a positive light, given the later extremes of German history. The other side of this idealism of the cosmos inside oneself, the provinciality and the narrow-minded arrogance that soon followed, is appropriately targeted by outsiders. In *Deutschland: Ein Wintermärchen* (Germany. A Winter's Tale, 1844), Heinrich Heine puts it in a nutshell:

> [...]
> O deutsche Seele, wie stolz ist dein Flug
> In deinen nächtlichen Träumen!
>
> Die Götter erbleichen, wenn du nahst!
> Du hast auf deinen Wegen
> Gar manches Sternlein ausgeputzt
> Mit deinen Flügelschlägen!
>
> Franzosen und Russen gehört das Land,
> Das Meer gehört den Briten,
> Wir aber haben im Luftreich des Traums
> Die Herrschaft unbestritten.
> Hier üben wir Hegemonie,
> Hier sind wir unzerstückelt;
> Die andern Völker haben sich
> Auf platter Erde entwickelt. (*Werke* 1: 452)

> [(...)]
> O German Soul, in your nightly dreams
> How haughtily you fly!
>
> The gods grow pale at your approach!
> And everywhere you go
> With beating pinions you snuff out
> Many a starlet's glow.
>
> The French and the Russians rule the land;
> The British rule the sea;
> But in the realms of dreams we own
> Unchallenged mastery.
>
> Here we become one mighty state,
> Here, in dreams, we are crowned —
> While other peoples build their realms
> Upon the level ground. (*Poetry and Prose* 246–47)]

The German soul was naturally not supposed to snuff out with its wings the other, secularized god; it circled it rather more like a moth around a flame. Just as it is impossible to understand the secularized rhetoric of the anti-Napoleonic liberation movement without the religious vacuum left by the enlightenment, what binds the Goethean be-one-and-become-everything philosophy of life and his sphere of influence is not only a conspiratorial fan club of Germanic chauvinists, literary critics, and dilettante practical philosophers, but also the rift running through the modern, Cartesian world. It is impossible to explain the strangely messianic context of the veneration of Goethe in the pantheon at the Frauenplan without acknowledging the post-enlightenment role of a theology of the poet.

> Wo in den metaphysischen Systembauten der Schlußstein des Absoluten und in den Schriften der Apokalyptiker der feurige Weltuntergang am Ende der Tage erscheint, steht hier [in der Dichtertheologie] das Bild des Kosmos als berstende Universalbibliothek. (Timm 30; also 13–30)
>
> [Whereas for the metaphysical system things end at the keystone of the absolute and in apocalyptic texts they conclude in the fiery last days of the earth, here (in the theology of the poet) the cosmic image is of an exploding universal library.]

The coincidence of politically legitimated salvation narrative and a secularized theology of the poet (an exceptionally creative one) with the demand of a micro-megalomanic, dialectic presence grants Weimar the aura of a mythic cultural landscape. The virulence of the Weimar myth through the years can be seen in the ambivalent reception of Goethe and his works. The history of Goethe parodies allow us to trace seismographically the forces of this specific myth. Indeed the distance of the parodist to the cultural phenomenon of Weimar, the quintessence of which is Goethe, allows the plotting of a fever curve of aversion or of the self-emancipation of the creative spirit from Weimar. The highpoints on the curve correspond exactly with those historical moments in which the quest for philosophical positions and the parodists' search for self-expression react to the hypertrophic paralysis of national-cultural identity.

In his 1939 novel *Lotte in Weimar*, Thomas Mann — the twentieth century's own Goethe — has his fictional poet-prince refer to the parodic attitude toward the past as "taking leave with a grin," a nod perhaps toward the paling of an inherited Goethean culture in a postmodern age. Ernst Cassirer described this image of Goethe in his last essay as follows:

> All das [die Berichte über Goethe in den ersten Kapiteln des Romans] gibt ein zwar buntes und vielfältiges, aber ein bloß mittelbares und in dieser Mittelbarkeit quälendes Bild. Goethe erscheint nirgends als er selbst; er erscheint nur als aufgefangen in einem fremden Medium. [...] Der einzelne Erzähler kann nur aussprechen, was Goethe *ihm* gewesen und wozu er für *ihn* geworden ist. Hier also stehen Erfüllung und Mangel sich nahe zur Seite. Die Bewunderung und Verehrung für Goethe, ja die Liebe zu ihm, wird zum Quell immer neuer Enttäuschung. Jeder, der sich in seinem Kreis aufgenommen sieht, fühlt zugleich, daß er diesen Kreis zwar berühren, aber niemals erfassen oder durchdringen kann. So wird die Anziehung selbst zur Abstoßung; Hingabe wird zur Entsagung; und in die Entsagung mischt sich eine tiefe Bitterkeit. (127)

[All of this (the descriptions of Goethe in the first six chapters of the novel) do indeed offer a colorful and diverse picture, but one that ultimately remains only oblique, and in this obliqueness the image is agonizing. Goethe never appears as himself; he only appears caught in a strange medium. (...) The single narrator can only express what Goethe has meant *to him*, what he has become *for him*. Thus fulfillment and insufficiency are both at hand. The admiration and veneration of Goethe, indeed even love for him, become the source of continually new disappointment. Everyone taken up into Goethe's circle feels that he can touch the circle, but never either understand it or penetrate it. In this way attraction becomes rejection; devotion becomes renunciation; and in this renunciation lies a deep bitterness.]

Cassirer's precise psychoanalytical portrayal is no less adequate a description than the experience of seeking god and of experiencing rejection within a limited personal circle. Thomas Mann's image of Goethe confirms again the state of being trapped in a religion of art on the eve of the Second World War — another example of secularized mythology.

Fragments — Building Blocks

Seeing danger in statistics might be a particularly German trait: magic no longer binds together what fashion keeps strictly apart. For several years now a steady demographic trend has been in evidence in the visitor statistics of Weimar attractions: the visitors are getting older and older. Not surprisingly, scholars at the latest national meeting of Germanists found that the continuously lamented "sudden aging of literature" is a sign of a decrease in the value of literary education. On the other hand, says Raimar Zons, one ought to be amazed at the stamina of German literary education in general and the school subject "Deutsch" in particular, for

> sicherlich [hat] die Nachkriegszeit mit ihren neuen Sinnbedürfnissen und den literarischen Antwortversuchen auf den Nationalsozialismus, der ja zum ersten Mal in der Geschichte statt auf die totale Mobilmachung der Herzen auf Massenmedien gesetzt hat, die weitere Ausdifferenzierung und Evolution der Medien zunächst unterbrochen. (257)

> [Surely in Germany, the postwar period, in need of meaning and attempting literarily to respond to National Socialism (which for the first time ever bet on mass media rather than a total mobilization of the people's hearts) interrupted further differentiation and evolution of the media.]

It is not erroneous, then, to posit, much like the delayed differentiation and development of the media in East and West Germany, historically determined cultural and scientific inhibitions with respect to the noble demands of Weimar humanity. In a lonely look at the situation — "Goethe und Einer seiner Bewunderer" (Goethe and One of His Admirers, 1958) — West German Jacobin Arno Schmidt sums up the lack of interest just as precisely as he does the helplessness and the unwillingness of postwar Germans to engage Goethean humanism in the face of both culturally syncretic perversions thereof and of genocide. In East Germany antifascist purging of Weimar Classicism became an inherited duty; its own real-socialist grumpiness did not lag behind the pathos of the early Wilhelmine years. In West Germany the displacement was effected in textual criticism. On the other hand the historical force and vitality of the Weimar myth is confirmed by the existence of a single all-German Goethe Society and work on the Schiller Nationalausgabe during the period of a divided Germany. These cooperative projects formed the only long-term officially tolerated cultural bridges across the ideologically driven cultural monopolies and squabblings of the Cold War.

Yet the trend toward older visitors shows plainly what movement toward national unity could not cover up: interest in the heroes of German intellectual culture is permanently dropping, not only among the video kids but also among the educated middle class critics of computer-driven consumer society. What has happened to the great exponents of classical literature in the Information Age? Here too we can agree with Zons's analysis:

> Erst recht aber suspendieren Datenverbundsysteme wie Internet, Conference-Areas, E-Mail, Datenserver, elektronische Newsletter — kurz alle vieldiskutierten kybernetischen "Räume" — nicht nur die alteuropäische Parochie des Marktplatzes, sondern auch jene Öffentlichkeit, in der Literatur konsumiert und räsoniert wird. In dieser Popkultur sind die großen Rahmenerzählungen, die Grundlagen der Bildung buchstäblich zerfallen: Die Bibel, die antike Mythologie, die klassische deutsche Literatur. "Zerfallen" heißt nicht verschwunden! Was ihnen verloren gegangen ist, ist — sozusagen — ihre Grammatik, die Einheit ihrer Erzählung. Nun lagern ihre dissoziierten Elemente neben solchen ostasiatischer Weisheit, afrikanischer Stammeskultur, amerikanischer Popmythologie, westlicher Werbebotschaften, östlicher Denkruinen und vielen anderen im globaldörflichen Kramladen des Glücks. (260)

> [Only now do we find that both the old European, parochial marketplace as well as the public that is both consumed and expatiated in literature, has been suspended by networked data systems such as the Internet, conference areas, e-mail, data servers, electronic newsletters, in short, by all these much discussed cybernetic spaces. In our pop culture the great frame narratives, the foundations of education — the Bible, classical mythology, and classical German literature — have literally fallen into ruin. But 'ruin' does not mean disappearance! What

is gone, one could say, is their grammar, their unity of narration. And now their dissociated elements lie in storage next to Far Eastern wisdom, African tribal culture, American pop mythology, Western ad campaigns, Eastern ruins, and all the rest in the global village thrift shop of happiness.]

So Goethe's "fragments of a great confession" have become fragments of a great confusion: the myth has disappeared, it seems. Is the *genius locii* passing over the city of Weimar only to set in the West at the threshold of the new millennium?

The weight of the fragmentary and the disordered also seems to be in evidence in the corporate logo of "Weimar 1999 — Culture City of Europe, Inc.": a battered package, ready for shipping, is supposed to contain all the town's cultural patrimony, all the archival and intellectual inventory from Cranach to Bauhaus, from classicism to the constitution (Fig. 1). As the accompanying press release has it:

> Der Aufschriften des Pakets sind so viele, wie sie die Geschichte und die Hoffnungen dieser Stadt bereithalten. Es steht für Empfangen und Versenden, es kann ungeöffnet bleiben und liegengelassen werden. Sein Inhalt ist keine billige Handelsware, ist nie "schrankfertig", immer anders, kann erschrecken, verführen, Freude und nachdenklich machen. Es wechselt die Farbe und die Aufschriften und eignet sich für jede Art Transportgut. (*Presseerklärung* of March 1997)

> [The package can have as many addresses as this town's history and its hopes provide. It stands for receiving and for sending; it can remain unopened and be left standing. Its contents are no cheap commercial wares, never ready to wear, always different, they can cause a fright, seduce, give joy, or prompt introspection. Its colors and labels change and it is suitable for shipping any sort of goods.]

The package's labels with various names and institutions represented are always changing but logically must always have someone in Weimar as the sender: Bach, Liszt, Schiller, Wieland, Nietzsche, Bauhaus, Wildenbruch, Lenz, Ettersburg, Anna Amalia, Weimarer Klassik .... A unique mixture of content in a colorful and variable design concept, the logo is presented in so many different forms it seems as if the organizers want to tempt the viewers' naïveté with so many options. But it is more complicated than this. What if the package, metaphorically speaking, were not delivered? Merchandise not accepted! Return to sender! Addressee unknown!

Explanations might lie in the declining numbers of visitors. Art and culture have never been pure gifts and not merchandise shipments; that one should have to earn what one is given by one's forebears is probably one of Goethe's best-known quips. But how does one *earn* a *gift*, one of those priceless gems pried out of the setting called classical education during the second modern era? The precondition for answering this question is quite clearly to accept the present (or more simply, to be able even to ask this question). And this is the secret wish of the packaging artists in Weimar: they want to get rid of the goods at all costs. More subtly: they make an offer so the matter can be discussed and thus the burden of the acquisition can be shared. *Carry your brother's burden*. This sort of pious pragmatism is necessary above all on site since there can never be a fire sale. Not even under the protective label "avant-garde" would the people in Weimar risk being publicly impeached on the count of incompetence.

Nevertheless, theoretically the accent in the business of Weimar has long since shifted: no longer does place stand at the center of things, but the word. Now one is supposed to move from an archaeology of the place to an archaeology of the word, in order to do justice finally to interpretations of the poets. From the representation to the essence of things.

The question whether such a heavily symbolic place ought to be the private matter of a cultural nation defining itself and an aesthetic alibi in German lessons at school is a question of the last century. Perhaps world culture today can be defined like this, too: a piece of magical incommensurability, a mystery without national guardians, which *can* (not must) offer every person enjoyment and inspiration, even counsel and tips for living a good life. For "consensus is nonsensus" (Bolz); not everyone has to like everything. In this respect it is understandable why the town's cultural activists declared the packages to be a bonus on the trial balloon.

The secret wish of the packaging artists must have been so urgent that, for the sake of complete presentation and of piquing foreign interests, they resorted to the heavily laden label "Germany" and began declaring the package to have all possible contents. They did this even amid the danger of false advertising and improper packaging. Because what the label on the black box says is not necessarily what is inside it. For who can know anything specific when the *Presseerklärung* [press release; better termed strategy paper] offers a package on a scale of possibilities ranging from Cracker Jacks to Pandora's box? Luis Buñuel received similar responses about the ominous box in his film *La Belle du Jour*. His box prompts wonder and fear in the story and it provoked the most curiosity of all in viewers. Like Buñuel, who does not know himself what is supposed to be in the box and encourages viewers to find their own solutions, the Weimar euphemism ought to be accepted as the best-suited answer to the packaged national and world culture.

Here is a nation which allowed its most important politically representative historical building to be wrapped up by a foreign artist, and did so to emphatic applause. Should one not also imagine it capable of shipping out, for the world to judge, the intellectual goods that legitimate it as a nation?

The Reichstag in Berlin, laden with negative connotations like most historically significant symbols in Germany, only got better through its aesthetic alienation. When the pathetic mixture of idealism and historicism was made magically to disappear under an enormous veil only the militant shadows of the stone monument vanished. The re-awakening of the so-called spirit of Potsdam, feared by many as a reaction to the spectacle at the Reichstag, was something that needed neither to be feared nor purged in the face of such a scene of aesthetic whimsy. The spirit of Potsdam was officially pronounced dead in 1945. Now it has died its natural death through the increasing dismantling of its material foundations and the disappearance of the nation state in the context of growing internationalization. Globalization as exorcism.

However, the ambivalence of the Weimar package campaign makes clear one thing above all: by understanding with Freud the motif of the package in such a way that both acceptance and rejection are wrapped up and then (as a sign of advanced mobility or of heightened post-Freudian possibilities of repression) *mailed off*, one can see something being acknowledged. The riddles of the world, the mysteries of life that the collective term "Weimar culture" so often posited in the abstract and described in aesthetic and philosophical ways, are neither solved nor settled, because they are obsolete. But this is saying nothing more than that the Weimar myth is as vital as ever. Only in the age of nomadic moderns has the myth of place become the mythic word. In addition, the world is always in need of antidotes to its own demystification through the abolition of reality by virtual worlds and the experience of the deceptive nature of signs. Finally, the age of Goethe appears just as legendary to us today as did ancient Greece to eighteenth-century Germans. And just as German hellenophiles avoided setting foot in modern Greece out of fear that the ideal and reality would be too far apart, Weimar simply packed up all its treasures, locked and sealed them up in the hope and fear that there might be something in there which would grab us, cause dissolution, or be too much for us. Incommensurable in the best Goethean sense and isolated because of contemporary thoughts about security, *the package* just stands there on the playing field of art, in order that it might be used in some trial and error method of living a cultured and artistic life. If we do choose to use it in this way, which would be just the opposite of making a deposit of culture in some anxious anticipation of a glowing future, then Weimar culture would indisputably become a healing force for diagnosed cases of global thinking.

—Weimar 1999 – Kulturstadt Europas GmbH

—Translated by Scott Denham

Notes

[1] Reference thanks to Steffen Dietzsch, Berlin.

[2] See here Friedrich Ebert's speech to the constitutional convention at Weimar on 11 February 1919: "[...] müssen wir hier in Weimar die Wandlung vollziehen, vom Imperialismus zum Idealismus, von der Weltmacht zur geistigen Größe. [...] Jetzt muß der Geist von Weimar, der Geist der großen Philosophen und Dichter, wieder unser Leben erfüllen" [We must accomplish a transformation here in Weimar, from imperialism to idealism, from being a world power to being spiritually great. [...] Now the spirit of Weimar, the spirit of the great philosophers and poets, must once again fill our lives" (qtd. in Mandelkow 2: 9).

[3] See here Ronell's original work, unfortunately almost unnoticed in Germany.

Works Cited

Assmann, Aleida. "Zur Metaphorik der Erinnerung." *Mnemosyne: Formen und Funktionen der kulturellen Erinnerung*. Eds. Aleida Assmann and Dietrich Harth. Frankfurt a. M.: Fischer, 1991. 13–35.

Berghahn, Klaus L. "Von Weimar nach Versailles. Zur Entstehung der Klassik-Legende." *Klassik -Legende*. Eds. Reinhold Grimm and Jost Hermand. Frankfurt a. M.: Athenäum, 1971. 50–78.

Bolz, Norbert, Cordula Meier, Birgit Richard, and Susanne Holschbach, eds. *Riskante Bilder. Kunst. Literatur. Medien*. Munich: W. Fink, 1996.

Borchmeyer, Dieter. "Der ganze Mensch ist wie ein versiegelter Brief. Schillers Kritik und Apologie der Hofkunst." *Schiller und die höfische*

Welt. Eds. Achim Aurenhammer et al. Tübingen: Niemeyer, 1990. 460–75.

Borges, Jorge Luis. *Borges und Ich: Gedichte und Prosa 1960.* Trans. Karl A. Horst. Ed. Gisbert Haefs and Fritz Arnold. Frankfurt a. M.: Fischer, 1993.

Cassirer, Ernst. "Thomas Manns Goethe-Bild. Eine Studie über Lotte in Weimar." *Geist und Leben: Schriften.* Ed. Ernst Wolfgang Orth. Leipzig: Reclam, 1993. 123–65.

Freud, Sigmund. *Das Motiv der Kästchenwahl.* Ed. Ilse Grubrich-Simitis. Rpt. Frankfurt a. M.: Fischer, 1977.

Fuhrmann, Manfred. "Die Querelle des Anciens et des Modernes, der Nationalismus und die Deutsche Klassik." *Brechungen: Wirkungsgeschichtliche Studien zur antik-europäischen Bildungstradition.* Stuttgart: Klett-Cotta, 1982. 129–49.

Heine, Heinrich. *Poetry and Prose.* Eds. Jost Hermand and Robert C. Holub. New York: Continuum, 1982.

———. *Werke und Briefe in zehn Bänden.* Ed. Hans Kauffmann. Berlin and Weimar: Aufbau, 1980.

Hörisch, Jochen. *Die andere Goethezeit: Poetische Mobilmachung des Subjekts um 1800.* Munich: W. Fink, 1992.

Laube, Heinrich. *Reise durch das Biedermeier.* Ed. Franz Heinrich Körber. Hamburg: Hoffmann and Campe, 1965.

Mandelkow, Karl Robert. *Goethe in Deutschland. Rezeptionsgeschichte eines Klassikers.* 2 vols. Munich: C. H. Beck, 1980, 1989.

Mann, Thomas. *Königliche Hoheit. Lotte in Weimar.* Frankfurt a. M.: Fischer, 1986.

Mayer, Hans. *Richard Wagner in Bayreuth: 1876–1976.* Frankfurt a. M.: Suhrkamp, 1978.

Ortega y Gasset, José. "Um einen Goethe von innen bittend." 1932. *Ästhetik in der Straßenbahn. Essays.* Eds. Karl-Heinz Barck and Steffen Dietzsch. Berlin: Volk and Welt, 1987. 167–201.

Presseerklärung der Weimar 1999 — Kulturstadt Europas GmbH. 20 March 1997.

Ronell, Avital. *Der Goethe-Effekt: Goethe — Eckermann — Freud.* Trans. U. Dünkelsbühler. Munich: W. Fink, 1994.

Scherer, Wilhelm. *Geschichte der deutschen Literatur.* 8th ed. Berlin: Weidmann, 1899.

Schlaffer, Hannelore. *Wilhelm Meister. Das Ende der Kunst und die Wiederkehr des Mythos.* Stuttgart: Metzler, 1980.

Schmidt, Arno. "Goethe und Einer seiner Bewunderer." *Bargfelder Ausgabe. Werkgruppe I (Studienausgabe)*. Ed. Arno Schmidt Stiftung, Bargfeld. Vol. 2. 2nd ed. Zurich: Haffmanns Verlag, 1992. 189–220.

Schulz, Gerhard. "Epilog." *Die deutsche Literatur zwischen französischer Revolution und Restauration*. Vol. 2. Munich: C. H. Beck, 1989. 809–20.

Seidler, Luise. *Erinnerungen der Malerin Louise Seidler*. Ed. Hermann Uhde. Weimar: G. Kiepenheuer, 1965.

Timm, Hermann. *Dichtung des Anfangs: die religiösen Protofiktionen der Goethezeit*. Munich: W. Fink, 1996.

Wellbery, David E. "Schopenhauers Bedeutung für die moderne Literatur." *Themen 67*. Munich: Carl-Friedrich-von-Siemens-Stiftung, 1998.

Wiedemann, Conrad. "Deutsche Klassik und nationale Identität. Eine Revision der Sonderwegsfrage." *Klassik im Vergleich. Nationalität und Historizität europäischer Klassik*. DFG-Symposium 1990. Ed. Wilhelm Voßkamp. Stuttgart: Metzler, 1993. 541–69.

———. "Römische Staatsnation und griechische Kulturnation. Zum Paradigmenwechsel zwischen Gottsched und Winckelmann." *Kontroversen, alte und neue*. Akten des VII. Internationalen Germanisten-Kongresses. Göttingen 1985. Vol. 9. Eds. F. N. Mennemeiner and Conrad Wiedemann. Tübingen: Niemeyer, 1986. 173–78.

Wyss, Beat. "Das Kunstdenkmal. Die Erfindung der Vergangenheit." *Riskante Bilder. Kunst. Literatur. Medien*. Eds. Norbert Bolz, Cordula Meier, Birgit Richard, and Susanne Holschbach. Munich: W. Fink, 1996. 190–215.

Zabka, Thomas. *Faust II — Das Klassische und das Romantische: Goethes Eingriff in die neueste Literatur*. Tübingen: Niemeyer, 1993.

Zons, Raimar. "Literarische Bildung in der Medienkonkurrenz." *Germanistik: Disziplinäre Identität und kulturelle Leistung*. Ed. Ludwig Jäger. Weinheim: Beltz Athenäum, 1995. 248–61.

Fig. 1: Kunstpaketserie (Series of Art Packages; courtesy of Weimar 1999 — Kulturstadt Europas GmbH).

Index

absolutism, 295, 302
Adorno, Theodor W., 286–7
aesthetics, classical, 28, 213, 214, 216–7, 222, 227, 228
Allgemeine Literaturzeitung, 37
Althoff, Gabriele, 259
Amazons, 181–3
anal fixation, 274–6
Anderson, Emily, 107
Andreas, Willy, 296
Anna Amalia, Duchess, 1, 6, 69, 113, 114, 233, 296, 310; court circle, 98; court theater, 98; "Freundschaftsloge," 234; musical ability 100–103, 113, 114, 116; musical identity, 97; instrumental pieces, 101;
Anna Amalia, Duchess, musical works by: *Das Jahrmarktsfest zu Plundersweilern*, 101, 102; *Die Zigeuner*, 101; *Erwin und Elmire*, 101, 102, 103, 104; portraits, 115; Tafelrunde, 28, 266–7; Tiefurt, summer residence, 71; and von Göchhausen, 238; works by: "Gedanken über die Musik," 99
anthropology, social, 195
anus, euphemism for, 175; *see also Kreuz*
army, Prussian, 162, 163
art packages, 323, 328
Aspelmeyer, Franz: melodrama by: *Pygmalion*, 106
Assmann, Aleida, 66, 312–3
authoritarianism, 295
autonomy, of art, 213, 218

balls, *see masquerade*

Bakhtin, Mikhail, 247, 254, 257, 259
Bamberg, Eduard von, 197
Barth, Ilse-Marie, 194, 207
Barthes, Roland: *metalanguage*, 19
Bauer, Dale, 261
Bauman, Thomas, 110, 116
Bayreuth, 315
Beaumont, Chevalier d'Eon de, 168
Beck, Franz: melodrama by: *Pandore*, 106, 118
Becker-Cantarino, Barbara, 192, 218, 228
Beckett, Samuel, 273–93, 316; comparisons to "Rat Man," 275–6; Germany, trip to, 274–5; letter to Mary Manning, 273; works by: *Molloy*, 286
belles lettres, 213, 215, 223
Benda, Georg, 106, 118; melodrama by: *Ariadne auf Naxos*, 106, 107, 118; similarities to *Proserpina* and *Pygmalion*, 110; similarities to *Medea*, 107, 108
Benjamin, Walter, on reproducibility of art; 43
Berghahn, Klaus L., 312
Berlin (Prussian Berlin), 311
Berlin Reichstag, *see Reichstag*
Bertuch, Friedrich Justin, 36, 41, 98, 105; as entrepreneur, 36–55; as Goethe's Doppelgänger, 37; as Klauer's commercial representative, 69; Industrie-Comptoir, founding of, 70; marketing of Weimar, 6; on England, 49; on Enlightenment, 52;

Bertuch, Friedrich Justin, works by: *Allgemeine Literaturzeitung*, 37; *Don Quichote*, translation of, 15; *Journal des Luxus und der Moden*, 17; *London und Paris*, 37; *Polyxena*, 99
Beutler, Ernst, 76
Biedermann, Karl, 306
Biedrzynski, Effi: works by: *Goethe's Weimar*, 5–6, 238, 239, 241, 258
Birmingham School, 5
Birtsch, Günter, 302
Bismarck, Otto von, 296
Blackall, Eric A., 108
Blackwell, Jeannine, 228
Bloom, Barbara: artistic work by: *Weimar. Vergangenheit... Zukunft. Und jetzt?*, 2, 10, 11
Boardman, John, 74
Bode, Johann Joachim Christoph: sculpture of, 76, 79, 197
Bode, Wilhelm, 68, 75, 77, 79, 197, 305; works by: *Die Gouvernante*, 197
Bödeker, Hans Erich, 302
Bohm, Arnd, 199, 228, 256, 292
Bolz, Norbert, 323
Bonaparte, Napoleon, 148
Borchert, Angela, 261
Borchmeyer, Dieter, 158, 305, 310
Borges, Jorge Luis, 316
Borghese, Scipione Cardinal, 50
Bosse, Heinrich, 215
Bourdieu, Pierre, 30, 222; concept of capital, 25, 213
bourgeoisie, German, 214, 215
Bovenschen, Silvia, 192, 216
Boyle, Nicholas, 100
Brachmann, Louise, 218, 219
Bray, William, 50
Brentano, Clemens, 81
Brinker-Gabler, Gisela, 228
Brockt, Johannes, 117

Bruegel, Pieter the elder, 252
Bruegel, Pieter the younger, 252
Bruford, W. H., 81, 82, 193, 258; works by: *Culture and Society in Classical Weimar*, 5
Buchenwald, 3, 22
Buñuel, Luis, works by: *La Belle du Jour*, 323
Bürger, Christa, 218, 222, 228
Bürger, Peter, 228
Bürgin, Hans, 307
Burkhardt, C. A. H., 99
Burns, Rob, 261
Butler, Judith, 203

Calhoun, Craig, 30
Camper, Petrus (surgeon), 75
Candide, 275–6
Cannabich, Christian, works by: *Elektra*, 118
Carl August, Duke, 1, 6, 172, 175, 276–7, 279, 295; class dinstinctions under, 193; depictions of, 240; monument of, 70; portrait busts, 76; theater patron, 147; war service, 153, 162
Carlson, Marvin, 162, 163, 207
carnival procession, 195–96
Cassirer, Ernst, 319
Castle, Terry, 194, 195
censorship, 299–302, 305
Christo, 4
clothing, 40, 50, 58–62, 195
Coade, "Artificial-Stone-Manufactory," 69
Cocalis, Susan, 192, 199, 218, 226, 228
Congress of Vienna, 297
Consilium medicum, 236–7
consumer culture, 36–56
Cooke, Lynn, 71
corporeal wholeness, 80
costume, 50, 166, 171, 193–5; Basko, 174–5; Crugantino,

174–5; Götz, 174–5; Werther, 166, 170–2
court jesters, 246
Craig, Gordon, 151
cross-dressing: Beaumont, Chevalier d'Eon de, 168; Bonny, Anne; 168; Charke, Charlotte, 168; Read, Mary, 168; in Weimar Theater, 166–86; of Weimar elite, 175
Cumberland, works by: *The West Indian*, 104, 197
cultural imperialism, 310
Cultural Studies, 2, 5, 45, 191–2

Dahl, Helma, 306
d'Angers, Pierre Jean David: sculpture of Goethe by, 82
Dawson, Ruth, 230
DC Comics, 287
Deetjen, Werner, 244, 251, 258, 259
De Lauretis, Teresa, 191
Deneke, Toni, 226, 238, 239, 258
Denham, Scott, 30
Derks, Paul, 167, 185
Dietrick, Linda, 226, 256
Diezmann, August, 306
dilettantism, 218–22
Döblin, Alfred, works by: *Berlin Alexanderplatz*, 78
Dollimore, Jonathan, 284
Dotzler, Bernhard, 228
Dresden, antiquities collection, 74
Duden, Barbara, 228
Düntzer, Heinrich, 207
During, Simon, 30, 191, 192, 203

Ebeling, Friedrich, 259
Eberhardt, Hans, 193
Ebers, Johann Jakob Heinrich, 226
Ebersbach, Volker, 15
Ebert, Friedrich, 325
Eberwein, Karl, 103
Eckermann, Johann Peter, 66

Economics, Thuringian Ministry of, 23
Ehrenreich, Barbara, 163
Eigler, Friederike, 261
Einsiedel, August von, 7
Einsiedel, Emilie von, 7
Einsiedel, Friedrich Hildebrand von, 98, 105, 233, 235, 259; works by: *Die Zigeuner* (text); 101
Eisenach, 233, 299
Elias, Norbert: on luxury goods, 52
Engelsing, Rolf, 222
Enlightenment, 41–2, 52, 215, 275, 302
Enzensberger, Hans Magnus, works by: *Nieder mit Goethe: Eine Liebeserklärung* 2, 23, 32

fashion, 58–62; *Modejournal*, views of, 40, 42, 50; *see also clothing*
Feldmann, Wilhelm, 55, 70
feminism, 214, 249
Femmel, Gerhard, 261
Ferns, Lesley, 204
Fichte, Johann Gottlieb, 297, 301; works by: *Grundriß des Familienrechts*, 193
Fielitz, Wilhelm, 224
Fischer, Rotraut: physiognomy, 75
Fisher, Richard, 155
Flemming, Willi, 162
Flögel, Karl Friedrich, 245, 246, 249
Flügel, J. C.: on eighteenth century masculine costume, 50
Forberg, Karl Friedrich: "Hospitäler der Menschheit," 310
fragmentation, 80
Frederick II of Prussia, 77, 150, 162, 313
free speech, 297–8, 302
Freitagsgesellschaft, 73

Freud, Sigmund, 324
Freud, Sigmund, works by: "Character and Anal Eroticism," 273; "Rat Man," 274–292; "On Transience," 80
Freundschaftsloge, 234
Frevert, Ute, 228
Friedell, Egon, 171
Friedenthal, Richard, 171, 173
Friedrich II: see Frederick II
Fuhrmann, Manfred, 327

Gallas, Helga, 228
Garber, Marjorie, 166, 167, 168, 184, 198, 204
Garve, Christian, 41
Gebauer, Gunter, 192, 195
Geertz, Clifford, 147, 162
Geese, Walter, 67, 68, 71, 74, 76, 81
Geitner, Ursula, 196
Genast, Anton, 154, 159
Genast, Eduard, 197–8
gender hierarchies, 191–209, 215–18
Gerassimov, Michail, 3
Gerber, Ernst Ludwig, 116
German Goethe Society, 321
Gervinus, Georg Gottfried, 311
Gilman, Sander, 186
ginkgo biloba, 21
Göchhausen, Louise, 7, 77, 233, 249, 250; called "Thusnelda," 238; descriptions of, 234–45; Italian journey, 241; paintings of, 235, 247, 248, 264–5, 269; works by, 249–56
Göres, Jörn, 56
Goethe International, 23
Goethe, Johann Wolfgang von: and masquerades, 194, 195; arrival in Weimar, 1; as commodity, 15–30; as Mignon, 170; as war observer, 148, 155, 163; Bertuch, opinion of, 45; brandy named after, 15, 26, 33–5; busts of, 27, 76, 89, 92–6; drawings, 235, 247, 264–5; early romantic theory, opinion of, 257; French Revolution, opinion of, 152; "Freundschaftsloge," 234; Gartenhaus, 22; heritage, 16; home at Frauenplan square, 16, 88; Klauer, opinion of, 70; lecture to Freitagsgesellschaft, 73; letters to: Kestner, 172; Knebel, 170; Lavater, 170; Merck, 170; Schiller, 219, 221; Sömmerring, 205; Stein, 71, 119, 170, 299; Stolberg, 172;
musical contributions by, 98; mythification of, 28, 322; on anti-fashion, 48; on artistic creation, 47; on consumer culture, 47; on luxury, 47; on Prince Borghese, 50–51; on sculpture, 66, 67, 81; Schiller, relationship with, 20; secret society, 7; sexual preference, 170, 198; Stein, relationship with, 21, 205; *Teutscher Merkur*, 52; theater, 8, 45, 147–63;
Goethe, Johann Wolfgang, works by:
Amtliche Schriften, 298, 300;
Briefe aus der Schweiz, 186;
Der Bürger-General, 154;
Campagne in Frankreich, 152, 155–6;
Dichtung und Wahrheit, 16;
"Erlkönig," 103;
Erwin und Elmire (text), 101;
"Euphrosyne," 198;
Faust, 21, 25–26, 160, 240;
Die Fischerin (text), 102, 103, 116;
"Frauenrollen auf dem römischen Theater von Männern gespielt," 203;

Götter, Helden und Wieland, 117;
Götz von Berlichingen, 118, 173–4, 177, 197, 207;
Der Großkophta, 197;
La Guerra, prologue to, 152;
Herrmann und Dorothea, 222;
Iphigenie auf Tauris, 25–26, 77, 105, 118, 199, 208, 299;
Italienische Reise, 185;
Das Jahrmarktsfest zu Plundersweilern, 101;
Jery und Bätely (text), 112;
"Kunst und Handwerk," 43;
Die Leiden des jungen Werthers, 54, 110;
Lila, 103, 104;
Das Neueste von Plundersweilern, 304;
prologues, theatrical, 151;
Propyläen, introduction to, 42, 72;
Proserpina, 102–03, 106, 107, 108–112, 118, 142–4;
"Regeln für Schauspieler," 158;
Stella, 197;
Der Triumph der Empfindsamkeit, 108–9;
"Über epische und dramatische Dichtung" (with Schiller), 152–3;
Die Vögel, 105;
Wilhelm Meisters theatralische Sendung, 148, 161, 197;
Wilhelm Meisters Lehrjahre, 148–150, 158, 163, 176–7
Goethe, Katherina, 250
Goethe Society, German, 321
Goldoni, works by: *La Locandiera*, 204
Goodman, Katherine R., 216, 228, 256
Greek artistic taste, 70
Grey, Margaret E., 293
Grimm, Jacob and Wilhelm, works by: *Deutsches Wörterbuch*, 175
Grosz, Elisabeth, 259
Grotesque, 233–63; and feminism, 249; in L. von Göchhausen's works, 249–56
Groth & Consorten, 23–5
Gustafson, Susan, 7, 207, 291

Hackert, Philipp, 6
Hahn, Barbara, 259
Hall, Stuart, 192
Hammer, Stephanie, 293
Handrick, Willy, 80
Haraway, Donna, 259
Harpham, Geoffrey Galt, 248, 257, 260; "the taboo compromise," 248–9
Hart Nibbrig, Christian L., 259
Haskell, Francis, 66
Haswell, Jock, 151
Hauptmann, Anton, 194
Hausen, Karin, 192, 228
Haydn, Joseph, 99
Hegel, Georg Wilhelm Friedrich, 311; on portrait statues, 78
Heilmann, Christoph, 50
Heine, Heinrich, works by: *Deutschland: Ein Wintermärchen*, 317
Henning, Hans, 162
Herder, Johann Gottfried von, 22, 72, 82, 90, 106, 169, 193, 287, 297; Bertuch, opinion of, 70; Göchhausen, relationship with, 233; Seckendorf, influence on, 114; sculpture, 65, 66;
Herder, Johann Gottfried, works by: *Osterkantate*, 99; "Plastik," 73; "Tanz und Melodrama," 100; "Über die Oper," 100
Herman, Judith Lewis, 291
Herrmann, Ernst, 103
Hesse, 303, 304

INDEX

Hiller, J. A., 101, 116, 117; works by: *Wöchentliche Nachrichten und Anmerkungen die Musik betreffend*, 115
Hinck, Walter, 159
Hinderer, Walter, 154
Hitler, Adolf, 3, 296
Hörisch, Jochen, 316
Hoffmann, Volker, 228
Hofnarren, *see court jesters*
Hohenstein, Siglinde, 17
Holtzhauer, Helmut, 298
Homer, works by: *Iliad*, 48
homosexuality, 166, 207; in *Don Karlos*, 284, 291; punishable by law, 166–7, 185; terms for, eighteenth century, 167; *see also theater, sexuality in*
Honegger, Claudia, 192
Horkheimer, Max, 286–7
"Hospitäler der Menschheit," 310
Houben, Heinrich Hubert, 306
Hufeland, Christian, 77
Hull, Isabel, 185
humanism, 320
Humboldt, Wilhelm von, 192–3, 311; works by: "Über den Geschlechtsunterschied und dessen Einfluß auf die organische Natur," 192–3

Idealism, German, 301
Imhoff, Amalie von, 217, 219, 220–22, 223; work by: *Die Schwestern von Lesbos*, 220, 221
"Incorrigibility," 219–21
Industrie-Comptoir, 70
informants, 296
intelligentsia, German, 42
Intelligenzblatt, 17, 68

Jagemann, Karoline, 197
Jarrell, Randall, 160
Jena, 315; University of, 298, 300–1
Johnson, Richard, 191–2

Joseph II, Emperor, 297
Journal der Romane, 223
Journal des Luxus und der Moden, 17, 36–55, 68–9; contents, 38; *Intelligenzblatt* as supplement to, 17, 68; long term goal of, 53; *see also Bertuch, Friedrich Justin; also Modejournal*
Journal von Tiefurt: see Tiefurt Journal
Juno Ludovisi, 65, 85

Kacandes, Irene, 30
Kalb, Charlotte von, 291
Kamper, Dietmar, 262
Kampf, 289
Kant, Immanuel, 198, 216
Kauffmann, Angelika, drawing by: *Die Musen des Dramas huldigen Goethe*, 82
Kauffmann, Bernd, 29
Kayser, Wolfgang, 245–7, 248, 252, 260
Keller, Gottfried, 195
Kern, Bärbel, 217
Kern, Horst, 217
Kessler, Harry Graf, 3
Kiceluk, Stephanie, 262
Kindermann, Heinz, 207
Kirby, Frank, 114
Kittler, Friedrich, 208, 292
Klauer, Gottlieb Martin, 6, 17, 68, 73; advertisement for sculpture, 68; appointed court sculptor, 69; busts of Goethe, 76, 89, 92, 94–5; busts of Weimar notables, 67, 76; Goethe's opinion of, 70; sculpture of Fritz von Stein, 70–1, 78
Klauß, Jochen, 162, 171
Kleist, Heinrich von, 276
Klingemann, August, 159
Klinger, Maximilian, 67
Klippel, Diethelm, 302

Knebel, Karl Ludwig von, 170, 226, 233, 240, 241, 252
Knowlson, James, 274
Köpke, Wulf, 150
Kord, Susanne, 199, 200, 201, 202, 222–3, 259, 256
Korff, H. A., 314–15
Kostümstreit, 78
Kotzebue, August von, works by: *Die Weiber nach Mode*, 6
Kraus, Georg Melchior, 235
Kräuter, Friedrich Theodor, 15
Kreuz (euphemism for anus), 175
Krimmer, Elisabeth, 7
Kristeva, Julia, 282
Kroeber, Hans Timotheus, 82
Kröll, Christina, 56
Kuczynski, Jürgen, 150
Kühn, Paul, 193, 195, 205
Kulturpolitik, 80
Kunstautonomie, concept of, 44
Kuzniar, Alice, 82, 186

Lacan, Jacques, 65–6, 73
Laermann, Klaus, 198
Lange, Sigrid, 192, 199, 219, 242, 244, 257, 259
Laqueur, Thomas, 192
Larkin, Eduard T., 163
Latzel, Klaus, 150, 163
Laube, Heinrich, 314
Lavater, Johann Kaspar, 17, 69, 71, 74–5, 90, 170
Lavater, Johann Kaspar, works by: *Physiognomische Fragmente*, 69, 75, 82, *Animalitätslinie*, 76
League of Princes, 162
Lessing, Gotthold Ephraim, works by: *Minna von Barnhelm*, 104; *Hamburgische Dramaturgie*, 148
Liebhabertheater, 241
Linder, Jutta, 155, 159, 160
linguistic authority, 213–28
Liszt, Franz, 3
London und Paris, 37

Ludwig, Emil, 170
luxury, 39, 41; Goethe on, 47
Lyncker, Karl Freiherr von, 194–5

MacLeod, Catriona, 6, 177, 181, 184
Mainz, siege of, 148
male-male desire: Goethe as object of, 169–70; in *Claudine von Villa Bella*, 174–5; in *Götz von Berlichingen*, 173–4, 177; in *Wilhelm Meisters Lehrjahre*, 176–8, 184
Mandelkow, Karl Robert, 311
Mann, Thomas, works by: *Lotte in Weimar*, 319
Mannheim, 118, 285; Antikensaal, 72
Marburg, exhibition of Klauer busts, 80
Martens, Wolfgang, 296
Marwitz, Ulrich, 150
masquerade, 170, 184, 191–6, 206; anonymity, 194; carnival procession, 195–6; exclusion of third estate, 192, 195; musicians, 195; rules for, 194; subscription tickets, 195
masturbation, 217
Maul, Gisela, 82
Mayer, Hans, 315
McKendrick, Neil, 56
Meer, Theo van der, 185
melodrama, 106–7
Mengs, Anton Raphael, 74
mercenaries, 303–4
Merck, Johann Heinrich, 233
Mereau, Sophie, 217
Merkur, see *Teutscher Merkur*
Meßner, Paul, 207
metalanguage, 19
Mode, 39
Modejournal, 17, 36–55, 68–9; see also *Journal des Luxus und der Moden*
Moi, Toril, 213

Mournier, Jean Joseph, 6
Mozart, Amadeus Wolfgang, 24, 99, 118; on Benda, 106, 118
musico-dramatic works, 104

Napoleonic Wars, 6
Natur- und Konversationston, 157
Neefe, Christian Gottlob, works by: *Sophonisbe*, 107
Neumann, Christiane, 197–8, 207
Newspaper for the Elegant World, 49
Nietzsche, Friedrich, 2
Nochlin, Linda, 81

Oellers, Norbert, 163
Oken, Lovenz, 298, 301
operas-comiques, French (German adaptations), 105–106
Oppel, Margarete, 82
Ortega y Gasset, José, 8, 311, 315; works by: *The Dehumanization of Art*, 8

Paret, Peter, 150
Passage, Charles, 278
Pendle, Karin, 106, 112
Penny, Nicholas, 66
Petersen, Julius, 120
Petropoulos, Jonathan, 30
Pfeiffer, Joachim, 186
physiognomy, 69, 75
private theater, 98, 104, 117, 139–40; repertoire, 104–5
Privy Council, 295, 297–9, 306, 307
Propyläen, 42, 70, 72, 81
Proserpina, 97, 102–4, 106–7, 108–112, 118, 122–34; collaboration on, 112; similarities with *Pygmalion*, *Ariadne auf Naxos*, and *Medea*, 110
protest, political, 299–302, 305
Prussian Berlin, 311
Pruys, Karl Hugo, 167, 169

Purdy, Daniel, 6, 68

Rabelais, 247, 248
Rasch, William, 228
"Rat Man," 274–90, 291, 292
Rechtsstaat, 302
Reichardt, J. F., 117, 163, 196, 207
Reichardt, J. F., works by: *Ino*, 107, *Monolog der Iphigenia*, 117
Reichstag, wrapping by Christo, 4
Revolution, American, 303
Revolution, French, 152, 192, 196, 215, 296, 299, 302; Weimar theater's focus against, 161
Rey, Alain, 25
Rey, Michel, 185
Rheinische Thalia, 277–9
Richter, Simon, 186, 217
Rilke, Rainer Maria: "Weltinnenraum," 311, 316
Romanticism, German, 257, 301, 311
Ronell, Avital, 274, 289, 325
Rost, art dealership, 74
Rothenberg, Gunther E., 150, 151, 163
Rousseau, Jean Jacques, 107; works by: *La Nouvelle Héloïse*, 110
Runge, Anita, 228
Russell, Gillian, 162
Russo, Mary, 261

Saine, Thomas P., 152
Satori-Neumann, Bruno, 195, 206, 207
Sauder, Gerhard, 292
Schadow, Johann Gottfried: sculpture of Goethe, 78, 82, 96
Scharnhorst, Gerhard von, 151
Scherer, Wilhelm, 313, 316

Schiller, Friedrich von, 6, 148,
162, 192, 193, 216–7, 234,
277, 314; Beckett, comparisons to, 275–91; Goethe,
relationship with, 20; homosocial attachments, 279;
legitimacy, quest for, 286;
letters to: Huber, 281; Körner,
278, 285, 288, 290;
Süvern, 292;
move to Weimar, 275, 287;
sculpture, 66;
Schiller, Friedrich von, works by:
Die Braut von Messina, 158;
Demetrius, 286–7;
Don Karlos, 275–93; malemale desire in, 284, 291;
Die Horen, 222, 228;
Die Jungfrau von Orleans, 291,
Kabale und Liebe, 279;
Macbeth, adaptation of, 197;
Musenalmanach, 220, 226;
Neue Thalia, 222;
"Über Anmut und Würde,"
216;
*Über die ästhetische Erziehung
des Menschen*, 65;
"Über epische und dramatische
Dichtung" (with Goethe),
152–3, 156;
Über naive und sentimentalische Dichtung, 292;
"Was kann eine gute stehende
Bühne eigentlich wirken?,"
148;
Wilhelm Tell, 198, 291;
"Würde der Frauen," 207
Schiller, Charlotte von, 116, 207,
222, 223–7, 228: works by:
"Der Prozeß. Eine Erzählung,"
228
Schiller Nationalausgabe, 321
Schlaffer, Hannelore, 73, 316
Schlegel, Caroline, 223
Schlegel, Dorothea, 223

Schmidt, Arno, 313; works by:
"Goethe und Einer seiner
Bewunderer," 320
Schmidt, Georg, 162
Schmidt, Martin H., 73, 78
Schmölders, Claudia, 84
Schneider, Klaus, 74
Schön, Erich, 213–5
Schrickel, Leonhard, 196, 198
Schröter, Corona, 97, 100, 102,
107, 108, 112–4, 116, 134;
Schröter, Corona, works by: "Die
Fischerin," 117; "Der
Taucher," 116; "Würde der
Frauen," 116
Schulte-Sasse, Jochen, 218
Schulz, Gerhard, 315
Schulze, Sabine, works by:
Goethe und die Kunst, 82
Schweitzer, Anton, 99, 114;
collaborations with Wieland,
98; melodrama by: *Pygmalion*,
106, 107, 110
Schwind, Klaus, 159, 160, 161
sculpture in Classical Weimar, 65–
84
Seckendorff, Karl von, 98, 100,
106, 113, 114, 118, 233;
musical collaboration, 112;
scores by: *Jery und Bäteley*,
112, 118; *Die Laune des
Verliebten*, 118; *Proserpina*,
104, 118, 122–35, 135–8,
143–4
secret societies, 7, 300
SED (Sozialistische Einheitspartei),
sixth party conference, 80
Seidel, Siegfried, 219, 220
Seidler, Luise, 313
Seuffert, Bernhard, 259
Seyler troupe, repertoire, 105,
107, 117
Shakespeare, William, 316;
Shakespeare, William, works by:
Henry V, 147; *The Life and
Death of King John*, 198

Sharpe, Lesley, 294
Sherry, John F., 26
Sichardt, Gisela, 77, 207
Simon, Michael, works by:
    Urfaust Rap, 2
Sinfield, Alan, 292
Sirmen, Maddalena Lombardini, 102
Smith, Clifford Neal, 303
Sojourner Truth, 239
Sozialistische Einheitspartei, *see* SED
Spain, 284
Spirit of Weimar, 312, 314
Stafford, Barbara Maria, 75
Stallybrass, Peter, 248
Steakley, James D., 187
Steiger, Robert, 220
Stein, Charlotte von, 71, 193, 199–203, 206, 208, 220, 223–32, 256, 304–5;
Stein, Charlotte von, works by:
    "An den Mond," 207–8; *Dido*, 199, 200, 207, 226, 228; *Ein neues Freiheitssystem oder Verschwörungen gegen die Liebe*, 200–3, 208; *Die Probe*, 208; *Rino*, 225
Stein, Fritz von, 70–1, 77, 86
Stiftung Weimarer Klassik, 8, 18; *see also* Weimar Classics Foundation
Stoll, Karin, 99
Storey, John, 191
Stumpp, Gabriele, physiognomy, 75
sumptuary law, 37–8, 193

Tafelrunde, 28, 266–7
Tasso, Torquato, works by:
    Jerusalem Delivered, 178–80
Terence, works by:
    The Brothers, 158
Terry, Jennifer, 259

Teutscher Merkur, 52, 67, 68, 77, 99, 117, 203; on music, 100, 103, 108, 114
Thälmann, Ernst, 4
theater, 8, 45, 98, 104, 117, 277; commission of, 163; cross-dressing in, 166–86, 196, 197; gender roles in, 166–86; laws, 158–60; musico-dramatic works, 104; sexuality in, 166–86; women in, 196
Thiel, Erika, 81
third estate, 192
Tieck, Ludwig, 16, 81, 82, 311
Tiefurt, 71, 234, 243
Tiefurt Journal, 99, 234, 239; Eduard von der Hellen, annotation, 258
Timm, Hermann, 314
Tischbein, 27
Tobin, Robert D., 184, 186, 207
Trippel, Alexander, 77, 82, 93
Truth, Sojourner, 239
Tümmler, Hans, 6, 162, 296, 305, 306

Unger, periodical by:
    Flora, 223, 228
Urlichs, Carl, 117
Urlichs, Ludwig, 223, 226

Verdun, siege of, 155
Villa Borghese, 50
Vischer, Friedrich Theodor, 311
Voigt, Christian Gottlob, 300, 306
Voltaire, works by: *Nanine*, 104
Vulpius, Christiane, 20

Wagner, Richard, 315
Wahl, Hans, 79, 307, 325
Wallace, Michele, 191
Ward, Albert, 222
wars: of Bavarian Succession, 162; Seven Years', 163; and theater, 147–63; Thirty Years', 154

Weber, Max, works by: *The Protestant Ethic and Spirit of Capitalism*, 280
Wedgwood, Josiah, 45
Weeks, Jeffrey, 185
Weichberger, Alexander, 207
Weimar: as Athens on the Ilm, 1; class distinction in, 193; consumer culture, 17–29; defined by Goethe's presence, 314; government, 295–305; Hilton, Goethesaal, 19; Kulturstadt Europas 1999, 1, 29, 322; music in, 97–121; reform in, 297; sculpture in, 65–84; theater, *see theater*; tourist information, 18; women authors, 256; women's inferiority in, 192
Weimar Classicism, 43–4, 66, 70, 73, 75, 79, 81, 206, 310, 321
Weimar Classics Foundation, 18; *see also Stiftung Weimarer Klassik*
Weimar Grotesque, 7, 245–7, 249
Weimar Lied, 103
Weimar Republic, 295; founding of, 79
Weissberg, Liliane, 20
Wellbery, David E., 316
Weltinnenraum (Rilke), 311, 316
Werther, 166, 171–2, 174–5, 176, 186
Werthern, Christian Ferdinand von, 7
Wette, Wolfram, 165
Wiedemann, Conrad, 327
Wieland, Christoph Martin, 22, 98, 99, 105, 114, 117, 169, 243, 245, 252, 291, 296–7; Göchhausen, relationship to, 233, 238;
Wieland, Christoph Martin, works by: *Diogenes*, 296; *Der Teutsche Merkur*, see *Teutscher Merkur*; "Versuch über das Teutsche Singspiel, und einige dahin einschlagende Gegenstände," 105, 114, 245
Wiese, Benno von, 276, 280, 291, 292
Wigley, Mark, 47
Wilhelmsburg Palace, 194
Williams, Raymond; works by: *Culture and Society*, 5, 21, 191
Wilson, W. Daniel, 7, 296, 305, 306, 314
Winter, Gundolf, 78
Winter, Peter; works by: *Lenardo und Blandine*, 106
Witkowski, Georg, 160, 163
Wolf, Caroline, 98
Wolf, Ernst Wilhelm, 98–100, 105, 113;
Wolf, Ernst Wilhelm, works by: *Der Abend im Walde*, 105; *Ceres*, 105; *Die Dorfdeputierten*, 105; *Ehrlichkeit und Liebe*, 117; *Das Gärtnermädchen*, 117; *Das grosse Loos*, 105; *Das Rosenfest*, 105; *Sei Sonate per il Clavicembalo Solo*, 114; *Die treuen Köhler*, 105
Wollen, Peter: *Visual Display*, introduction to, 71
Wolzogen, Karoline von, 217, 219, 220, 222; works by: *Agnes von Lilien*, 219
work ethic, Puritan, 280
Wranitzky, Paul; opera by: *Oberon*, 197
Wyss, Beat, 312

Xenien, 310

Zabka, Thomas, 311
Zantop, Susanne, 228
Zeitung für die elegante Welt, 49
Žižek, Slavoj, 73
Zons, Raimar, 320, 321